PSYCHOLOGICAL PERSPECTIVES ON WOMEN'S HEALTH

Edited by

Vincent J. Adesso,
Diane M. Reddy,
and Raymond Fleming
University of Wisconsin–Milwaukee

Taylor & Francis
Publishers since 1798

USA	Publishing Office:	Taylor & Francis 1101 Vermont Avenue, N.W., Suite 200 Washington, DC 20005-3521 Tel: (202) 289-2174 Fax: (202) 289-3665
	Distribution Center:	Taylor & Francis 1900 Frost Road, Suite 101 Bristol, PA 19007-1598 Tel: (215) 785-5800 Fax: (215) 785-5515
UK		Taylor & Francis Ltd. 4 John St. London WC1N 2ET Tel: 071 405 2237 Fax: 071 831 2035

PSYCHOLOGICAL PERSPECTIVES ON WOMEN'S HEALTH

1 2 3 4 5 6 7 8 9 0 BRBR 9 8 7 6 5 4

This book was set in Times Roman by Harlowe Typography, Inc. The editors were Karen D. Taylor and Elisabeth Magnus; the production supervisor was Peggy M. Rote. Cover design and cover photo by Michelle Fleitz.
Printing and binding by Braun-Brumfield, Inc.

A CIP catalog record for this book is available from the British Library.
∞ The paper in this publication meets the requirements of the ANSI Standard Z39.48-1984 (Permanence of Paper)

Library of Congress Cataloging-in-Publication Data
Psychological perspectives on women's health / edited by Vincent J.
  Adesso, Diane M. Reddy, and Raymond Fleming.
     p. cm.
  Includes bibliographical references and index.
    1. Women—Health and hygiene. 2. Clinical health psychology.
  I. Adesso, Vincent J. II. Reddy, Diane M. III. Fleming, Raymond.
  RA564.85.P89   1994
  613'.04244—dc20
                                                93-29062
ISBN 0-89116-848-6 (case)   CIP
ISBN 1-56032-335-3 (paper)

PSYCHOLOGICAL PERSPECTIVES ON WOMEN'S HEALTH

Contents

v

PART 2: STRESS, CORONARY HEART DISEASE, AND CANCER

PART 3: BODY IMAGE AND WEIGHT REGULATION AND DRUG USE

PART 4: MENSTRUATION AND PAIN

PART 6: DIRECTIONS FOR RESEARCH IN WOMEN'S HEALTH

Contributors

VINCENT J. ADESSO, Ph.D.
Department of Psychology
Garland Hall
P.O. Box 413
University of Wisconsin
Milwaukee, WI 53201

KAREN L. CALDERONE
Department of Psychology
University of Rhode Island
Kingston, RI 02881

HELEN L. COONS, Ph.D.
Department of Mental Health Sciences
Hahnemann University
Philadelphia, PA 19102

APRIL E. FALLON, Ph.D.
Department of Psychiatry
Medical College of Pennsylvania
EPPI
3200 Henry Avenue
Philadelphia, PA 19129

RAYMOND FLEMING, Ph.D.
Department of Psychology
Garland Hall
P.O. Box 413
University of Wisconsin
Milwaukee, WI 53201

MARIANNE FRANKENHAEUSER,
   Ph.D.
Psychology Division
Department of Psychiatry and Psychology
Karolinska Institutet
University of Stockholm
S-10691 Stockholm
Sweden

SHERYLE J. GALLANT, Ph.D.
Department of Medical Psychology
Uniformed Services University of the
   Health Sciences
4301 Jones Bridge Road
Bethesda, MD 20814

SHARON M. HALL, Ph.D.
Center for Social and Behavioral Sciences
University of California, San Francisco
1350 7th Avenue (CSBS-207)
San Francisco, CA 94143
and San Francisco Veterans
   Administration Medical Center, 116A
4150 Clement Street
San Francisco, CA 94121

JEFFREY A. KELLY, Ph.D.
Department of Psychiatry and Mental
   Health Sciences
Medical College of Wisconsin
Milwaukee, WI

PAMELA KATO KLEBANOV, Ph.D.
Educational Testing Service,
   Mail Stop 10-R
Rosedale Road
Princeton, NJ 08541

ELAINE A. LEVENTHAL, M.D., Ph.D.
Department of Medicine
University of Medicine and Dentistry of
   New Jersey
Robert Wood Johnson School of Medicine
One Robert Wood Johnson Place, CN 19
New Brunswick, NJ 08903

SANDRA M. LEVY, Ph.D.
University of Pittsburgh
Western Psychiatric Institute and Clinic
3811 O-Hara Street
Pittsburgh, PA 15213-2593

PATRICIA J. MOROKOFF, Ph.D.
Department of Psychology
University of Rhode Island
Kingston, RI 02881

DEBRA A. MURPHY, Ph.D.
Community Health Behavior Program
Department of Psychiatry and Mental
   Health Sciences
Medical College of Wisconsin
8701 Watertown Plank Road
Milwaukee, WI 53226

PEGGY J. OTT, Ph.D.
University of Pittsburgh
Western Psychiatric Institute and Clinic
3811 O-Hara Street
Pittsburgh, PA 15213-2593

ANTHONY E. READING, Ph.D.
Department of Psychiatry
UCLA School of Medicine
Center for Reproductive Medicine
Cedars-Sinai Medical Center
444 S. San Vicente Boulevard
Los Angeles, CA 90048

DIANE M. REDDY, Ph.D.
Department of Psychology
Garland Hall
P.O. Box 413
University of Wisconsin
Milwaukee, WI 53201

DIANE N. RUBLE, Ph.D.
Department of Psychology
New York University
6 Washington Place, 7th Floor
New York, NY 10003

GERDI WEIDNER, Ph.D.
Department of Psychology
State University of New York at Stony
   Brook
Stony Brook, NY 11794

Preface

This book is an outgrowth of several developments. First, significant scientific advances have been made in understanding psychological aspects of women's health. Second, there is increasing recognition that the investigation of questions in health psychology with special relevance to women is not only important to women's health, but essential to the promotion of health and prevention and treatment of illness of all people. These developments formed the impetus for this volume.

Two goals guided the preparation of this book. First, we wanted to provide a rich, scholarly resource that not only presented cutting-edge research on the important topics in women's health but also identified new directions and insights for research. The dual focus on current and future research is integrated throughout the book, and the concluding chapter specifically discusses the future challenges and directions in which the investigation of psychological aspects of women's health is likely to move. Our hope is that the book offers much needed, timely information and stimulates new thinking and research devoted to women's health.

A second goal in preparing this volume was to create a thorough book on the vitally important topics in women's health. To accomplish this goal, we recruited internationally respected experts to carefully discuss the topics in considerable depth from a biopsychosocial perspective. The resulting compilation of thorough, state-of-the-art chapters highlights the complex interplay of biological, psychological, and social factors in all health matters. It is our hope that readers find this balanced, in-depth approach valuable.

The book is intended for scholars, practitioners, and students in the social sciences, medicine, and nursing. It addresses in detail the most recent developments in research on important topics such as psychological aspects of aging, stress, coronary heart disease, cancer, drugs, weight regulation and body image, pain, menstruation, sexuality and infertility, and AIDS. Special features include presentation of a biopsychosocial framework to understanding stress in women, an overview of the unique process of aging as experienced by women, discussion of new reproductive technologies such as gamete intrafallopian transfer (GIFT), and examination of research and policy on AIDS prevention in women.

We wish to acknowledge the contributions of Frederick P. Begell, who encouraged us to undertake this work initially and who provided valuable guidance until his untimely death; and of Taylor & Francis editors Ron Wilder and Carolyn Ormes, whose support and patience helped us continue with the project. The many contributors to this work should also be thanked for their patience and scholarly efforts. We especially thank Diane Ellefson and Anna Morehouse for their untiring assistance with the many tedious details involved in completing this book. Finally, we want to thank our families for giving us their enduring love and support, even when it entailed delaying gratification of their own needs.

Vincent J. Adesso, Ph.D.
Diane M. Reddy, Ph.D.
Raymond Fleming, Ph.D.

Chapter 1

Psychological Perspectives on Women's Health: An Introduction and Overview

Vincent J. Adesso
Diane M. Reddy
Raymond Fleming

Heart disease, cancer, and human immunodeficiency virus infection are major causes of mortality for both men and women throughout the world.[1] Yet as Gerdie Weidner in Chapter 4 and Debra Murphy and Jeffrey Kelly in Chapter 11 in this volume point out, most studies have focused on men and have under-emphasized the extent of these problems in women. That males have higher age-adjusted death rates than females for all major causes of death including heart disease (1.89 males die for every 1 female), cancer (1.47 males die for every 1 female), and human immunodeficiency virus infection (9.09 males die for every 1 female) may partially explain this neglect (Adams & Hardy, 1989). However, the major causes of morbidity and mortality that primarily affect women, such as osteoporosis and breast cancer, have been given disproportionately little scientific attention relative to their toll. Compelling questions related to the etiology, treatment, and prevention of these serious diseases remain, yet the rate of sci-

---

[1]Most people do not actually die from human immunodeficiency virus infection or from AIDS, but succumb to opportunistic infections resulting from the progression of AIDS.

entific advances in these research literatures is low. One reason for the lack of attention given to women's health problems and the underrepresentation of females found in almost all health research may be that males have been treated as the standard for health. Although there is no prototypic person, research has suggested that for some clinicians the healthy male may be synonymous with the healthy adult (Broverman, Broverman, Clarkson, Rosenkrantz, & Vogel, 1970). Not only clinicians but researchers, too, have tended to treat males as representative of people, generalizing findings based solely on males to all people, excluding women as subjects of study, and exaggerating the importance of trivial differences observed between male and female subjects (e.g., Grady, 1981; Levy & Richey, 1988).

This perspective of the male as the standard for health has justified the exclusion of women in research, contributed to the myth of women's specialness and uniqueness, focused attention on sex steroids and other genetic factors as the determinants of differences in life expectancy and mortality rates between males and females, and discouraged policy formation and funding for disease prevention and health promotion. Although it is known that many differences between males and females have more to do with the social construction of gender than they do with genetic and hormonal factors related to sex, researchers, by focusing on the male as the standard, have avoided undertaking serious study of the sociocultural and behavioral factors that influence these differences until recently.

A fact often cited to justify the search for genetic and hormonal rather than sociocultural and behavioral differences between men and women is that males fare worse than females in life expectancy and mortality in all technologically based countries. Elaine Leventhal in Chapter 1 of this volume provides a detailed examination of the hypothesized explanations for this difference. In a similar vein, we argue in a recent review of gender and health that this gender differential arises, in part, from the cumulative effects of the different social worlds that men and women experience from the moment of their birth (Reddy, Fleming, & Adesso, 1992) and is reflected in important health-related behaviors.

The impact of living in different social worlds is dramatically evidenced by behavioral differences between men and women. In general, men tend to engage in more negative health-related behaviors than women. For example, Sharon Hall in Chapter 6 of this volume points out that more men than women drink alcohol and use illicit drugs such as crack, cocaine, and heroin. And, until recently, more men than women smoked cigarettes. Moreover, men traditionally have been more likely than women to be heavier users of these substances. Cigarette smoking alone has been estimated to account for between 40 and 60% of the gender differences in total mortality across the adult lifespan (Waldron, 1986). More than four times as many men (13.1%) as women (3.0%) are classified as being heavy drinkers (Nelson & McLemore, 1988). Heavy drinking has been linked with chronic liver disease and cirrhosis, cardiovascular and neural damage, and stomach cancer. Alcohol is also involved in a high percentage of homicides, suicide attempts, and traffic fatalities. For each of these causes of death men outnumber women. Overall, alcoholism increases the mortality rate for men by a factor from 2 to 3 and for women by a factor from 2.7 to 7 (Kilbey & Sobeck, 1988).

Complementing this tendency to engage in negative health-related behaviors, fewer men than women engage in positive health-related behaviors such as sleeping more than six hours per day, eating breakfast (Nelson & McLemore, 1989), taking vitamins (Moss, Levy, Kim, & Park, 1989), and brushing their teeth (Verbrugge, 1982). These positive and negative health-related behavioral tendencies may stem from the ascribed "appropriateness" of the relevant behaviors for men and women.

Traditional sex roles dictate that men should be less nurturant, less person-oriented, and less concerned with family well-being than women. The relative deemphasis for men compared to women on caring may extend to health matters, contributing to fewer health promotion practices in men. Similarly, views of women as lifegivers and moral guardians have led to more extensive and negative reactions to substance use in women than men, which may reflect the current lower use of illicit drugs in women and their lower rate of alcoholism (Gomberg, 1982; Marsh, Colten, & Tucker, 1982). Even cigarette smoking was considered unacceptable for "ladies" not that long ago, as one cigarette manufacturer reminds us with the slogan, "You've come a long way, baby!" If a woman in the early 1900s smoked, she typically did not begin smoking regularly until she was in her thirties. In contrast, her male counterpart began to smoke regularly before his twentieth birthday (Harris, 1983).

Reflecting the current acceptability of cigarette smoking in women, males and females today initiate and become regular users of cigarettes at about the same ages (Glynn, Leventhal, & Hirschman, 1986). Intoxication and addiction to illicit drugs like heroin are another matter. These behaviors are still viewed as more reprehensible in women than men. The double standard appears to stem from two sources (Gomberg, 1982). First, observers may perceive that a drunk woman or female addict high on drugs has irresponsibly impaired her ability to function as a nurturer, a primary role assigned to women. Second, observers may conceptually link female drunkenness, female alcoholism, and female addiction to illicit drugs with sexual vulnerability and promiscuity. In any case, even though health behaviors predict each other only modestly, research suggests that men and women do differ in health practices and, as noted, these differences may result from the social construction of differences between genders.

The outcome of the social construction of differences between men and women is well illustrated by research on the menstrual cycle, particularly work on mood differences between men and women across the month (Tavris, 1992). It is commonly accepted that hormonal variations associated with the menstrual cycle "cause" women's moods to vary and that men do not have the same hormonal or emotional variations. Thus there are strong societal beliefs regarding gender differences in mood across the month and the hormonal basis for these differences. Men and women attest to these beliefs. However, Pamela Kato Klebanov and Diane Ruble in Chapter 8 of this volume present convincing documentation of the consistent failure of research to find any difference in reports of mood across the month. True, there may be some individual differences in monthly mood variations; but, as groups, men and women evidence similar amounts of mood variation across the month. The search for hormone-based differences in mood across the month illustrates the tendency of researchers to favor biologic explanations for health-related gender differences over sociocultural and behavioral ones.

So although gender is a socially constructed variable, researchers have focused on a search for genetic, hormonal, and physiological rather than sociocultural and behavioral differences as the primary causes of the health differences between men and women. For example, genetic factors often are implicated in the shorter life expectancy and higher rates of mortality for men. Indeed, infant mortality data show that boys have higher rates of death than girls from most major causes of mortality (E. G. Hammond, 1965). However, greater male infant mortality appears to contribute only minimally to the excess in male mortality. Greater male vulnerability to infectious diseases has also been noted (Preston, 1976). This gender difference might contribute moderately to the higher rates of male mortality in that at least five of the 15 leading causes of death may relate to infectious agents.

Similarly, the contribution of sex hormones to the excess in male mortality relates primarily to coronary heart disease risk. Limited support exists for the detrimental function of testosterone in coronary heart disease risk in males (Amos, Odake, & Ambrus, 1969; Johnson, Ramey, & Ramwell, 1975, 1977), whereas stronger support exists for the protective function of estrogen in coronary heart disease risk in females (e.g., Barrett-Conner, Brown, Turner, Austin, & Criqui, 1979; Gordon, Kannel, Hjortland, & McNamara, 1978; C. B. Hammond & Maxson, 1982; Kannel, Hjortland, McNamara, & Gordon, 1976).

Thus genetic and hormonal factors appear to play a role in gender differences in mortality, but the extent of their role is unknown and their contribution is significantly modulated by sociocultural and behavioral factors (Waldron, 1983). The causes of death with the largest gender differentials (human immunodeficiency virus infection, suicide, homicide, and legal intervention) relate to behaviors rather than genetics.

It has also been argued that gender differences in psychophysiological reactivity to stress might contribute to the excess in male mortality, especially in regard to coronary heart disease. As discussed by Marianne Frankenhaeuser in Chapter 3 of this volume, men in general show greater catecholamine (especially epinephrine) reactivity to stress than women. However, the work of Frankenhaeuser and her colleagues suggests that this difference may be a learned coping response, that is, a product of sociocultural influences. Males may learn social role expectations that teach them to cope with stressors in an excessively competitive and achievement-oriented fashion. These learned coping responses may combine with other risk factors to increase male coronary heart disease risk and mortality. For example, as Gerdie Weidner in Chapter 4 of this volume indicates, the Type A behavior pattern and hostility, which have been linked to increased risk for coronary heart disease, are more prevalent in men than in women (Baker, Dearborn, Hastings, & Hamberger, 1984; Weidner, Friend, Ficarroto, & Mendell, in press). Both hostility and the Type A behavior pattern may represent coping practices that men are socialized to develop.

In conclusion, behavioral, genetic, and, possibly, hormonal factors play important roles in the shorter life expectancy of males and their excess mortality from most major causes of death. Psychophysiological factors may also significantly influence the gender difference in life expectancy and mortality, although the evidence at this time is less than conclusive. In any case, the gender difference in life expectancy and mortality appears to have as much to do with the social construction of gender and the effects of this construction on individuals' behavior as it does with genetic factors related to sex. Starting to treat gender as an independent variable can be seen as a step forward for research. However, it is clear that gender is more than a single or multilevel independent variable. Researchers must move away from viewing gender as a unidimensional construct and begin to work to understand its multidimensional nature. Failure to adopt a multidimensional conception of gender will only continue to restrict our thinking about health. In contrast, adopting a multidimensional view of gender will encourage both clinicians and researchers to move away from viewing the male as the standard for health and abet our attempts to advance our understanding of the complex relations existing between behavior and health in general, and women's health in particular.

In an effort to create a needed scholarly resource on psychological perspectives on women's health, we called on recognized experts to contribute chapters on ten critically important areas of women's health. Each of these 10 chapters aims at illustrating the multifaceted nature of gender, illuminating the role of psychological factors, broadly construed as encompassing behavioral and sociocultural influences, and demonstrating the ways in which psychological and biological factors interact to influence women's health. The first section of this book presents a sweeping overview of gender, health, and aging. The second section covers stress, coronary heart disease, and cancer. The third section is devoted to substance use and weight. The fourth section reviews menstruation and pain. The fifth section examines sex and infertility and AIDS. The concluding chapter in the book considers the challenges and future directions for research on women's health.

REFERENCES

Adams, P. E., & Hardy, A. M. (1989). *Current estimates from the National Health Interview Survey, 1988. Vital and Health Statistics, Series 10, No. 173.* Hyattsville, MD: National Center for Health Statistics.

Amos, S., Odake, K., & Ambrus, C. M. (1969). Effect of sex hormones on the serum-induced thrombosis phenomenon. *Proceedings of the National Academy of Science, 62,* 150–154.

Baker, L., Dearborn, M., Hastings, J. E., & Hamberger, K. (1984). Type A behavior in women: A review. *Health Psychology, 3,* 477–497.

Barrett-Connor, E., Brown, W. V., Turner, J., Austin, M., & Criqui, M. H. (1979). Heart disease risk factors and hormone use in postmenopausal women. *Journal of the American Medical Association, 241,* 2167–2169.

Broverman, I. K., Broverman, D. M., Clarkson, F. E., Rosenkrantz, P. S., & Vogel, S. R. (1970). Sex-role stereotypes and clinical judgments of mental health. *Journal of Consulting and Clinical Psychology, 34,* 1–7.

Glynn, K., Leventhal, H., & Hirschman, R. (1986). *A cognitive developmental approach to smoking prevention.* National Institute on Drug Abuse/Research Analysis and Utilization System RAUS Research Monograph Series. Monograph No. 63, pp. 130–152. Rockville, MD: U.S. Department of Health and Human Services.

Gomberg, E. S. L. (1982). Historical and political perspective: Women and drug use. *Journal of Social Issues, 38,* 9–23.

Gordon, T., Kannel, W. B., Hjortland, M. C., & McNamara, P. M. (1978). Menopause and coronary heart disease: The Framingham study. *Annals of Internal Medicine, 89,* 157–161.

Grady, K. E. (1981). Sex bias in research design. *Psychology of Women Quarterly, 54,* 628–636.

Hammond, C. B., & Maxson, W. S. (1982). Current status of estrogen therapy for the menopause. *Fertility and Sterility, 37,* 15.

Hammond, E. G. (1965). Studies in fetal and infant mortality. II. Differentials by sex and race. *American Journal of Public Health, 55,* 1152–1163.

Harris, J. E. (1983). Cigarette smoking among successive birth cohorts of men and women in the United States during 1900–1980. *Journal of the National Cancer Institute, 71,* 473–479.

Johnson, M., Ramey, E., & Ramwell, P. W. (1975). Sex and age differences in human platelet aggregation. *Nature, 253,* 355–357.

Johnson, M., Ramey, E., & Ramwell, P. W. (1977). Androgen mediated sensitivity in platelet aggregation. *American Journal of Physiology, 232,* 381–385.

Kannel, W. B., Hjortland, M. C., McNamara, P. M., & Gordon, T. (1976). Menopause and risk of cardiovascular disease: The Framingham Study. *Annals of Internal Medicine, 85,* 447–452.

Kilbey, M. M., & Sobeck, J. P. (1988). Epidemiology of alcoholism. In C. B. Travis (Ed.), *Women and health psychology: Mental health issues* (pp. 92–107). Hillsdale, NJ: Erlbaum.

Levy, R. L., & Richey, C. A. (1988). Measurement and research design. In E. A. Blechman & K. D. Brownell (Eds.), *Handbook of behavioral medicine for women* (pp. 421–438). New York: Pergamon Press.

Marsh, J. C., Colten, M. E., & Tucker, M. B. (1982). Women's use of drugs and alcohol: New perspectives. *Journal of Social Issues, 38,* 1–8.

Moss, A. J., Levy, A. S., Kim, I., & Park, Y. K. (1989). *Use of vitamin and mineral supplements in the United States: Current users, types of products, and nutrients.* Advance data from *Vital and Health Statistics*, No. 174 (DHHS Pub No. PHS 89-1250). Hyattsville, MD: National Center for Health Statistics.

Nelson, C., & McLemore, T. (1988). *The National Ambulatory Medical Care Survey: 1975–81 and 1985. Vital and Health Statistics*, Series 13, No. 93 (DHHS Pub No. PHS 88-1754). Hyattsville, MD: National Center for Health Statistics.

Preston, S. H. s (1976). *Mortality patterns in national populations.* New York: Academic Press.

Reddy, D. M., Fleming, R., & Adesso, V. J. (1992). Gender and health. In S. Maes, H. Leventhal, & M. Johnson (Eds.), *International review of health psychology* (pp. 3–32). London: Wiley.

Tavris, C. (1992). *The mismeasure of women.* New York: Simon & Schuster.

Verbrugge, L. M. (1982). Sex differentials in health. *Prevention, 97,* 417–437.

Waldron, I. (1983). Sex differences in human mortality: The role of genetic factors. *Social Science and Medicine, 17,* 321–333.

Waldron, I. (1986). The contribution of smoking to sex differences in mortality. *Public Health Reports, 101,* 163–173.

Weidner, G., Friend, R., Ficarroto, T. J., & Mendell, N. R. (In press). Hostility and cardiovascular reactivity in women and men. *Psychosomatic Medicine.*

Part One

Gender, Health, and Aging

We selected Elaine Leventhal's chapter on gender, aging, and health to open this book because it provides a comprehensive overview of health changes in the major bodily systems as a function of aging. We believe that the reader will find this review of physical systems a useful orientation to the topics discussed throughout the remainder of this book. More importantly, Leventhal has marshalled a host of empirical evidence to argue cogently that psychosocial factors contribute substantially to gender differences in morbidity and mortality by influencing symptom formation and reporting, utilization of health care resources, and emotional distress. From her own research, Leventhal also introduces the interesting concept of illness burden, which is "used as an evaluation of the impact of chronic illness status on a host of health-related behaviors and perceptions." Her research indicates fascinating age by gender interactions on illness burden. Her data also suggest the importance of an individual's emotional state in both the causes and the effects of symptom reports, illness, and illness burden. Finally, Leventhal eloquently elaborates the theme that gender cannot be viewed as an independent variable. Rather, it is a "window" through which a multitude of other important mechanisms that control health and longevity may be viewed.

Chapter 2

Gender and Aging: Women and Their Aging

Elaine A. Leventhal

"Each passing year confirms one of the great events of modern times: the triumph of survivorship. . . . The increase in the absolute number and the relative proportion of people over the age of 65 in our nation and around the world has been an extraordinary historical phenomenon—with fundamental social, economic, cultural and personal consequences. Within our own lifetimes, the trend has been clear: marked reductions in childhood and maternal mortality and, more recently, reductions in later-life mortality."

Robert Butler (1980).

INTRODUCTION

The chances of reaching the age of 65 has increased from 4% in 1900 to 12% today and is projected to rise to 20% by 2020. Not only are people living longer, but more people are living longer and more of these aging Americans are women (Waldron 1976, 1983). Women averaged a life span 2–4 years longer than men throughout the 19th century, and by 1980, the difference was 7.5 years (U.S. Department of Health and Human Services, 1980). What are the implications of increased total life span for the physical and mental health of the population?

Completion of this chapter was aided by grant AG 03501 from the National Institute on Aging. I would like to thank Linda Cameron and Howard Leventhal for critical readings of early drafts.

Will the increase in numbers of old women have any special implications for health and utilization of the health care system?

The goal of this chapter is to discuss the biological changes of aging, the factors related to gender difference in physical health, and the possible relationship of these aging and gender factors to symptoms and health behaviors. Not only are there differences between the sexes in longevity, but throughout the life span there are many other biological, psychological and social factors that are correlated with and comprise gender diversities. Moreover, many of these gender differences change over the life span. In adolescence and early adulthood, there are gender differences in diet and exercise practices that reflect current standards of attractiveness and assumptions regarding activities that are life extending. For example, body building, intense physical exercise, steroid use, and increased dietary intake are adopted for these purposes by males, and fasting and exercise for the attainment of anorectic slimness are frequently adopted by females. These behaviors may persist throughout the life span for women whereas they may decline for males.

Complaints and reports of symptoms and the seeking of medical care also reflect concerns about health, illness, and longevity. Such illness behaviors have been described in the medical literature for centuries. They have been observed more frequently in women than in men and are usually attributed to differences in "socialization." Yet there may be gender- specific biological processes such as physical differences in immune resistance or hormonal responsivity, differential exposure to environmental hazards, and different health habits, such as smoking, that are responsible for or that modulate these behaviors for both men and women. The latter argument has been strengthened as greater numbers of females smoking over the past two to three decades have so increased the incidence of lung cancer (the most common cancer of men) that this disease overtook breast cancer as the most common female malignancy in 1987.

It is also probable that behaviors typical in women can be "learned" by males or not expressed by females. Practicing clinicians have little trouble recounting anecdotes of "feminine-type" illness behaviors in males just as they can recall the absence of such "typical" behaviors in some females. One should not assume that there is a sex bias implicit in the attribution of gender difference to female rather than male patterns of behavior. When only two patterns are involved, a coin flip can best determine which pattern is "normative."

It has also been suggested that unique personality styles of women may affect longevity. Women react differently to illness and disability because of their greater experience and more adaptive behavior toward illness, which includes their willingness to access health care (Lewis, 1985). Nathanson (1975) examined various models designed to account for gender differences in illness behavior and rejected those proposing that: (1) sex role is compatible with sick role ("home" work duties allow for being ill), and (2) many female roles are stressful and may be more illness inducing than those of men. Nathanson has proposed that women are less likely to be rejected for exhibition of emotional symptoms and less likely to be held to standards of independent behavior, so that it is easier for them to report symptoms and seek help. She has also pointed out that role hypotheses do not generalize to all women since only *some* females are intensive users of the health system. More symptomatology is seen in unemployed women. Both working women and women with young children have fewer symptoms, yet working women with young children are more likely to use medical care if they are single parents. Nathanson suggests that this may be because they need to protect income and can afford fewer days of disability. Women appear to have accepted a help-seeking role, whereas males appear to have always had difficulty being incapacitated.

Given the great variety of factors associated with gender differences and given the changes in these factors over the life span, it may be appropriate to treat gender as a marker for analysis and for sampling, and inappropriate to treat it as a scientific variable. The differences between the sexes may be better thought of as a window through which one can obtain an interesting view of biological and social-psychological processes and the interactions among these processes. It has been suggested that chronological age should also be used as a window through which to view process rather than as a scientific variable (Leventhal, Leventhal, & Schaefer, 1991), an outlook similar in some respects to that of developmental psychologists who have drawn sharp distinctions between chronological and mental age. Thus comparisons between both age and gender should enhance our understanding of social and biological processes since they allow us to examine these processes from two different vantage points.

To better speculate about the processes visible through the gender window and to present hypotheses organizing apparently contradictory findings between gender differences in mortality, morbidity, and health behavior, I will review the biological changes associated with aging and briefly describe current beliefs about gender and psychological and social aging. Then I will review data on health and illness behaviors that may provide clues to the reasons for the presumed excess of illness behaviors evidenced by women and the health care provided for them. It is my hope that these data and the conclusions based upon them may be helpful to clinicians in the care of their older patients, both male and female, as well as encouraging further research.

BIOLOGICAL AGING

Primary aging or *senescence* is a result of a lifetime of exposure to the environment and the accumulation of illnesses and injuries and is characterized by changes in adaptive capacities at the organismic, organ system, and cellular levels. The specific examples of biological aging included here have been chosen because they are relevant to our discussion of gender differences in illness behavior. We can think of human aging as a series of biological clocks that start to tick at conception and stop at death. They are set at different rates for different organ systems and also at different rates for the sexes. Decrements in overall reserve, the ability to respond to stress and recover from illnesses, represent losses in regenerative ability and deterioration in function. In senescence, there is a general quantitative loss of cells as well as changes in many of the enzymatic activities within cells. Most enzymatic syntheses continue, although for some, rates of production and clearance decline and there may be decreased response to demands for increased activity. In both sexes, the normal kidneys, lungs, and skin age much more rapidly than the heart and liver, whereas the musculoskeletal system and the gonads become atrophic at different times in the life span of males and females (Finch & Schneider, 1985, p. 589).

Epidermal System

Aging of the skin is a reflection of a lifetime of physical changes, environmental exposures, and personal behaviors. The skin as a whole atrophies, with loss of the subcutaneous cushion of fat and decrease in the size of dermal organs. There are fewer blood vessels in the skin and the rate of healing slows, so that older people may adopt behaviors to protect themselves from injury. Elastin, one of the structural elements responsible for the "stretch" in tissues, fragments. However, not all senescent changes represent cell or tissue loss or deterioration. Accumulations of another structural element, collagen, may thicken organs or organ parts. Examples of these age-related changes in elastin and collagen can be seen in wrinkling (Kligman, Grove, & Balin, 1985).

Though there are few innate gender differences in the aging of the skin, such changes that do occur may have different implications for males and females. The skin acts as a major barometer of visible age and is used as a "marker" to judge attractiveness and desirability. It becomes a continuous reminder of the passage of time for both males and females. Although women are assumed to be more reactive emotionally to these particular stigmas of aging and therefore more active in seeking remedies for them, there is a paucity of data on male responses to such changes. It would appear, however, that the recent dramatic increase in advertisements for male cosmetics and hair preparations signals that there is a significant market for products designed to "turn back the clock" for men.

Cardiovascular System

The age-related decline in the cardiovascular system has been assumed to be the critical component in decreased tolerance for exercise and loss of conditioning that contributes to feelings of agedness and overall decline in reserve. However, there is more than heart and blood vessel involvement in loss of reserve. There are important interactions between the cardiovascular system and the musculoskeletal and pulmonary systems. The behavioral complexities of these relationships become apparent when one looks at the gender differences in the rates of aging of these particular organ systems. In the heart, changes occur in the heart chambers, blood vessels, and heart valves. With time, the ventricular myocardium thickens, the chambers within the heart become smaller, and the amount of blood pumped per contraction (the cardiac output) decreases. Heart rate also slows with time. The decrease in rate may be related to "down regulation," or decreased responsiveness of adrenergic receptors on heart muscle, since synthesis and clearance of epinephrine do not decline (Rodeheffer, Gerstenblith, Becker, Fleg, Weisfeldt & Lakatta, 1984; Lakatta, 1987). Another cause may be decreased baroreceptor sensitivity. Thus the heart becomes incapable of generating rate accelerations in response to increased activity and stress demands. These anatomic changes in the vascular system have a detrimental effect on function by causing a decline in cardiac output and a decrease in response to work demands. The level of physical activity for most women in the current "elderly" cohort has been less than for men. They are less conditioned and may experience a greater sense of being old than their male peers even though males are at greater risk for cardiovascular disease because of genetic predisposition, diet, and higher incidence of cigarette smoking.

Blood vessels narrow because of the thickening of endothelial linings and changes in smooth muscle mass. Calcium may be deposited in vessel walls if vascular muscle injury occurs, making blood vessels more rigid and contributing to the slow elevation in blood pressure seen over time. In the absence of cardiovascular disease this may never reach a pathological range, and an individual can be very old and not be hypertensive. When coronary artery disease is superimposed onto normal cardiac aging, function is further compromised. Women appear to enjoy a slower rate of progression of arteriosclerotic disease while exposed to circulating estrogens. This is reflected in the lower incidence of coronary artery disease in premenopausal women. (National Center for Health Statistics, 1982; Kannel & Abbott, 1984).

Anecdotally, individuals state that they are aware of changes in their heart rates and claim that they are attentive or vigilant to them in a variety of settings; they monitor anxiety or the effort of exercise by heart rate and respiratory rate; they are aware of increases in their heart rates when upset, excited, stressed, or exerting physical effort. They perceive rate changes, the presence of ectopic beats, and dysrhythmias. They believe that they can tell when their blood pressure is going up or down, and they use these symptoms to direct health behaviors (Bauman & H. Leventhal, 1985; Meyer, H. Leventhal, & Gutmann, 1985).

Pulmonary System

The aging changes in the cardiovascular system are mirrored by an even more rapid decline in respiratory function due to changes in the muscles and bones of the chest as well as changes in the lungs. There is less work capacity as smooth muscle mass in the bronchi, the diaphragm and chest wall declines, as collagen thickens, and as elastin fragments. If the thoracic cage becomes smaller because of fractures of osteoporotic vertebrae in women, there is a further decrease in chest capacity and thus in pulmonary function. Within the lung itself, single cell layers or septa separate the air-filled alveoli from their vascular supply. The septa are critical as the exchange site for oxygen and carbon dioxide. With aging and pollution exposure, random disruptions or areas of thickening in the septal walls occur that interfere with gaseous exchange. This form of "senile emphysema" may limit the amount of exercise and energy that can be expended. Thus, in many older people, pulmonary aging may have even more impact than cardiac aging on exercise tolerance and response to stress. It is difficult to determine how much respiratory functional decline is age related and how much is environmentally induced since most individuals are exposed to air pollution. There are no studies on nonsmokers living in nonpolluted environments, but it is clear that use of cigarettes or other inhaled substances exaggerates the aging changes described above. Smoking produces an acceleration of the emphysematous changes described above, leading to decreased gas exchange, increased secretions, and increased rates of chronic infection such as those frequently present in middle- aged smokers. These changes in the lungs can be reversed or stabilized if smoking stops (Hermanson, Omenn, Kronmal, & Gersh, 1988).

Musculoskeletal System

Accelerated skeletal aging and the loss of muscle mass are responsible not only for diminished exercise capacity in females but also for the greater vulnerability of women to fractures and immobilization. Skeletal aging, involving the bones and muscles as well as the ligaments and tendons, probably accounts for most of the common symptoms responsible for limitations of activities in work, recreation, and daily living. Males maintain an advantage in greater musculoskeletal strength after pubescence though they, like women, lose significant muscle mass over time. Joint and muscle aches and stiffness symptoms are frequently ascribed to getting old yet are also characteristic of degenerative joint disease, one of the most common diseases of the elderly. Musculoskeletal symptoms are responsible for the most time lost on the job and the high use of pain medications.

The most common form of loss of bone mass or osteopenia is calcium demineralization or osteoporosis. The decline in skeleton mineralization, which occurs over the life span for both men and women, evolves more rapidly for females. This can be especially prominent in the vertebral column of women and is important not only for posture but, as noted above, for respiratory function as well. This rate difference in bone mass loss represents an approximate 10-year advantage for males, though men may become osteoporotic earlier because of concurrent disease. The gender-specific rate of demineralization has a complex metabolic etiology that includes the permissive effect of circulating estrogens and progesterone on remodeling of the bones of the vertebral spine. In contrast, calcium and Vitamin D metabolism and weight-bearing activity appear to be more critical for the integrity of the cortical types of bones of the extremities. Thus postmenopausal women are more vulnerable to fractures of the spine than same- aged males, whereas both men and women are at risk for fractures of the long bones—although women are fracture prone 10 years earlier than are men of the same age.

Reproductive System

Although other organ systems have unique gender-relevant aging characteristics, the remainder of this discussion will focus on the reproductive system, where gender differences are most pronounced. Aging begins in utero and continues throughout the life span. Potential germ cells reach maturation in the female's ovaries during fetal development and undergo a massive attrition prior to birth, declining from a population of 10 ▪▪▪ 10[T67,SUP + /;6,A1] cells during ovarian organogenesis to 10[T67,SUP + /;6,A1] at birth. This steady decline in functional cell number continues until pubescence, when a population of about 10,000 cells remains available for fertilization. The attrition of ova continues, but at a slower rate, through the active reproductive period of the female's life with its monthly cyclicity and interruptions for pregnancy (Nicosia, 1983). The maturation of germ cells and the production of sex hormones are controlled by a negative feedback loop between the brain and the gonads, whereby hormones such as luteinizing hormone (LH) and follicular stimulating hormone (FSH) are secreted by the anterior pituitary to regulate the follicular ripening of ova and the production of estrogen and progesterone. Follicles that can produce a mature ovum and are capable of synthesizing estrogen and progesterone continue to decline in number, so that at the climacteric there are too few remaining to produce adequate circulating hormones to stimulate and protect not only gonad- dependent end organs such as the breasts and genitalia but trabecular bone of the vertebrae and blood vessels as well. Thus, as estrogenic stimulation declines, females begin to experience the effects of hormonal deficiency, including atrophy of the breasts and genitalia and vasomotor instability. The reduction in estrogen and progesterone results finally in the cessation of menstruation, or the menopause, and the uninhibited production of the pituitary gonadotropic hormones because there is inadequate hormone to participate in the negative feedback cycling with the pituitary. All women show elevations in circulating pituitary gonadotropic hormones (LH and FSH) after they enter the perimenopausal period between the ages of 40 and 55, the physiologic significance of this development is not clear (Barbo, 1987; Mastroianni & Paulsen, 1986). After the menopause, there is a relatively rapid rise in the appearance of diseases such as stroke and coronary artery disease and osteoporosis-related fractures indicative of the loss of the protective effects of estrogen and progesterone.

Males, on the other hand, show minimal loss of testicular structures or declines in hormonal synthesis and secretion. In the testes, potential sperm cells remain arrested at the primitive spermatogonium stage. The process of maturation to mature sperm continues throughout the male lifetime, with declines occurring only very late in the seventh to eighth decades. Hormonal function also remains relatively stable, and in many men the negative feedback mechanisms with the anterior pituitary are unchanged until the eighth decade; elevated gonadotropic hormones are rarely seen before the age of 70 (Stearns, Mac-Donnell, Kaufman, Padua, Lucman, Winter, & Faiman, 1974).

Summary

Despite their apparent accelerated aging in many organ systems, women outlive their male partners. These old women have more acute and chronic illnesses but die at a lesser rate. The biological changes discussed above are reflected in these mortality figures. For example, the risk for death from coronary heart disease (CHD) is much higher among men, and a majority of male deaths occur during the 45- to 65-year age range, during the early part of which women are still under or just moving out of the presumable protective influence of estrogen. Women "catch up" in cardiovascular disease risk in the 65- to 75-year-old range. And although overall patterns of cardiovascular morbidity are eventually similar, the clinical pictures vary by sex. Men present most frequently with an acute myocardial infarction, whereas more than half of women with CHD present with symptoms of angina. In addition, silent infarcts are more common in women (Kannel & Abbott, 1984). Women have more hypertension, yet males die more frequently from stroke and hypertensive heart disease.

There is a higher incidence of diabetes in women, but female mortality rates are only slightly higher than the rates for males for this disease. Women are commonly thought to be the more frail and less healthy sex, yet they live longer than males and many will spend a significant portion of their lives alone, coping with the physical as well as the psychosocial changes of aging (Stoney, Davis, & Matthews, 1987).

Finally, the biological data suggest that among the oldest old, those 80 years and up, females may suffer more from osteoporotic conditions, but males may be the more frail, with more heart disease and malignancy.

PSYCHOSOCIAL AGING AND DISEASE IN WOMEN

We can generate some hypotheses regarding the biological factors responsible for the greater longevity of women over men, but the data do not provide a sufficiently coherent picture to attribute all of the female advantage to biological factors. Indeed, there is still the puzzle as to why women's greater longevity should be associated with increased symptom reporting and health behavior. Can it be that the same factors that lead to longevity are protective for chronic debilitating diseases (Stoney et al., 1987)? Is it possible that these protective factors are biological, or might they be behavioral? Are they more symptomatic only at certain times in women's lives such as during pregnancy or at the menopause, and do women report more symptoms and make more use of the health care system at these times?

Some of the above questions have been addressed, for example, the data showing that women have lower mortality rates yet report more illness holds without the inclusion of obstetrical and gynecological conditions (Nathanson, 1977). Other questions remain, however. Thus we do not know why the gender difference in reporting exists: is it because women, as the primary caregivers in most family groups, learn coping strategies that alert them to illness and prepare them to provide care for others and as a consequence become more sensitive to their own symptomatology? Do their illness and wellness behaviors help them maintain their own health because they are more vigilant and more open to seeking care? Do social expectations about the behavior and health of women determine what women anticipate from treatment as well as how they are treated (Verbrugge & Steiner, 1981)?

Emotional Factors: Do They Create a Gender Bias in Symptom Reports and Health Care Utilization?

For many centuries patterns of female illness have been attributed to emotional rather than physical factors, with the emotional upset seen as arising from the strain between women's role expectations and their life experiences. In the late 1500s and early 1600s, the physician-astrologer Ralph Napier wrote that of the many patients that sought relief from mental distress, two-thirds were female. He believed that women were more distressed by unexpected ills of life because of their greater powerlessness. In 1604, Thomas Wright wrote that females have greater emotional travail because of their inability to resist adversities or any injury offered to them. It appears that in a society where many forms of expression and action were denied to them, women were often seen as resorting to using illness as a "voice" (Tomes, 1990, pp. 143–171).

The contemporary view that women perceive psychological distress as symptomatic of illness and seek medical help can be interpreted as the consequence of professional and intellectual developments in 19th century medicine that expanded medical authority over a variety of human behaviors and conditions previously thought of in moral or religious terms. This medicalization of social and psychological problems (Fox, 1977) led women to think of symptoms of emotional distress as symptoms of medical conditions rather than as moral failings or spiritual crises requiring guidance of the priest. Thus, in the era of

Social Darwinism, women were encouraged by physicians and the larger culture to "somaticize" their feelings of distress with the promise that medicine, not religion, would provide the surer form of relief. This was the time in Western history when character, class, race and gender traits were given physiological or somatic explanations. Indeed, women's complaints were not believed to be diseases at all, but dysfunctions of the womb, continuing a concept that originated in the ancient Greek belief that "hysteria" and aberrant behavior in women resulted from the activities of the "wandering womb" (Rosenberg, 1976; Rosenberg & Smith-Rosenberg, 1976). It is interesting to speculate that until the 19th century, highly religious women might have assumed that stress and malaise were due to sinful actions and avoided medical advice, whereas nonreligious females with symptoms of irritable bowel, diiffuse arthralgias, migraine headaches, or ennui might have been the subjects of the anecdotal examples described above.

Given this historical perspective, it is not surprising that gender differences in use of health care have been found most extensively in studies of the use of mental health services. This literature assumes that the high use of services by females is due almost exclusively to women's more ready translation of nonspecific feelings of distress into the conscious recognition that they have emotional problems. Between 10 and 28% of excess female morbidity measured in treatment statistics appears to be explained by this gender difference in the recognition of mental health problems (Kessler, Brown, & Broman, 1981), and the 1978 President's Commission on Mental Health reported more use of the health system by females and a greater willingness to seek help for emotional problems. This survey also documented that 76% of all prescriptions written for psychotropics (e.g., Librium, Valium) were prescribed for women (Lewis, 1985). In a Canadian study, females were shown to take twice as many drugs as males, with minor tranquilizers and sedative hypnotics making up 45% of all prescriptions. Females reported more symptoms of anxiety and generalized discomfort and inhibition of behaviors than males (Cooperstock, 1978). There were similar findings from a Scandinavian study (Hemminki, 1974) though an interesting age effect was also seen. Once treated, middle- aged but not elderly women were more likely to be retreated with minor psychotropics within 3 years. The gender difference in treatment was largest for those between the ages of 30 and 49, less for those below age 13 and over age 50, and lowest for those over 60. Within the female ranks, housewives were more likely to be retreated than were married females and married working females, though all three groups were more likely to be retreated than were males. So, as in medieval Europe, women continue to appear to account for disproportionately larger proportions of the physician's clientele, present with a greater proportion of stress-related illnesses, and continue to receive a greater percentage of pharmacologic interventions (Morantz-Sanchez, 1985).

A variety of hypotheses have been advanced in efforts to explain such gender differences in treatment of mental health problems. Coopersmith (1971), for example, advanced a social- perception hypothesis suggesting that physicians expected emotional distress, expressiveness, and upset in females and tended to treat female but not male patients with medication. Additional data consistent with this hypothesis were collected by Russo (1977). He found that women recounted experiencing more anxiety and depression than men and were more likely to seek help for these feelings. Most were seen by generalists who were likely to prescribe psychotropic drugs. Females used 66% of all prescribed medications, 63% of all tranquilizers, and 71% of all antidepressants. There were gender differences for expression of and response to emotional stress: females became depressed, avoiding exciting activities, whereas males turned to alcoholism and drug abuse and exhibited personality disorders that were associated with an acting out of distress. Females were more likely to interpret distress as a sign of illness and to be judged sick. Males were more apt to be labeled "bad" because of the aggressive ways they manifested emotional discomfort (Russo, 1984).

An alternative approach is offered by Rosenfield's (1980, 1989, in press) analyses of a subsample of married couples from the 1965 psychiatric epidemiology study conducted in the Washington Heights section of New York City, and her analyses of three large data sets (the Fifty Community Study by Fischer, 1982, Americans View Their Mental Health by Veroff, Douvan & Kulka, 1976, and a survey of 500 Southern California residents by Rosenfield, 1989; Baldassare et al., 1984). She presents clear evidence of contrasting gender effects for depressive symptoms as a function of marital status and employment. Specifically, as in prior studies, women reported more depressive symptomatology than men. This gender difference was greatest and was confined to comparisons of nonworking housewives to their husbands. When the wife was employed, the differences reversed, with husbands reporting more depressive symptoms than their wives (Rosenfield, 1980). The increase in depressive symptomatology by males is exacerbated when the wife's income comprises a greater proportion of total family income, and this effect is strongest for higher income families (Rosenfield, 1993). These findings are generally supported by the analyses of the two West Coast samples and the nationally representative sample (Rosenfield, 1989), with a qualification: working women facing competing demands of work and homemaking tend to be more symptomatic than working women not facing such demands. Similarly, depressive symptoms are most intense among men who report sharing homemaking responsibilities. Further analyses show that these gender effects are largely due to feelings of personal control, with a poor sense of personal control apparently responsible for high rates of symptom reporting and for the above-mentioned gender differences.

In summary, the data indicate the existence of a psychological or emotional path to symptoms for both men and women. The psychological and emotional factors generating symptoms are activated by role- and conflict-related factors for each gender, though the operational definitions for each are somewhat dif-

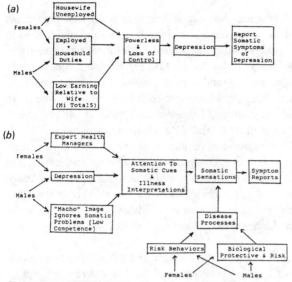

Figure 2.1   Social structural and situational factors producing a sense of powerlessness and loss of control generate depressed affect and symptoms for both sexes (Panel a). These same situational factors, along with a wide variety of situational variables ranging from illness in peers to media messages, can affect self monitoring and readiness to interpret somatic sensations as signs of illness (Panel b).

ferent (see Figure 2.1a). As Coopersmith (1971) proposes, it seems likely that social stereotypes can build upon and enhance these effects.

Physical Illness as a Source of Gender Differences in Symptom Reports and Health Care Utilization

The above findings raise two important questions. First, are gender differences confined primarily to mental health conditions, and can these conditions account for virtually all of the excess morbidity reported by women? Second, if gender differences persist after controlling for mental health problems, we are left with our original problem, namely, how to account for the excess morbidity reported by women and the higher levels of mortality among men.

   In his comprehensive examination of the bases for perceived gender differences, Kessler (1985) pointed out that assumptions about gender differences and perceptions of health problems are *not* firmly based on data, and clear distinctions have not been made between conditions that differ in chronicity, severity, or symptom clarity. Thus we do not know whether women report more symptoms than men when the symptoms are of long rather than short duration, mild or intense in severity, and psychological or psychophysiological (such as headache or fatigue) rather than physical (such as rashes or bleeding). We also do not know whether women are more likely than men to use medical services for each of these types of symptom. Much has been made of findings from large utilization surveys or self-report studies that are relatively insensitive to the nonadditive effects between symptoms and other predictors. They do not take into account the biologic factors just reviewed and also fail to provide validating information based upon medical examinations to confirm the presence or absence of illness for comparison to self-reports of health status. As previously noted, most deal only with mental health symptomatology.

A comprehensive study of a nationally representative sample of men and women, the National Health Survey (National Center for Health Statistics, 1982), reported gender differences in reports of physical symptoms and diagnoses as part of an effort to examine health care practices in the United States. This survey found gender and age differences in the incidence of acute and chronic conditions, with the highest incidence of illnesses occurring in early childhood, at greater than 300 illnesses per year per 100 children and decreasing to less than 100 illnesses per year per 100 persons among those over age 65. Although the incidence of virtually every chronic condition rose steadily with age, the extremely high incidence of acute, infectious diseases in the young was responsible for this group's having the highest overall incidence rates. Women showed a slightly higher incidence of illness than men, though the difference seemed small relative to that in studies focusing on mental and emotional complaints. Although some of the excess illness in women is due to certain diseases of the later years that are *unique* to females, for example, gynecological malignancies such as uterine cancer, there are increases for women in the incidence of non-gender-specific acute and chronic illnesses such as hypertension, stroke, and diabetes, as well as senile dementia of the Alzheimer's type, arthritis, and urinary incontinence (Barbo, 1987).

The National Health Survey data continue to support the hypothesis that compared to males, females have a greater burden of physical illness, though the data suggest that the excess morbidity for women for "physical" health problems is far smaller than that for "psychological" complaints. The survey data are also very clear in showing life span changes in both the frequency and types of physical illnesses afflicting cohorts of different ages. But these data are still inconsistent with mortality findings since they do not tell us why women outlive their male counterparts if they are afflicted with a greater number of chronic conditions.

One possibility is that females are exposed to a greater number of environmental conditions that are disease inducing. As a group, women are socioeconomically less well off than men, may have greater role conflict and be subject to more stress, have less favorable life styles (are more likely to be overweight and are less physically active) and have more difficulties making effective use of health care due to lower rates of insuredness and difficulty taking time off due to competing demands of family and work. In her detailed examination of data from the Health in Detroit Study (Verbrugge, 1984; Verbrugge & Depner, 1981), Verbrugge (1989) found that controlling for social factors such as those just mentioned greatly reduced and for some indicators actually reversed the excess morbidity reported by women. For example, the statistically significant excess morbidity of women relative to men was substantially reduced for 24 of 27 indicators (derived from retrospective data obtained at a baseline health survey and prospective data obtained from daily diaries) after controlling for a wide array of social factors. Moreover, on 3 indicators the gender difference was reversed: that is, men had greater morbidity than women. And for 10 indicators that initially showed no statistically significant gender difference, 3 became smaller and 6 reversed, with males now showing more health deficits than females. On 4 of the 6 indicators that showed initially higher levels of morbidity for men than women, controlling for social factors led to increases in the magnitude of these differences.

Verbrugge's (1989) careful examination of the Detroit data strongly suggests that males may indeed be at greater risk of morbidity than previously thought. But as she points out, the inconsistency still remains. Even after controlling for social factors, estimates of morbidity are still somewhat higher for women than men and gender ratios for mortality are little changed: that is, men still show higher mortality rates after controlling for the same factors. This is the case for three data sets: the Alameda County data (Wingard, 1982), the Rancho Bernardo data (Wingard, Suarez, & Barrett-Connor, 1983), and the San Francisco-Oakland data (Friedman, Loring, & Ury, 1979). Indeed, even after controlling for smoking history and alcohol consumption, risk factors that are greater sources of mortality for men than for women, the risk ratios for all causes and for coronary disease mortality remain surprisingly stable, with men having higher death rates than women. Verbrugge (1989, p. 295) concludes that "given that all these studies cover a wide range of social factors we are left with an old but powerful hypothesis—that biological factors are at work in men's poorer long-run health and higher mortality." These paths are represented in Figure 2.1b.

Steps toward a Resolution of the Inconsistency

Factors That May Affect Gender Differences in Symptom Reporting
The contrast between excess mortality among men and excess morbidity among women, the provocative analyses conducted by Rosenfield (1989, in press) and Verbrugge (1989), and the data obtained in one of our recent studies have led us to make several suggestions that may help us to understand these contrasting gender effects. The basic ideas are simple. First, like others (Costa & McCrae, 1985; Schroeder & Costa, 1984; Watson & Pennebaker, 1989), we strongly suspect that the symptom reports obtained in most epidemiological studies do not adequately discriminate between symptoms that are attributable primarily to psychological factors, such as depressed affect, and symptoms that are attributable to either acute or chronic physical pathology. This discrimination is not

easily made since physiological disruption can generate emotional change (Aneshensel, Frerichs, & Huba, 1984) and emotional states can, in turn, affect symptomatology.

Second, it appears that somewhat different factors will affect the emotional-symptom complex and the symptoms and signs of disease-specific pathology. Depression is a source of somatic symptoms (Barsky & Klerman, 1983), and the factors producing it, such as a sense of loss of control (Rosenfield, 1989), are symptom generating. But the same variables identified by Rosenfield and Verbrugge, such as role expectations, perceptions of control, and work demands, may affect the reporting of symptoms caused by physical pathology by affecting psychological factors such as somatic awareness or introspection (Hansell & Mechanic, 1991), rumination over symptoms (Cameron, Leventhal, & Leventhal, in press), and the interpretation of somatic sensations. Symptomch awareness, symptom interpretation, and other similar factors can be influenced by a wide variety of contextual factors such as illness in peers, media messages, (e.g., President Reagan's colonoscopy), and so on, which can enhance awareness of and readiness to report somatic sensations as physical events (Cioffi, 1991; H. Leventhal, 1986; Leventhal & Everhart, 1979; Leventhal, Leventhal, Shacham, & Easterling, 1989). Gender differences in symptom reporting may reflect a combination of these factors, in that women, particularly in roles with low levels of control, will be more emotionally distressed, more somatically attentive and aware of both emotionally and physically generated somatic sensations, and more likely to interpret these sensations as reflections of illness (see Figure 2.1b).

Third, several factors such as trait anxiety and depression (Costa & McCrae, 1985; Watson & Pennebaker, 1989) and some situational stressors related to somatic awareness and the interpretation and reporting of symptoms are related to gender and are relatively stable. These factors will generate relatively consistent gender differences in symptom reporting, and gender will serve as a proxy or window through which to view the effect of these factors on symptom reports in both cross-sectional and longitudinal studies.

Fourth, it is highly likely that the social and psychological factors affecting psychological and physical symptom sets operate over quite different time frames. We would expect the time frame to be long (years) for symptoms associated with slow-onset chronic illnesses such as cancer, and relatively short for symptoms associated with emotional states.

Finally, it is important to note that gender differences in morbidity and symptom reporting may reflect interactions among specific disease processes and the various factors favoring symptom awareness and reporting. For example, the chronic diseases of later life, such as cancer and atherosclerotic disease, are typically asymptomatic at their early stages and become symptomatic only gradually. If the socialization of females makes them more attentive to somatic states and more likely to interpret these states in medical terms, and if the roles women occupy provide the opportunity for self-observation and permission for reporting, women may be more likely to detect chronic illness in its early stages. If so, the duration of a chronic disease as a psychologically and socially recognized illness will be longer for women than for men, and increases in duration will necessarily increase estimates of prevalence.

It appears, therefore, that the increased morbidity of female relative to male respondents in epidemiological studies is due in part to the use of symptom checklists since these checklists do not sharply differentiate between symptoms generated by somatic disruptions or disease and symptoms generated by social psychological and emotional factors. Moreover, the environmental factors (role factors leading to reduced control) and personal factors (trait depression and anxiety) that generate social-psychological and emotional symptoms are more prevalent among women than men (Wallston, Wallston, & DeVellis, 1978). In addition, women seem to have higher levels on measures such as body awareness and readiness to report somatic distress, which will increase symptom reports (and morbidity estimates) for somatic sensations generated by disease. Thus, even if women's verifiable morbidity is not greater than that of men, estimates of morbidity filtered through the multiple factors affecting self-report and self-referral behavior will inflate morbidity estimates for women. It is worth noting the gender bias in the prior sentence, and indeed in every statement claiming "excess" morbidity in women, in that such statements attribute the difference between genders to an active biasing process in women. Is it not possible that the bias is in men, namely that men are unaware of or unable to accurately report their physical condition?

Some Evidence for These Factors in Data from our Research Group
The studies conducted by our research group have examined the relationship between gender and symptoms for cohorts of different ages and done so in both cross-sectional and longitudinal analyses; thus they may be of some relevance to the resolution of the apparent inconsistency between morbidity and mortality ratios for males and females. In one recently completed investigation, we assessed perceived health status, symptom reports, utilization of the health system, and a variety of factors such as life events, mood states, and coping strategies (for both health and non-health problems) in a sample of 366 middle-aged to elderly (45 to 93 years) community-dwelling respondents. The participants were also interviewed whenever one of them made a patient-initiated clinic visit to their health care system, a University Hospital General Internal Medicine and Geriatrics Clinic. Thus the data provided us with both a short- and a long-term time frame for examining the relationship of age and gender to symptoms and utilization. Since there were many diseases represented in this patient population, an illness burden index was generated from a comprehensive review of each subject's chart by an internist-geriatrician. The score represented a 5-point rating of diseases by severity, chronicity, and potential for functional compromise and was used as an evaluation of the impact of chronic illness status on a host of

health-related behaviors and perceptions. Since medical ratings of illness burden are not typically found in epidemiological studies, these ratings provided an interesting touchstone against which to compare gender differences in symptom reporting.

Data covering a long time frame were obtained from five interviews conducted at 3-month intervals. Each of the interviews covered current symptoms (conducted in the form of a review of systems that allowed us to code over 250 separate symptoms in response to 26 open-ended questions); an interpretation of the most significant symptoms and the unfolding of the most significant symptom episode, including the emotional distress and coping responses it provoked and whether it led to the use of health care; the presence of major and minor life events; the subject's perceptions of whether events and age in general could contribute to the onset of illness; and several personality factors.

The gender and age differences observed in these data are consistent with the assumption that symptom reports reflect both the physical and psychological status of the respondent and that both components are involved in gender differences. First, we found significant gender and age differences in physician-rated illness burden. Illness burden increased with age for both sexes, but there was a crossover with increasing age. Whereas younger women had higher illness burdens than younger males, males over 75 years of age had higher physician ratings of illness burden and more severe illnesses than did the females of similar age; the crossover produced a significant sex by age interaction and a significant contrast in the oldest old group: that is, the illness burden was greater for the oldest old males than for the oldest old females.

Consistent with the assumption that symptom reports reflect physical status, gender differences in symptom reporting paralleled the differences in illness burden. The total number of symptoms increased with the age of the cohort for both genders, and women had a greater total number of symptoms than men. There was a significant increase in symptoms among the middle-aged females, an effect not seen in males, consistent with probable menopausal symptoms. As with medically rated illness burden, the gender differences reversed in the oldest old cohort, with the oldest old males reporting more symptoms than were reported by the females in this cohort. Thus, compared to women, the oldest old males were more frail, had a greater burden of chronic illness, and reported increased symptomatology. We also found that females made significantly more visits to the medical clinic than did males, though among the oldest old cohort the data showed a greater number of spontaneous (i.e., patient-initiated) clinic visits among males than females. Thus both symptom reports and patient-driven visits parallel the illness burden ratings for the overall gender differences and the crossover showing higher response rates for the oldest old males. The symptom data clearly reflect medical need.

The above cross-sectional data make clear that symptom reports reflect disease. The data also reveal a link from affect to gender and from affect and gender to symptom reports. Scores on the mood adjective scales used to measure emotional states were higher for females than males, indicating greater distress parallel to the higher level of symptom reporting by females, and emotional states of anxiety and depression were correlated with symptom reports for both sexes. When asked how they felt about their symptoms, females also reported stronger emotional responses to symptoms than did males. Thus, as Rosenfield and Verbrugge's analyses would suggest, gender is a predictor of symptoms if we do not first correct for the association of gender with variables such as anxiety and depression that influence symptom reporting or when we do not correct for current symptom load with later symptom load. If we correct for variables such as those studied by Rosenfield and Verbrugge, we can identify their effect on morbidity data.

We computed a model of the relationships among gender, age, and illness burden to emotional reactions (anxiety and depression) and symptoms over three occasions: the baseline, 6- month, and 1-year interviews. The cross-sectional relationships are as described above: females reported higher levels of anxiety and depression and higher levels of symptomatology. The model also showed that depression at baseline was related to increases in symptom reports from baseline to the 6-month follow-up, and that *increases* in symptom reporting over this period by female respondents were accounted for by their higher levels of depression at baseline. The data suggest, therefore, that emotional states can affect symptom reports over an "intermediate" (6-month) term, and that emotional state may account in part for the increase of symptom reporting by women. Of course, we do not know whether this path reflects the effect of depression on later disease or on sensitivity to somatic changes. We suspect the former since there was no increase in symptom reporting related either to gender or to depression over a longer (1- year) time period, suggesting that high levels of depression were related to a slight excess of acute illness episodes.

The data also suggested that illness and symptoms can increase negative emotions. That this may occur over relatively long time periods was seen in data showing increases in negative affect with increases in the incidence of chronic illness. This relationship occurred despite the sharp decreases in emotional distress with increasing age for both genders. This may seem a contradiction since the incidence of chronic illness increases with age. But the two differences are compatible since they reflect that in comparison to older respondents, younger respondents were far more emotionally reactive to symptoms of both acute and chronic illness, whereas all respondents were more distressed in response to symptoms of chronic illness. Moreover, the age-related decline in emotional distress to symptoms was much more pronounced for individuals with a low illness burden. When there was a high illness burden associated with a severe chronic illness, the decrease with age was much less.

When we looked at symptom cognitions (interpretations) and emotional factors as motivators of health care, we found that both symptom cognitions and emotional (life events) factors predicted utilization (Cameron et al., 1993). But whereas symptom cognitions (perceived seriousness and disruption) increased negative affects, neither negative affects nor life stresses affected symptom cognitions. Moreover, the only gender difference in the data was the typical increase in symptom reports for females. Thus, at least in these data, emotional reactions did not appear to have an effect on the appraisal of ongoing somatic symptoms.

Finally, we found small but consistent gender differences in types of coping strategies for personal health problems versus for the health problems of others that were noted in the life events section of the interviews. Although females, overall, generated more clinic visits than males, they also adopted other, primarily *passive* tactics, including diversion, suppression of emotion, and the seeking of religious support for their own significant life events. Males were *active* in their choice of coping behaviors. They solicited information, advice, and social support from peers, sought either catharsis or relaxation, or used some form of stimulant (i.e., cigarettes, alcohol, chocolate, drugs), and appeared to be more accepting of their problem. Both males and females sought support and advice from social contacts for their *own* health problems with equal frequency, but males looked for information when talking to peers, whereas women looked for social support and advice about seeking care. Married and widowed females solicited advice more frequently than single and divorced women, and married females were most likely to talk to peers when faced with a symptomatic problem. Thus, for themselves, females developed avoidance tactics whereas males took action. For coping with *another* person's medical needs, females were the active caretakers; males were more likely to offer social support, but offered little actual service. These are similar to the findings, including drug use in response to health problems, of Pennebaker (1982).

Summary of Hypotheses Accounting for Gender Differences

My review of the published literature and our own findings strongly suggest that multiple factors affect symptom reports and that no single variable is the key to gender differences. Thus, as indicated at the outset of this chapter, gender is not a scientific variable, but is a proxy for many variables. Male and female populations serve as windows or divergent vantage points for viewing the biological and social-psychological processes involved in the generation of disease and reporting of symptoms. As these various factors are identified, incorporated, and logically sequenced in a multifactorial model of gender and health, the paradox of higher levels of symptom reporting and lower mortality for women will vanish since these different endpoints will be seen as consequences of different sets of antecedent factors driving partially overlapping and partially independent mechanisms. The association of increased symptom reporting with increased longevity will disappear as a paradox and emerge as an obvious outcome of differential mechanisms.

Figure 2.1b summarizes the suggestions made from the studies here reviewed. It is important to note that the figure says as much about male symptom reporting as it does about female symptom reporting! An account of the difference between two groups cannot be valid if it focuses on the processes in only one group. First, social roles such as involvement in work, child care, and the double demands of jobs and home can affect an individual's sense of control, increase negative affect, particularly depressed mood, and increase reporting of psychological symptoms. *These factors operate for both men and women!* But traditional social structure enhances their potency for women, whereas "modern" role reversals enhance their potency for men (Rosenfield, 1989, in press). At present, there is no reason to assume that the mechanism involved is gender specific.

Second, it appears that women may be more accurate and sensitive reporters of somatic sensations related to disease. The factors that may be at work in this area are both social and biological. Women's roles are more closely linked to caring. Across widely varying cultures it is women who bear primary responsibility for child care. This is vividly illustrated in the account of the apportionment of responsibilities in an Ecuadorian family with an injured 6- year-old girl (Price, 1987). To get to the clinic each day for months, the mother carried the youngster on her back down 200 steps to the local bus stop four blocks away. Neither she nor her husband, a bus driver whose bus was parked near the home, would think of his taking them both to the clinic; his concern was with the economic burden of the treatment. But whether in the United States or in Ecuador, the individual responsible for child care must attend to and cope with childhood illnesses: *the mother develops expertise in health management.* So, too, with a woman's biology: the monthly menstrual cycle and the changes of menopause require attention to and management of somatic problems. Thus, for both social and biological reasons, women are poised to be the experts at monitoring and coping with somatic problems.

Men, on the other hand, lack the life experience that is likely to generate expertise in monitoring and caring for systemic, somatic states. The active, dominating and controlling male role, its "machismo," is equated with the absence of fear and the absence of symptoms. Male athletes are treated and taught to blunt symptoms and to continue competing, and they falsely believe that monitoring and becoming aware of symptoms will disrupt their performance (Morgan & Pollock, 1977). Their mental processes are environmentally focused and they ignore their bodies and emotions. The only acceptable somatic symptoms are those related to sports injuries that they master and overcome. Therefore, it comes as no surprise that males may be slow to detect somatic changes and to identify them with disease. For example, Type A men are slow to recognize the presence of cardiac symptoms (Matthews, Siegel, Kuller, Thompson,

& Varat, 1983; Robbins & Contrada, in preparation), a behavior that puts them at greater risk of death. Thus the very same behavior that may lower the prevalence of morbidity estimates may be responsible for males' increased mortality. It also appears that males may lack the skills needed to access and use the health care resources necessary for coping with the chronic illness and frailty that are intrinsic to the later years.

It would appear that variations in health behaviors evolve over time and are meant to preserve well-being and optimize aging. Because of the gender differences in psychobiological developmental patterns, it is to be expected that the two sexes will exhibit different health and illness behaviors. The biological gender differences are present at birth, but the behaviors they generate probably become relevant for women before adulthood, at puberty, and continue to be important throughout the life span. Awareness of body cues becomes salient for the female at menarche and is inexorably linked to the *rhythmicity* of feminine adulthood with its cyclical physical and emotional sensations related to normal body functioning. Through their lifetime, women accumulate a "history" of awareness of internal physical cues and emotional responses and experiences in coping with reproduction, illness, injury, infection, and malignancy. Males repress such internal body cues. Women become familiar with seeking medical care during the reproductive years and use the health system more consistently than men for the evaluation of their symptoms, regardless of etiology, pathological or functional. Although women experience more symptoms without having a greater incidence of chronic illness, they are not hypochondriacal because women report neither more illness nor a greater perceived illness burden. Thus they do not see themselves as less well than their male peers. It may be that the psychosocial roles that women adopt both mold and direct these behaviors in response to either their own or others' physical symptoms. Well older persons and especially older females may increase the number and variety of health practices they undertake, even when they may have doubts about the efficacy of some of these strategies, because they may feel increasingly vulnerable to disease and disability. Because they are symptomatic and feel vulnerable as they age, they make systematic efforts to avoid stress and the worry associated with potential illness. Using health care and engaging in preventative behaviors, etc. are ways of controlling such worry. When sick, it is the elderly patient who is more compliant with medical regimens as diverse as antihypertensive treatment and cancer chemotherapy (Leventhal, E., 1986). They delay less in seeking care for serious illness (E. Leventhal, Leventhal, Schaefer, & Easterling, in review). Whether older females are more compliant than older males with medical regimens or more active participants in preventive health practices needs to be studied in the clinical setting.

We suggest that the longevity of older women reflects their ability to adapt and maintain functional independence by the vigilance and prudent interpretation of bodily symptoms and the judicious use of the superimposition of their particular illness history onto their aging clock. However, their ability to self-monitor and attend to body cues and report symptoms has also made them vulnerable to possible over-treatment when their presentations of symptoms are interpreted as evidence of neurotic behavior that demands psychological treatments or psychotropic medications.

Both illness and the accumulation of an illness burden effect clinic utilization for males and females, but it is clear that it is symptomatology that determines frequency of clinic visits: when symptoms increase, visits go up. The use of the health system depends on the presence of illness and on perceptions and interpretations that are ascribed to symptoms by physicians as well as patients. Women of all ages, report more emotional distress and symptoms yet are not less healthy than their male counterparts. These gender differences in clinical presentation reflect biological as well as behavioral patterns that need to be understood in order to provide comprehensive and appropriate health care to both males and females.

REFERENCES

Aneshensel, C. S., Frerichs, R. R., & Huba, G. J. (1984). Depression and physical illness: A multiwave, nonrecursive causal model. *Journal of Health and Social Behavior*, *25*, 350-371.

Baldassare, M., Rosenfield, S., & Rook, K. (1984). Types of social relations predicting elderly well-being. *Research on Aging, 6*, 549–559.

Barbo, D. M. (1987). The physiology of the menopause in the postmenopausal woman. *Medical Clinics of North America*, *71*, 11–22.

Barsky, A. J., & Klerman, G. L. (1983). Overview: Hypochondriasis, bodily complaints, and somatic styles. *American Journal of Psychiatry*, *140*, 273–283.

Baumann, L. J., & Leventhal, H. (1985). "I can tell when my blood pressure is up, can't I?" *Health Psychology*, *4*, 203–218.

Butler, R. N. (1979). Aging research: Needs research: Needs and Leads. *American College of Physicians Observer*, *2*, 716–725.

Cameron, L., Leventhal, E. A., Leventhal, H., and Schaefer, P. (1993). Symptom representations and affects as determinants of care-seeking. *Health Psychology, 12*, 171–199.

Cioffi, D. (1991). Beyond attentional strategies: A cognitive-perceptual model of somatic interpretation. *Psychological Bulletin*, *109*, 25–41.

Coopersmith, R. (1971). Sex differences in the use of moodmodifying drugs: An explanatory model. *Journal of Health and Social Behavior*, *12*, 238–244.

Cooperstock, R. (1978). Sex differences in psychotropic drug use. *Science and Medicine*, *12B*, 179–186.

Costa, P. T., & McCrae, R. R. (1985). Hypochondriasis, neuroticism, and aging: When are somatic complaints unfounded? *American Psychologist*, *40*, 19–28.

Department of Health and Human Services. (1980). *Life Tables. Vol. II. Section 5. Vital Statistics of the United States*, Washington, D. C.: U. S. Government Printing Office.

Finch, C. E., & Schneider, E. L. (Eds.). (1985). *Handbook of the biology of aging* (2nd ed., p. 959). New York: Van Nostrand Reinhold.

Fox, R. C. (1977). The medicalization and demedicalization of American society. In J. H. Knowles (Ed.), *Doing better and feeling worse* (pp. 9–22). New York: W. W. Norton and Company, Inc.

Friedman, G. D., Loring, G. D., & Ury, H. K. (1979). Mortality in middle-aged smokers and nonsmokers. *New England Journal of Medicine, 300*, 213–217.

Hansell, S. & Mechanic, D. (1990). Body awareness and self assessed health among older adults. Manuscript submitted for publication.

Hemminki, E. (1974). Disease leading to psychotropic drug therapy. *Scandinavian Journal of Society and Medicine, 2*, 129–134.

Hermanson, B., Omenn, G. S., Kronmal, R. A., & Gersh, B. J. (1988). Beneficial six-year outcome of smoking cessation in older men and women with coronary artery disease. *New England Journal of Medicine, 319*, 1365–1369.

Kannel, W. B. & Abbott, R. D. (1984). Incidence and prognosis of unrecognized myocardial infarction: An update on the Framingham Study. *New England Journal of Medicine, 311*, 1144–1147.

Kessler, R. (1985). Sex differences in the use of health services. In S. McHugh & T. M. Vallis (Eds.), *Illness behavior: A multidisciplinary model* (pp. 135–148). New York: Plenum Press.

Kessler, R. C., Brown, R. L., & Broman, C. L. (1981). Sex differences in psychiatric help-seeking: Evidence from four large-scale surveys. *Journal of Health and Social Behavior, 22*, 49–64.

Kligman, A. M., Grove, G. L., & Balin, A. K. (1985). The anatomy and pathogenesis of wrinkles. *British Journal of Dermatology, 113*, 37.

Lakatta, E. G. (1987). Cardiovascular function and age. *Geriatrics, 42*, 84–94.

Leventhal, E. A. (1986). The dilemma of cancer in the elderly. In J. M. Vaeth & J. Meyer (Eds.), *Cancer and the elderly: Vol. 20. Frontiers of radiation therapy and oncology* (pp. 1–13). Basel: Karger.

Leventhal, E. A., Leventhal, H., Schaefer, P., & Easterling, D. (1993). Conservation of energy, uncertainty reduction and swift utilization of medical care among the elderly. *J. Gerontology, 48*, 78–86.

Leventhal, E. A., Leventhal, H., Shacham, S., & Easterling, D.V. (1989). Active coping reduces reports of pain from childbirth. *Journal of Consulting and Clinical Psychology, 57*, 365–371.

Leventhal, H. (1986). Symptom reporting: A focus on process. In S. McHugh & T. M. Vallis (Eds.), *Illness behavior: A multi-disciplinary model* (pp. 219–237). New York: Plenum Press.

Leventhal, H., & Everhart, D. (1979). Emotion, pain, and physical illness. In C. E. Izard (Ed.), *Emotions and psychopathology* (pp. 263–299). New York: Plenum Press.

Leventhal, H., Leventhal, E. A., & Schaefer, P. (1990). Vigilant coping and health behavior: A life span problem. In M. Ory & R. Abeles (Eds.), *Aging, health, and behavior*. Baltimore: The Johns Hopkins Press.

Lewis, M. (1985). Older women and health: An overview. In S. Golub & R. J. Freedman, *Health needs of women as they age. Women and health: Vol. 10* (pp. 1–16). New York: Haworth Press.

Mastrioanni, L. & Paulsen, C. A. (1986). *The climacteric*. New York: Plenum Press.

Matthews, K. A., Siegel, J. M., Kuller, L. H., Thompson, M. & Varat, M. (1983). Determinants of decisions to seek medical treatment by patients with acute myocardial infarction symptoms. *Journal of Personality and Social Psychology, 44*, 1144–1156.

Meyer, D., Leventhal, H., & Gutmann, M. (1985). Common-sense models of illness: The example of hypertension. *Health Psychology, 4*, 115–135.

Morantz-Sanchez, R. M. (1985). *Sympathy and science: Women physicians in American medicine*. New York: Oxford University Press.

Morgan, W. P., & Pollock, M. L. (1977). Psychological characterization of the elite distance runner. *Annals New York Academy of Science, 301*, 382–403.

Nathanson, C. A. (1975). Illness and the feminine role: A theoretical review. *Social Science and Medicine, 9*, 57–62.

Nathanson, C. A. (1977). Sex, illness, and medical care: A review of data, theory, and method. *Social Science and Medicine, 11*, 13–25.

National Center for Health Statistics. (1982). *Current estimates from the National Health Interview Survey. Vital and Health Statistics* (Series 10, No. 150). Washington, D. C.: U. S. Government Printing Office.

Nicosia, S. V. (1983). Morphological changes in the human ovary throughout life. In G. B. Serra (Ed.), *The ovary* (pp. 57–81). New York: Raven Press.

Pennebaker, J. W. (1982). *The psychology of physical symptoms*. New York: Springer-Verlag.

Price, L. (1987). Ecuadorian illness stories: Cultural knowledge in natural discourse. In D. Holland & N. Quinn (Eds.), *Cultural models in language and thought* (pp. 313–342). New York: Cambridge University Press.

Robbins, M. & Contrada, R. L. (In preparation). Hurry-up and wait: The role of type A behavior in decisions to seek treatment for cardiovascular symptoms.

Rodeheffer, R. J., Gerstenblith, G., Becker, L. C., Fleg, J. L., Weisfeldt, M. L., & Lakatta, E. G. (1984). Exercise cardiac output is maintained with advancing age in healthy human subjects: Cardiac dilatation and increased stroke volume compensate for a diminished heart rate. *Circulation, 69*, 203–213.

Rosenberg, C. (1976). The bitter fruit: Heredity, disease, and social thought. In C. Rosenberg (Ed.), *No other gods: On science and American social thought*, (pp. 332–56). Baltimore: Johns Hopkins Press.

Rosenberg, C., & Smith-Rosenberg, C. (1976). The female animal: Medical and biological views of women and her role in nineteenth century America. In C. Rosenberg (Ed.), *No other gods: On science and American social thought* (pp. 54–70). Baltimore: Johns Hopkins Press.

Rosenfield, S. (1980). Sex differences in depression: Do women always have higher rates? *Journal of Health and Social Behavior, 21*, 33–42.

Rosenfield, S. (1989). The effects of women's employment: Personal control and sex differences in mental health. *Journal of Health and Social Behavior, 30*, 77–91.

Rosenfield, S. (1992). The costs of sharing: Wives' employment and husbands' mental health. *Journal of Health and Social Behavior, 33*, 299–315.

Russo, N. (1984). Women and the mental health delivery system: Women in mental health policy. In L. Walker (Ed.), (pp. 2262–2350). Beverly Hills: Sage Publications.

Schroeder, D. H. & Costa, P. T. (1984). Influence of life event stress on physical illness: Substantive effects or methodological flaws? *Journal of Personality and Social Psychology*, *46*, 853–863.

Stearns, E. L., MacDonnell, J. A., Kaufman, B. J., Padua, R., Lucman, T. S., Winter, J. S. D., & Faiman, C. (1974). Declining testicular function with age. *American Journal of Medicine*, *57*, 761–766.

Stoney, C. M., Davis, M. C., & Matthews, K. (1987). Sex differences in physiological response to stress and in coronary heart disease. *Psychophysiology*, *24*, 127–131.

Tomes, N. (1990). *Historical perspectives on women and mental medicine in America* (pp. 143–171). New York: Garland.

Verbrugge, L. M. (1984). Health diaries-problems and solutions in study design. In C. F. Cannell, & R. F. Groves (Eds.), *Health survey research methods* (Research Proceedings Series, DHHS Publ. No.(PHS) 84-3346, pp. 171–92). Rockville, MD: National Center for Health Research.

Verbrugge, L. M. (1989). The twain meet: Empirical explanations of sex differences in health and mortality. *Journal of Health and Social Behavior*, *30*, 282–304.

Verbrugge, L. M., & Depner, C. E. (1981). Methodological analyses of Detroit health diaries. In S. Sudman (Ed.), *Health survey research methods— Third Conference* (Research Proceedings Series, DHHS Publ. No. (PHS) 81-3268, pp. 144–58). Hyattsville, MD: National Center for Health Services Research.

Verbrugge, L., & Steiner, R. P. (1981). Physician treatment of men and women patients—Sex bias or appropriate care? *Medical Care*, *19*, 609–632.

Waldron, I. (1976). Why do women live longer than men? *Social Science and Medicine*, *10*, 349–362.

Waldron, I. (1983). Sex differences in human mortality: The role of genetic factors. *Social Science and Medicine*, *17*, 321–333.

Wallston, K. A., Wallston, B. S., & DeVellis, R. (1978). Development of the multidimensional health locus of control (MHLC) scales. *Health Education Monographs*, *6*. 160–170.

Watson, D., & Pennebaker, J. W. (1989). Health complaints, stress, and distress: Exploring the central role of negative affectivity. *Psychological Review*, *96*, 234–254.

Wingard, D. L. (1982). The sex differential in mortality rates. *American Journal of Epidemiology*, *115*, 205–216.

Wingard, D. L., Suarez, L., & Barrett-Connor, E. (1983). The sex differential in mortality from all cause and ischemic heart disease. *American Journal of Epidemiology*, *117*, 165–172.

Part Two

Stress, Coronary Heart Disease, and Cancer

Part Two focuses on a biopsychosocial approach to stress in women and men and biopsychosocial mechanisms influencing the development of coronary heart disease and cancer progression in women. Heart disease and cancer are the two leading causes of mortality for women (and men) in the United States and all other technologically advanced countries. Accordingly, the authors, Marianne Frankenhaeuser (stress), Gerdie Weidner (coronary heart disease), and Peggy Ott and Sandra Levy (cancer) discuss complex mechanisms potentially involved in either the development or the progression of these significant diseases: for example, biopsychosocial influences on stress responses in women and men; the role of psychosocial variables in coronary heart disease risk in women; and the influence of psychosocial factors such as personality, coping style, social support, and cognitive/attitudinal functioning on cancer survival in women. Thus the three chapters in this section clarify the basic mechanisms by which psychological and behavioral factors may be linked to disease.

Marianne Frankenhaeuser provides a lucid discussion of psychophysiological reactivity to stress. She presents findings from her laboratory showing striking gender differences in catecholamine responses to cognitive achievement stressors. When challenged, males (including boys) showed consistent marked increases in epinephrine excretion and to a lesser extent norepinephrine increases. In contrast, females (including girls) consistently showed no psychoendocrine response to cognitive achievement stressors or only slight increases. Franken-haeuser points out that the males and females in these studies performed equivalently. Consequently, differential performance cannot explain the gender differences in psychophysiological reactivity exhibited. Moreover, she informs us that interactions between sex steroids and stress hormones do not appear to account for this gender difference. Supporting the thesis that psychosocial factors shape these reactivity differences, Frankenhaeuser found increases in epinephrine and norepinephrine secretion to cognitive achievement stressors similar to those observed among men for women employed in what were considered "male" occupations (e.g., bus driving and engineering). Complementing this finding, lower epinephrine increases in men than women have been found in a traditional female sphere (i.e., interpersonal relations). Fathers showed less of an increase than mothers in the interpersonally demanding context of bringing their 3-year-old child to a hospital for a physical examination. These findings provocatively suggest that the gender differences often observed in catecholamine output to stressors may be learned coping responses.

In the next chapter in this section, Gerdie Weidner examines coronary risk in women. The bulk of her chapter is devoted to a thorough and clear discussion of three psychosocial variables (Type A behavior, occupational stress, and hostility) that have been identified as independent risk factors for coronary risk in women in at least one prospective study. In addition to reviewing the scientific evidence connecting these psychosocial variables to coronary heart disease risk in women, Weidner discusses possible biopsychosocial mechanisms linking each variable to coronary heart disease and gender differences in the prevalence of these psychosocial variables. After reading this chapter one wonders what it is about being male that predisposes men to smoke more cigarettes, be less flexible in food choices, and score higher on Type A behavior and cynical hostility than women. As our present limiting conceptions of maleness and femaleness change, the gender differential in mortality from coronary heart disease and other major causes of death may disappear.

The concluding chapter in this section (Ott and Levy) discusses representative examples of psychological and behavioral research in oncology focusing on breast cancer and uterine and cervical cancer. The main topics covered are psychological distress and adjustment to cancer, the relationship between psychosocial variables and cancer survival rates, and the psychological sequelae of treatment and living with cancer. The authors also discuss significant findings from their own work in the area of psychoneuroimmunology. The aggregated findings reviewed in this chapter suggest that the expression of distress may not only be psychologically adaptive for women with cancer, but also have survival value. Unfortunately, the traditional conception of femaleness may foster emotional passivity in women facing negative, serious events such as breast cancer and uterine and cervical cancer.

Chapter 3

A Biopsychosocial Approach to Stress in Women and Men

Marianne Frankenhaeuser

CORNERSTONES IN STRESS RESEARCH

Stress is a vague concept that eludes a strict definition. Still, the concept has proved useful as an "umbrella" for research on a wide range of conditions, experiences, and responses relevant to health and well-being. Outside the scientific community the stress concept enjoys great popularity, since it captures essential aspects of people's daily hassles as well as critical life events.

The stress under which people in contemporary society live should be viewed in an evolutionary perspective. For our ancestors, survival called for adaptability to physical hazards. It was the "wisdom of the body" (Cannon, 1932), that is, ingenious mechanisms of adaptation, that enabled our ancestors to overcome hardships. The nature of today's demands, however, is generally psychological rather than physical, and our bodily responses have not changed. It is this mismatch between our old biology and the demands of new sociotechnical environments that makes stress a central issue in modern life.

This chapter is based, in part, on earlier reviews by the author: see list of references.

Acknowledgments: The research reported in this chapter has been supported by grants to the author from the J. D. & C. T. MacArthur Foundation's Research Network on Health and Behavior, the Swedish Work Environment Fund, and the Swedish Medical Research Council.

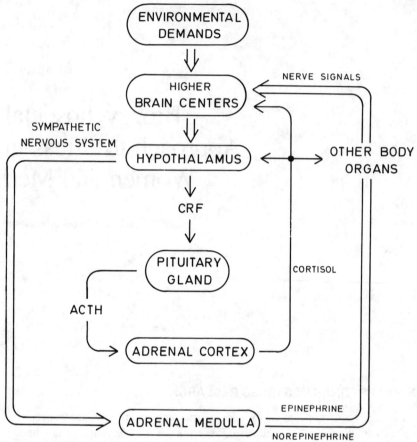

Figure 3.1 Schematic representation of pathways from the brain to the adrenal system involved in stress: (1) the sympathetic–adrenal medullary system and (2) the pituitary–adrenal cortical system.

Since the early days of research on human adaptation, before the term stress had been introduced, psychobiological approaches to adaptive and emotional processes centered on two systems that are still cornerstones in stress research: the sympathetic–adrenal medullary system and the pituitary–adrenal cortical system (Figure 3.1).

The susceptibility of the sympathetic–adrenal medullary system to psychological factors was first demonstrated early in this century by Walter B. Cannon and his associates at Harvard. Results from a series of experiments in which cats were exposed to barking dogs led Cannon (1914, 1932) to formulate the emergency-function theory of adrenal medullary activity, which states that many of the physiological effects of the adrenal-medullary hormone, later termed epinephrine, serve the goal of preparing the organism to meet threatening situations involving fear or rage or pain. Some decades later, von Euler (1946, 1956) showed that norepinephrine, the nonmethylated homologue of epinephrine, was the adrenergic neurotransmitter as well as an adrenal-medullary hormone.

Hans Selye, endocrinologist and pioneer in research on the pituitary–adrenal cortical system, introduced the term "stress" (Selye, 1936, 1956). He argued that various of diseases were associated with a common set of physiological and hormonal reactions, the general adaptation syndrome (G.A.S.). These reactions are triggered by different threatening stimuli (stressors) and involve mobilizing bodily resources to deal with the threat.

Selye's model soon proved too inflexible to explain the complexity of interacting factors linking physiological responses to disease. Mason (1975) argued that there is no general, nonspecific response to threat. On the contrary, different types of stressors elicit different patterns of hormonal responses. Moreover, he argued that the "nonspecific" pituitary-adrenal response should be interpreted as a reaction to the anxiety-inducing elements common to most stress situations, rather than to the physical demands per se. Mason et al. (1976) presented empirical evidence in support of these ideas, showing that emotional stimuli are among the most potent stimuli to the adrenal-cortical response (see also reviews by Mason, 1968a, b).

In 1966 Lazarus put forward a psychological theory of stress that had a strong impact on stress research. The focus in this theory is on the individual's cognitive appraisal of the threat or challenge and the transactional processes by which he or she deals with the challenging situation (see also Lazarus & Folkman, 1984). Today most researchers in the field emphasize the transactional/relational nature of stress rather than describing stress as a stimulus or a state or an outcome (see Appley & Trumbull, 1986; Baum & Singer, 1987).

In line with this tradition, our laboratory has adopted a transactional view of stress, emphasizing the interplay between the biological, psychological, and social levels (see reviews by Frankenhaeuser, 1979, 1980a, 1983, 1986, 1989, 1991a). The measurement of psychological and physiological reactions is seen as a tool by which new insights can be gained into the dynamics of the relationships between environmental demands and their health outcomes.

NEW AVENUES IN STRESS RESEARCH

Recent advances in the understanding of how the brain regulates endocrine functions have brought about a reorientation of psychophysiological stress research. Until recently, the brain and the endocrine system were generally viewed as separate entities. The brain was seen as mediating the organism's relation to the external environment, whereas the endocrine system was considered to be oriented toward the body's internal environment, regulating growth, metabolism, and reproduction. New insights have been gained into the pathways and neuroendocrine mechanisms by which the brain controls the endocrine system. We are beginning to grasp the coordinated functioning of the nervous system and the endocrine system in the adaptation of the whole human being to the environment (Hamburg, Elliot, & Parron, 1982).

Progress in biomedical techniques has opened new avenues for the study of stress, both in the laboratory and in field settings (Lundberg, Melin, Fredrikson, Tuomisto, & Frankenhaeuser, 1991). With ambulatory recording techniques, physiological reactions can be monitored under real-life conditions without interfering with ordinary activities (Frankenhaeuser, 1991b). In this way, aversive aspects of the psychosocial environment can be identified as well as protective factors or "buffers" against potentially harmful influences. It is an exciting task for stress research to identify those factors in the environment that either increase or dampen physiological responses and then to determine when these responses are either adaptive and health promoting or maladaptive and potentially health damaging.

DIMENSIONS OF STRESS: ACTIVITY AND AFFECT

Factor analysis of self-reports from subjects in a large number of studies in our laboratory led us to focus on two dimensions of the stress experience: an activity dimension, ranging from a passive to an active state, and an affective dimension, ranging from a negative to a positive mood state (Frankenhaeuser, 1980; Lundberg & Frankenhaeuser, 1980).

The active state involves effort, engagement, and determination to reach a goal. It is often associated with positive affect. A passive state is characterized by negative affect, distress, helplessness, and giving up.

In studies at different work sites (reviewed by Frankenhaeuser & Johansson, 1986), we have identified specific characteristics of work processes that promote active, positive attitudes as distinguished from passive and negative mood states. The interesting point is that activity vs. passivity and negative vs. positive affect tend to be associated with different neuroendocrine response patterns (Frankenhaeuser, 1983, 1986). The psychobiological relationships can be conceptualized as shown in Figure 3.2, which tells us the following:

Effort and positive affect is a productive, happy state. This is experienced in the performance of demanding tasks that allow a high degree of personal control, the use of creativity, and deep involvement in the job. This state is accompanied by increased catecholamine secretion, whereas cortisol is generally low and may even be suppressed. Examples of occupations in which these characteristics may be found are crafts, arts, science, and entrepreneurial activities. We find them also among top executive jobs. In other words, these are occupations that allow a high degree of autonomy and personal control.

Effort and negative affect is a state characteristic of pressure to produce while control over the situation is low. This is a state typical of the hassles of

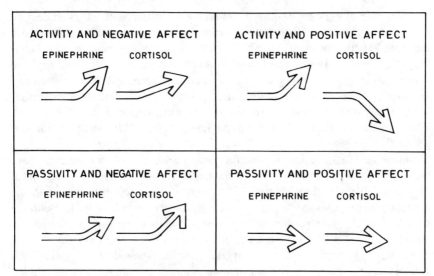

Figure 3.2 Schematic representation of epinephrine and cortisol release associated with activity versus passivity and positive versus negative affect.

everyday life. In working life the stte is common among people engaged in repetitious, machine-paced jobs. This type of work demands effort, which is accompanied by increased catecholamine secretion, and it evokes negative affects, which tend to increase the secretion of both catecholamines and cortisol.

Passivity and positive affect implies feeling pleasantly relaxed. Both mind and body are at rest, and stress-hormone output remains low.

Passivity and negative affect implies a lack of control, feeling helpless, and giving up. This is the prisoner's situation. The unemployed are at risk, and so are people in extremely coercive jobs. Feelings of helplessness are likely to develop when people experience that events and outcomes are uninfluenced by their actions. Helplessness is accompanied by an outflow of stress hormones, particularly cortisol.

In sum, the psychoendocrine pattern typical of the different conditions depicted in Figure 3.2 tells us *first* that the endocrine profile varies with the psychological significance of the situation, and *second* that epinephrine is a more general (less specific) response than cortisol to different situational demands. Thus epinephrine, but not cortisol, increases in pleasantly engaging as well as in distressing situations.

Empirical evidence suggests that the ability to exert control is an important modulating factor in achieving a state of effort and positive affect (Frankenhaeuser, 1989). A lack of control is almost invariably associated with negative affect, whereas personal control tends to stimulate positive affect. Similarly, a lack of control tends to make people passive, whereas high personal control stimulates activity.

The role of personal control in achieving a positive state has been demonstrated in a laboratory experiment in which subjects were exposed to performance demands in both low- control and high-control situations (Frankenhaeuser, Lundberg, & Forsman, 1980). The low-control situation induced effort and negative affect. Accordingly, both epinephrine and cortisol increased. The high-control situation induced effort and positive affect. Accordingly, epinephrine increased, but cortisol was suppressed. Similar results were obtained in real-life work situations that differed with regard to the level of control (Johansson & Sanden, 1989).

A possible mechanism for the favorable health effects of work conditions that allow personal control could be the catecholamine/cortisol balance typical of controllable situations (Figure 3.2). There is evidence that damage to the myocardium requires the simultaneous release of catecholamines and cortisol (Steptoe, 1981). Hence, the fact that cortisol tends to be low in controllable situations could account for the buffering effects of personal control. Such a neuroendocrine mechanism could explain epidemiological data (Karasek, 1979; Karasek & Theorell, 1990) from national surveys in Sweden and the United States showing that high job demands and work overload have adverse health consequences only when combined with low control over job-related decisions. According to the Karasek (1979) model, the combination of work overload and low decision latitude is dangerous to the cardiovascular system, whereas the risk of work overload leading to heart disease is reduced when people are given a high degree of personal control over a heavy workload.

Personal control and workload are key concepts in both Karasek's job strain model and our effort-affect model. The latter adds a psychological and a physiological dimension. It emphasizes the experience of positive versus negative affect induced by different environmental demands as the determinants of the physiological-hormonal responses evoked. These stress responses, in turn, influence health outcomes. In this model, personal control is seen as a mediator of the quality of the affect experienced, high control inducing positive affect and low control inducing negative affect.

A BIOPSYCHOSOCIAL APPROACH TO SEX DIFFERENCES IN STRESS

The biopsychosocial approach outlined in Figure 3.3 provides a framework for the study of relationships between environmental demands and individual health, well-being, and efficiency. The combination of biological, psychological, and social factors helps us to understand the mechanisms by which psychosocial factors exert an influence at the individual level. This approach is also well suited for locating and analyzing sex differences in stress reactions as well as sex differences in mediating and outcome variables.

A biopsychosocial model

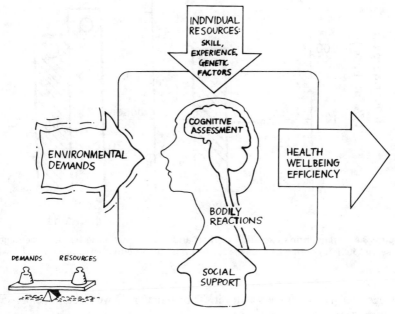

Figure 3.3 Schematic representation of a biopsychosocial framework for stress–health interactions.

A key concept is cognitive assessment. When the individual is challenged by demands, he or she appraises their nature and strength. This cognitive process involves weighing the importance and the severity of the demands against one's own coping abilities. Any stimulus or situation that is perceived as a threat to something one values or as a challenge requiring effort generates signals from the brain's cortex that trigger the release of stress hormones (see Figure 3.1). The measurement of stress hormones plays a dual role in stress research. First, it helps to assess the impact of a particular environment on a person, pinpointing aversive as well as protective factors. Second, it provides early warnings of long-term health risks. For both these reasons, the study of biological mediators plays a key role in early intervention and prevention of health damage.

The mediating variables, as shown in Figure 3.3, include individual characteristics as well as social support systems. The interaction of these variables with external demands determines the outcome in terms of health, well-being, and efficiency.

One of the key notions in the biopsychosocial approach is that physiological responses to the psychosocial environment reflect its emotional impact on the individual. It follows that changes in attitudes and values will be reflected in

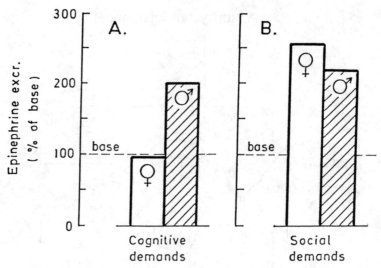

Figure 3.4 Epinephrine excretion of men and women expressed as a percentage of baseline (100): (a) during a performance task and (b) in a situation requiring social skills.

changes on the physiological level. The studies reviewed below demonstrate such changes.

Studies of men and women performed in the author's laboratory during the 1970s showed striking differences in the epinephrine increase induced by achievement stress. During rest and relaxation, gender differences in catecholamine output were slight (provided body weight was taken into account), but challenging performance situations gave consistent sex differences, particularly in epinephrine secretion (see reviews by Collins, 1985; Frankenhaeuser, 1983, 1988, 1991b). The common feature of a series of experiments with cognitive achievement demands was a pronounced rise in epinephrine excretion in males as compared with a slight increase or no response at all in females. This is illustrated in Figure 3.4a. The picture was similar for norepinephrine, although the sex differences were less marked. The age range of the subjects participating in these experiments was 13 to 35 years. Similar results were obtained for 3- to 6-year-old children studied during play activities, both at a daycare center and in their home settings (Lundberg, 1983). Epinephrine excretion was significantly higher in the boys under both conditions.

A point of interest is the fact that the women's lower epinephrine secretion during achievement stress did not affect their level of performance. In fact, the females performed as well as or slightly better that the males in all our experiments. Whereas performance level and epinephrine secretion generally show a positive correlation in men, in women the correlations tend to be close to zero (see review by Frankenhaeuser, 1988).

Women's lower epinephrine response when faced with pressure to achieve can be interpreted as a more "economical" way of coping. Thus their "cost" of adapting to achievement demands could be lower than that of men.

GENETIC VERSUS SOCIAL INFLUENCES

The hypothesized relation between vulnerability to coronary heart disease and catecholamine reactivity in men prompts the question of the extent to which gender differences are genetically determined rather than learned. Insofar as sex hormones and catecholamines interact, reasonable hypotheses would be that estrogens inhibit or that androgens facilitate catecholamine secretion. A study of postmenopausal women exposed to the same performance demands before and after estrogen replacement therapy (Collins et al., 1982) showed that estrogens did not markedly modify catecholamine secretion. The same appears to hold for androgens, as shown in a study of stress responses of women with hirsutism and oligomenorrhea, before and after anti-androgen therapy (Lundberg et al., 1984). In other words, manipulations of hormone levels did not support the assumption that interactions between sex hormones and stress hormones would account for the sex differences in reactivity.

To the extent that reactivity patterns are influenced by social factors, sex differences are likely to be reduced as the social and occupational roles of men and women become more similar. We approached this problem by studying women who had entered traditional male occupations: bus drivers, lawyers, engineers, and managers. The hypothesis was that these women would exhibit the psychoendocrine stress responses typical of men. The results showed that, on the whole, these groups of "nontraditional" women did tend to respond to achievement demands by almost as sharp an increase in epinephrine secretion as did men.

There is no straightforward interpretation of the results. The similarity between the sexes in these occupational groups might arise from these women's greater constitutional similarity to men in terms of responding to achievement demands. This could also be the reason for their choice of occupation. The other possibility is that these women had been conditioned by their work roles.

Next, we approached this question by studying men and women in a situation that challenges a traditionally female area of competence, namely, managing interpersonal relations. All situations considered so far had challenged the traditional male field of competence, which emphasizes self-assertion, achievement, and output. We now wanted to test the hypothesis that women are more vulnerable than men when challenged in situations that emphasize social skills. We had the opportunity to perform a well-controlled study within a traditional female sphere of responsibility (Lundberg, de Chateau, Winberg, & Frankenhaeuser, 1981), comparing mothers and fathers who took their 3-year-old child to a hospital for a medical check-up. In this demanding but noncompetitive situation the women secreted more epinephrine than did the men (Figure 3.4b). These results show that interpersonal confrontations are effective triggers of epinephrine release in women.

PRODUCTIVE BEHAVIOR

The changing neuroendocrine reactivity patterns of women entering men's occupations, combined with the fact that increasing job involvement generally does not reduce involvement in home and family, raises important questions about the stress associated with women's multiple roles and its possible health consequences.

The evaluation of stress effects of multiple-role strain on women's health requires an assessment of the total workload, that is, the combined load of paid work and other duties, mostly related to household and family.

Kahn and his associates at the University of Michigan have introduced the term "productive behavior" to define all the things that people do that contribute to the goods and services that other people use and value (Kahn, 1984, 1991). Answers from 3,600 employed American men and women showed that, throughout the life cycle, women perform more productive activity than men. The total of paid and unpaid productive activity approximates 80 hours a week for women and 68 hours for men. As Kahn points out, this means that men have, on average, 2–2.5 hours more free time per day than women. A questionnaire study with 1,200 Swedish men and women (Mardberg, Lundberg, & Frankenhaeuser, 1991) shows general agreement with the Michigan study and adds interesting information about the relation between the number of children and the parents' workload. In essence, women's but not men's productive behavior increases with the number of children.

In spite of their heavy workload, some women rise to managerial positions. Insofar as the stresses and strains from different roles add up, married women managers carry a particularly heavy load. This was demonstrated in a study of male and female white-collar workers in managerial and nonmanagerial positions at Volvo in Gothenburg, Sweden (Frankenhaeuser et al., 1989). Answers to a questionnaire showed that the women carried the main responsibility for shopping, cooking, laundry, sewing and mending, daily cleaning, and major house cleaning, whereas the men were responsible for the car and finances. Thus the division of labor followed the traditional pattern. Not only are women responsible for a greater number of activities at home, but the nature of their responsibilities differs in that their duties (e.g., cooking) have to be performed daily at a fixed time, whereas managing money and fixing the car give more flexibility.

The general picture was the same for managers and nonmanagers. However, combining the paid and unpaid work was more of a burden for the women managers, as shown by answers to the question: "How much does work outside paid work contribute to your total workload?" (Figure 3.5). Whereas the female

HOW MUCH DOES WORK OUTSIDE PAID
WORK CONTRIBUTE TO THE TOTAL WORKLOAD?

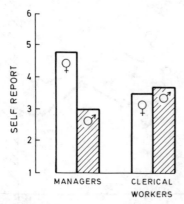

Figure 3.5   Self-reports of men and women in managerial and nonmanagerial positions in response to the question, "How much do duties outside your paid work contribute to your total workload?" (Based on Frankenhaeuser et al., 1989.)

clerical workers spent more hours in unpaid work than any other group, the female managers felt more torn between demands related to their profession and their family. Male managers also reported occasional conflicts between work and home but perceived this as less of a problem than their female colleagues did.

The conflict experienced by the women managers between incompatible demands from paid work and duties at home was reflected in their inability to unwind in the evening after work. This lack of unwinding was manifested in measurements of blood pressure, heart rate, catecholamine secretion, and self-reports of stress, wakefulness, and mood. Whereas sex differences in the level of physiological arousal were rather small at the place of work, the differences were pronounced in the evening at home, particularly between male and female managers. The men's norepinephrine level dropped sharply after 5 PM, when they returned home from work, whereas the women's level continued to rise (Figure 3.6). In other words, women managers tended to "wind up" in the evenings, whereas male managers "wound down". For blood pressure, the sex difference after 5 PM was similar, though less pronounced (Figure 3.7). The tendency was also seen in epinephrine secretion, but the picture was obscured by the pronounced diurnal variations in the release of this hormone.

THE BUFFERING EFFECTS OF SOCIAL SUPPORT AND PERSONAL CONTROL

There is general agreement among stress researchers that social support can serve as a buffer protecting people from damaging effects of stress. This appears to

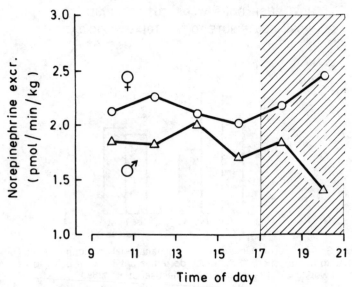

Figure 3.6 Norepinephrine excretion in male and female managers during and after a day at work. (Based on Frankenhaeuser et al., 1989.)

MANAGERS AT WORK

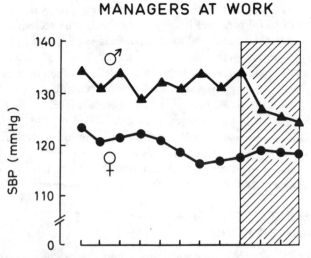

Figure 3.7 Systolic blood pressure in male and female managers during and after a day at work. (Based on Frankenhaeuser et al., 1989.)

SOCIAL SUPPORT ON THE JOB

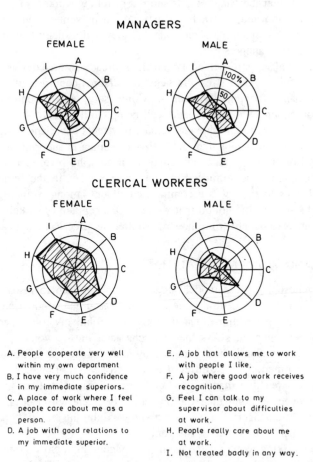

Figure 3.8 Self-reports of social support at work. Scores represent the percentages of males and females in managerial and nonmanagerial positions agreeing to each statement (A-I). The dark area in each diagram depicts the average total amount of social support reported by the group. (Based on Frankenhaeuser et al., 1989.)

apply to women in particular (Repetti, Matthews, & Waldron, 1989). In view of the heavy workload and slow unwinding of women managers, it was important to find out to what extent they are protected by a social network. In Figure 3.8, self-reports of nine aspects of social support in the female managers are compared with those of male managers as well as with those of male and female clerical workers. The larger the shaded area in each of the four diagrams, the stronger the support experienced at the workplace. In this respect the women clerical workers were far better off than any other group. The female managers, like the two male groups, did not have the support of a strong network. This raises the question of whether they had lost the support of fellow workers on their way up in the organization and, if so, how this may be prevented. One of the chief complaints of the women managers was that they had difficulty communicating with higher level managers.

Beside social support, personal control, as already pointed out, is considered to be a powerful buffer of stress. In general, personal control facilitates adjustment and enhances coping effectiveness. Conversely, lack of control may have negative consequences for health and well-being. In the Volvo study (Frankenhaeuser et al., 1989), both male and female managers experienced significantly more control over their jobs than did men and women in subordinate positions. The comparison between male and female managers, however, showed that the sense of autonomy and influence at work was weaker in the female group. "Nobody listens to me" was a common complaint among women managers. These results support the notion that women managers are less likely than their male colleagues to benefit from the stress-buffering effects of personal control.

STRESS AND WOMEN'S HEALTH

The biopsychosocial stress model suggests new approach to research on sex differences in health. A central issue is the increased neuroendocrine reactivity of women entering traditionally male jobs. The relatively low catecholamine response to achievement stress that was characteristic of women until a few decades ago has gradually been replaced by more "male-like" stress responses in employed women. The sex difference in reactivity is still evident in children, girls being less reactive than boys (Lundberg, 1983), as well as in male and female employees in nonmanagerial positions (Frankenhaeuser et al., 1989). It is the women in managerial positions who now exhibit the reactivity pattern that was earlier considered typical of men only.

Another striking feature is the women managers' high physiological arousal level in the evening. Measurements of catecholamines and blood pressure in the Volvo employees (Figures 3.6 & 3.7) indicate that unwinding in the evening after work is a male manager's privilege. Slow unwinding was first demonstrated in our laboratory by Rissler (1977) in a study of female clerks during a period of intense overtime at work. During this period epinephrine levels were significantly elevated in the evenings that were spent under nonwork conditions at home. In agreement with the women managers vs. nonmanagers at Volvo, the women whose epinephrine secretion rose markedly during the overtime period reported being more "career-oriented" than did the women whose epinephrine increase was less pronounced. It seems plausible that the elevated evening epinephrine level was related not to job demands as such, but rather to the intrapsychic conflict associated with letting duties in the occupational role "invade" the time ordinarily reserved for the home and family. This interpretation agrees with the data from the Volvo study, showing that the high catecholamine levels in the evening reflected the conflict between incompatible demands from dual roles.

In this connection it is of interest that Alfredsson, Spetz, and Theorell (1985) found that even moderate amounts of overtime were detrimental to women's cardiovascular health, whereas men suffered ill effects only when the overtime load was heavy. This indicates that women, because of their heavy total work-load, have a smaller margin.

Insofar as high catecholamine levels are a risk factor for cardiovascular disease, women in leadership roles may constitute a vulnerable group. Not only do they react with a catecholamine increase to acute achievement demands just as readily as men, they also stay in "high gear" long after their male colleagues and female subordinates have subsided to their physiological baseline. However, it is still an open question whether the rather modest catecholamine increase typical of stress in daily life is likely to cause structural damage of blood vessels and increase the risk of developing cardiovascular disease. There is no indication of increased cortisol secretion in women in leadership positions, and their cate-cholamine/cortisol balance seems favorable. It is encouraging that a critical review (Repetti et al., 1989) of research on the health of employed women leads to the conclusion that the net effect of employment on women's health is positive (see also Frankenhaeuser et al., 1991; Baruch, Biener, & Barnett, 1987; Graves & Thomas, 1985; Rodin & Ickovics, 1990; Waldron, Herold, Dunn, & Staum, 1982). Up to now, interest has been focused on the cardiovascular system, where damaging stress effects are less likely to occur in the short term. Studies of muscoloskeletal disorders now in progress (Lundberg et al., in preparation) suggest that stress-induced complaints, particularly common among women, may show up after a few years of, for example, bue-collar work.

In conclusion, until a deeper insight has been gained into causal links be-tween stress and disease, the stress responses of women managers should be viewed as warning signals of possible long-term health consequences. Role conflict may add more to the total load than either the paid job or the other duties per se. Therefore, the future sex differential in morbidity and mortality is likely to be influenced by numerous factors relating to the multiple roles of women and men. If we are to come to grips with the sources of stress in both women and men, it will be necessary to take their total workload into account and to consider interactions between work role and other life roles.

REFERENCES

Alfredsson, L., Spetz, C.-L., & Theorell, T. (1985). Type of occupation and near-future hospitalization for myocardial infarction and some other diagnoses. *International Journal of Epidemiology, 14,* 378–388.

Appley, M. H., & Trumbull, R. (Eds.). (1986). *Dynamics of stress* (pp. 101–116). New York: Plenum Press.

Baruch, G. K., Biener, L., & Barnett, R. C. (1987). Women and gender in research on work and family stress. *American Psychologist, 42*, 130–136.

Baum, A., & Singer, J. E. (Eds.). (1987). *Handbook of psychology and health. Vol. 5. Stress.* Hillsdale, NJ: Erlbaum.

Cannon, W. B. (1914). The emergency function of the adrenal medulla in pain and the major emotions. *American Journal of Physiology, 33*, 356–372.

Cannon, W. B. (1932). *The wisdom of the body.* New York: W. W. Norton.

Collins, A. (1985). Sex differences in psychoneuroendocrine stress responses: Biological and social influences. Doctoral thesis, University of Stockholm, Sweden.

Collins, A., Hanson, U., Eneroth, P., Hagenfeldt, K., Lundberg, U., & Frankenhaeuser, M. (1982). Psychophysiological stress responses in postmenopausal women before and after hormonal replacement therapy. *Human Neurobiology, 1*, 153–159.

Frankenhaeuser, M. (1979). Psychoneuroendocrine approaches to the study of emotion as related to stress and coping. In H. E. Howe & R. A. Dienstbier (Eds.), *Nebraska symposium on motivation 1978* (pp. 123–161). Lincoln: University of Nebraska Press.

Frankenhaeuser, M. (1980a). Psychoneuroendocrine approaches to the study of stressful person–environment transactions. In H. Selye (Ed.), *Selye's guide to stress research* (Vol. 1, pp. 46–70). New York: Van Nostrand Reinhold.

Frankenhaeuser, M. (1980b). Psychobiological aspects of life stress. In S. Levine & H. Ursin (Eds.), *Coping and health* (pp. 203-223). New York: Plenum Press.

Frankenhaeuser, M. (1983). The sympathetic-adrenal and pituitary-adrenal response to challenge: Comparison between the sexes. In T. M. Dembroski, T. H. Schmidt, & C. Blumchen (Eds.), *Biobehavioral bases of coronary heart disease* (pp. 91–105). New York: Karger.

Frankenhaeuser, M. (1986). A psychobiological framework for research on human stress and coping. In M. H. Appley & R. Trumbull (Eds.), *Dynamics of stress* (pp. 101–116). New York: Plenum Press.

Frankenhaeuser, M. (1988). Stress and reactivity patterns at different stages of the life cycle. In P. Pancheri & L. Zichella (Eds.), *Biorhythms and stress in the physiopathology of reproduction* pp. 31–40). Washington, DC: Hemisphere.

Frankenhaeuser, M. (1989). A biopsychosocial approach to work life issues. *International Journal of Health Services, 19*, 747–758.

Frankenhaeuser, M. (1991a). The psychophysiology of sex differences as related to occupational status. In M. Frankenhaeuser, U. Lundberg, & M. A. Chesney (Eds.), *Women, work and health: Stress and opportunities* (pp. 31–40). New York: Plenum Press.

Frankenhaeuser, M. (1991b). The psychophysiology of workload, stress, and health: Comparison between the sexes. *Annals of Behavioral Medicine, 4*, 197–204.

Frankenhaeuser, M., & Johansson, G. (1986). Stress at work: Psychobiological and psychosocial aspects. *International Review of Applied Psychology, 35*, 287–299.

Frankenhaeuser, M., Lundberg, U., & Chesney, M. A. (Eds.). (1991). *Women, work, and health: Stress and opportunities.* New York: Plenum Press.

Frankenhaeuser, M., Lundberg, U., & Forsman, L. (1980). Dissociation between sympathetic-adrenal and pituitary-adrenal responses to an achievement situation characterized by high controllability: Comparison between Type A and Type B males and females. *Biological Psychology, 10,* 79–91.

Frankenhaeuser, M., Lundberg, U., Fredrikson, M., Melin, B., Tuomisto, M., Myrsten, A.-L., Hedman, M., Bergman-Losman, B., & Wallin, L. (1989). Stress on and off the job as related to sex and occupational status in white-collar workers. *Journal of Organizational Behavior, 10,* 321–346.

Graves, P. L., & Thomas, C. B. (1985). Correlates of midlife career achievement among women physicians. *Journal of the American Medical Association, 254,* 781–787.

Hamburg, D. A., Elliot, G. R., & Parron, D. L. (1982). *Health and behavior: Frontiers of research in the biobehavioral sciences.* Washington, DC: National Academy Press.

Johansson, G., & Sanden, P.-O. (1989) *Mental load and job satisfaction of control room operators* (Report No. 698). Stockholm: University of Stockholm, Department of Psychology.

Kahn, R. L. (1984). Productive behavior through the life course: An essay on the quality of life. *Human Resource Management, 23,* 5–22.

Kahn, R. L. (1991). The forms of women's work. In M. Frankenhaeuser, U. Lundberg, and M. Chesney (Eds.), *Women, work, and health: Stress and opportunities* (pp. 65–83). New York: Plenum.

Karasek, R. A. (1979), Job demands, job decision latitude, and mental strain: Implications for job redesign. *Administration Science Quarterly, 24,* 285–308.

Karasek, R. A., & Theorell, T. (1990). *Healthy work.* New York: Basic Books.

Lazarus, R. S. (1966). *Psychological stress and the coping process.* New York: McGraw-Hill.

Lazarus, R. S., & Folkman, S. (1984). *Stress, appraisal, and coping.* New York: Springer.

Lundberg, U. (1983). Sex differences in behavior pattern and catecholamine and cortisol excretion in 3–6-year-old daycare children. *Biological Psychology, 16,* 109–117.

Lundberg, U., de Chateau, P., Winberg, J., & Frankenhaeuser, M. (1981). Catecholamine and cortisol excretion patterns in three-year-old children and their parents. *Journal of Human Stress, 7,* 3–11.

Lundberg, U., & Frankenhaeuser, M. (1980). Pituitary-adrenal and sympathetic-adrenal correlates of distress and effort. *Journal of Psychosomatic Research, 24,* 125–130.

Lundberg, U., Fredrikson, M., Wallin, L., Melin, B., & Frankenhaeuser, M. (1989). Blood lipids as related to cardiovascular and neuroendocrine functions under different conditions in healthy males and females. *Pharmacology, Biochemistry, and Behavior, 33,* 381–386.

Lundberg, U., Hanson, U., Eneroth, P., Frankenhaeuser, M., & Hagenfeldt, K. (1984). Anti-androgen treatment of hirsute women: A study of stress responses. *Journal of Psychosomatic Obstetrics and Gynaecology, 3,* 79–92.

Mason, J. W. (1968a). A review of psychoendocrine research on the pituitary-adrenal cortical system. *Psychosomatic Medicine, 30,* 576–597.

Mason, J. W. (1968b). A review of psychoendocrine research on the sympathetic-adrenal medullary system. *Psychosomatic Medicine, 30,* 631–653.

Mason, J. W. (1975). Emotion as reflected in patterns of endocrine integration. In L. Levi (Ed.), *Emotions: Their parameters and measurement* (pp. 143–181). New York: Raven Press.

Mason, J. W., Maher, J. T., Hartley, L. H., Mougey, E. H., Perlow, M. J., & Jones, L. G. (1976). Selectivity of corticosteroid and catecholamine responses to various natural stimuli. In G. Serban (Ed.), *Psychopathology of human adaptation* (pp. 147–172). New York: Plenum Press.

Mardberg, B., Lundberg, U., & Frankenhaeuser, M. (1991). The total workload of parents employed in white-collar jobs: Construction of a questionnaire and a scoring system. *Scandinavian Journal of Psychology, 32,* 233–239.

Repetti, R. L., Matthews, K. A., & Waldron, I. (1989). Effects of paid employment on women's mental and physical health. *American Psychologist, 44,* 1394–1401.

Rissler, A. (1977). Stress reactions at work and after work during a period of quantitative overload. *Ergonomics, 20,* 13–16.

Rodin, J., & Ickovics, J. R. (1990). Women's health: Review and research agenda as we approach the 21st century. *American Psychologist, 45,* 1018–1034.

Selye, H. (1936). A syndrome produced by diverse nocuous agents. *Nature, 139,* 32.

Selye, H. (1956). *The stress of life.* New York: McGraw-Hill.

Steptoe, A. (1981). *Psychological factors in cardiovascular disorders.* London: Academic Press.

von Euler, U. S. (1946). A specific sympathomimetic ergone in adrenergic nerve fibres (sympathin) and its relation to adrenaline and noradrenaline. *Acta Physiologica, 12,* 73–97.

von Euler, U. S. (1956). *Noradrenaline: Chemistry, physiology, pharmacology, and clinical aspects.* Springfield, IL: Charles C Thomas.

Waldron, I., Herold, J., Dunn, D., & Staum, R. (1982). Reciprocal effects of health and labor force participation among women: Evidence from two longitudinal studies. *Journal of Occupational Medicine, 24,* 126–132.

Chapter 4

Coronary Risk in Women

Gerdi Weidner

Heart disease is a major factor in morbidity and mortality in both sexes. According to statistics presented by the U.S. Bureau of the Census (1991), the heart disease death rate in 1988 was 301.2 among women and 321.9 among men per 100,000 residents of the United States. Comparable rates for the other major cause of death, cancer, were 180.0 for women and 215.5 for men. Thus heart disease presents the number one health threat for both women and men. When mortality rates for coronary heart disease (CHD), the major form of heart disease, are examined, a similar pattern emerges (U.S. Bureau of the Census, 1991, pp. 83, 84). For example, of 100,000 persons in the 55- to 64-year-old age group, 147.1 women and 401.3 men died of CHD in 1988. Table 4.1 presents death rates due to CHD and the major forms of cancer in women and men. As can be seen, women's death rates for CHD and most major forms of cancer are lower than those of men. However, among women as a group, CHD is the primary cause of death.

Although heart disease is a major health problem for women, most studies have focused on men and have underemphasized the extent of the problem in

Preparation of this manuscript was supported in part by funds from the National Heart, Lung, and Blood Institute (grants HL 3426103 and HL 403601), Biomedical Research Support (grant RR 076721), and a grant from the Deutscher Akademischer Austauschdienst (DADD). I thank Margaret Chesney and Ron Friend for their helpful comments on an earlier version of this chapter.

Table 1   Death rates from coronary heart disease and cancer by sex and age[a] in 1988

	Women	Men
Persons 45-54 years old:		
Coronary Heart Disease	36.8	134.5
Major Cancers		
respiratory	35.0	65.7
digestive organs	22.4	39.5
breast	45.3	0.3
genital organs	18.5	3.1
Persons 55-64 years old:		
Coronary Heart Disease	147.1	401.3
Major Cancers		
respiratory	102.2	229.5
digestive organs	69.8	125.9
breast	81.8	0.4
genital organs	41.3	25.1
Persons 65-74 years old		
Coronary heart disease	453.1	956.9
Major Cancers		
respiratory	164.1	425.4
digestive organs	155.6	257.3
breast	109.4	1.1
genital organs	71.3	111.8

[a] Deaths per 100,000 population in specified age groups.
(Adapted from U.S. Bureau of the Census, 1991.)

women. One reason for this oversight is that mortality rates for heart disease are greater for men than for women, accounting for 41% of the gender difference in overall mortality in the United States (Lerner & Kannel, 1986; Wingard, 1984).[1,2]

There is some controversy as to why women are at lower risk for coronary heart disease (CHD) than men. In a critical and comprehensive review of the literature on the role of genetic factors, Waldron (1983) concludes that "for both violent death and ischemic (coronary) heart disease it appears that any genetic contribution to sex differences in mortality are strongly reinforced by the cultural influences that foster more risky behavior in males. . . . " (p. 321).

Further, if women's advantage were biological, we would expect gender differences in CHD to be stable and universal. This, however, is not the case.

[1] Although heart disease is the main contributor to the sex mortality differential at older ages, accidents are mainly responsible for the differential in younger age groups (Wingard, 1984).

[2] The major type of heart disease is coronary heart disease (CHD), accounting for 66.3% of all heart disease deaths (based on figures given on p. 78, U.S. Bureau of the Census, 1991). Therefore, this chapter focuses on CHD. Only where statistics for CHD alone are not available, statistics for the entire category of heart diseases are given.

Women's relative protection from CHD does not seem to be stable over time or universal. For example, in 1920, the age-adjusted ratio of male to female heart disease deaths was approximately equal, but between 1975 and 1978, it had increased to a level of 3.47 in the United States (Verbrugge, 1980; Wingard, 1984). In addition, sex mortality ratios for heart disease differ widely across countries, ranging from 5:1 in Finland to 1.87:1 in the former Yugoslavia (Thom, Epstein, Feldman, & Leaverton, 1985). Thus relying on biological differences alone when explaining this gender differential is neither sufficient nor convincing.

The Framingham study indicates that among the factors predicting CHD in both women and men (aside from age) are elevated levels of plasma cholesterol, cigarette smoking, and high blood pressure (Stokes, Kannel, Wolf, Cupples, & D'Agostino, 1987; Truett, Cornfield, & Kannel, 1967). Consistent with the observation that women are less likely to die of CHD than men is the fact that they also exhibit lower levels of every one of these traditional risk factors when compared to men (Gordon & Shurtleff, 1973; Lerner & Kannel, 1986; Stokes et al., 1987).

Traditional risk factors appear to be strongly influenced by behavior. Smoking is purely behavioral. Also, plasma cholesterol level and blood pressure are linked to dietary choices and habits, such as excessive consumption of foods high in salt, cholesterol, and saturated fats (Connor & Connor, 1985; Stamler, Stamler, & Liu, 1985).[3] It follows, therefore, that gender differences in behavior may explain gender differences in traditional coronary risk factors. For example, 33% of the population of adult men smoked in 1987. The percentage for women was 28% (American Cancer Society, 1989). Gender differences in dietary intake of foods related to elevated blood pressure and cholesterol have not been systematically investigated. There is some evidence that women report more flexibility in their food choices, which may make them more open to changing their dietary habits (Hollis, Carmody, Connor, Fey, & Matarazzo, 1986). Women, too, indicate greater awareness of the role that diet plays in the prevention of disease than men (Hollis et al., 1986). Consistent with the latter is the finding that women report more improvements in their diet than men in response to a community program designed to prevent heart disease (Griffin, Schneider, Eitel, Connor, & Weidner, 1992). In conclusion, it is possible that gender differences in behavior contribute to gender differences in traditional coronary risk factors, which in turn may explain the gender differential in CHD.

One problem with focusing on traditional coronary risk factors to explain the CHD gender differential is that these risk factors are not solely responsible for CHD etiology. In fact, they account for less than half of new CHD cases (Jenkins, 1971). This problem has prompted investigators to search for other

---

[3]It is of interest to note that women's levels of the protective high-density-lipoprotein cholesterol appear to be affected by lower levels of alcohol consumption than those of men (Weidner et al., 1991). This raises the question of gender-specific effects of diet on coronary risk factors.

variables that influence the development of CHD. Over the past 25 years, some progress has been made in identifying psychosocial variables as independent predictors of CHD. It is conceivable that gender differences in these psychosocial variables, in addition to primary risk factors, contribute to the observed gender differential in coronary heart disease.

To conclude, it is important to study coronary risk among women for two reasons. First, coronary heart disease presents a major health problem among women and must be recognized as such despite the greater prevalence in men. Second, by trying to understand why women are at lesser risk for CHD than men we may be able to improve our knowledge of CHD risk in men, and ultimately reduce CHD among both women and men.

Although we have information on the role that *traditional* coronary risk factors play in the development of coronary heart disease among women (e.g., Stokes et al., 1987), we know relatively little about women's *psychosocial* risk for CHD. Therefore, a major purpose of this chapter is to discuss what evidence exists for psychosocial coronary risk factors in women. Only those variables showing an independent contribution to CHD in at least one prospective study with women will be included. This criterion is met by *Type A behavior* (Eaker, Abbott, & Kannel, 1989; Eaker & Castelli, 1988; Haynes, Feinleib, & Kannel, 1980), *occupational stress* (Haynes & Feinleib, 1980; LaCroix & Haynes, 1987), *hostility* (Barefoot et al., 1987), and *social support* (Berkman & Syme, 1979; Orth-Gomer & Johnson, 1987).[4] The following sections will discuss the first three of these variables, their prospective association with CHD, and possible mechanisms linking each of them to CHD.[5]

TYPE A BEHAVIOR

Type A behavior has been conceptualized as a coping style that is characterized by extremes of competitive achievement striving, time urgency, and aggressiveness. The strongest evidence for a Type A-CHD association among women comes from the Framingham Heart Study. In this study, a psychosocial questionnaire was administered from which the Framingham Type A Scale (FTAS; Haynes, Levine, Scotch, Feinleib, & Kannel, 1978) was derived. Haynes et al. (1980) report a positive relationship of Type A behavior to the 8-year incidence of coronary heart disease. The 14-year follow-up found that when compared to Type B women, Type A women were more likely to develop CHD when angina

---

[4]A detailed discussion of the role of social support in cardiovascular disease in both women and men is available in *Social support and cardiovascular disease*, edited by Shumaker & Czajkowski (in press).

[5]Because most research on psychosocial risk factors has dealt with CHD, the focus of this chapter will be on coronary heart disease. Mattson and Herd (1988) have reviewed gender differences in other cardiovascular diseases such as stroke, sudden cardiac death, and mitral valve prolapse syndrome.

pectoris, or angina pectoris without any other manifestation of CHD, was included in the criteria. (Eaker & Castelli, 1988). Type A women were not significantly more likely to develop CHD in the absence of angina symptoms. Specifically, 15.9% of the women classified as Type As developed total CHD compared to 9.2% of the women classified as Type Bs. The incidence of angina pectoris was 7.8% among Type A women and 3.3% among Type B women. Although the percentage of Type A women who developed CHD without angina symptoms was greater than that of Type B women (8.3 vs. 5.6), this difference was not statistically significant.

Based on these findings, it appears that the FTAS is related to symptoms of angina among women rather than to "hard" indicators of coronary artery disease, such as myocardial infarction. It is noteworthy that the FTAS correlates with measures of neuroticism (Chesney, Black, Chadwick, & Rosenman, 1981) and that generally anxiety and neuroticism appear to be more consistently related to angina symptoms than to "hard endpoints" (Costa, 1986; Jenkins, 1976).[6],[7]

In spite of this problem, the follow-ups of the Framingham Heart Study women suggest that Type A behavior is independently associated with CHD outcome. That is, Type A behavior does not seem to assert its influence via the traditional coronary risk factors. Findings from a few studies suggest that Type A women like Type A men) engage in behaviors that might elevate their risk for CHD. For example, Type A women ignore signs of fatigue and other symptoms when engaged in a stressful task (Weidner & Matthews, 1978). Ignoring symptoms of fatigue and chest pain, the prodromal symptoms of myocardial infarction, may lead to delay in seeking medical care and thus increases the risk of death due to CHD. Generally, Type A women—like Type A men—report more stress in their lives and indicate difficulties with coping. Weidner and Chesney (1985) and Weidner and R. L. Collins (1992) review this research.

With regard to physiological characteristics, it has been suggested that heightened physiological reactivity to stress may be implicated in CHD etiology (e.g., Krantz & Manuck, 1984; Matthews, Weiss, Detre, Dembroski, Falkner, Manuck, & Williams, 1986). Specifically, the assumption is that Type As chronically react to environmental stressors with greater activity of the sympathetic-adrenomedullary system and possibly also the pituitary-adrenocortical system (Henry & Meehan, 1981).[8] Of the studies on cardiovascular reactivity to stress

[6]Contrary to the notion that measures of neuroticism predict only "soft" endpoints, the most recent follow-up report of women in the Framingham study found indicators of neuroticism (e.g., symptoms of tension and anxiety) to be independent predictors of the 20-year incidence of myocardial infarction and coronary death among homemakers (Eaker, Pinsky, & Castelli, 1992).

[7]We do not intend to minimize the importance of angina symptoms. To the contrary, it should be kept in mind that angina pectoris is a powerful predictor of coronary mortality in women (e.g., Campbell, Elwood, Abbas, & Waters, 1984; LaCroix, Haynes, Savage, & Havlik, 1989).

[8]A meta-analysis of studies concludes that there are gender differences in cardiovascular stress reactivity (Stoney, Davis, & Matthews, 1987). However, several other studies indicate that gender roles, social roles, and stress characteristics are more powerful determinants of cardiovascular

Table 2   Blood pressure changes, hostility and Type A behavior in women[a]

a) behavior type defined by the Framingham Type A Scale

	SBP		DBP	
	hi Host	lo Host	hi Host	lo Host
Type A	.92	2.70	4.92	3.25
	┌──p = .005──┐		┌──p = .058──┐	
Type B	6.07	−.54	6.06	2.05

b) behavior type defined by the Jenkins Activity Survey

	SBP		DBP	
	hi Host	lo Host	hi Host	lo Host
Type A	3.49	3.11	5.92	4.22
			┌──p = .014──┐	
Type B	2.44	−.89	4.72	1.22

[a] All analyses were based on residualized change scores to control for the effect of baseline on change.

that have included women, most have employed either the Structured Interview (SI; Chesney, Eagleston, & Rosenman, 1980) or the Jenkins Activity Survey (JAS; Jenkins, Rosenman, & Zyzanski, 1974). Although some studies support the notion of heightened cardiovascular stress reactivity among Type A men, the evidence for SI- or JAS-defined female Type As is weak. Houston (1988) reviews this research in more detail.

Unfortunately, very few studies have employed the FTAS, the only measure that has been prospectively linked to CHD in women. The few studies using the FTAS (Chesney & Black, 1988; Houston, T. W. Smith, & Zurawski, 1986; MacDougall, Dembroski, & Krantz, 1981; T. W. Smith, Houston, & Zurawski, 1985; our study reported below in this chapter) report inconsistent findings. Comparing subjects selected on the basis of extreme FTAS scores, T. W. Smith et al. (1985) found significantly greater systolic blood pressure responses to stress in both Type A women and men. In a reanalysis of data collected in T. W. Smith et al.'s study, Houston et al. (1986) report increased systolic blood pressure responses among women and men who scored high on competitive drive (a factor derived from the FTAS). In contrast, our data (below) did not reveal Type A-B (FTAS) differences in cardiovascular stress reactivity in either women (Table 4.2a) or men. Also, MacDougall et al. (1981) and Chesney and Black (1988) failed to find differences in blood pressure or heart rate reactivity in their female samples of FTAS-defined Type As and Bs.

Drawing on these results, we can conclude that there is inconsistent evidence for increased cardiovascular reactivity to stress among FTAS-defined Type A

reactivity than biological sex of subject (see Frankenhaeuser, Chapter 3, this volume; Frankenhaeuser, 1991; Girdler, Turner, Sherwood, & Light, 1990; Weidner & Messina, 1993).

women (and men). Thus the mechanisms by which Type A behavior asserts its influence on CHD in women are presently unclear. Future studies may benefit from focusing on lipid and lipoprotein responses as a mechanism linking personality variables with increased risk for coronary heart disease (see Doornen & Orlebeke, 1982; Stoney, Matthews, McDonald, & Johnson, 1988; Weidner, Sexton, McLellarn, Connor, & Matarazzo, 1987).

With regard to gender differences in Type A behavior, most studies find that Type A behavior is more prevalent in men than in women in the United States (e.g., Chesney, 1983; Baker, Dearborn, Hastings, & Hamberger, 1984). This difference is also apparent in children who are rated on Type A behavior by their teachers (Corrigan & Moskowitz, 1983; Lundberg, 1983; Matthews & Angulo, 1980). However, when self-ratings or a structured interview (administered by trained interviewers) are used to assess Type A behavior in children, this gender difference disappears (e.g., Kirmil-Gray et al., 1987; Kliewer & Weidner, 1987; Siegel & Leitch, 1981; Weidner, McLellarn, Sexton, Istvan, & Connor, 1986). This suggests that teachers' higher ratings of Type A behavior may be influenced by a sex bias.

Although there is no consistent evidence for gender differences in Type A behavior in children, several studies suggest that parental correlates of Type A behavior differ in boys and girls. For example, Type A boys are likely to have fathers who also score high on Type A behavior (Bracke, 1986; Matthews, Stoney, Rakaczky, & Jamison, 1986; Thoresen & Patillo, 1988; Weidner, Sexton, Matarazzo, Pereira, & Friend, 1988). In contrast, daughters' Type A scores are not consistently related to their fathers' or mothers' Type A scores.

In addition to a father-son similarity in Type A behavior, fathers' aspirations predict their sons' Type A scores (Kliewer & Weidner, 1987). In this study, fathers of Type A boys reported setting high goals for their Type A sons and perceived that these goals were not attained by them. Neither parent's aspirations were related to Type A behavior in daughters; instead of specific parental behaviors, a general family climate characterized by high conflict was predictive of girls' Type A behavior, specifically aggression (Weidner, Hutt, Connor, & Mendell, 1992).

In sum, the findings from the above studies suggest that fathers may encourage Type A behavior in their sons by modeling Type A behavior, communicating unrealistically high goals, and expressing discontentment when their sons do not achieve these goals.

Parental influences on the development of Type A behavior in girls are still unclear. A family environment characterized by high conflict appears to promote Type A behaviors in girls. To what extent these differences in parental behaviors and family environments of Type A children influence the gender gap in the prevalence of Type A behavior in adults still needs to be determined.

Although adult women as a group score lower on Type A behavior when compared to men, controlling for employment status eliminates this gender difference (e.g., Haynes, Feinleib, Levine, Scotch, & Kannel, 1978; Waldron, Zyzanski, Shekelle, Jenkins, & Tannebaum, 1977). Comparisons of Type A scores in female samples by employment reveal that employed women score significantly higher on Type A behavior than women not working outside the home (e.g., Lawler, Rixse, & Allen, 1983; Morell & Katkin, 1982). Thus gender differences in Type A scores might have less to do with gender and more to do with environmental circumstances related to employment. Alternatively, it is possible that Type A women are more likely to seek employment than their Type B counterparts. Further, as we will see in the next section, certain occupational characteristics are associated with increased coronary risk, and Type A women may be more likely to choose high-strain occupations than their Type B counterparts, thereby confounding the relationship between job strain and coronary risk (see Chesney, 1983). Unfortunately, studies on the role of interactive aspects of personal and environmental characteristics in coronary risk are rare.

To conclude, Type A behavior as measured by the FTAS is an independent predictor of angina pectoris, a major symptom of CHD. Prospective studies determining the relationship of angina symptoms to hard endpoints are clearly needed. The mechanisms by which Type A behavior asserts its influence on CHD etiology are still unclear. Studies on cardiovascular stress reactivity among Type A women are too few, and the findings are too inconsistent to permit any conclusions. The higher prevalence of Type A behavior in adult men when compared to women may contribute to women's lower CHD risk in general. Although we currently do not know when the gender difference in Type A behavior emerges developmentally, we do have enough evidence to suggest that there are gender differences in socialization of Type A behavior.

OCCUPATIONAL STRESS

The increasing number of women in the United States labor force (from 37.7% in 1960 to 57.5% in 1990; U.S. Bureau of the Census, 1991, p. 386) has raised the question of whether women will lose their survival advantage over men. As discussed in the previous section, employed women also score higher on Type A behavior when compared to women working inside the home. If Type A behavior is related to both employment and increased risk for coronary disease, one should expect a higher incidence of CHD among women who have been employed for most of their lives. This, however, does not seem to be the case. No difference in CHD incidence was found between employed women and women working inside the home (Haynes & Feinleib, 1980). In fact, women who were employed the longest period of time (single working women) had the lowest rate of CHD.

In addition, there is evidence from two large studies (Health and Nutrition Examination Survey I [HANES I]; San Antonio Heart Study) that employed women are at *lower* risk for coronary heart disease than women working inside the home. Analyses based on data from the HANES I indicate a lower prevalence of elevated plasma cholesterol among employed women than among women working inside the home (Slaby, 1982). Consistent with this observation, employed women in the San Antonio Heart Study had a more favorable lipid profile and consumed a less atherogenic diet than women working inside their home (Hazuda et al., 1986). It is unlikely that the above findings are due to the selection of certain women into the labor force because of their relatively good health (i.e., the "healthy worker effect") because both studies took initial health status into account. In sum, there is little evidence that employment per se is unhealthy for women.

Several factors are important in predicting CHD among employed women. One is family size, the other is the type of job a women holds. Employed mothers with more than three children are more likely to develop CHD than employed women without children (Haynes & Feinleib, 1980). With regard to job type, it appears that women holding clerical jobs are at increased risk. In the Framingham Heart Study, women holding clerical jobs had CHD rates twice as great as women working inside the home or or women in other occupation groups. Similar results were reported in Tecumseh, Michigan (House, Strecher, Metzner, & Robbins, 1986). These findings are of particular interest because clerical work is associated with high demands and lack of control over the work environment (Stellman, 1978).

Other studies also support the notion that specific job characteristics reflecting low personal control and high demand (e.g., time pressure) are related to CHD in both women and men (Alfredsson, Spetz, & Theorell, 1985; Haan, 1985; Karasek, Baker, Marxer, Ahlbom, & Theorell, 1981; Karasek et al., 1988; LaCroix, 1985; LaCroix & Haynes, 1987). In Alfredsson et al.'s study (1985), hospitalization rates for myocardial infarction among women were greatest for women reporting hectic and monotonous work one year prior to hospitalization. Unfortunately, of the three traditional coronary risk factors—hypertension, elevated levels of plasma cholesterol, and smoking—only smoking was controlled for. Therefore, it is not clear to what extent job characteristics contributed independently to hospitalization.

Analyses of Framingham Heart Study data revealed that employed women who described their jobs as high in strain (high job demand combined with low control) exhibited a threefold relative risk of CHD compared to women with low-strain jobs (LaCroix & Haynes, 1987). These findings were particularly strong among female clerical workers: those in high-strain jobs had more than five times the risk of CHD than those in low-strain jobs. These associations persisted even after controlling for age, blood pressure, and cholesterol levels.

It is presently unclear how the association between job strain and high CHD rates can be explained. Controlling for traditional risk factors generally reduces the relationship between job strain and CHD (Karasek, personal communication, 1988). Conceivably, job stress induces behaviors such as eating fatty foods and smoking, which then enhance levels of traditional coronary risk factors.

Several studies support a link between psychosocial job characteristics and traditional coronary risk factors. For example, men increase their smoking under heavy workload (Conway, Vickers, Ward, & Rahe, 1981), smoke when work demands are high and control is low (Pieper, Karasek, & Schwartz, 1985), smoke to lower feelings of stress (Ikard & Tomkins, 1973), smoke to increase stress coping capacity (Nesbitt, 1973), and have difficulty stopping smoking in stressful jobs (Caplan, Cobb, & French, 1975). A relationship between job stress and smoking was also found among female hospital nurses (Tagliacozzo & Vaughn, 1982). In a further study, greater smoking (combined with coffee consumption) was observed among clerical workers when compared to other occupational groups within a university setting (Weidner, Istvan, & McKnight, 1989).

Plasma cholesterol and blood pressure also seem to be associated with job stress. For example, plasma cholesterol is elevated in stressful job settings (Friedman, Rosenman, & Carroll, 1958) and in situations of low job control (Pieper et al., 1985). Men employed in blue-collar occupations (presumably lacking control) have higher blood pressure than those employed in white-collar jobs (U.S. Department of Health, Education, and Welfare, 1977). Also, increased blood pressure has been found in workers exposed to "high stress," including air traffic controllers managing heavy air traffic (e.g., Cobb & Rose, 1973; Kasl & Cobb, 1970).

In sum, although there is evidence that the type of job a woman holds is associated with increased risk for coronary heart disease, it is not clear to what extent this effect is mediated by primary coronary risk factors. The exact nature of the effect of job strain on CHD (i.e., interactive or additive) needs to be determined. Also, most studies examining the relationship of job stress to traditional coronary risk factors are based on men, and systematic investigations among women are only beginning.[9]

It is also conceivable that certain job characteristics are associated with increased sympathetic nervous system arousal, which could be damaging to the cardiovascular system in the long run (see Matthews et al., 1986b). Support for this relationship comes from experimental studies that have manipulated work demands and control and then measured increases in sympathetic nervous system arousal (e.g., heart rate, blood pressure, and excretion of catecholamines). With a few exceptions these studies find increases in heart rate and blood pressure (e.g., Bohlin, Eliasson, Hjemdahl, Klein, & Frankenhaeuser, 1986; DeGood, 1975; Ettema & Zielhuis, 1971; Hokanson, DeGood, Forrest, & Brittain, 1971)

---

[9]Haynes, LaCroix, and Lippin (1987) report results from the North Carolina Occupational Safety and Health Project (1985), the first epidemiologic study to systematically investigate health among office workers: highest self-reported angina symptoms were found among visual display terminal workers with low control on the job.

and catecholamine output (Frankenhaeuser, 1983). In most of these studies, however, the effects of control and demand are studied separately, or, when they are combined, control is confounded with demand. For example, in conditions where subjects have control, they also have control over demands (e.g., work pace), which may lower demands compared to conditions in which subjects have no control. If it is the combination of low control/high demand that is most predictive of CHD, then control and demand will have to be manipulated independently in order to assess possible pathogenic responses associated with this combination.

Some support for the postulated effects of job strain on physiological and affective responses to stress was found in a recent experimental study that manipulated control and demand independently (Hutt & Weidner, 1992; also see Burns, Hutt, & Weidner, 1990). Briefly, strain together with subjective feelings of having little control predicted increased systolic blood pressure among women, and the absence of strain was associated with improved affect in both sexes (Hutt & Weidner, 1992).

To summarize, in spite of the higher prevalence of Type A behavior among women working outside the home, employment per se is not unhealthy for women. Rather, specific job characteristics as proposed by Karasek and his colleagues (high demand, low control; Karasek et al., 1981) is related to coronary heart disease in women, especially among clerical workers. However, the mechanisms by which these job characteristics assert their influence on CHD are not clear. Although the relationship of job strain to CHD remained after controlling for the traditional coronary risk factors in the Framingham Heart Study, the effect of job strain on traditional coronary risk factors as well as on sympathetic nervous system activity needs to be further examined.

HOSTILITY

Early indications that variables related to anger and hostility (i.e., anger that is not shown or discussed) predict CHD in women and men were based on analyses of Framingham Heart Study data (Haynes et al., 1980). Since then, several prospective studies have linked hostility as measured by the Cook Medley hostility scale (Cook & Medley, 1954) to mortality in general, including death due to CHD in men (e.g., Barefoot, Dahlstrom, & Williams, 1983; Shekelle, Gale, Ostfeld, & Paul, 1983). This scale is a subscale of the MMPI and assesses suspiciousness, resentment, and cynical mistrust (T.W. Smith & Frohm, 1985). It is not a measure of overt aggressive behaviors, which are more characteristic of Type As (Weidner, Istvan, & McKnight, 1989).

Cynical hostility has also been implicated in atherosclerosis and coronary risk among women (Weidner et al., 1987; Williams, Haney, Lee, Kong, Blumenthal, & Whalen, 1980). The first prospective evidence linking cynical hostility to CHD among women as well as men was reported only recently (Barefoot et al., 1987). Hostility in this study was assessed by Factor L of Cattell's 16PF Inventory, a measure of suspiciousness that is closely related to the Cook Medley hostility scale (Barefoot et al., 1987), the measure employed in most of the studies linking hostility to CHD among men. Findings from the 15-year follow-up of older adults indicated that both women and men scoring high on suspiciousness had greater mortality risk than those scoring low on suspiciousness. The leading cause of death in this sample was coronary heart disease.

It is not clear how Cook Medley-type hostility asserts its influence on the disease process. Although in some studies the cynical hostility/mortality relationship remains significant after controlling for traditional risk factors, the relationship of cynical hostility to these risk factors is inconclusive.[10] Several investigators found cynical hostility to be associated with smoking (Scherwitz et al., 1992; Shekelle et al., 1983; Siegler, Peterson, Barefoot, & Williams, 1992). In the only prospective study on mortality that has included women (Barefoot et al., 1987), cynical hostility was unrelated to any of the traditional risk factors. In sum, the role of hostility as an independent risk factor for CHD still needs to be determined.

It is of interest to note that cynical hostility is associated with a variety of unhealthy behaviors (in addition to smoking) that may contribute to increased coronary risk. For example, both men and women scoring high on the Cook Medley scale report poorer health habits (e.g., physical fitness) than their low-hostile counterparts (Leiker & Hailey, 1988; Scherwitz et al., 1992; Siegler et al., 1992).

With regard to physiological mechanisms linking cynical hostility to CHD, the following speculation is offered: It is possible that highly mistrustful people spend a substantial amount of time in a high arousal state, overreacting to stimuli that arouse their suspiciousness. This elevated arousal may be associated with increased sympathetic nervous system activity, which in the long run may contribute to atherosclerosis and CHD. Several studies have attempted to demonstrate heightened cardiovascular arousal in response to stress among men (e.g., Hardy & T. W. Smith, 1988; M. A. Smith & Houston, 1987; T. W. Smith & Allred, 1989; Suarez & Williams, 1989), and two studies have included women (Sallis, Johnson, Trevorrow, Kaplan, & Hovell, 1987; Weidner, Friend, Ficarrotto, & Mendell, 1989). From their findings it appears that the stressor has to elicit suspiciousness and mistrust in order to obtain elevated cardiovascular arousal from highly hostile men and women. For example, Weidner et al. (1989a) gave subjects unsolvable anagrams that were falsely described as "fairly easy" and capable of being "solved with little difficulty by most people." The studies that did not find an effect of cynical hostility on cardiovascular arousal employed

---

[10]Measures of hostility have been linked to elevated levels of plasma total and low-density-lipoprotein cholesterol in both sexes (Dujovne & Houston, 1991).

mental tasks where a right or wrong answer was possible and recognizable (M. A. Smith & Houston, 1987; Sallis et al., 1987).

In sum, suspiciousness and mistrust are related to CHD in both women and men. Also, highly suspicious women react to ambiguous stressful situations with increases in blood pressure just as their male counterparts do. However, of particular importance for explaining the gender difference in CHD is the fact that women as a group score lower on suspiciousness and mistrust when compared to men (Scherwitz, Perkins, Chesney, & Hughes, 1991; Swenson, Pearson, & Osborne, 1973; Weidner et al., 1989a; Williams et al., 1980). Thus it is possible that this difference in cynical hostility contributes to women's lower CHD risk.

One problem with the cynical hostility-CHD association found in prospective studies is that hostility also predicts death due to other causes and thus may not be related to CHD mortality alone. Type A behavior, on the other hand, appears to be more specifically linked to CHD. Since both variables, however, have been linked to CHD independently, their joint effect may be even more detrimental to one's health. In other words, it is conceivable that Type A behavior displayed by highly hostile people predisposes to CHD. Support for this notion comes from a study by Williams et al. (1980), who found that male as well as female cardiac patients who had at least one coronary artery occlusion greater or equal to 75% also scored highest on Type A behavior and hostility. In addition, Weidner et al. (1987) found that hostility among Type As was significantly related to elevated levels of plasma total and low-density-lipoprotein cholesterol in a community sample of adult women and men.

The above findings suggest that cynical hostility may also potentiate cardiovascular reactivity to stress among Type A women and men. One of our studies examined this hypothesis. Cynical hostility was assessed by the Cook Medley scale, and Type A behavior was measured by the Framingham Type A scale (FTAS; Haynes et al., 1978b) and the student version of the Jenkins Activity Survey (JAS; Krantz, Glass, & Snyder, 1974). Fifty-six female and 56 male college students participated in the study. Blood pressure and heart rate responses to an unsolvable anagram task were assessed. Among men, highly hostile Type As responded with greater increases in blood pressure when compared to low-hostile Type A men. Specifically, in JAS-defined Type A men as compared to their Type B counterparts, cynical hostility was associated with significantly greater increases in diastolic blood pressure and marginally significant increases in systolic blood pressure. When the FTAS was used as a classification instrument, marginally significant increases in diastolic blood pressure were obtained among Type A men. Hostility did not potentiate reactivity among Type B men. In fact, Type B men were quite reactive regardless of their level of hostility.

In contrast, cynical hostility did not increase cardiovascular reactivity to stress in either JAS- or FTAS-defined Type A women. However, highly hostile

Type B women had greater increases in blood pressure when compared to their low hostile Type B counterparts. Table 4.2 presents mean increases in systolic and diastolic blood pressure among both JAS- and FTAS-defined Type A and B women.

In sum, cynical hostility did potentiate blood pressure responses to stress among Type A men, but not among Type A women. Type A women were reactive regardless of their level of cynical hostility. However, cynical hostility potentiated blood pressure responses among Type B women. Thus being female and having either one of the male sex role characteristics (Type A behavior *or* hostility) may be associated with increased blood pressure reactivity to stress as compared to lacking both of these characteristics (i.e., being a non-hostile Type B woman). Being male, on the other hand, is associated with blood pressure reactivity to stress in general and in particular when both characteristics are present (Type A behavior *and* hostility).

Considering that measures of Type A behavior have consistently been associated with measures of masculinity (Blascovitch, Major, & Katkin, 1981; DeGregorio & Carver, 1980; Grimm & Yarnold, 1985; Nix & Lohr, 1981; Stevens, Pfost, & Ackerman, 1984; Zeldow, Clark, & Daughterty, 1985), and that men display more aggression, hostility, and anger than women do, our findings raise the question of whether gender roles interact with sex to influence cardiovascular stress reactivity. Embracing the male gender role stereotype may be unhealthy for both women and men. However, scoring low on these male gender role characteristics may be protective only when sex "appropriate," i.e., for women. Being a low-hostile Type B man in a society that encourages aggressiveness, competitiveness, and hostility among men may actually be associated with negative health consequences.[11]

To conclude, cynical hostility has emerged as an independent predictor of mortality among women in one prospective study to date. It is not clear whether hostility is specifically linked to CHD. The extent to which hostility is associated with traditional coronary risk factors is unclear. However, hostility is linked to elevated blood pressure reactivity to stress in women and men, which may present a possible pathway to CHD. Further, the effect of cynical hostility on stress reactivity appears to be moderated by Type A behavior and sex in a way that suggests an influence of gender roles.

SUMMARY AND CONCLUSIONS

Although the prevalence of coronary heart disease is greater in men than in women, CHD is a major cause of premature death among women. When com-

---

[11]As discussed in Chapter 3 of this volume, Frankenhaeuser and her colleagues find neuroendocrine responses to stress to be influenced by gender roles. For example, women with nontraditional career goals such as engineering are more similar to men in their urinary catecholamine response to stress than women with more traditional career goals (A. Collins & Frankenhaeuser, 1978).

pared to men, women as a group score lower not only on traditional coronary risk factors, but also on all three psychosocial risk factors reviewed in the present chapter: women score lower on Type A behavior and cynical hostility, and are less likely to be exposed to job strain because fewer women than men are employed outside the home. Thus women's lower risk for CHD may be partly accounted for by these gender differences in psychosocial risk factors.

Despite the gender differences in absolute risk factor levels, the link between each risk factor and CHD is apparent in both women and men. Both Type A women and Type A men are at elevated risk for CHD; both women and men who are highly hostile are more likely to develop CHD; both women's and men's coronary risk is affected by job strain. It is not clear, however, to what extent these psychosocial factors are independently associated with CHD. The evidence for an independent contribution to CHD is strongest for Type A behavior. With regard to occupational stress, there are some findings that suggest that job stress may be related to traditional coronary risk factors. The evidence is least clear for an independent contribution of cynical hostility to CHD among women. One of the major problems in this area is that few studies have included women; we do not have the data bases available that would allow us to determine the extent to which psychosocial variables contribute independently to CHD. New large-scale epidemiologic studies that include female samples are clearly needed.

Several laboratory studies have attempted to elucidate alternative ways by which psychosocial risk factors could assert their influence on the disease process. Results from these studies suggest that certain behaviors may contribute to elevated coronary risk in predisposed women and men (e.g., not acknowledging physical symptoms when under stress among Type As; poor health habits among highly hostile people).

One particularly promising set of studies focuses on cardiovascular reactivity to stress as a mechanism linking Type A behavior and cynical hostility to increased CHD risk. Unfortunately, most studies in this area exclude women as subjects. One reason for this could be that it is still unclear whether the variation of reproductive hormones during the menstrual cycle has an effect on cardiovascular responses to stress. Although some studies have found differences in cardiovascular responses according to cycle phase, these differences have not been consistent (e.g., Hastrup & Light, 1984; Polefrone & Manuck, 1988). The majority of studies do not find any differences in blood pressure and heart rate responses to stress across the menstrual cycle (e.g., Carroll, Turner, Lee, & Stephenson, 1984; A. Collins, Eneroth, & Landgren, 1985; Stoney, Langer, & Gelling, 1986; Stoney, Owens, Matthews, Davis, & Caggiula, 1990; Strauss, Schultheiss, & Cohen, 1983). Further, the lack of phase differences in a study that employed a male control group (yoked to the women's cycle phases) and a cover story that eliminated subjects' awareness of participation in a "menstruation study" suggests that the phase differences in stress reactivity found in some studies may be methodological artifacts (Weidner & Helmig, 1990). Thus, there is no convincing evidence that blood pressure and heart rate reactivity to stress varies across the menstrual cycle.

The results from the studies that have employed both women and men show many noteworthy *similarities* between the sexes. For example, Type As of both sexes report more stress. Hostility among both Type A women and Type A men is related to elevated levels of plasma total and low density lipoprotein cholesterol. And high-hostile women and men respond with greater cardiovascular arousal to stress when compared to low-hostile individuals.

In spite of the many similarities, there are also important gender *differences* that need further investigation. Type A behavior interacts with hostility on cardiovascular stress reactivity in a different manner in women than in men. In addition, socialization patterns associated with Type A behavior in boys are not associated with Type A behavior in girls. By investigating environmental correlates that encourage Type A behavior and cynical hostility in both boys and girls, we may learn to alter the conditions that contribute to the greater prevalence of Type A behavior and cynical hostility among men.

Finally, not much is known about gender differences in health behaviors associated with CHD risk. Studying health behaviors is important for several reasons. First, health behaviors such as eating a diet high in cholesterol and saturated fats may impact on traditional coronary risk factors. Second, some health behaviors are specific to women and may by themselves or in combination with other risk factors contribute to women's coronary risk. For example, oral contraceptive use elevates the risk for thromboembolic disease and myocardial infarction (e.g., Mann, Inman, & Thorogood, 1976; Mann, Vessey, & Thorogood, 1975; Vessey & Doll, 1969). Heavy smoking in combination with oral contraceptive use greatly exacerbates the risk for myocardial infarction (Jain, 1976; Ory 1977) and is related to elevated blood pressure reactivity to stress (Emmons & Weidner, 1988; Davis & Matthews, 1990).

In sum, progress has been made in identifying risk factors for coronary heart disease, the number one killer among both women and men. Given that most of these risk factors are behavioral or have behavioral components, it should be possible to reduce the rates of CHD among both men and women through behavioral interventions. However, the origin of these risk factors and the mechanisms by which they assert their influence on CHD etiology have yet to be identified. Since CHD has multiple causes that are interrelated (e.g., job stress and hypertension), a multidisciplinary approach combining perspectives from medicine, epidemiology, and psychology is mandatory to further our understanding, and ultimately control, of CHD.

REFERENCES

Alfredsson, L., Spetz, C.L., & Theorell, T. (1985). Type of occupation and near-future hospitalization for myocardial infarction and some other diagnoses. *International Journal of Epidemiology, 14*, 378–388.

American Cancer Society. (1989). *Cancer facts and figures*. New York: Author.

Baker, L., Dearborn, M., Hastings, J.E., & Hamberger, K. (1984). Type A behavior in women: A review. *Health Psychology, 3*, 477–497.

Barefoot, J. C., Dahlstrom, G., & Williams, R. B. (1983). Hostility, CHD incidence, and total mortality: A 25-year follow-up study of 255 physicians. *Psychosomatic Medicine, 45*, 59–63.

Barefoot, J. C., Siegler, I. C., Nowlin, J. B., Peterson, B. L., Haney, T. L., & Williams, R. B. (1987). Suspiciousness, health, and mortality: A follow-up study of 500 older adults. *Psychosomatic Medicine, 49*, 450–457.

Berkman, L. F., & Syme, S. L. (1979). Social networks, host resistance, and mortality: A nine-year follow-up study of Alameda County residents. *American Journal of Epidemiology, 109*, 186–204.

Blascovitch, J., Major, B., & Katkin, E. S. (1981). Sex-role orientation and Type A behavior. *Personality and Social Psychology Bulletin, 7*, 600–604.

Bohlin, G., Eliasson, K., Hjemdahl, P., Klein, K., & Frankenhaeuser, M. (1986). Pace variation and control of work pace as related to cardiovascular, neuroendocrine, and subjective responses. *Biological Psychology, 23*, 247–263.

Bracke, P. E. (1986). Parental child-rearing practices and the development of Type A behavior in children. (Doctoral dissertation, Stanford University. 1986, Vol. 46, p. 4421-B.)

Burns, J. W., Hutt, J., & Weidner, G. (1990). Hostility, task demand, and decision latitude as determinants of cardiovascular and affective reactivity in women and men. *Psychophysiology, 27*, S–20. (Abstract)

Campbell, J. J., Elwood, P. C., Abbas, S., & Waters, W.E. (1984). Chest pain in women: A study of prevalence and mortality follow-up in South Wales. *Journal of Epidemiology and Community Health, 38*, 17–20.

Caplan, R. D., Cobb, S., & French, J. R. P. (1975). Relationships of cessation of smoking with job stress, personality, and social support. *Journal of Applied Social Psychology, 60*, 211–219.

Carroll, D., Turner, J. R., Lee, H. J., & Stephenson, J. (1984). Temporal consistency of individual differences in cardiac response to a video game. *Biological Psychology, 19*, 81–93.

Chesney, M. A. (1983). Occupational setting and coronary-prone behavior in men and women. In T.M. Dembroski, T. H. Schmidt, & G. Bluemchen (Eds.), *Biobehavioral bases of coronary heart disease* (pp. 79–90). New York: Karger.

Chesney, M. A., & Black, G. W. (1988). Coronary-prone behavior and cardiovascular reactivity in women. Paper presented at the meeting of the American Psychological Association, Atlanta.

Chesney, M. A., Black, G. W., Chadwick, J. H., & Rosenman, R. H. (1981). Psychological correlates of the coronary prone behavior pattern. *Journal of Behavioral Medicine, 4*, 217–229.

Chesney, M. A., Eagleston, J. E., & Rosenman, R. H. (1980). The Type A structured interview: A behavioral assessment in the rough. *Journal of Behavioral Assessment, 2,* 255–272.

Cobb, S., & Rose, R. M. (1973). Hypertension, peptic ulcer, and diabetes in air traffic controllers. *Journal of the American Medical Association, 224,* 489–492.

Collins, A., Eneroth, P., & Landgren, B. M. (1985). Psychoneuroendocrine stress response and mood as related to the menstrual cycle. *Psychosomatic Medicine, 47,* 512–527.

Collins, A., & Frankenhaeuser, M. (1978). Stress responses in male and female engineering students. *Journal of Human Stress, 4,* 43–48.

Connor, W. E., & Connor, S. L. (1985). The dietary prevention and treatment of coronary heart disease. In W. E. Connor & J. D. Bristow (Eds.), *Coronary heart disease: Prevention, complications, and treatment* (pp. 43–64). New York: J. B. Lippincott.

Conway, T. L., Vickers, R. R., Ward, H. W., & Rahe, R. H. (1981). Occupational stress and variation in cigarette, coffee, and alcohol consumption. *Journal of Health and Social Behavior, 22,* 155–165.

Cook, W. W., & Medley, D. M. (1954). Proposed hostility and pharisaic-virtue scales for the MMPI. *Journal of Applied Psychology, 38,* 414–418.

Corrigan, S. A., & Moskowitz, D. S. (1983). Type A behavior in preschool children: Construct validation evidence for the MYTH. *Child Development, 54,* 1513–1521.

Costa, P. T. (1986). Is neuroticism a risk factor for CAD? Is Type A measure of neuroticism? In T. Schmidt, T. M. Dembroski, & G. Bluemchen (Eds.), *Biological and psychological factors in cardiovascular disease* (pp. 85–95). New York: Springer-Verlag.

Davis, M. C., & Matthews, K. A. (1990). Cigarette smoking and oral contraceptive use influence women's lipid, lipoprotein, and cardiovascular responses during stress. *Health Psychology, 9,* 717–736.

DeGood, D. E. (1975). Cognitive control factors and vascular stress responses. *Psychophysiology, 12,* 399–401. DeGregorio, E., & Carver, C. S. (1980). Type A behavior, sex role orientation, and psychological adjustment. *Journal of Personality and Social Psychology, 39,* 286–293.

Doornen, L. J. P. van, & Orlebeke, J. F. (1982). Stress, personality and serum cholesterol level. *Journal of Human Stress, 8,* 24–29.

Dujovne, V. F., Houston, B. K. (1991). Hostility-related variables and plasma lipid levels. *Journal of Behavioral Medicine, 14,* 555–565.

Eaker, E. D., Abbott, R. D., & Kannel, W. B. (1989). Frequency of uncomplicated angina pectoris in Type A compared to Type B persons (the Framingham Study). *American Journal of Cardiology, 63,* 1042–1045.

Eaker, E. D., & Castelli, W. P. (1988). Type A behavior and coronary heart disease in women: Fourteen-year incidence from the Framingham Study. In B. K. Houston & C. R. Snyder (Eds.), *Type A behavior pattern: Research, theory and intervention* (pp. 83–97). New York: John Wiley.

Eaker, E. D., Pinsky, J., & Castelli, W. P. (1992). Myocardial infarction and coronary death among women: Psychosocial predictors from a 20-year follow-up of women in the Framingham Study. *American Journal of Epidemiology, 135,* 854–864.

Emmons, K. M., & Weidner, G. (1988). The effects of cognitive and physical stress on cardiovascular reactivity among smokers and oral contraceptive users. *Psychophysiology, 25,* 166–171.

Ettema, J. H., & Zielhuis, R. L. (1971). Physiological parameters of mental load. *Ergonomics, 14,* 137–144. Frankenhaeuser, M. (1983). The sympathetic-adrenal and pituitary-adrenal response to challenge: Comparison between the sexes. In T. M. Dembroski, T. H. Schmidt, & G. Bluemchen (Eds.), *Biobehavioral bases of coronary heart disease* (pp. 91–105). New York: Karger.

Frankenhaeuser, M. (1991). The psychophysiology of workload, stress, and health: Comparison between the sexes. *Annals of Behavioral Medicine, 13,* 197–204.

Friedman, M., Rosenman, R. H., & Carroll, V. (1958). Changes in serum cholesterol and blood clotting time in men subjected to cyclic variation of occupational stress. *Circulation, 17,* 582–861.

Girdler, S. S., Turner, J. R., Sherwood, A., & Light, K. C. (1990). Gender differences in blood pressure control during a variety of behavioral stressors. *Psychosomatic Medicine, 52,* 571–591.

Gordon, T., & Shurtleff, D. (1973). *Means at each examination and interexamination variation of specified characteristics: Framingham Study, Exam 1 to Exam 10.* Washington, DC: U.S. Government Printing Office.

Griffin, K., Schneider, T., Eitel, P., Connor, S. L., & Weidner, G. (1992). Type A behavior and Health Locus of Control as predictors of dietary change and plasma cholesterol-lowering. Paper presented at the Annual Meeting of the American Psychological Association. San Francisco, CA.

Grimm, L. G., & Yarnold, P. R. (1985). Sex typing and the coronary-prone behavior pattern. *Sex Roles, 12,* 171–177.

Haan, M. (1985). Job strain and cardiovascular disease: A ten-year prospective study. *American Journal of Epidemiology, 122,* 532 (abstract).

Hardy, J. D., & Smith, T. W. (1988). Cynical hostility and vulnerability to disease: Social support, life stress, and physiological response to conflict. *Health Psychology, 7,* 447–459.

Hastrup, J. L., & Light, K. C. (1984). Sex differences in cardiovascular stress responses: Modulation as a function of menstrual cycle phases. *Journal of Psychosomatic Research, 28,* 175–183.

Haynes, S. G., & Feinleib, M. (1980). Women, work, and coronary heart disease: Prospective findings from the Framingham Heart Study. *American Journal of Public Health, 70,* 133–141.

Haynes, S. G., Feinleib, M., & Kannel, W. (1980). The relationship of psychosocial factors to coronary heart disease in the Framingham study III. Eight-year incidence of coronary heart disease. *American Journal of Epidemiology, 111,* 37–58.

Haynes, S. G., Feinleib, M., Levine, S., Scotch, N., & Kannel, W. B. (1978a). The relationship of psychosocial factors to coronary heart disease in the Framingham study II. Prevalence of coronary heart disease. *American Journal of Epidemiology, 107,* 384–402.

Haynes, S. G., LaCroix, A. Z., & Lippin, T. (1987b). The effect of high job demands and low control on the health of employed women. In J. C. Quick, R. S. Bhagat, J. Dalton, & J. D. Quick (Eds.), *Work stress: The role for health care delivery systems* (pp. 93–110). New York: Praeger.

Haynes, S. G., Levine, S., Scotch, N., Feinleib, M., & Kannel, W. B. (1978). The relationship of psychosocial factors to coronary heart disease in the Framingham study: Methods and risk factors. *American Journal of Epidemiology, 107,* 362–383.

Hazuda, H. P., Haffner, S. M., Stern, M. P., Knapp, J. A., Eifler, C.W., & Rosenthal, M. (1986). Employment status and women's protection against coronary heart disease: Findings from the San Antonio Heart Study. *American Journal of Epidemiology, 123,* 623–640.

Henry, J. P., & Meehan, J. P. (1981). Psychosocial stimuli, physiological specificity, and cardiovascular disease. In H. Weiner, M. A. Hofer, & A. J. Stunkard (Eds.), *Brain, behavior, and bodily disease* (pp. 305–333). New York: Raven Press.

Hokanson, J. E., DeGood, D. E., Forrest, M. S., & Brittain, T. M. (1971). Availability of avoidance behaviors in modulating vascular stress responses. *Journal of Personality and Social Psychology, 19,* 60–68.

Hollis, J. F., Carmody, T. P., Connor, S. L., Fey, S. G., & Matarazzo, J. D. (1986). The Nutrition Attitude Survey: Associations with dietary habits, psychological and physical well-being, and coronary risk factors. *Health Psychology, 5,* 359–374.

House, J. S., Strecher, V., Metzner, H. L., & Robbins, C. A. (1986). Occupational stress and health among men and women in the Tecumseh community health study. *Journal of Health and Social Behavior, 27,* 62–77.

Houston, B. K. (1988). Cardiovascular and neuroendocrine reactivity, global Type A, and components of Type A behavior. In B. K. Houston & C. R. Snyder (Eds.), *Type A behavior pattern: Research, theory, & intervention* (pp. 212–253). New York: John Wiley.

Houston, B. K., Smith, T. W., & Zurawski, R. M. (1986). Principal dimensions of the Framingham Type A Scale: Differential relationships to cardiovascular reactivity and anxiety. *Journal of Human Stress, 12,* 105–112.

Hutt, J., & Weidner, G. (1992). The effects of task demand and decision latitude on cardiovascular reactivity to stress. *Behavioral Medicine, 18,* 181–188.

Ikard, F. F., & Tomkins, S. (1973). The experience of affect as a determinant of smoking behavior. *Journal of Abnormal Psychology, 8,* 172–181.

Jain, A. K. (1976). Cigarette smoking, use of oral contraceptives, and myocardial infarction. *American Journal of Obstetrics and Gynecology, 126,* 301–307.

Jenkins, C. D. (1971). Psychologic and social precursors of coronary disease. *New England Journal of Medicine, 284,* 244–255.

Jenkins, C. D. (1976). Recent evidence supporting psychologic and social risk factors for coronary disease. *New England Journal of Medicine, 294,* 987–994, 1033–1038.

Jenkins, C. D., Rosenman, R. H., & Zyzanski, S. J. (1974). Prediction of clinical coronary heart disease by a test for the coronary-prone behavior pattern. *New England Journal of Medicine, 290,* 1271–1275.

Karasek, R. A., Baker, D., Marxer, F., Ahlbom, A., & Theorell, T. (1981). Job decision latitude, job demands and cardiovascular disease. *American Journal of Public Health, 71,* 694–705.

Karasek, R. A., Theorell, T., Schwartz, J. E., Schnall, P. L., Pieper, C. F., & Michela, J. L. (1988). Job characteristics in relation to the prevalence of myocardial infarction in the U.S. Health Examination Survey (HES) and the Health and Nutrition Examination Survey (HANES). *American Journal of Public Health, 78,* 910–918.

Kasl, S. V., & Cobb, S. (1970). Blood pressure changes in men undergoing job loss: A preliminary report. *Psychosomatic Medicine, 2,* 19–38.

Kirmil-Gray, K., Eagleston, J. R., Thoresen, C. E., Heft, L., Arnow, B., & Bracke, P. (1987). Developing measures of Type A behavior in children and adolescents. *Journal of Human Stress, 13,* 5–15.

Kliewer, W., & Weidner, G. (1987). Type A behavior and aspirations: A study of parents' and children's goal setting. *Developmental Psychology, 23,* 204–209.

Krantz, D. S., Glass, D. C., & Snyder, M. L. (1974). Helplessness, stress levels, and the coronary prone behavior pattern. *Journal of Experimental Social Psychology, 10,* 284–300.

Krantz, D. S., & Manuck, S. B. (1984). Acute psychophysiologic reactivity and risk of cardiovascular disease: A review and methodologic critique. *Psychological Bulletin, 96,* 435–464.

LaCroix, A. Z. (1985). High demand/low control work and coronary heart disease incidence in the Framingham cohort. Unpublished doctoral dissertation, Department of Epidemiology, School of Public Health, University of North Carolina at Chapel Hill. Vol. 45, p. 2521-B.

LaCroix, A. Z., & Haynes, S. G. (1987). Gender differences in the health effects of workplace roles. In R. C. Barnett, L. Biener, & G. K. Baruch (Eds.), *Gender and stress* (pp. 96–121). New York: Macmillan.

LaCroix, A. Z., Haynes, S. G., Savage, D. D., & Havlik, R. J. (1989). Rose questionnaire angina among United States black, white, and Mexican-American women and men: Prevalence and correlates from the second National and Hispanic Health and Nutrition Examination surveys. *American Journal of Epidemiology, 129,* 669–686.

Lawler, K. A., Rixse, A., & Allen, M. T. (1983). Type A behavior and psychophysiological responses in adult women. *Psychophysiology, 20,* 343–350.

Leiker, M., & Hailey, B. J. (1988). A link between hostility and disease: Poor health habits. *Behavioral Medicine, 14,* 129–133.

Lerner, D. J., & Kannel, W. B. (1986). Patterns of coronary heart disease morbidity and mortality in the sexes: A 26-year follow-up of the Framingham population. *American Heart Journal, 111,* 383–390.

Lundberg, U. (1983). Sex differences in behavior and catecholamine and cortisol excretion in 3–6 year old day-care children. *Biological Psychology, 16,* 109–117.

MacDougall, J. M., Dembroski, T. M., & Krantz, D. S. (1981). Effects of types of challenge on pressor and heart rate responses in Type A and B women. *Psychophysiology, 18,* 1–9.

Mann, J. I., Inman, W. H. W., & Thorogood, M. (1976). Oral contraceptive use in older women and fatal myocardial infarction. *British Medical Journal, 2,* 445–447.

Mann, J. I., Vessey, M. P., & Thorogood, M. (1975). Myocardial infarction in young women with special reference to oral contraceptive practice. *British Medical Journal, 2,* 241–245.

Matthews, K. A., & Angulo, J. (1980). Measurement of the Type A behavior pattern in children: Assessment of children's competitiveness, impatience-anger, and aggression. *Child Development, 51,* 466–475.

Matthews, K. A., Stoney, C. M., Rakaczky, C. J., & Jamison, W. (1986a). Family characteristics and school achievements of Type A children. *Health Psychology, 5,* 453–467.

Matthews, K. A., Weiss, S. M., Detre, T., Dembroski, T. M., Falkner, B., Manuck, S. B., & Williams, R. B. (Eds.). (1986b). *Handbook of stress, reactivity, and cardiovascular disease*. New York: John Wiley.

Mattson, M. E., & Herd, J. A. (1988). Cardiovascular disease. In E. A. Blechman & K. D. Brownell (Eds.), *Handbook of behavioral medicine for women* (pp. 160–177). New York: Pergamon.

Morell, M. A., & Katkin, E. (1982). Jenkins Activity Survey scores among women of different occupations. *Journal of Consulting and Clinical Psychology, 4*, 588–589.

Nesbitt, P. D. (1973). Smoking, physiological arousal, and emotional response. *Journal of Personality and Social Psychology, 25*, 137–144.

Nix, J., & Lohr, J. M. (1981). Relationship between sex, sex-role characteristics and coronary-prone behavior in college students. *Psychological Reports, 48*, 739–744.

North Carolina Occupational Safety and Health Project and North Carolina Communications Workers of America. (1985). *Office workers stress survey results*. Washington, DC: Author.

Orth-Gomer, K., & Johnson, J. V. (1987). Social network interaction and mortality: A six year follow-up study of a random sample of the Swedish population. *Journal of Chronic Disease, 40*, 949–957.

Ory, H. W. (1977). Association between oral contraceptives and myocardial infarction: A review. *Journal of the American Medical Association, 237*, 2619–2622.

Pieper, C., Karasek, R. A., & Schwartz, J. (1985). The relationship of job dimensions to coronary heart disease risk factors. Paper presented to the Society for Epidemiological Research, Chapel Hill, NC.

Polefrone, J. M., & Manuck, S. B. (1988). Effects of menstrual phase and parental history of hypertension on cardiovascular response to cognitive challenge. *Psychosomatic Medicine, 50*, 23–36.

Sallis, J. F., Johnson, C. C., Trevorrow, T. R., Kaplan, R. M., & Hovell, M. F. (1987). The relationship between cynical hostility and blood pressure reactivity. *Journal of Psychosomatic Research, 31*, 111–116.

Scherwitz, L. W., Perkins, L. L., Chesney, M. A., & Hughes, G. H. (1991). Cook-Medley Hostility Scale and subsets: Relationship to demographic and psychosocial characteristics in young adults in the CARDIA Study. *Psychosomatic Medicine, 53*, 36–49.

Scherwitz, L. W., Perkins, L. L., Chesney, M. A., Hughes, G. H., Sidney, S., & Manolio, T. A. (1992). Hostility and health behaviors in young adults: The CARDIA Study. *American Journal of Epidemiology, 136*, 136–145.

Shekelle, R. B., Gale, M., Ostfeld, A. M., & Paul, O. (1983). Hostility, risk of coronary heart disease, and mortality. *Psychosomatic Medicine, 45*, 109–114.

Shumaker, S. A., & Czajkowski, S. M. (Eds.). (In press). *Social support and cardiovascular disease*. New York: Plenum Press.

Siegel, J. M., & Leitch, C. J. (1981). Behavioral factors and blood pressure in adolescence: The Tacoma Study. *American Journal of Epidemiology, 113*, 171–181.

Siegler, I. C., Peterson, B. L., Barefoot, J. C., & Williams, R. B. (1992). Hostility during late adolescence predicts coronary risk factors at mid-life. *American Journal of Epidemiology, 136*, 146–154.

Slaby, A. R. (1982). Cardiovascular risk factors in women by their working status. Paper presented at the 22nd Conference on Cardiovascular Disease Epidemiology, San Antonio, TX.

Smith, M. A., & Houston, B. K. (1987). Hostility, anger expression, cardiovascular responsivity, and social support. *Biological Psychology, 24,* 39–48.

Smith, T. W., & Allred, K. D. (1989). Blood pressure responses during social interaction in high and low cynically hostile males. *Journal of Behavioral Medicine, 12,* 135–143.

Smith, T. W., & Frohm, K. D. (1985). What's so unhealthy about hostility? Construct validity and psychosocial correlates of the Cook Medley Ho Scale. *Journal of Health Psychology, 4,* 503–520.

Smith, T. W., Houston, B. K., & Zurawski, R. M. (1985). The Framingham Type A Scale: Cardiovascular and cognitive-behavioral responses to interpersonal challenge. *Motivation & Emotion, 9,* 123–134.

Stamler, J., Stamler, R., & Liu, K. (1985). High blood pressure. In W. E. Connor & J. D. Bristow (Eds.), *Coronary heart disease: Prevention, complications, and treatment* (pp. 85–109). New York: J. B. Lippincott.

Stellman, J. M. (1978). Occupational health hazards of women: An overview. *Preventive Medicine, 7,* 281–293.

Stevens, M. J., Pfost, K. S., & Ackerman, M. D. (1984). The relationship between sex-role orientation and the Type A behavior pattern: A test of the main effect hypothesis. *Journal of Clinical Psychology, 40,* 1338–1341.

Stokes, J., Kannel, W. B., Wolf, P. A., Cupples, L. A., & D'Agostino, R. B. (1987). The relative importance of selected risk factors for various manifestations of cardiovascular disease among men and women from 35 to 64 years old: 30 years of follow-up in the Framingham Study. *Circulation, 75*(Suppl. V), V-65-73.

Stoney, C. M., Davis, M., & Matthews, K. (1987). Sex differences in physiological responses to stress in coronary heart disease: A causal link? *Psychophysiology, 24,* 127–131.

Stoney, C. M., Langer, A. W., & Gelling, P. D. (1986). Effects of menstrual cycle phase on cardiovascular and pulmonary responses to behavioral and exercise stress. *Psychophysiology, 23,* 393–402.

Stoney, C. M., Matthews, K. A., McDonald, R. H., & Johnson, C. A. (1988). Sex differences in lipid, lipoprotein, cardiovascular, and neuroendocrine responses to acute stress. *Psychophysiology, 25,* 645–656.

Stoney, C. M., Owens, J. F., Matthews, K. A., Davis, M. C., & Caggiula, A. (1990). Influences of the normal menstrual cycle on physiologic functioning during behavioral stress. *Psychophysiology, 27,* 125–135.

Strauss, B., Schultheiss, M., & Cohen, R. (1983). Autonomic reactivity in the premenstrual phase. *British Journal of Clinical Psychology, 22,* 1–9.

Suarez, E. C., & Williams, R. B. (1989). Situational determinants of cardiovascular and emotional responses in high and low hostile men. *Psychosomatic Medicine, 51,* 404–418.

Swenson, W. M., Pearson, J. S., & Osborne, D. (1973). *An MMPI source book: Basic item, scale, and pattern data on 50,000 medical patients.* Minneapolis: University of Minnesota Press.

Tagliacozzo, R., & Vaughn, S. (1982). Stress and smoking in hospital nurses. *American Journal of Public Health, 72,* 441–448.

Thom, T. J., Epstein, F. H., Feldman, J. J., & Leaverton, P. E. (1985). Trends in total mortality and mortality from heart disease in 26 countries from 1950 to 1978. *International Journal of Epidemiology, 14,* 510–520.

Thoresen, C. E., & Pattillo, J. R. (1988). Exploring the Type A behavior pattern in children and adolescents. In B. K. Houston & C. R. Snyder (Eds.), *Type A behavior pattern: Research, theory, and intervention* (pp. 98–145). New York: John Wiley.

Truett, J., Cornfield, J., & Kannel, W. B. (1967). A multivariate analysis of the risk of coronary heart disease in Framingham. *Journal of Chronic Disease, 20,* 511–524.

U.S. Bureau of the Census. (1991). *Statistical abstract of the United States* (111th ed.). Washington, DC: U.S. Government Printing Office.

U.S. Department of Health, Education, and Welfare. National Health Service. (1977). *Hypertension in adults 24–74 years of age, United States, 1971–75* (DHEW Publication No. PHS 79-1310, Series 11, No. 221). U.S. Government Printing Office. Hyattsville, MD.

Verbrugge, L. M. (1980). Recent trends in sex mortality differentials in the United States. *Women & Health, 5,* 17–37.

Vessey, M. P., & Doll, R. (1969). Investigation of the relationship between use of oral contraceptives and thromboembolic disease: A further report. *British Medical Journal, 2,* 651–657.

Waldron, I. (1983). Sex differences in human mortality: The role of genetic factors. *Social Science and Medicine, 17,* 321–333.

Waldron, I., Zyzanski, S., Shekelle, R. B., Jenkins, D., & Tannebaum, S. (1977). The coronary-prone behavior pattern in employed man and women. *Journal of Human Stress, 2,* 2–18.

Weidner, G., & Chesney, M. A. (1985). Stress, Type A behavior, and coronary heart disease. In W. E. Connor & J. D. Bristow (Eds.), *Coronary heart disease: Prevention, complications, and treatment* (pp. 157–172). Philadelphia: J. B. Lippincott.

Weidner, G., & Collins, R. L. (1992). Gender, coping and health. In H. W. Krohne (Ed.), *Attention and avoidance* (pp 241–265). Toronto: Hogrefe & Huber.

Weidner, G., Connor, S. L., Chesney, M. A., Burns, J. W., Connor, W. E., Matarazzo, J. D., & Mendell, N. R. (1991). Sex differences in high density lipoprotein cholesterol among low-level alcohol consumers. *Circulation, 83,* 176–180.

Weidner, G., Friend, R., Ficarrotto, T. J., & Mendell, N. R. (1989a). Hostility and cardiovascular reactivity to stress in women and men. *Psychosomatic Medicine, 51,* 36–45.

Weidner, G., & Helmig, L. (1990). Cardiovascular stress reactivity and mood during the menstrual cycle. *Women & Health, 16,* 5–21.

Weidner, G., Hutt, J., Connor, S. L., & Mendell, N. R. (1992). Family stress and coronary risk in children. *Psychosomatic Medicine, 54,* 471–479.

Weidner, G., Istvan, J., & McKnight, J. D. (1989b). Clusters of behavioral coronary risk factors in employed women and men. *Journal of Applied Social Psychology, 19,* 468–480.

Weidner, G., & Matthews, K. A. (1978). Reported physical symptoms elicited by unpredictable events and the Type A coronary-prone behavior pattern. *Journal of Personality and Social Psychology, 36,* 1213–1220.

Weidner, G., McLellarn, R., Sexton, G., Istvan, J., & Connor, S. L. (1986). Type A behavior and physiological coronary risk factors in children of the Family Heart Study: Results from a one year follow-up. *Psychosomatic Medicine, 48,* 480–488.

Weidner, G., Messina, C. R. (1993). The effects of gender-typed tasks and gender-roles on cardiovascular reactivity. Presentation to the Society of Behavioral Medicine, San Francisco, CA.

Weidner, G., Sexton, G., Matarazzo, J. D., Pereira, C., & Friend, R. (1988). Type A behavior in children, adolescents, and their parents. *Developmental Psychology, 24,* 118–121.

Weidner, G., Sexton, G., McLellarn, R., Connor, S. L., & Matarazzo, J. D. (1987). The role of Type A behavior and hostility in an elevation of plasma lipids in adult women and men. *Psychosomatic Medicine, 49,* 136–146.

Williams, R. B., Haney, T. L., Lee, K. L., Kong, Y. H., Blumenthal, J. A., & Whalen, R. E. (1980). Type A behavior, hostility, and coronary atherosclerosis. *Psychosomatic Medicine, 42,* 539–549.

Wingard, D. (1984). The sex differential in morbidity, mortality, and lifestyle. *Annual Review of Public Health, 5,* 433–458.

Zeldow, P. B., Clark, D., & Daughterty, S. R. (1985). Masculinity, femininity, Type A behavior, and psychosocial adjustment in medical students. *Journal of Personality and Social Psychology, 48,* 481–492.

Chapter 5

Cancer in Women

Peggy J. Ott and Sandra M. Levy

This chapter discusses psychological aspects of cancer in women, focusing in particular on breast and gynecological cancers. Of the hundreds of publications on psychology and oncology during the past decade on psychology and oncology, approximately 85% were on gynecological and breast cancers, almost as if women were spared all other forms of this disease. This finding would stand out as singularly odd if it were not for two significant factors—the increasing incidence of breast cancer and certain gynecological cancers and the uniqueness of these types of cancer in terms of their psychological ramifications.

Breast cancer is second only to lung cancer as the most common form of cancer in women. The incidence rate has been recently revised to be one in nine women will develop breast cancer at some time in her life (Hofer, 1992). Furthermore, this incidence rate has been increasing for decades. The dramatic rise in this particular form of cancer led one physician to question who sets our research priorities. In his words, "if testicular cancer had reached such proportions, and if it were still increasing, we would by now have seen an unprecedented commitment of resources to its cure" (Konner, 1988, p. 66). As noted in the introductory and concluding chapters in this book, breast cancer and other significant forms of disease affecting large numbers of women have only recently begun to get the research attention they deserve.

The increasing incidence of breast and certain gynecological cancers coincides with profound social changes that have occurred over the past several decades. Epidemiological studies have cited specific changes in society (e.g., women's roles, child-rearing practices, sexual freedom) as contributory risk factors in the increased incidence of breast and cervical cancer. Risk factors cited for cervical cancer include cigarette smoking, sexually transmitted diseases such as venereal warts, multiple sexual partners, and early and frequent sexual activity (Hofer, 1992). The increasing incidence of breast cancer partly reflects earlier detection of tumors (contributing to more diagnoses) and partly reflects several risk factors that are a consequence of the changing roles of women in our society. That is, among other factors, higher risk of breast cancer is associated with no children and with first childbirth after age 30 (Hofer, 1992). Other risk factors for breast cancer include menstruation before age 12, family history of breast cancer, diet high in fat, certain forms of benign breast disease, and previous personal history of breast cancer.

A second factor that makes intelligible the seemingly inexplicable overrepresentation of these types of cancer in the psychology and oncology research literature is their uniqueness in terms of psychological sequelae. That is, breast and gynecological cancers, and the traditional surgical interventions to treat them, often have serious consequences for psychological well-being. In addition to the general psychological consequences of cancer are the assaults to female identity, sexuality, self-esteem, and body image, with their ensuing impact on psychosocial adjustment.

Psychological research on cancer generally clusters into the following classifications: prevention and compliance, the psychological sequelae of treatment and living with cancer, psychosocial adjustment, and psychological contributors to increased survival rates. After we review representative research on each of these topics, our focus will be on recent research in this area, namely, on our own research in the area of behavioral immunology.

PREVENTION AND COMPLIANCE

Based on the fact that many deaths from cancer can be prevented by prophylactic surveillance (e.g., breast self-examination, mammography, and the Pap smear), it is important to understand the factors that predispose women to engage or not engage in these early detection behaviors. In addition to the demographic characteristics of each group, it is important to ascertain the roles of attitude, motivation, and emotions as they affect behavior. This is a specific area in which psychology can make a significant contribution to medicine and health care.

Huguley, Brown, Greenberg, and Clark (1988) investigated the relationship between breast self-examination and survival rates. Results of this study of 2,093 newly diagnosed breast cancer patients from 14 different hospitals revealed that, compared with nonexaminers, self-examiners had smaller primary tumors at time of diagnosis, with less lymph node involvement. In addition, women who practiced breast self-examination were "younger, more educated, and more likely to be premenopausal, white, and married than nonexaminers" (Huguley et al., 1988, p. 1391). Women in this group also had an almost three times greater frequency of having obtained a mammogram. Although this study certainly provides further evidence to support the relationship between breast self-examination and longer survival rates, it falls short of understanding the psychological factors preventing initiation and maintenance of breast self-examination and making specific recommendations to enhance compliance with this simple, noninvasive technique.

In a similar vein, the results of a recent nationwide telephone survey ($N = 4,659$) evaluating the incidence of cervical and breast cancer screening identified specific demographic groups at risk due to decreased incidence of preventive care (e.g., breast examinations, Pap smears, mammography). In this extensive survey, Hayward, Shapiro, Freeman, and Corey (1986) found that "being older, uninsured, and having lower socioeconomic status are independent risk factors for receiving less preventive care" (p. 1181). Age, as one significant variable, means that "women with the greatest risk of developing breast cancer are receiving the least intense surveillance for the condition" (p. 1180). Beyond demographic particulars (risk groups) and overt reasons (lack of financial wherewithal and/or education), additional research is needed to decipher underlying psychological factors involved in not seeking preventive care. The results of this survey suggest that psychological interventions to enhance compliance need to be tailored to the needs of specific risk groups. What might be an effective intervention with one group might completely fail with another.

In an attempt to understand the underlying factors in seeking medical care, Timko (1987) examined cognitive/attitudinal factors affecting motivation to seek or delay examination of breast cancer symptoms. By comparing delayers versus nondelayers using Ajzen and Fishbein's theoretical model of attitude-behavior relations (Ajzen & Fishbein, 1980), Timko identified specific beliefs that were counterproductive in seeking medical attention. Substantiating the results of several other studies, Timko found that "postponing medical care may increase perceptions of control in that the delayer, rather than the doctor, monitors the characteristics and development of symptoms" (Timko, 1987, p. 321). This finding, that is, perceived control over one's health, is also affected by some women perceiving themselves as invulnerable to cancer. Based on these findings, Timko recommended the use of "persuasive communication" to counter dysfunctional beliefs. Whereas some external factors (e.g., demographic characteristics) cannot be changed or manipulated, attitude can be manipulated. And, according to this theoretical model, a change in attitude corresponds with a change in behavior. However, what specific form this "persuasive communication" could take remains unclear. Also, a limitation of this cognitive/attitudinal model is that it underestimates the influence of psychodynamic factors (e.g., anxiety, denial, rationalization) on health-related behaviors.

Using the same theoretical model of Ajzen and Fishbein in which behavioral intentions correspond with volitional behavior, Rassaby, Hill, and Gardner (1985) also examined the predisposing factors for performing breast self-examination and having regular Pap tests in a study of 123 women. To this end, Rassaby et al. used three measures to predict this behavior: the Theory of Reasoned Action (TRA), the Health Belief Model (HBM), and the Subjective Probability Model (SPM). The results showed that each assessment instrument was a significant predictor of behavioral intentions to engage in preventive care. In addition, Rassaby et al. also suggested that "persuasive communication" would be effective in increasing the desirable behavior. Moreover, they identified specific beliefs that should be targeted. To increase breast self-examination the intention would be to "persuade the target audience that doing breast self-examination will give reassurance about cancer, increase the probability of it being curable, and not cause false alarms" (Rassaby et al., 1985, p. 77). And, to increase compliance with obtaining Pap smears, the persuasive communication would have to undo barriers arising from embarrassment, indignity, and fears of discomfort.

Based on the assumption that health intentions positively correlate with health behavior, this study targeted specific beliefs that can undermine this relationship. In this way, the results can have an impact on the direction of health education. However, as in Timko's (1987) study, the direct application of these results remains unclear. Future research needs to focus on other psychological factors impeding health behavior, as well as test certain hypotheses as they are applied via intervention studies. Issues regarding prevention and compliance are complex:

> not only across patient populations but within patient populations and across stages of disease, from prevention of illness to terminal care. Little is known specifically about cancer patients' (or physicians') motives to comply or to seek out alternative arrangements to accepted practice. We have begun to map out parameters within patient, physician, and treatment settings that affect the care delivery process aimed at cancer control. We have only begun to understand such behaviors as indirect contributors to cancer outcome. (Levy, 1985, p. 119)

PSYCHOLOGICAL SEQUELAE OF TREATMENT AND LIVING WITH CANCER

The majority of cancer patients live five years beyond initial diagnosis. With the increased survival rates of cancer patients comes an increased need for psychological interventions targeted at coping with the side effects of cancer treatment, as well as adjusting to living with the uncertainty of a potentially fatal disease. This body of research also raises the issue of the quality of life for patients who are faced with disfiguring surgical interventions and toxic forms of treatment that might result in infertility, for example, as well as damage to other healthy organs.

One body of research in this area is oriented toward the direct treatment of the toxic side effects of the chemotherapeutic treatment of cancer. Conditioned aversive reactions to treatment, especially nausea and vomiting, are thought to be the result of respondent conditioning, and once they develop as such are as resistant to treatment as drug-induced, pharmacologic side effects. Numerous animal and human studies provide ample evidence to support the classical conditioning paradigm to explain these non-drug-induced reactions. In addition, more recent research by Burish and Carey (1986; Burish, Carey, Krozely, & Greco, 1987) and others has pointed to the role of anxiety as a possible moderating variable in explaining the anticipatory nausea and vomiting that can occur prior to the injection of chemotherapeutic agents. That anxiety seems to be a contributing factor in either the development or maintenance of conditioned nausea and vomiting receives further support from the success of clinical interventions aimed at reducing stress and anxiety. That is, behavioral interventions, such as progressive muscle relaxation, hypnosis, and systematic desensitization are effective in either the prevention, or reduction in the severity, of symptoms of aversive conditioned responses. Early identification of the types of individuals with particular personality profiles or maladaptive coping strategies who are at high risk for developing aversive conditioned reactions and appropriate behavioral interventions would certainly reduce the incidence of these distressing symptoms.

Beyond the immediate consequences of cancer treatment are the more long-lasting and distressing psychological sequelae. As a result of the necessarily aggressive and toxic chemotherapeutic agents and surgical treatments that curb the disease, survivors are faced with the aftermath of the treatment, such as learning to adjust to disfigurement or accepting sterility, to give two devastating examples. The consequences of especially aversive forms of treatment have recently led the Food and Drug Administration to include quality of life measures as part of experimental cancer treatment protocols (e.g., McCartney & Larson, 1987). Another significant psychological stressor is living with the uncertainty of recurrence. Living in dread of the recurrence of disease, for the patients and their families, has been described as the Damocles Syndrome (Koocher & O'Malley, 1981).

Not surprisingly, the incidence rate of diagnosable psychological distress in cancer patients is quite high. Derogatis et al. (1983), in a multicenter study of 215 cancer patients (equal numbers of males and females), reported a 47% incidence rate of patients with psychiatric diagnoses as assessed by the American Psychiatric Association's DSM-III-R diagnostic criteria. The rate varied between

24% and 69%, with the higher rate positively correlated with advanced disease. Approximately 68% of the sample with psychiatric disorders were diagnosed with adjustment disorders, 13% were diagnosed with major affective disorders, and the remainder had organic mental disorders, personality disorders, and anxiety disorders. A significant finding of this research was that more than two thirds of the diagnosable disorders are amenable and responsive to psychological interventions and that the major depressive episodes (13% incidence) are successfully treated by pharmacologic agents. It is also significant to note that the 47% incidence rate of psychiatric disorders among cancer patients far exceeds the psychiatric prevalence rates among other medical and general practice populations.

In a more recent assessment of psychological distress in medical patients, Derogatis and Wise (1989) identified the phenomena of anxiety and depression as the predominant disorders of this population. In individuals with chronic medical illnesses, such as cancer, "concern and uncertainty about the future, coupled with dysphoria about illness-induced losses of function or capacity, represent the optimal 'breeding ground' for reactive anxiety and depressive disorders" (p. ix). Another study by Lansky et al. (1985) compared the nature of depression in psychiatric patients as contrasted with oncology patients. Compared to psychiatric patients, oncology patients reported no symptoms of a psychotic depression, depersonalization, or paranoia. However, "depressed oncology patients appeared to experience more frequent insomnia, greater gastrointestinal disturbance (appetite, weight loss), and felt more anxious, helpless, and concerned about the future" (Lansky et al., 1985, p. 1558). Along these lines, Massie and Holland (1984) have stressed the "diagnostic challenge" of depression in cancer patients. Depressive symptoms can be an artifact of the disease as well as the direct result of chemotherapeutic drugs to treat the disease. "[Whereas] the diagnosis of depression in physically healthy patients depends heavily on somatic symptoms of anorexia, fatigue, and weight loss, . . . these indicators are of little diagnostic value in the cancer patient, since they are common to both cancer and depression" (Massie & Holland, 1984, p. 26). Thus, the management of depression in cancer patients needs to be refined.

Aside from psychological distress associated with most forms of cancers, sexual dysfunction is prevalent after treatment of certain gynecological and breast cancers, with the degree of dysfunction highly associated with the most radical treatments (e.g., vulvectomy, radical mastectomy, pelvic exenteration). Recent research efforts to develop more comprehensive quality of life measures in cancer now include sexuality as a significant component.

Research by Derogatis (1980), among others, in the area of sexual dysfunction paved the way for the inclusion of sexuality as integral to understanding psychological adjustment after treatment for cancer. Derogatis asserted that breast and gynecological cancers are unique because "not only do they inflict pain, suffering and the potential for death, but carry with them a special liabil-

ity—by attacking a woman directly in her genital organs they possess the capacity to devastate her feminine identity'' (p. 10). Based on his assertion that body
image and sexuality are essential components of psychological well-being, Derogatis evaluated the psychological adjustment of 40 women with breast cancer
three months postmastectomy. Results of this study revealed that ''patients with
sexual difficulties reported higher levels of anxiety, depression and general symptomatic distress, and lower mood balance and global adjustment'' (Derogatis,
1980, p. 6).

Other investigators have also reported the incidence and prevalence of psychological distress secondary to disturbed body image and sexuality posttreat-
ment for breast and gynecological cancers. Silberfarb (1978) discussed the psychological issues involved in women's adjustment postmastectomy. He stressed
that the psychological meaning of the breast in our culture is not only a ''badge
of female sexuality,'' but it is also associated with a woman's role as mother. A
woman who has had a mastectomy, then, is not only ''coping with a cancer and
all the charged feelings of death, disfigurement, pain, and the very real possibility
of a long and lingering illness; but she is also coping with an attack on her
gender'' (Silberfarb, 1978, p. 161). It is interesting to note, in light of our review
of the literature on seeking or delaying medical treatment, that Silberfarb raises
the issue of the psychological meanings of the breast as a possible factor in
explaining why women might delay seeking prevention or treatment.

In an earlier work, Polivy (1974) reviewed the literature on the psychological
reactions of women who had undergone hysterectomy. After her extensive review, Polivy concluded that, for many women, ''the uterus (and its functions)
seems to be an important symbol of femininity. Loss of this organ is perceived
as a threat or injury to femaleness'' (p. 435). As such, factors that can interfere
with psychological adjustment posthysterectomy emerge from ''expected loss of
childbearing ability . . . loss of menstruation, effects on sexual activity, loss of
strength, and aging and appearance changes'' (Polivy, 1974, p. 24). Based on
her findings, Polivy recommended improved methodological and statistical research in categorizing and predicting psychological distress posthysterectomy,
the elimination of medically unwarranted operations, and improved preoperative
psychological and physical education.

In another study, Polivy (1977) investigated the psychological consequences
of mastectomy for women's self-concept. This study attempted to evaluate
changes in body image, self-concept, and total self-image in women who had
undergone mastectomy versus women in two control groups (biopsy and other
surgery controls). One counterintuitive result of this study was that for mastectomy patients, there was no change in body image or total self-image immediately
after the surgery. However, two months postmastectomy, scores on both scales
were significantly elevated, suggesting a significant loss of self-esteem. Polivy
interpreted this finding as a function of denial. As compared with biopsy patients,
mastectomy patients ''still needed the denial after surgery, and thus reported

feeling the same (or minutely better) about themselves as before the operation. Over time, of course, this denial broke down by the reality of the loss, and self-image reflects this'' (Polivy, 1977, p. 86). Based on the findings of these studies, we would agree with Derogatis' conclusion that in a society that has moved rapidly toward an expanded awareness of sexuality at all ages, these patients will demand, not without justification, that medical science possess both appreciation and expertise concerning this dimension of their disease. They will require and expect therapeutic interventions which will assist them in becoming psychosexually as well as physically rehabilitated.

In response to this need, Andersen (1987) outlined specific research directions as well as preventive and rehabilitative treatments to decrease the incidence of sexual dysfunction in women with gynecologic cancer. In an earlier work, Andersen (1985) reported a 30 to 90% incidence rate of significant sexual dysfunction in women with gynecologic cancer, with the variability of the estimate correlating with the site of the disease and the nature of the treatment. Given the prevalence of sexual dysfunction in this population, Andersen suggested that future research identify patterns of difficulty and specific subtypes as they occur in the female sexual response cycle (i.e., from loss of desire to nonorgasmia). This more refined investigation might then point to specific interventions to alleviate the difficulty. Along these lines, Andersen also suggested that behavioral sex therapy techniques that are effective with healthy individuals might be modified to address the needs of this population. Other recommendations included refining medical interventions to enhance sexual functioning, providing informed education to dispel myths and misconceptions, focusing on sexual lifestyle alternatives, treating affective disorders secondary to the surgery, etc. In short, there is still much work to be done to refine interventions that respond to the needs of this population.

PSYCHOLOGICAL ADJUSTMENT TO CANCER

In her extensive review of the literature on the psychological correlates of breast cancer and mastectomy, Meyerowitz (1980) found that, generally speaking, most women will experience ''(a) some degree of depression, anxiety, and/or anger; (b) some disruption in everyday life patterns, including marital and/or sexual relationships; and (c) considerable fear regarding the danger and mutilation of cancer and mastectomy'' (p. 114). Furthermore, Meyerowitz found that the degree and length of this distress was influenced by preoperative factors. That is, postoperative adjustment was affected by ''the age of the woman at the time of surgery, the importance that physical appearance has played in the formation of her self-concept, and the expectations of outcome with which she enters surgery'' (Meyerowitz, 1980, p. 118). However, Meyerowitz found that premorbid psychological adjustment was less significant in postoperative adjustment than the success of specific coping strategies employed in dealing with breast

cancer. Along these lines, Meyerowitz cited the role of denial, when not interfering with treatment, as a healthy coping strategy.

In other work stemming from Project Omega at Massachusetts General
Hospital, Weisman, Worden, and Sobel (1980) described what they call the
existential plight of cancer patients and recognized the critical 100-day period
postdiagnosis as a pivotal period in well-being. They based their results on
clinical interviews and psychological tests of 120 newly diagnosed cancer patients. By assessing such factors as disturbance in affect, coping strategies, and
quality of social support, the investigators were able to predict, within limits,
who would cope effectively and who would fail to cope with the disease. Good
copers sought information and resolution through confrontation and redefinition.
In contrast, poor copers were characterized by suppression, passivity, and stoic
submission. In short, those patients who successfully survived the emotional
distress in the two to three months after treatment were those who had taken an
active approach to well-being.

Another important factor that affects psychosocial adjustment is the support
of significant others in coping with this trauma. Dunkel-Schetter and Wortman
(1982) stressed that an aversion even to the topic of cancer can impede communication between family members or friends and the person with cancer. That
is, significant others may avoid the topic of cancer out of their own fears and
thus compound the alienation of the cancer patient.

In a more recent study by Friedman et al. (1988), 57 women with breast
cancer were asked to complete assessments of family cohesion, marital adjustment, and psychosocial adjustment. The results indicated that the women who
reported the highest psychosocial adjustment to breast cancer, including marital
adjustment, were the women who reported the highest levels of family cohesion.
The findings of this study suggest that "while extreme degrees of family closeness may be dysfunctional for families under other circumstances, women with
breast cancer have a need for family closeness that goes beyond the norm for
medically healthy persons" (Friedman et al., 1988, p. 536).

In another study investigating social support after surgery for breast cancer,
Neuling and Winefield (1988) completed a longitudinal study of 58 breast cancer
patients. They used the Multi-Dimensional Support Scale (MDSS) to assess
psychological, social, and physical adjustment, and one finding of their study
was that those patients who were satisfied with support from family members
were also significantly less likely to experience anxious or depressive symptomatology. Furthermore, "the mere presence of support is not sufficient unless the
person for whom it is provided sees it as accessible" (Neuling & Winefield,
1988, p. 385). This study also revealed that "patients require empathic and
informational support from health professionals for at least three months after
surgery" (Neuling & Winefield, 1988, p. 391).

Meyerowitz (1981) also recognized that the reactions to people with breast
cancer by family, friends, and medical personnel can have a significant impact

on the person's psychological well-being. She asserted that an individual's re-action to someone who has had a mastectomy "cannot be separated from cultural attitudes specific to the individual's ethnic background or from the attitudes of the majority culture" (p. 126). Based on this view, Meyerowitz cautioned psychologists who work with breast cancer patients to be sensitive to the stereotypic views of women that may be detrimental to psychological well-being. In her words, past approaches, perhaps based on stereotypic views of women as dependent and passive, have stressed the "right" way to adjust and react rather than appreciating women's abilities for self-determination. Maximization of patient control may have particularly strong implications for the psychological well-being of breast cancer patients, who may experience a sense of loss of control in relation to cancer.

PSYCHOLOGICAL FACTORS AND CANCER SURVIVAL RATES

Studies have documented specific psychological variables that correlate with longer cancer survival rates. For example, Derogatis, Abeloff, and Melisaratos (1979), in their research on the psychological status of women with metastatic breast cancer, revealed significantly higher levels of anxiety, hostility, and alienation among those who survived the longest. Similarly, Greer & Morris (1979) also reported that a "fighting spirit," in comparison to passive acceptance, was positively correlated with longer survival. In addition, a study by Rogentine et al. (1979) reported a psychological predictor of relapse at one year in melanoma patients, independent of biological status.

In a more recent prospective study examining the relationship between psychological factors and the progression of breast cancer, Jensen (1987) investigated a sample of 52 women with a history of breast cancer and 34 healthy controls. In brief, the results of her study revealed "neoplastic spread to be associated with a repressive personality style, reduced expression of affect, helplessness-hopelessness, chronic stress, and comforting daydreaming . . . (the) psychological variables accounted for 56% of the observed variance" (Jensen, 1987, p. 317). In general, this body of research contributes to an understanding of the clinical lore that passive, submissive, stoic, and emotionally inhibited patients fare the worst.

However, in 1979, a study of survival time in advanced breast cancer patients was initiated at the National Cancer Institute (NCI Protocol #80-C-49; Levy et al., 1975). Thirty-four patients with first-recurrent breast cancer, who had had no previous chemotherapy (mean age 52 years), were administered a structured interview and were given a self-report psychiatric rating instrument, the Symptom Checklist-90 (SCL-90; Derogatis, 1977), as well as a mood measure, the Affect Balance Scale (ABS). The patients were rated on a brief behavioral rating form, the Global Adjustment to Illness Scale (GAIS; Morrow, Chiarello, & Derogatis, 1978), which has also been shown in previous research to be a valid measure of psychological function in cancer patients (Morrow et al., 1981). Patients were also rated by observers on the Karnofsky Scale (Karnofsky & Burchenal, 1949), a measure of physical disability status.

Biological prognostic factors that have been shown to be associated with length of survival were recorded from patients' charts. These factors included the disease free interval (DFI), number and direness of metastatic site(s), numbers of nodes positive at primary diagnosis, and age. Patients were assessed at baseline and again at three months, and were followed until recurrence of disease. Twenty-four patients in the original sample have died.

When stratified by living longer than, versus shorter than, two years, long survivors had significantly more positive affect at baseline ($t = 2.3$, $p < .03$), a longer physician's prognosis ($t = 2.0$, $p < .05$), significantly more joy ($t = 3.0$, $p < .009$), and less depression ($t = 1.8$, $p < .08$) than did shorter survivors. Using a Cox's survival hazards model (Kalbfleisch et al., 1980), DFI, number of metastatic sites, age, and cell histology were always entered into the stepwise analysis. We then also attempted to enter psychological factors significantly associated, by Pearson correlations or by simple t-tests, with survival time. The most significant model predicting length of survival included the variables DFI, joy, physician's prognosis, and number of metastatic sites ($X^2 = 23.0$, p < .0001). A long DFI, more joy expressed at baseline (measured by the Affect Balance Scale), longer physician's prognosis, and fewer metastatic sites were significantly associated with longer survival.

In all likelihood, the affect variable labeled joy had overlapping variance with a number of biologically relevant factors such as host resilience, vigor, stamina, etc. But the psychological expression associated with this undoubtedly complex phenomenon was joy. This finding is consistent with recent epidemiological data reported by Reynolds and Kaplan (1986). Cancer mortality data from their Alameda county cohort showed that well-being and happiness predicted reduced cancer incidence and mortality from hormonally dependent tumors for women in that large population study.

BEHAVIORAL IMMUNOLOGY AND CANCER

Behavioral immunology, as applied to oncology, attempts to identify and understand mediating pathways that connect higher cortical function and behavior with cancer and survival rates. The overarching intention of this research is not only to identify biological pathways linking psychological factors and tumor cause, but also, based on these empirical findings, to recommend specific psychological interventions to reduce such biological risk.

At the onset, it is important to note that the major determiner of cancer outcome is the biology of the tumor, the histopathology of the cell, the stage of diagnosis, and the biological therapeutics that the patient receives. The question here is whether central nervous system factors affect the course of some tumors. Laboratory and clinical evidence suggest that this may be the case and provide the base for the essentially biological questions being asked in our program of studies.

It is also important to note that some tumors are more likely candidates of study than others. Tumors with a wide range of response patterns, and with known control by endocrine and/or immune factors, are reasonable to study in this regard. In 1981, we began gathering data on early-stage breast cancer patients who were being treated at the National Cancer Institute. Because our study has been published (Levy, Herberman, Maluish, Schlien, & Lippman, 1985), the findings are briefly summarized.

We investigated the predictive power of natural killer (NK) cell activity as well as selected psychological and demographic factors on breast cancer prognostic risk status. It was found that NK activity predicted the presence or absence of cancer spread to the axillary lymph nodes. Those patients with higher NK activity tended to have fewer nodes positive with cancer.

We then investigated the relative contribution of both clinically and theoretically derived behavioral, psychological, and demographic variables to NK activity at the time of primary treatment by stepwise multiple-regression analysis. After the observer rating (by GAIS), a measure of perceived social support, and the Profile of Mood States (POMS) subscale Fatigue were entered into the equation, the other variables, including delay in diagnosis and age, accounted for only a very small amount of additional NK variance. With all of the variables entered into the equation [$F(3, 41) = 14.3$, $p < .0001$), we could account for 52% of the NK activity variance. However, 51% of the NK variance could be accounted for by the first three variables alone. Patients who were rated as well adjusted, who reported having less than desirable support in their environment, and who responded with fatigue-like symptoms (lack of vigor, listless, apathetic, etc.) tended to have lower NK activity. We have also replicated these findings in a three month follow-up (Levy, Herberman, Lippman, & D'Angelo, 1987).

We are continuing to follow the NCI samples, tabulating instances of recurrence and deaths. Final analyses will be performed in the next year. In the meantime, an expansion of the NCI investigation has been initiated at the University of Pittsburgh School of Medicine. The biological mediators that are being examined now include various hormones—urinary catecholamine, cortisol, and endogenous opioids—as well as measurements of lymphocyte phenotypes and functional assays of NK cells. We have also refined the psychological measures of coping and social support. To date, we have recruited approximately 125 patients for this study.

As an outgrowth of the breast cancer work, a pilot study of stress, coping, and biological outcome in melanoma patients and normal volunteers (NCI Protocol #84-C-09) was initiated at the NCI. We expanded the biological mediators measured to include not only NK activity, but also urinary catecholamine excretion as a general distress index.

For the advanced melanoma patients (stage III), although the pilot sample was quite small ($N = 13$), we found significant correlations between natural immunity and distress indicators. Negative associations were found between NK activity and tension (-0.87), depression (-0.61), fatigue (-0.85), total Profile of Mood States (POMS) score (-0.64), and state anxiety (-0.69). Interestingly, positive correlations were found between NK activity and vigor ($+0.70$), state curiosity ($+0.55$), state anger ($+0.60$), and trait curiosity ($+0.74$). Given the size of this pilot sample, such clusters of strong correlations are somewhat surprising. But on the whole, these findings make clinical sense. These results also indicated to us that psychosocial factors may also play a role even in advanced disease. Because of these findings, we are also prospectively studying intermediate and advanced melanoma patients to identify factors predicting differential outcome of disease in these samples.

For the healthy volunteer sample, the most interesting finding from work in Japan (Aoki, Usuda, Miyakoshi, Tamura, & Herberman, 1986) was the identification of a subgroup at particular risk for follow-up infectious illness severity. These individuals were characterized as having persistently lower levels of NK activity (LNK syndrome, operationally defined as below the group mean NK function across serial assessment) at all three baseline times of measurement. Individuals with normal functional levels of natural immunity were much less likely to report serious follow-up illness than subjects with persistently low NK activity. Individuals with LNK tended to be younger and to report more hassles and less vigor than those with more normal levels of NK activity. These individuals with LNK also tended to have higher levels of norepinephrine excretion across the three baseline measurements, potentially reflecting higher levels of emotional distress in this subsample.

We are currently pursuing this line of investigation at the University of Pittsburgh. We are studying a normal population to identify and characterize such immunologically compromised hosts and to develop intervention strategies—both immunological and behavioral—that will enhance immunological status.

In a previous article we outlined some specific directions for empirical investigation in areas that might then have clinical application. These areas, which are on the frontier of psychological research, include the potential of various behavioral therapies to contribute to tertiary prevention, particularly to counter stress, loneliness, and passive responses associated with increased risk. There is speculation, based on existing animal and human data, that replacing passive coping patterns with active, problem-solving strategies will produce direct effects on the endocrine and immune systems, and thus lead to prolonged disease remission.

CONCLUSION

A cautionary clinical consideration is that a possible consequence of behavioral medicine research in oncology is iatrogenically induced stress and guilt in patients with cancer. In our clinical practice, we have often seen patients with cancer who have become exceedingly self-critical when they do not maintain a positive/optimistic attitude in the face of their disease or are not the "exceptional cancer patient" touted in the popular self-healing literature. Families often exacerbate the patient's sense of "failure" with continual admonishments to try harder, to use visual imagery more often, or whatever. Oftentimes these "failures" end up seeing psychologists. They are demoralized not only by the burden of the disease, and its often quite aversive treatments, but also by the guilt of believing they are causing their cancer and recurrences because of their negative attitude, inadequate personality, poor coping skills, etc. Clinically, we are not benefitting these people with this popular interpretation of this area of research.

However, if we can offer specific psychological interventions that have been *empirically* proven to enhance the immune system and ultimately lengthen and/ or enhance the quality of survival, whether by increasing the use of more effective coping skills, alleviating depressive symptomatology, or increasing a sense of control over the unpredictable course of the disease, then we have achieved our goal.

REFERENCES

Ajzen, I., & Fishbein, M. (1980). *Understanding attitudes and predicting social behavior*. New Jersey: Prentice-Hall.

American Psychiatric Association. (1987). *Diagnostic and Statistical Manual of Mental Disorders* (DSM-III-R).

Andersen, B. L. (1985). Sexual functioning morbidity among cancer survivors: Present status and future research directions. *Cancer, 55*, 1835–1842.

Andersen, B. L. (1987). Sexual functioning complications in women with gynecologic cancer. *Cancer, 60*, 2123–2128.

Aoki, R., Usuda, T., Miyakoshi, H., Tamura, K., & Herberman, R. B. (1987). Low NK Syndrome (LNKS): Clinical and immunologic features. *Natural Immunity and Cell Growth Regulation, 6*, 116–128.

Burish, T. G., & Carey, M. P. (1986). Conditioned aversive responses in cancer chemotherapy patients: Theoretical and development analysis. *Journal of Consulting and Clinical Psychology, 54*, 593–600.

Burish, T. G., Carey, M. P., Krozely, M. G., & Greco, F. A. (1987). Conditioned side effects induced by cancer chemotherapy: Prevention through behavioral treatment. *Journal of Consulting and Clinical Psychology, 55*, 42–48.

Derogatis, L. R. (1977). Administration, scoring, and procedures manual for the SCL-90-R. Clinical psychometric research. *Journal of Clinical Oncology*.

Derogatis, L. R. (1980). Breast and gynecologic cancers. *Frontiers of Radiation Therapy and Oncology, 14*, 1–11.

Derogatis, L. R. (1986). Psychology in cancer medicine: A perspective and overview. *Journal of Consulting and Clinical Psychology, 54*, 632–638.

Derogatis, L. R., Abeloff, M., & Melisaratos, N. (1979). Psychological coping mechanisms and survival time in metastatic breast cancer. *Journal of the American Medical Association, 242*, 1504–1509.

Derogatis, L. R., Morrow, G. R., Fetting, et al. (1983). The prevalence of psychiatric disorders among cancer patients. *Journal of the American Medical Association, 249*, 751–757.

Derogatis, L. R. & Wise, T. N. (1989). *Anxiety and depressive disorders in the medical patient*. Washington, DC: American Psychiatric Press.

Dunkel-Schetter, C. A., & Wortman, C. B. (1988). The interpersonal dynamics of cancer: Problems in social relationships and their impact on the patient. In H. S. Friedman & R. DiMatteo (Eds.), *Interpersonal issues in health care* (pp. 69–100). New York: Academic Press, 1982.

Friedman, L. C., Baer, P. E., Nelson, D. V., Lane, M., Smith, F. E., & Dworkin, R. J. (1988). *Psychosomatic Medicine, 50*, 529–540.

Greer, S., & Morris, T. (1975). Psychological attributes of women who develop breast cancer: A controlled study. *Journal of Psychosomatic Research, 19*, 147–153.

Hayward, R. A., Shapiro, M. F., Freeman, H. E., & Corey, C. R. (1987). Who gets screened for cervical and breast cancer? *Archives of Internal Medicine, 148*, 1177–1181.

Hofer, M. (1992). Lifesaving facts about female cancers. *Special Report Home Library, 1*, 3–14.

Huguley, G. M., Brown, R. L., Greenberg, R. S., & Clark, W. S. (1988). Breast self-examination and survival from breast cancer. *Cancer, 62*, 1389–1396.

Jensen, M. R. (1987). Psychobiological factors predicting the course of breast cancer. *Journal of Personality, 55*, 317–342.

Kalbfleisch, J. D., & Prentice, R. C. (1980). *The statistical analysis of failure time data*. New York: Wiley.

Karnofsky, D., & Burchenal, J. (1949). The clinical evaluation of chemotherapeutic agents in cancer. In C. MacLead (Ed.), *Evaluation of chemotherapeutic agents* (pp. 191–205). New York: Columbia University Press.

Konner, M. (1988). Civilization's cancer. *New York Times Magazine, 137*, 66–67.

Koocher, G., & O'Malley, J. (1981). *The Damocles syndrome: Psychosocial consequences of surviving childhood cancer*. New York: McGraw-Hill.

Lansky, S. B., List, M. A., Herrmann, C. A., Ets-Hokin, E. G., KasGupta, T. K., Wilbanks, G. D., & Hendrickson, F. R. (1985). Absence of major depressive disorder in female cancer patients. *Journal of Clinical Oncology, 3*, 1553–1560.

Levy, S. M. (1985). *Behavior and cancer*. San Francisco: Jossey-Bass.

Levy, S., Ewing, G., & Lippman, M. (1988). Gynecological cancers: Direct and indirect contributors to outcome. In E. Blechman & K. Brownell (Eds.), *Behavioral medicine for women*. New York: Erlbaum.

Levy, S. M., Herberman, R. B., Lippman, M., & D'Angelo, T. (1987). Correlation of stress factors with sustained depression of natural killer cell activity and predicted prognosis in patients with breast cancer. *Journal of Clinical Oncology, 5*, 348–353.

Levy, S. M., Herberman, R. B., Maluish, A. M., Schlien, B., & Lippman, M. (1985). Prognostic risk assessment in primary breast cancer by behavioral and immunological parameters. *Health Psychology*, *4*, 99–113.

Levy, S. M., Lee, J. K., Bagley, C., & Lippman, M. (1988). Survival hazards analysis in first recurrent breast cancer patients: Seven-year followup. *Psychosomatic Medicine*, *50*, 520–528.

Levy, S. M., Seligman, M., Morrow, L., Bagley, C., & Lippman, M. (1988). Survival hazards analysis in first recurrent breast cancer patients: Seven-year follow-up. *Psychosomatic Medicine*, *50*, 520–528.

Massie, M. J., & Holland, J. C. (1984). Diagnosis and treatment of depression in the cancer patient. *Journal of Clinical Psychiatry*, *45*(3), 25–28.

McCartney, C. F., & Larson, D. B. (1987). Quality of life in patients with gynecologic cancer. *Cancer*, *60*, 2129–2136.

Meyerowitz, B. E. (1980). Psychosocial correlates of breast cancer and its treatments. *Psychological Bulletin*, *87*(1), 108–131.

Meyerowitz, B. E. (1981). The impact of mastectomy on the lives of women. *Professional Psychology*, *12*(1), 118–127.

Meyerowitz, B. E., Watkins, I. K., & Sparks, F. C. (1983). Psychosocial implications of adjuvant chemotherapy: A two year follow up. *Cancer*, *52*, 1541–1545.

Morrow, G., Chiarello, R., & Derogatis, L. R. (1978). A new scale for assessing patients' psychosocial adjustment to medical illness. *Psychological Medicine*, *8*, 605–610.

Morrow, G., Feldstein, M., Adler, L., Derogatis, L. R., Enelow, A., Gates, C., et al. (1981). Development of brief measures of psychosocial adjustment to medical illness applied to cancer patients. *General Hospital Psychiatry*, *3*, 79–88.

Neuling, S. J., & Winfield, H. R. (1988). Social support and recovery after surgery for breast cancer: Frequency and correlates of supportive behaviours by family, friends and surgeon. *Social Science and Medicine*, *27*, 385–392.

Polivy, J. (1974). Psychological reactions to hysterectomy: A Critical review. *American Journal of Obstetrics and Gynecology*, *118*, 417–426.

Polivy, J. (1977). Psychological effects of mastectomy on a woman's feminine self-concept. *The Journal of Nervous and Mental Disease*, *164*(2), 77–87.

Rassaby, J., Hill, D., & Gardner, G. (1985). Factors predisposing women to take precautions against breast and cervical cancer. *Journal of Applied Social Psychology*, *1*, 59–79.

Reynolds, R., & Kaplan, G. (1986, March). *Serialconnections and cancer: A prospective study of Alameda county residents*. Presented at the meeting of the Society of Behavioral Medicine, Washington, D.C.

Rogentine et al. (1979).

Silberfarb, P. M. (1978). Psychiatric themes in the rehabilitation of mastectomy patients. *International Journal of Psychiatry in Medicine*, *8*(2), 155–168.

Timko, C. (1987). Seeking medical care for a breast cancer symptom: Determinants of intentions to engage in prompt or delay behavior. *Health Psychology*, *6*, 305–328.

Weisman, A. D., Worden, J. W., & Sobel, H. J. (1980). Psychosocial screening and intervention with cancer patients. *Project Omega Research Report*.

Body Image and Weight Regulation and Drug Use

Part Three covers research related to two significant forms of appetitive behavior: eating and drug use. Biological factors are involved in the regulation of weight and drug use and abuse. However, both weight and drug use and abuse also are strongly influenced by sociocultural and behavioral factors. Accordingly, Sharon Hall in Chapter 5 and April Fallon in Chapter 6 present balanced overviews of the biological, sociocultural, and behavioral factors influencing these two forms of appetitive behavior.

Sharon Hall, in her well-written review of current knowledge of drug use among women, calls for greater understanding and cooperation among biological and psychological researchers so that an integrative model of addiction may be developed. Although we know a fair amount about the epidemiology of drug use among women, Hall makes it quite clear that we know relatively little about the etiological and treatment factors that might differentiate the genders. She does highlight some of the factors that need to be taken into account when designing treatments for women and men, particularly social support.

Hall describes as regrettable the failure of alcohol research to emulate the methodological sophistication of cigarette smoking research in its attempts to answer important questions about treatment and outcome, and states that this is probably due to the doctrinnaire beliefs that prevail in the field. Even more regrettable, perhaps, is the relative dearth of research on women's use of other licit and illicit drugs. Given the major contributions to illness of cigarettes, alcohol, and other drugs of abuse, the importance of stimulating high-quality research on the use of these substances in women and men is overwhelming.

Reinforcing our introductory comments, Fallon's discussion of the factors influencing weight regulation provides a concrete illustration of the complex interactions among behavior, psychosocial factors, and biological factors. Not only does she carefully review the neurochemical, neuroanatomical, and biological mechanisms controlling weight, but she also discusses the impact of social class, culture, and behavior. Indeed, the need for additional cross-cultural research on weight is evident from her review. Reading her chapter, one is struck by the idealization of thinness in women. Most women (and men) have been raised to value an unrealistically thin body image in women. Television advertisements, fashion magazines, and even many parents who themselves are not free from the thin ideal exert pressure on girls to diet. Some girls may attempt to emulate Miss America winners, who as a group weigh only 82.5% of average in recent years and still symbolize for many the ideal woman. This training undoubtedly contributes to the dissatisfaction that most women have with their bodies and their strong desire to weigh less. Moreover, the conflict and stress created by the struggle to conform to a culturally prized yet unrealistic image may itself foster and encourage compulsive overeating, uncontrolled binge eating and/or purging, and self-starvation in females. Fallon's comprehensive review of research on body image and the regulation of weight makes it clear that as a society we must nurture healthful eating habits in children and adolescents, regardless of gender.

Chapter 6

Women and Drugs

Sharon M. Hall

There has been increasing awareness by governmental agencies and others that drug use and abuse among women may merit special study and treatment efforts (e.g., Ray & Braude, 1986). There are many reasons for increased attention to women's drug involvement. First is the concern that the use of some drugs is becoming more prevalent among women. Traditionally, men have been more likely to be cigarette smokers than women. Recently, however, smoking prevalence rates have been converging for the sexes (Fiore et al., 1989). There is also fear that alcohol use may be increasing among women, although this fear may be unfounded (see R. W. Wilsnack, S. C. Wilsnack, & Klassen, 1984). Second, there is mounting evidence that some variables may play different roles in the etiology, maintenance, and treatment of drug abuse in women and in men. For example, although both men and women benefit from social support when they attempt to maintain abstinence from cigarettes, the extent of the benefit they receive may differ (Ginsberg, Hall, & Rosinski, 1987). Third, the serious implications of women's drug use for children have become sadly evident in the transmission of the Human Immunodeficiency Virus, the etiologic agent of the Acquired Immune Deficiency Syndrome, from infected women drug abusers to

Preparation of the chapter was supported by Grants R01 DA02538, R01 DA03082, DA06097, and K02 DA00065, all from the National Institute on Drug Abuse, and by a Research Career Scientist Award from the Department of Veterans Affairs.

their fetuses. They are also evident in the problems of children born to women who abuse crack cocaine, nicotine, alcohol, and other drugs prenatally. Lastly, women who abuse drugs, including alcohol, may be more likely to be victims of other social disturbances. Alcohol and other drug problems are implicated in homelessness in women (Basuk & Rosenberg, 1988) and in an increased possibility of a woman's being the recipient of violence (Blume, 1982).

In this chapter, I focus on two legal drugs, alcohol and nicotine, to exemplify drugs of abuse. This choice is largely pragmatic. There is less scientific literature on the use and abuse of illicit drugs by women.

CONSUMPTION TRENDS

Alcohol

National surveys indicate that about one-third of the population of the United States does not drink alcohol. Of the remaining two-thirds, about one-third are light drinkers and one-third moderate or heavy drinkers (U.S. Department of Health and Human Services [USDHHS], 1987). In every age group, more men than women drink, and the men who do drink are more likely to be heavier drinkers than women (USDHHS, 1987). Exact determination of drinking rates is hampered by definitional differences among studies. Many investigators (e.g., Clark & Medanik, 1982; Malin, Coakley, Kaelber, Musseh, & Holland, 1982) define level of drinking in mean amount of pure alcohol ingested. For example, in these studies, 1 ounce of pure alcohol per day is the lower limit for heavy drinking (USDHHS, 1987). This is the approximate equivalent of two mixed drinks, two glasses of wine or two bottles of beer. Other investigators use the criterion of number of drinks per occasion. In this scheme, heavy drinking would be the consumption of five or more drinks per occasion at least once a week (USDHHS, 1987).

Evidence gathered during the 1960s and 1970s suggested alcohol use among women might be increasing, especially when compared with drinking rates earlier in the century (U.S. Department of Health, Education, and Welfare [USDHEW], 1978). A large-scale study failed to provide convincing evidence of increasing drinking among women. Nevertheless, it did provide interesting data about drinking problems and patterns in women. Using a national sample, R. W. Wilsnack et al. (1984) interviewed 917 women who were selected from 4,032 households across the country. The original sample was stratified on the basis of a screening interview to include 500 moderate to heavy drinkers (four or more drinks per week) and 500 light drinkers and abstainers. In comparing these data with earlier data, the investigators found no dramatic increases in drinking in general, or in heavy drinking among women between 1971 and 1981. R. W. Wilsnack et al. (1984) attributed perception of an "epidemic" to a delayed reaction to long-standing changes in women's drinking behavior and to greater visibility of women's drinking problems. They suggested that social discomfort about women's liberation from traditional sex roles also contributed to this perception, in that some had assumed that liberation from traditional sex roles would be stressful and that stress would increase alcohol use. The implication of these two assumptions was that movement away from traditional sex roles would increase alcohol use. However, the data supporting both the assumptions and the link between sex role change and alcohol use are lacking.

R. W. Wilsnack et al. (1984) did note that some subgroups of women showed limited increases in drinking. For example, they noted a modest recent increase in drinking among middle- aged women. Single, divorced, or separated women were more likely to be heavier drinkers than married women. Widows were least likely to be heavier drinkers. However, the relation of amount of alcohol consumed and marital status was confounded with age. Older women were more likely to be widows, and also to drink less.

As increasing numbers of women work outside the home, it could be argued their drug use patterns will come to resemble those of men. The implication is that working outside the home and increases in drinking are correlated. The data do not support this suggestion. R. W. Wilsnack et al. (1984) found that married women who did not work outside the home were more likely to be heavier drinkers than women who did work outside the home. Married women who worked outside the home were more likely to be moderate drinkers. Women's drinking patterns were likely to be similar to those of their husbands or partners. An exception was the wives of problem drinkers. They were less likely to be heavy drinkers than women who viewed their husbands as frequent drinkers, but not as problem drinkers.

Alcohol-related behavior problems are symptoms of alcohol dependence. As might be expected, R. W. Wilsnack et al. (1984) found some problems closely related to levels of alcohol consumption. A disturbing finding was that among women averaging 1 ounce or more of pure ethanol per day, 45% reported having driven while intoxicated in the last year. Also, at this level of consumption, 61% of the subjects reported at least one lifetime experience of feeling sad, depressed, or unresponsive for 2 weeks or more. Only 38% of long-term abstainers reported similar episodes.

Cigarettes

Historically, fewer women have smoked than men. In recent years, for both men and women, there has been a steady decline in smoking prevalence, as determined by the response to the question, "Do you smoke now?" Fiore et al. (1989) have described smoking trends from seven National Health Interview Surveys (NHIS; 1974 to 1985). The decline in smoking prevalence was greater for men than for women but both followed linear trends. The prevalence for men decreased by .91% per year to 33.5% in 1985. For women, the prevalence decreased by .33% per year to 27.6% in 1985.

In these studies, smoking cessation was measured by the quit ratio, that is, the proportion of eversmokers who are former smokers at a specific time. Eversmokers were defined as persons who reported they had smoked at least 100 cigarettes in their lifetime. They were identified as current smokers or former smokers based on their responses to the question, "Do you smoke now?" Quit ratios then included both long- and short-term quitters. Smoking cessation increased for both men and women, but cessation was at a slightly higher rate for women (.90% per year) than for men (.67% per year).

Smoking initiation occurs mostly during the teen years. Therefore, the indicator of initiation in each survey was the prevalence of smoking among the youngest age group included in NHIS, those 20–24 years old. Smoking initiation decreased among young men (-1.03% per year), but not young women ($+0.11\%$ per year). Fiore et al. (1989) concluded that smoking prevalence is decreasing for both sexes, although at a slower rate for women than for men, and that differences in smoking initiation are primarily responsible for converging smoking prevalence rates between men and women.

ETIOLOGY

Alcohol

Biological Factors   It has long been noted that alcoholism runs in families. Recently, there has been an accumulation of evidence that heredity plays a role in the transmission of at least some forms of alcoholism. The most direct evidence for a hereditary mode of transmission comes from studies where drinking patterns of adopted children are compared with those of their biological and adoptive parents. Such studies suggest there may be at least two forms of alcoholism that have heritable components. These two forms affect men and women differently.

A series of studies (Bohman, Sigvardsson, & Cloninger, 1981; Cloninger, Bohman, & Sigvardsson, 1981) examined alcoholism in children born out of wedlock in Sweden from 1930 to 1949. All children included in the sample were adopted at an early age by nonrelatives. There were 862 men and 913 women.

Most cases of alcoholism fell into the category of "milieu-limited." Milieu-limited alcoholism can be either severe or mild. This form of alcoholism is called milieu- limited because it also required that the adoptive father be of low socioeconomic status to be manifest. It is not associated with criminal behavior, and it occurs in both men and women.

The second category of alcoholism, "male-limited," occurs only in males. It is transmitted from father to son. In this subsample, alcohol abuse was increased ninefold in the adopted sons of alcoholics, independent of the drinking status of their adoptive parents. The biological fathers were characterized by adolescent onset of alcohol abuse, and had extensive treatment histories for both alcoholism and criminality. The biological mothers of these alcoholic sons were no more likely to be alcoholic than the biological mothers of nonalcoholics (Bohman et al., 1981).

Women with biological fathers with male-limited alcoholism had a high frequency of "diversiform somatization," a psychosomatic condition characterized by frequent medically unexplained complaints of pain or discomfort. However, they were not more likely to become alcoholic (Bohman, Cloninger, Von Knorring, & Sigvardsson, 1984).

One goal of the study was to look specifically at the women in the sample. Bohman et al. (1981) reported that there was a fourfold excess of alcohol abusers among the daughters of biological mothers who abused alcohol and biological fathers who did not over those daughters where neither biological parent abused alcohol. A similar excess of alcoholics was found if both parents abused alcohol. If only the biological father abused alcohol, no excess in alcohol abuse was found in the daughters. A discriminating variable about the adoptive parents themselves was the occupational status of the adoptive fathers. Fathers with less-skilled occupations were associated with greater risk of alcohol abuse in their daughters than in the daughters of fathers with more-skilled occupations. Their data suggest that in some cases, at least, environmental factors play a role.

Bohman et al. (1981) note that their investigation is the first to demonstrate that the susceptibility to alcoholism in adopted daughters may be inherited from either biological parent, but is more often inherited from the mother than from the father.

Although these investigations implicate hereditary factors in the transmission of alcoholism, they also suggest these factors differ for men and women, and that hereditary components of alcoholism may have a greater influence among men than among women. These studies do not explain the mechanism by which the genetic component exerts its influence. There are, however, other lines of research that may do so. For example, Schuckit has shown that nonalcoholic children of alcoholics become less intoxicated (Schuckit, 1984) and evidence greater tolerance after drinking a standard alcoholic dose (Schuckit, 1985) than children of nonalcoholics. Such studies may be helpful in carefully delineating the transmitted characteristics that put individuals at risk for alcoholism. The role of gender differences in these characteristics is not yet clear.

Psychological Factors   There has not been a great deal of attention paid to the development of alcoholism in women from a psychological perspective, although earlier psychoanalytic writers scoured the early years for etiologic factors, independent of gender. H. Barry (1982), however, in a review of the literature, suggested that the mother of future female alcoholics is typically cold, severe, and dominating. The father, on the other hand, was reported to be warm, gentle, and frequently alcoholic. These descriptions are not inconsistent with the factors that increase risk of alcoholism in men. These include a father who is seen as weak, distant, or absent, and a mother who is viewed as dominant and overprotective, and who discourages assertiveness. Whether these variables are specific to the prediction of alcoholism or predict general psychopathology is not clear. Also, the role of possible confounding sociodemographic factors is not well addressed by this literature.

Lang (1983) reviewed the evidence about the childhood personalities of children who later became heavy drinkers or alcoholics. He concluded that there is a pattern of rebelliousness and acting out that appears to be correlated with later heavy drinking or alcoholism. The pattern does not seem to differ greatly for men or for women.

Traditional personality theorists thus have assumed that alcoholism has its roots in the experiences of early childhood. Other writers have suggested that experiences at midlife or in the later years can precipitate alcoholism (Maletta, 1982). In women, the most frequently mentioned events are life crises, especially those involving interpersonal conflict and loss (Beckman, 1975; Plant, 1980; Schindler, 1987). Allan and Cooke (1985) have persuasively argued that the studies that contribute to this literature cannot support a causative link between life events and alcoholism onset. Events thought to precipitate alcoholism may actually result from it (for example, loss of a spouse through divorce). Also, reports of the impact of an event can be colored by the occurrence of alcoholism, or a causative link assumed between the event and the onset of alcoholism when none exists.

Osgood (1987) has suggested that depression caused by the problems of aging increases the risk of alcoholism. Again, there is only indirect evidence to support this proposition. Alcoholism and suicide independently are both serious problems in the elderly (Osgood, 1987). The correlation between the two becomes especially strong in later life. Osgood notes that many older persons lose important social roles in work, family, politics, and community. They also undergo profound physical and personal losses. Since a large proportion of the old are women, these observations are especially relevant to the consideration of alcoholism in women. Again, however, the complex nature of the relationship among losses, suicide, and alcoholism does not allow assignment of causality.

S. C. Wilsnack (1982) reviewed the literature on other potential causative factors of alcoholism in women. She notes these include dependency needs, power needs, sex role conflicts, low self-esteem, and a history of sexual abuse (Julian, Mohr, & Lapp, 1980). All of these variables have some evidence to support them. None, however, appears preeminent. As yet, there has been no attempt to form these variables into a comprehensive model of the etiology of alcoholism in women. For example, it seems plausible that childhood sexual abuse by an alcoholic father could lead both to increased dependency needs, low self-esteem, and a compensating need to assert power over others. The alcoholic father could also provide a model for solving emotional problems by alcohol abuse.

Cigarettes

Biological Factors   Like alcoholism, cigarette smoking is known to run in families. Hughes (1986) reviewed results from several studies on the contribution of heredity to the adoption and maintenance of cigarette smoking. He surveyed studies from four genetic methodologies: twin studies, adoption studies, association studies (those that show a behavior's association with a known genetic trait), and trait marker studies (those designed to discover a behavioral trait, such as response to nicotine, that differs between subjects with family history of nicotine abuse and subjects without a family history). Hughes concluded that association and twin studies indicated heredity influences on cigarette smoking. There were few adoption and trait marker studies, but the data tended to be consistent with the hypothesis that there is an hereditary contribution to smoking behavior, albeit a small one. Hughes suggested that the mechanism by which this might occur could be personality traits that have been found to be associated with smoking, including extroversion and differential responsivity to the reinforcing, punishing, and dependence-producing properties of nicotine. As yet, gender differences have not been studied.

Psychosocial Factors   Smoking is usually initiated between the adolescent and preadolescent periods (USDHHS, 1988, 1989). Therefore, research on psychosocial factors correlated with cigarette smoking has focused on this time. The Surgeon General's report (USDHHS, 1980) noted that the data consistently highlight a relationship between lower parental educational status and income and smoking rates in adolescent girls. Also, for both boys and girls, parental smoking was found to be an important determinant of smoking. Peer group pressure to smoke and poor grades are also predictors. An important factor may be that smoking is a behavior that was suppressed for women by social norms for years (USDHHS, 1980). It may remain a way for adolescent girls who feel rebellious to express these feelings. For example, girls who smoke are also more likely to consider parties a favorite leisure activity, to have a boyfriend, and to have had sexual relationships. Leventhal and Cleary (1980) speculated that affect regulation, self-definition, and social compliance play major roles in smoking initiation for children, both male and female. As they note, these same variables may affect children of both genders. The path by which they facilitate smoking may differ for boys and girls, however. For example, smoking may enhance girls' self-image by keeping them slim, but it may add an aura of toughness to boys.

HEALTH EFFECTS

Alcohol

Most of the health effects of alcohol abuse for women parallel the effects for men. Alcoholics are more likely than nonalcoholics to develop chronic gastritis, alcoholic hepatitis, or cirrhosis. Alcohol abuse increases the risk of many cancers, including those of the oral cavity, tongue, pharynx, larynx, esophagus, stomach, liver, lung, pancreas, colon, and rectum (USDHHS, 1987). For both men and women, alcohol use can increase the risk of vascular problems. Diseases associated with increased alcohol use include venous thrombosis, pulmonary embolism, and brain ischemia (USDHHS, 1987). Moderate alcohol consumption, however, may decrease the risk of death from coronary artery disease.

Excessive alcohol use may be more dangerous for women than for men. Gynecological and obstetric dysfunctions have been reported for women who abuse alcohol (Mello, 1988). There is evidence that women alcoholics run a greater risk for developing liver disease at an early age than do men. This appears to follow a shorter period of heavy drinking and lower level of consumption. This more rapid development of diseases in women than men has been referred to as "telescoping" (Blume, 1986). Also, once the liver has been injured, women appear to have greater risk of increased mortality (USDHHS, 1980). Alcoholism in pregnant women may result in the Fetal Alcohol Syndrome, a cluster of physical deformities that are due to severe alcoholism. These include craniofacial, limb, and cardiovascular defects, growth deficiency and developmental delay, mental retardation, and hearing and vision problems. Some of these effects, including vision and hearing problems and mental retardation, last at least into middle childhood. The syndrome is uncommon, however, even for alcoholic women. Rates appear to be 1 to 3 cases per 1,000 live births in nonalcoholic women and 23 to 29 cases per 1,000 births in alcoholic women (USDHHS, 1987).

Cigarettes

Mortality rates for female smokers may be somewhat less than for male smokers. It has been hypothesized that this occurs because of differences in exposure to cigarette smoke between the sexes. Women have less exposure than men. They begin smoking at a later age (USDHHS, 1989), and more women smoke cigarettes with lower "tar" and nicotine content than men (USDHHS, 1989). Nevertheless, the same dose-response relationship between smoking and mortality and morbidity holds for women as for men. Death rates increase with number of cigarettes smoked per day, with a greater number of pack years, greater inhalation, and a higher "tar" and nicotine content of the cigarette.

Like men, women who smoke are more likely to have heart disease. Smoking also acts synergistically with other risk factors. The use of oral contraceptives by women smokers increases the risk of serious cardiac and vascular disease. As with men, smoking is associated with increased cancer of the lung, larynx, oral cavity, and esophagus (Steinfeld, 1980). The death rate because of chronic obstructive lung disease in women is increasing, probably because of increased smoking among women (USDHHS, 1980). Also in 1985, for the first time, the incidence of deaths because of lung cancer surpassed those for breast cancer (Gritz, 1986).

Women's smoking affects their fetuses. Babies born to smoking women are lighter than those to nonsmoking women, even when other risk factors are considered. Maternal smoking increases the risk of spontaneous abortion, fetal death, and neonatal death. It is also thought to increase the risk of Sudden Infant Death Syndrome and pregnancy complications (USDHHS, 1980).

DRUG EFFECTS

Hamilton (1986) notes that gender has been neglected in studies of behavioral pharmacology, pharmacodynamics, and pharmacokinetics. Most research about gender effects on smoking is conducted in the context of biological laboratory research. Scientists consider the study of gender differences to be applied, not basic, research. Basic research is considered more valuable by many laboratory scientists. Therefore, there are few definitive data about gender differences in drug effects.

Alcohol

Biggens (1988) reviewed the role of sex and gender differences in acute alcohol intoxication. As she notes, research on alcohol effects has focused almost exclusively on male subjects. It is only recently that gender differences have been of interest. Variables studied have been blood alcohol levels achieved per unit alcohol dose, body sway, social anxiety, physiological arousal, and performance on various tasks. The results have been inconsistent. Biggens attributes this to methodological difficulties, including failure to adjust for the greater volume of water per unit body weight in men, failure to monitor blood alcohol levels, and use of average measures of blood alcohol rather than time of peak blood alcohol level.

An emerging area of interest is the effects of the menstrual cycle on drug effects. (See Chapter 8 of this volume for a fuller discussion of the menstrual cycle.) Mello (1986) notes that there is evidence that alcohol use increases during the premenstruum in both alcoholic and nonalcoholic women. Why this occurs is not clear. It may be that drug effects differ at different phases of the menstrual cycle. Biggens (1988) reviewed this literature. She again noted inconsistent findings. She attributes these inconsistencies to failure to determine whether the cycle was in fact ovulatory, and failure to measure gonadal hormones directly. Recent studies seem to indicate that there are no differences in subjective or physiological *effects* of alcohol as a function of the menstrual cycle (Mello, 1986).

Cigarettes

It does not seem that the effects of the menstrual cycle on smoking behavior have been studied, nor is it known whether hormonal changes during the menstrual cycle effect nicotine metabolism.

There is some evidence that nicotine is cleared from the body more slowly for women than for men. If so, nicotine exposure per unit dose will be higher for women than for men (Benowitz & Jacob, 1984). As a result, one would expect greater drug and health effects, especially those linked directly to nicotine for women when compared to men. As yet, there is little if any evidence in this direction.

In summary, studies of the pharmacokinetics and pharmacodynamics of alcohol and nicotine in women are sparse. Although some of the sparsity may stem from lack of interest on the part of scientists, some of it must also be linked to a lack of data about fine-grained differences in alcohol and nicotine consumption patterns between men and women. Also lacking is a consistent theoretical rationale about why differences between men and women should occur, and the implications of such differences.

TREATMENT ISSUES

There is mixed evidence that women smokers and alcoholics have more difficulty in attaining abstinence than men. This was noted in the Surgeon General's Report on Smoking in Women (USDHHS, 1980) for nicotine, although more recent data find a trend in the opposing direction (Fiore et al., 1989). Poorer outcome has been reported for alcoholic women (Davidson, 1976), although others dispute the accuracy of this position (e.g., Vanicelli, 1984).

It may be that the variables controlling drug use and determinants of relapse differ for men and women, although the extent of these differences may not be great. Women smokers report they are more likely to smoke in response to negative emotions than men (e.g., Peterson, Longeran, Hardinger, & Teel, 1968). The predominance of negative affect smoking among women could be a factor in the higher relapse rates reported for them, since negative affect smokers have been found to be more likely to relapse than smokers who do not label negative affect as a primary determinant of smoking (Pomerleau, Adkins, & Pertschuck, 1978). The greater role of negative affect in use of alcohol for women has also been noted (Braiker, 1982).

Others have suggested that the treatments offered, rather than women's characteristics, explain possible differences in outcome. Several writers have suggested that chemical dependency treatment services are not designed for alcoholic women and may fail to recognize women's key difficulties. These difficulties include heavy familial responsibilities, child care, and active opposition to treatment from family and friends (Beckman & Amaro, 1986; Blume, 1982; Robinson, 1984). The issue of treatment suitability for women smokers has been little discussed.

Cigarettes

For the most part, variables controlling successful treatment outcome do not differ for men and women. Multicomponent programs appear useful for both (Hall, Hall, & Ginsberg, 1990). Pharmacological replacement strategies such as nicotine gum have been shown to be successful for heavier smokers of both genders, although this may not be so for all drug treatments of cigarette smoking. For example, Glassman et al. (1988) recently reported that Clonidine, an anti-hypertensive drug, appears to help women, but not men, remain abstinent.

Nevertheless, there are issues in smoking treatment that are especially important to consider when treating women. Recently, exploratory analyses have indicated that the importance of smoking history variables and work-related stresses may be greater for women than for men in treatment success (Swan et al., 1988). However, those issues most consistent in the literature are weight gain, affect management, and social support.

Weight Gain　There is ample evidence that smoking and body weight are consistently correlated. Of the 28 studies that have examined the phenomenon, 25 (89%) found that smokers weigh less than nonsmokers (USDHHS, 1988). Also, of the 43 studies examining changes in weight following smoking initiation or cessation, 37 (83%) found that smoking and weight were inversely correlated (USDHHS, 1988). That is, quitting smoking produced weight gain, and beginning smoking produced loss. Neither weight gains after quitting nor body weight differences between smokers and nonsmokers are great, however. The average weight gain after quitting smoking is 6.16 lbs; the average difference between smokers and non- smokers is 7.13 lbs (USDHHS, 1988). There is general agreement, however, that women are more concerned about excess body weight than are men (e.g., Hall & Havassy, 1981). (Chapter 7 of this volume contains a full discussion of weight regulation.) This concern extends to weight regulation by cigarettes. Recent evidence from surveys conducted in the United States and in England suggests that more females than males are aware that smoking controls weight. Overweight girls are more likely to take up smoking for weight-related reasons as compared with normal weight girls, but weight does not determine initiating smoking for boys (USDHHS, 1988).

Why smoking cessation-related weight gain occurs is not known. The most likely candidates for causative status are decreases in the rates at which food is converted to energy (metabolic rate) or increased caloric consumption. Some investigators (Dallaso & James, 1984; Hofstetter, Schutz, Jequir, & Wahren, 1986) have found significant decreases in energy expenditures after smoking cessation, while others have not (Burse et al., 1975; Stanford, Matter, Fell, & Papanek, 1986). The lack of consistency in outcomes suggests that changes in metabolic rates are not a central causative variable in cessation induced weight gain. The most consistent finding about eating behavior has been that the number of calories consumed changes after quitting (USDHHS, 1988). Laboratory studies have suggested that this increase in calories is because of increased consumption of sweet foods (e.g., Grunberg, Bowen, & Winder, 1985). Field studies have produced evidence generally congruent with the laboratory data. Rodin and Wack (1987) found that self-selected quitters who gained weight were likely to increase their intake of sugar, but that they did not increase total caloric intake. This is a puzzling finding since weight gain generally follows an increase in calories, not an increase in specific foods without a concomitant calorie increase. Hall, McGee, Tunstall, Duffy, and Benowitz (1989), in a random assignment study, found increases in sucrose, a sweet-tasting sugar, and fat intake after quitting. Total calories also increased. Consumption of non-sweet-tasting sugar (e.g., lactose) did not change. Increases in calories were correlated with later weight gain, especially for women. At 6 months postquitting, caloric intake returned to baseline levels, but the weight gain continued. These data suggest that a change in some as yet unidentified biological system that regulates weight occurs after quitting smoking.

How this weight gain affects quitting smoking is not clear. The two studies that have examined the effects of weight gain on quitting have produced surprising findings. Hall, Ginsberg, and Jones (1986) examined weight changes in smokers who had been abstinent for 6 months. They correlated these changes with smoking status at 1 year. Weight gain during the first 6-month period predicted abstinence at 1 year, not relapse, as might be expected. There were no differences between men and women. Similar findings have been reported by Gritz, Carr, and Marcus (1988). Whether these findings reflect the action of mechanisms that enhance the reinforcing properties of food deprivation (Carroll & Meisch, 1984) or the possibility that more motivated smokers ignore weight gain and concentrate on maintaining abstinence is not known. Also, smokers who greatly fear weight gain may relapse early since significant weight gain appears within 3 weeks of quitting (Hall et al., 1986). Such smokers may thus select themselves out of samples that examine long-term abstinence and weight gain.

Mood   Women are more likely to report affective distress, both in general (Frieze, Parsons, Johnson, Ruble, & Zellman, 1978, p. 444), and as a reason to relapse to cigarettes (Peterson et al., 1968). It is known that smokers reporting high levels of affective distress fail to quit smoking cigarettes and to maintain abstinence. A cluster of psychological characteristics including sadness, anxiety, low self-esteem, and anger consistently predict failure in quitting smoking (e.g., McArthur, Waldron, & Dickenson, 1958; Schwartz & Dubitsky, 1968). Also, retrospective evidence suggests that negative affect plays a role in specific relapse situations. For example, Marlatt and Gordon (1980) found that 43% of smokers reported negative affect as a determinant of relapse. Callers to a "hot-line" for smokers who relapsed or who feared they might reported that 71% of smoking-related crises were preceded by negative affect (Shiffman, 1982). However, recent work casts doubt on the causative status of these reports (Hall, Havassy, & Wasserman, 1990). In a prospective study in this area, Pomerleau et al. (1978) found that variables indicating the strength of dependence or habit (number of years smoked, number of cigarettes per day) predicted cessation at the end of treatment. Abstinence at 1 year follow-up, however, was related only to negative affect induced smoking. Only 26% of smokers who said they smoked in response to negative affect were abstinent at 1 year as compared with 50% of those who were not negative affect smokers.

In a related line of research, Glassman et al. (1988) reported that 61% of the smokers who entered a smoking treatment trial had histories of major depressive disorder. The rate of major depressive disorder in the general population is about 7–10%; thus the rate for depressed smokers was considerably higher than expected. Glassman et al. reported that smokers with a history of major depressive disorder were more likely to relapse than those who did not have such a history. Small sample sizes, especially for men, precluded definitive analyses of depression history, smoking abstinence, and gender. Thus despite the possibility of important relations between gender, mood, and smoking relapse, no studies have examined the intersection of the three.

Social Support   There is some suggestion that social support is important for both men and women, but it may play different roles for the two. There are two important dimensions of social support, structural and functional support. Structural social support is the existence and pattern of relationships with others, for example, marital status or number of relationships. Functional support is the degree to which interpersonal relationships provide emotional, intellectual, or material resources (Cohen & Wills, 1986). In general, there is correlational evidence that social support is important for abstinence in both men and women smokers. The presence of nonsmokers (Eisinger, 1971; Greenwald, Nelson, & Greene, 1971; Mermelstein, Cohen, Lichtenstein, Baer, & Kamarck, 1986; West, Graham, Swanson, & Wilkinson, 1977) and perceived supportiveness for abstinence by important people in the support network (Horwitz, Hindi-Alexander, & Wagner, 1985; Mermelstein et al., 1986; Mermelstein, Lichtenstein, & McIntyre, 1983; West et al., 1977) predict abstinence. Fisher and Bishop

(1986) found that women had higher 3-month quit rates in a social support treatment than in treatment emphasizing self-mastery and insight. Men had approximately equal quit rates in the two treatment conditions. In anecdotal comments about the value of treatment, women were more likely to cite social factors, whereas men referred to their own individual self-control attempts. In work in our laboratory, interventions involving social support tended to be more successful in producing short- term abstinence in women than in men, but this effect did not endure into long-term follow-ups (Ginsberg, Hall, & Rosinski, 1987).

In a pilot study using taped segments of smokers' conversations rather than self-report, Ginsberg et al. (1987) reported correlations between social support and abstinence for smokers of both genders, and differences between men and women. Contrary to the assumptions of social support interventions, discussions of self-help strategies were more effective in predicting abstinence than strategies that involved cooperation with a partner. This suggests that effective supportive behavior consists of reinforcing the smokers' own cognitive and behavioral coping efforts. These data also suggest that partner disengagement, that is, avoidance of involvement in the quitting process, had a negative impact on women, but not on men.

The best way to use social support in interventions for either men or women is unclear. Although intriguing correlations between levels of support and abstinence exist, interventions to increase levels of support have usually been ineffective for either gender (Glasgow, Klesges, & O'Neill, unpublished; Marlatt & Gordon, 1984; Mermelstein et al., 1986). Ginsberg et al. (1987) have suggested that the reason for this discrepancy is methodological. Usually smokers' self-reports of helpfulness from others are studied rather than actual behavior. Behavior and self-report may not correlate well. Differences in self-reported social support may reflect differences in perception of level of support that reflect underlying psychopathology (Dohrenwend, Dohrenwend, Dodson, & Shrout, 1984). For example, smokers who suffer from enduring dysphoria might perceive a particular behavior as less helpful than smokers who do not suffer from negative moods.

Alcoholism

The alcoholism treatment literature is not nearly so well developed as the smoking treatment literature. Little is known about effective interventions, much less about gender differences in outcome. The field has not evolved the tradition of rigorous, controlled outcome research that characterizes the smoking treatment literature, partly because of the doctrinnaire beliefs that have characterized the field. However, there is some information available to suggest that, as is the case with cigarette smoking, affective distress plays a role.

Mood   At least two psychiatric diagnoses are more prevalent among alcoholics than in the general population. These are antisocial personality and depressive disorders (e.g., Martin, Cloninger, & Guze, 1985). The rates of antisocial personality are low among women, and women alcoholics are no exception. However, there is some evidence that the rates of depressive disorders are disproportionately higher among alcoholic women than among alcoholic men or among the general population. S. C. Wilsnack (1982), for example, estimates that 25–30% of alcoholic women also have an affective disorder. For many female alcoholics, depressive symptoms are transitory, and disappear during sobriety. For some, however, a residual depression remains.

Many writers, especially psychiatrists, discriminate between depressive disorders (diagnosable syndromes that meet the criteria of the *Statistical Manual* of the American Psychiatric Association), and depressed mood. It should be noted that although the covariance of depressive *disorder* and alcoholism is well documented, the role of depressed *mood* and other negative affect in the role of alcoholism is not so clear. Turnbull and Gomberg (1988) constructed two indices of depression, one measuring low self- esteem, the other measuring current mood. In a sample of women in treatment for alcoholism ($N = 301$), these indices were correlated with earlier age of onset and earlier level of control over drinking. Binge drinking was correlated with current mood, and daily or weekend drinking with low self- esteem. On the other hand, Vaglum, Vaglum, and Larson (1987) studied level of depression and alcohol consumption in alcoholic women, nonalcoholic female psychiatric patients, and healthy women. Among women with depressive disorder, alcohol consumption was bimodally distributed. Among healthy women, there was a negative correlation between depression and alcohol consumption. The results for nonalcoholic psychiatric patients were complex, but generally support the conclusion that there is no general dose-response relationship between level of depression and alcohol consumption. Comparing mildly depressed and nondepressed male and female social drinkers, Berger and Adesso (1991) found depressed men more likely to drink than all other subjects.

Thus the role of depression in alcoholism is complex. Alcohol withdrawal can result in the symptoms that characterize depressive disorder, depressive symptoms without a diagnosable syndrome, and depressed mood. Depression can be caused by alcoholism and vice versa. Also, both depression and alcoholism increase in midlife. The perceived relationships between the two may be complicated by this illusory correlation (Schindler, 1987). Depression appears to be the only negative affect that has been studied extensively in alcoholic women. It would seem logical that anger, boredom, and fatigue would also play a role in the development and maintenance of alcohol dependence, yet they have not been studied.

Social Support   There is evidence that social support plays a role in alcoholism and in successful alcoholism treatment for women. Investigators have found that alcoholic women have poorer social support than nonalcoholic women (McCormack, 1985), that familial support is important in successful treatment for women (Billings & Moos, 1982), and that number of supportive relationships predicts treatment outcome (MacDonald, 1987). In our own work, we have found that social support, especially structural support, is important in predicting continued abstinence for both women and men (Havassy, Hall, & Tschann, 1987). Some clinical reports suggest that alcoholic women not only fail to receive active support for abstinence, but may encounter actual opposition to treatment from family and friends (Amaro & Beckman, 1984). The reasons for this opposition include problems with child care, with spouses who are overly dependent on alcoholic women, and with the fear of stigmatization.

The suggestive nature of these studies indicates that further research is needed to clarify the role of social support in alcoholism in women. For example, it is not known whether the poorer support systems observed in alcoholic as opposed to nonalcoholic women increase the risk of alcoholism or are the result of it. The depression and loneliness resulting from a poor support system could encourage drinking and thus be causative. On the other hand, writers have noted that alcoholic women are more likely to lose the support of family and friends than are men (Franks & Wiseman, 1980).

Writers have suggested that incorporation of the family into the treatment system is especially important for alcoholic women (e.g., Amaro & Beckman, 1984). The need for adequate child care to remove that barrier to treatment has also been expressed (Blume, 1982). Despite these recommendations, we found no reports of such programs in the alcoholism literature. Controlled research on the potential increments in outcome that such innovations might engender is not available.

SPECIAL ISSUES

Cross-Addictions

Many clinicians report that combined misuse of alcohol and other drugs is more common in women seeking treatment than men. A study of alcoholic women in medicine (Bissell & Skorina, 1987) supports this view. Of the 100 women interviewed, only 40% reported addiction to alcohol alone. These results must be viewed with caution, however, because of the easy accessibility physicians have to licit psychoactive drugs.

Of special concern with women from the general population is the use of diazepam (Valium) with alcohol. Cross-addiction is a serious problem because of the interactive effects of these two classes of drugs and the difficulties encountered in withdrawing from both of them simultaneously. Several scenarios could facilitate the development of cross-addiction in women. Women may be more sensitive to appearing intoxicated. Therefore, a working woman alcoholic might use prescription drugs during the day and alcohol in the evening when the alcohol will not be detected. Women are more likely to be prescribed diazepam and other psychoactive drugs. Also, women with undetected alcohol problems may be more likely to receive diazepam from a physician for physical or minor emotional complaints if their alcoholism is undetected (USDHEW, 1980).

Prescription Drug Misuse in the Elderly

An area of drug misuse of special concern for women is that of prescription drug misuse. Writers have suggested this is especially a problem in the elderly. Braude (1986) discussed the issue in detail. She defined drug misuse as the inappropriate use of drugs intended for therapeutic purposes. Inappropriate use includes inappropriate prescribing or use of drugs resulting from inadequate knowledge of the drug's effects by either the physician or the patient. It also includes self-medication by the patient in a manner inconsistent with the label information. Because of the longer life expectancy of women, the problems of the elderly are increasingly those of women. Future growth of the older population is expected to be substantial, and by the year 2000 the Census Bureau projects a population of 19 million older women versus 12.7 million older men. Potential problems are risk of adverse effects because of drug interactions, including alcohol, changes in drug disposition that come with age, and increased drug sensitivity in the elderly. Despite the problems that are known to occur and the potential for research, little is known about the specific problems of drug misuse in elderly women (Braude, 1986). As P. P. Barry (1986) has noted, elderly women are more likely to be widowed, live alone, or reside in an institution than elderly men. Many have reduced income. These variables, when considered together, would seem to put older women at higher risk for a variety of problems. Whether prescription drug misuse is one of them, and if so what variables control it, have not been studied.

Alcohol Abuse in the Elderly

Alcohol abuse is less prevalent among the elderly than among other age groups (USDHHS, 1987). The reasons for this lower prevalence are not clear. Statistics could reflect a real drop in consumption, underreporting, or premature death of heavy drinkers (USDHHS, 1987). Maletta (1982) argues the low prevalence is largely artifactual. He suggests it reflects the absence of role requirements that would bring older people to the attention of systems that diagnose alcoholism. For example, because the elderly are no longer employed, they are not identified by work absences. Many have stopped driving, so that the older person who abuses alcohol is less likely to be arrested for driving while drinking. Also, Maletta (1982) suggests that mental health workers are not comfortable in discussing drinking habits with elderly people.

Whether these factors significantly distort reporting of alcoholism in the aged has yet to be demonstrated. It is clear, however, that excessive use of alcohol can be particularly deleterious in the aged. Elderly people often take medications that can interact with alcohol. Also, even modest alcohol consumption may be a hazard for older individuals who have impaired metabolic and excretory function (Maletta, 1982).

Those few studies that have examined the correlates of heavy drinking in the aged seem to have focused exclusively on men. In a study of Finnish men, the only reliable correlate of heavy alcohol use was heavy cigarette smoking (Kivela, Nissinen, Punsar, Puska, & Karsonen, 1988). In another study with older male veterans, higher socioeconomic status and marital status were associated with moderate as opposed to heavy drinking (Glynn, de Labry, & Hou, 1988). The generalizability of these limited data to elderly women in this country seems questionable.

Illicit Drugs

This chapter has focused on cigarette smoking and alcohol use because the literature on gender differences and illicit drugs is both less voluminous and more complex than that for the two drugs we have considered. This is so for several reasons. One is the comparatively low prevalence of, and mortality because of, illicit drug abuse. Also, the term "illicit drugs" covers a range of drugs with diverse pharmacologic actions and social consequences. Thus the findings from studies on opiate abusers do not necessarily generalize to cocaine abusers. However, multiple drug abuse appears to be the rule rather than the exception. Most users of illicit drugs are also users of alcohol and cigarettes. For example, in a sample of heroin addicts in detoxification treatment, 90% responded that they had smoked cigarettes during the 6 months before treatment, and 81% responded that they had used alcohol during that period (Hall, Havassy, & Wasserman, 1990). Therefore, it seems likely that the variables that are important in the etiology and treatment of illicit drugs will be similar to each other and to those for licit drugs. For example, there is ample evidence that high levels of "psychiatric severity" predict poor treatment outcome for opiate addicts (e.g., Roundsaville, Kosten, Weissman, & Kleber, 1986; Roundsaville, Weissman, Wilber, Crits-Christoph, & Kleber, 1982) and alcoholics, (McClellan, Luborsky, Woody, O'Brien, & Droler, 1983) and perhaps for cigarette smokers. Nevertheless, with few exceptions (e.g., Griffin, Weiss, Mirin, & Lange, 1989), little attention has been paid to the interaction of gender and psychological problems in the treatment of illicit drug users. Also, writers have commented on the role of social support in both the initiation of addiction for women cocaine abusers and women opiate addicts (Beschner, Reed, & Mondanaro, 1981; Reed, Beschner, & Mondanaro, 1982). The few extant data indicate that this variable is as important for opiate and cocaine abusers as for alcoholics and cigarette smokers (Hall, Havassy, & Wasserman, 1991).

COMMENTARY AND DIRECTIONS FOR FUTURE RESEARCH

In a chapter that addresses as many diverse issues as does this one, many directions for future research can be targeted. A few issues, however, emerge as central.

The first is that in the search for the etiology of alcohol and other drug use among women, genetic factors are among the most promising. Clearly, they do not account for all of the variance in the occurrence of these disorders. Recent data, however, suggest they should be carefully considered. As the work of Cloninger's group indicates, equally important is the interaction of genetics with environmental influences.

A second direction for future research in almost all areas is design of studies so that potential gender differences can be examined. For example, if studies have large enough sample sizes, differential effects of gender on dependent variables can be determined even when the primary goals of the study are in other domains. This recommendation holds for studies of etiology, effects, and treatment outcome.

The research on the abuse of alcohol and other drugs suffers from a disciplinary schism wherein psychologically oriented investigators too often fail to acknowledge that the topic of study is a substance with pharmacologic and other biological effects. Biologically oriented investigators, on the other hand, often dismiss the psychological factors surrounding addiction as "adjuncts" or acknowledge the presence of such factors but fail to consider how they might interact with the drug. Studies on etiology and treatment of women drug users are no exception. For example, as we have discussed, women in general tend to report more negative affect than men. Nicotine is known to alleviate some symptoms that resemble those of depression. Yet we know little about how these pharmacological characteristics interact with the "psychological" characteristics of depression or how these variables might influence relapse. More research is needed that integrates these two perspectives if we are to derive a comprehensive model of addiction.

This chapter has emphasized those aspects of alcohol and nicotine dependence that may be especially important when considering causes and treatment of drug abuse in women. Two points are important. The first is that in an effort to fulfill the goal of the chapter, that is, to discuss the variables of special importance to women, I may have led the reader astray. Although there are special considerations unique to women in many important areas, pervasive differences between the genders do not seem to exist. For example, the smoking cessation literature reveals few differences between the genders in effective intervention techniques. Nicotine replacement and multicomponent behavioral programs still appear to be the most efficacious treatment interventions for both men and women. The addition of social support interventions may be more useful for women than for men, but the amount of variance explained in relation to other factors is not great. The second point is the lack of rigorous studies on gender differences in addictions. This lack reflects the field in general. For example, although the literature on negative events and alcohol use in women is flawed by reliance on retrospective data, these data reflect the methods used in the field to study the relationship between life events and alcohol use, and are not unique to studies of women or of gender differences.

For the most part, research on nicotine dependence has by far been the more elegant and methodologically rigorous when both alcohol and nicotine are considered. In designing studies of abusers of illegal drugs, researchers would do well to look to this literature for methodology, and to the two combined for common variables that suggest substantive areas to study.

REFERENCES

Allan, C. A., & Cooke, D. J. (1985). Stressful life events and alcohol misuse in women: A critical review. *Journal of Studies on Alcohol, 46,* 147–152.

Amaro, H., & Beckman, L. J. (1984). Patterns of women's use of alcohol treatment agencies. *Bulletin of the Society of Psychologists in Addictive Behaviors, 3,* 145–154.

Barry, H. (1982). A psychological perspective on development of alcoholism. In E.M. Pattison & E. Kaufman (Eds.), *Encyclopedic handbook of alcoholism.* New York: Gardner.

Barry, P. P. (1986). Gender as a factor in treating the elderly. In B. A. Ray & M. C. Braude, *Women and drugs: A new era for research. NIDA Research Monograph 65* (DHHS Publication No. ADM 87-1447). Rockville, MD: National Institute on Drug Abuse. 65–69.

Basuk, E. L., & Rosenberg, L. (1988). Why does family homelessness occur? A case-control study. *American Journal of Public Health, 78,* 783–788.

Beckman, L. J. (1975). Women alcoholics: A review of social and psychological studies. *Journal of Studies on Alcohol, 36,* 797.

Beckman, L. J. (1972). The self-esteem of alcoholic women: Myth or reality. *Journal of Abnormal Psychology, 87,* 408–417.

Beckman, L. J., & Amaro, H. (1986). Personal and social difficulties faced by women and men entering treatment. *Journal of Studies in Alcohol, 47,* 135–145.

Benowitz, N. L., & Jacob, P. (1984). Daily intake of nicotine during cigarette smoking. *Clinical Pharmacology & Therapeutics, 35,* 499–504.

Berger, B. D., & Adesso, V. J. (1991). Gender differences in using alcohol to cope with depression. *Addictive Behaviors, 16,* 315–327.

Beschner, G. M., Reed, G. B., & Mondanaro, J. (1981). *Treatment services for drug dependent women. Vol. 1* (DHHS Publication No. ADM 81-1177). Rockville, MD: National Institute on Drug Abuse.

Biggens, C. (1988). *The role of sex and gender differences in acute alcohol intoxication.* Unpublished manuscript, University of California, San Francisco.

Billings, A. G., & Moos, R. H. (1982). Social support and functioning among community and clinical groups: A panel model. *Journal of Behavioral Medicine, 5,* 295–311.

Bissell, L., & Skorina, J.K. (1987). One hundred alcoholic women in medicine. An interview study. *Journal of the American Medical Association, 21,* 2939–2944.

Blane, L. J. (1968). Women alcoholics: A review of social and psychological studies. *Journal of Studies on Alcohol, 36,* 797–824.

Blume, S. B. (1982). Alcohol problems in women. *New York State Journal of Medicine, 82,* 1222–1224.

Blume, S. B. (1986). Women and alcohol: A review. *Journal of the American Medical Association, 256,* 1467–1470.

Bohman, M., Cloninger, C. R., Von Knorring, A., & Sigvardsson, S. (1984). An adoption study of somatoform disorder. III. Cross fostering analysis and genetic relationship to alcoholism and commonality. *Archives of General Psychiatry, 39,* 872–878.

Bohman, M., Sigvardsson, S., & Cloninger, C. R. (1981). Maternal inheritance of alcohol abuse. *Archives of General Psychiatry, 38,* 965–969.

Braiker, H. B. (1982). The diagnosis and treatment of alcoholism in women. In *NIAAA Alcohol and health, Monograph 4: Special population issues* (DHHS Publication No. ADM 82-1192, pp. 111–139). Rockville, MD: National Institute on Alcohol Abuse and Alcoholism.

Braude, M. C. (1986). Drugs and drug interaction in the elderly. In B. A. Ray & M. C. Braude (Eds.), *Women and drugs: A new era for research. NIDA Research Monograph 65* (DHHS Publication No. ADM 87-1447). Rockville, MD: National Institute on Drug Abuse. 58–64.

Burse, R. L., Bynum, G. D., Pandolf, K. B., Goldman, R. F., Simms, E. A. H., & Danforth, E. R. (1975). Increased appetite and unchanged metabolism upon cessation of smoking with diet held constant. *Psychologist, 18,* 157.

Carroll, M., & Meisch, R. (1984). Increased drug-reinforced behavior due to food deprivation. In T. Thompson, P. B. Dews, & J. E. Barrett (Eds.), *Advances in behavioral pharmacology, 4,* 47–48. New York: Academic Press.

Clark, W., & Medanik, L. Alcohol use and problems among U.S. adults: Results of the 1979 national survey. In NIAAA, *Alcohol consumption and related problems,* (DHHS (PHS) 86-1214). Washington, D.C.: U.S. Government Printing Office. 3–52.

Cloninger, C. R., Bohman, M., & Sigvardsson, S. (1981). Inheritance of alcohol abuse. *Archives of General Psychiatry, 38,* 861–868.

Cohen, S., & Wills, T. A. (1985). Stress, social support and the buffering hypothesis. *Psychological Bulletin, 98,* 310–357.

Dallaso, H. M. & James, W. P. T. (1984). The role of smoking in the regulation of energy balances. *International Journal of Obesity, 8,* 365–375.

Davidson, A. F. (1976). An evaluation of the treatment and after-care of a hundred alcoholics. *British Journal of Addiction, 71,* 217–224.

Dohrenwend, B. S., Dohrenwend, B. P., Dodson, M., & Shrout, P. E. (1984). Symptoms, hassles, social supports, and life events: Problems of confounded measures. *Journal of Abnormal Behavior, 93,* 222–230.

Eisinger, R. A. (1971). Psychosocial predictors of smoking recidivism. *Journal of Health and Social Behavior*, *12*, 355–362.

Fiore, M. C., Novotny, T. E., Pierce, J. P., Hatziandreu, E. J., Patel, K. M., & Davis, R. M. (1989). Trends in cigarette smoking in the United States. *Journal of the American Medical Association*, *261*, 49–55.

Fisher, E. B., & Bishop, D. B. (1986). Gender, social support, and smoking cessation. Paper presented at the annual meeting of the Society of Behavioral Medicine, San Francisco.

Franks, V., & Wiseman, J. (1980). Discussion summary. In National Institute on Alcohol Abuse and Alcoholism, *Alcoholism and alcohol abuse among women* (Research Issues DHEW Publication No. ADM 80-835). Rockville, MD: USDHEW.

Frieze, I. H., Parsons, J. E., Johnson, P. B., Ruble, D. N., & Zellman, G. L. (1978). *Women and sex roles*. New York: W.W. Norton and Company, pp. 444.

Ginsberg, D., Hall, S. M., & Rosinski, M. (1987). Pilot study of social interaction and smoking cessation. Paper presented at the annual meeting of the Society of Behavioral Medicine, Washington, D.C.

Glasgow, R. E., Klesges, R. C., & O'Neill, H. K. Programming social support for smoking modification: An extension and replication. Oregon Research Institute, 195 West 12th Avenue, Eugene, Oregon 97401.

Glassman, A. H., Stetner, F., Walsh, B. T., Raizman, P. S., Fleiss, J. L., Cooper, T. B., & Covery, L. S. (1988). Heavy smoker, smoking cessation and clonidine. Results of a double-blind, randomized trial. *Journal of the American Medical Association*, *259*, 2863–2866.

Glynn, R. J., de Labry, L. O., & Hou, D. M. (1988). Alcohol consumption, type A behavior, and demographic variables. Results from the Normative Aging Study. *American Journal of Epidemiology*, *12*, 310–320.

Greenwald, P., Nelson, D., & Greene, D. (1971). Smoking habits of physicians and their wives. *New York State Journal of Medicine*, *71(3)*, 2096–2098.

Griffin, M. L., Weiss, R. D., Mirin, S. M., & Lange, U. (1989). A comparison of male and female cocaine abusers. *Archives of General Psychiatry*, *46*, 122–126.

Gritz, E. R. (1986). Gender and the teenage smoker. In B. A. Ray & M. C. Braude, *Women and drugs: A new era for research monographs* (DHHS Publication No. ADM 87-1447). Rockville, MD: National Institute on Drug Abuse. 70–79.

Gritz, E. R., & Brunswick, A. F. (1980). Psychosocial and behavioral aspects of smoking in women. In J. M. Pinney (Ed.), *The health consequences of smoking for women: A report of the Surgeon General*. Rockville, MD: USDHHS. 269–292.

Gritz, E. R., Carr, C. R., & Marcus, A. C. (1988). Unaided smoking cessation: Great American smoke out and New Year's Day quitters. *Psychosocial Oncology*, *6*, 217–234.

Grunberg, N. E., Bowen, D. J. & Winder, S. E. (1985). Effects of nicotine on body weight and food consumption in rats. *Psychopharmacology*, *90*, 101–105.

Hall, S. M., Ginsberg, D. G., & Jones, R. T. (1986). Smoking cessation and weight gain. *Journal of Consulting and Clinical Psychology*, *54(3)*, 342–346.

Hall, S. M., Hall, R. G., & Ginsberg, D. (1990). Pharmacological and behavioral treatment for cigarette smoking. In A. S. Bellach, M. Hersen, & A. E. Kazdin (Eds.), *International handbook of behavior modification and behavior therapy*. New York: Plenum Press.

Hall, S. M., & Havassy, B. E. (1981). The obese woman: Causes, correlates and treatment. *Professional Psychology, 12*, 163–170.

Hall, S. M., Havassy, B. E., & Wasserman, D. A. (1990). Commitment to abstinence and acute stress in relapse to alcohol, opiates, and nicotine. *Journal of Consulting and Clinical Psychology, 58*, 175–181.

Hall, S. M., Havassy, B. E., & Wasserman, D. A. (1991). Effects of commitment to positive moods, stress and coping in lapses to cocaine use. *Journal of Consulting and Clinical Psychology, 59*, 526–532.

Hall, S. M., McGee, R., Tunstall, C. D., Duffy, J. S., & Benowitz, N. (1989). Changes in food intake and activity after quitting smoking. *Journal of Consulting and Clinical Psychology, 57(1)*, 81–86.

Hamilton, J. A. (1986). An overview of the chemical rationale for advancing gender-related psychopharmacology and drug abuse research. In B. A. Ray & M.C. Braude (Eds.), *Women and drugs: A new era for research*. NIDA Monograph 65. (DHHS Publication No. ADM 87-1447). Rockville, MD: NIDA. 14–20.

Havassy, B. E., Hall, S. M., & Tschann, J. M. (1987). Social support and relapse to tobacco, alcohol, and opiates: Preliminary findings. 48th annual Scientific Meeting of the Committee on the Problems of Drug Abuse: National Institute on Drug Abuse Research Monograph Series, 76, 207–213.

Hofstetter, A., Schutz, Y., Jequir, E., & Wahren, J. (1986). Increased 24-hour energy expenditures in cigarette smokers. *New England Journal of Medicine, 314*, 79–82.

Horwitz, M. B., Hindi-Alexander, M., Wagner, T. J. (1985). Psychosocial mediators of abstinence, relapse, and continued smoking: A one-year followup of a minimal intervention. *Addictive Behaviors, 10*, 29–39.

Hughes, J. R. (1986). Genetics of Smoking: A brief review. *Behavior Therapy, 17*, 335–345.

Kivela, S. L., Nissinen, A., Punsar, S., Puska, P., & Karvonen, M. (1988). Determinants and predictors of heavy alcohol consumption among aging Finnish men. *Comprehensive Gerontology, 2*, 103–109.

Lang, A. R. (1983). Addictive personality: A viable construct? In P. K. Levison, D. R. Gerstein, & D. R. Maloff (Eds.), *Commonalities in substance abuse and habitual behavior*. Lexington, MA: Lexington Books.

Leventhal, H., & Cleary P. D. (1980). The Smoking Problem: A Review of Research & Theory in Behavioral Risk Modification. *Psych. Bulletin, 88*, 320–407.

Maletta, G. J. (1982). Alcoholism and the aged. In E. M. Pattison & E. Kaufman (Eds.), *Encyclopedic handbook of alcoholism*. Gardner Press: New York.

Malin, H., Coakley, J., Kaelber, C., Munch, N., & Holland, W. (1982). An epidemiological perspective on alcohol use and abuse in the United States. In NIAAA, *Alcohol consumption and related problems* (PHS 86-1214). Washington, D.C.: U.S. Government Printing Office. 99–153.

Marlatt, G. A., & Gordon, J. R. (1984). (Eds.) *Relapse prevention: Maintenance strategies in the treatment of addictive behaviors*. New York: Guilford Press.

Marlatt, G. A., & Gordon, J. R. (1980). Determinants of relapse: Implications for the maintenance of behavior change. In Davidson, P. O. (Ed.), *Behavioral medicine: Changing health lifestyles*. New York: Bruner-Mazel, 410–452.

Martin, R. L., Cloninger, R., & Guze, S. B. (1985). Alcohol misuse and depression in women criminals. *Journal of Studies on Alcohol, 46*, 65–71.

McArthur, C., Waldron, E., & Dickenson, J. (1958). The psychology of smoking. *Journal of Abnormal Psychology, 56*, 267–275.

McClellan, A. T., Luborsky, L., Woody, G. E. O'Brien, C. P., & Droler, K. (1983). Predicting response to alcohol and drug abuse treatments: The role of psychiatric severity. *Archives of General Psychiatry, 40*, 620–625.

McCormack, A. (1985). Risk for alcohol-related accidents in divorced and separated women. *Journal of Studies on Alcohol, 46*, 240–243.

MacDonald, J. G. (1987). Prediction of treatment outcomes for alcoholic women. *The International Journal of the Addictions, 22*, 235–248.

Mello, N. K. (1986). Drug use patterns and premenstrual dysphoria. In B. A. Ray and M. C. Braude (Eds.), *Women and drugs: A new era for research*. NIDA Research Monograph 65. (DHHS Publication No. ADM 87-1447). Rockville, MD: USDHHS. 31–48.

Mello, N. K. (1988). Effects of alcohol abuse on reproductive function in women. In M. Galanter (Ed.), *Recent developments in alcoholism* (Vol. 6, pp. 253–276). New York: Plenum.

Mermelstein, R., Cohen, S., Lichtenstein, E., Baer, J. S., & Kamarck, T. (1986). Social support and smoking cessation and maintenance. *Journal of Consulting and Clinical Psychology, 54*, 447–453.

Mermelstein, R., Lichtenstein, E., & McIntyre, K. (1983). Partner support and relapse in smoking cessation programs. *Journal of Consulting and Clinical Psychology, 51*, 465–466.

Osgood, N. J. (1987). The alcohol suicide connection in late life. *Postgraduate Medicine, 87*, 379–384.

Peterson, D. I., Longeran, L. H., Hardinger, M. G., & Teel, C. W. (1968). Results of a stop smoking program. *Archives of Environmental Health, 16*, 211–214.

Plant, M. (1980). Women with drinking problems. *British Journal of Psychiatry, 137*, 289–290.

Pomerleau, O. F., Adkins, D., & Pertschuck, M. (1978). Prediction of outcome and recidivism in smoking cessation treatment. *Addictive Behaviors, 3*, 65–70.

Ray, B. A., & Braude, M. C. (1986). *Women and drugs: A new era for researchers.* (NIDA Research Monograph, 65, DHHS Publication No. ADM 87-1447). Rockville, MD: National Institute on Drug Abuse. 1–99.

Reed, B. G., Beschner, G. M., & Mondanaro, J. (1982). *Treatment services for drug dependent women. Volume II.* (DHHS Publication No. ADM 82-1219. Rockville, MD: National Institute on Drug Abuse.

Robinson, S. D. (1984). Women and alcohol abuse factors involved in successful intervention. *International Journal of the Addictions, 19*, 601–611.

Rodin, J., & Wack, J. T. (1987). The relationship between cigarette smoking and body weight: A health promotion dilemma. In J. D. Matarazzo, S. M. Weiss, J. A. Herd, N. E. Miller, & S. M. Weiss (Eds.), *Behavioral health: A handbook of Health enhancement and disease prevention*, 671–690. New York: Wiley.

Roundsaville, B. J., Kosten, T. R., Weissman, M. M., & Kleber, H. D. (1986). Prognostic significance of psychiatric disorders in treated opiate addicts. *Archives of General Psychiatry, 43*, 739–743.

Roundsaville, B. J., Weissman, J. J., Wilber, C. H., Crits-Christoph, K., & Kleber, H. D. (1982). Diagnosis and symptoms of depression in opiate addicts: Course and relationship to treatment outcome. *Archives of General Psychiatry, 39*, 151–156.

Schindler, B. A. (1987). The psychiatric disorders of mid-life. The post menopause woman. *Medical Clinics of North America, 71*, 71–85.

Schuckit, M. A. (1985). Ethanol induced change in body sway in men at high alcoholism risk. *Archives of General Psychiatry, 42*, 375–379.

Schuckit, M. A. (1984). Subjective response to alcohol in sons of alcoholics and control subjects. *Archives of General Psychiatry, 41*, 879–884.

Schwartz, J. L., & Dubitsky, M. (1968). Requisites for success in smoking withdrawal. In E. F. Borgatta & R. R. Evans (Eds.), *Smoking, health and behavior*. Chicago: Aldine, 231–247.

Shiffman, S. (1982). Relapse following smoking cessation: A situational analysis. *Journal of Consulting and Clinical Psychology, 50*, 71–86.

Stanford, B. A., Matter, S., Fell, R. D., & Papanek, P. (1986). Effects of smoking cessation on weight gain, metabolic rate, calorie consumption and blood lipids. *American Journal of Clinical Nutrition, 43*, 486–494.

Swan, G. E., Denk, C. E., Parker, S. D., Carmelli, D., Furze, C. T., & Rosenman, R. H. (1988). Risk factors for late relapse in male and female ex-smokers. *Addictive Behaviors, 13*, 253–266.

Turnbull, J. E., & Gomberg, E. S. (1988). Impact of depressive symptomatology on alcohol problems in women. *Alcoholism: Clinical and Experimental Research, 12*, 374–381.

United States Department of Health and Human Services. (1989). *Reducing the health consequences of smoking: 25 years of Progress*, A Report of the Surgeon General. Rockville, MD: USDHHS.

United States Department of Health, Education and Welfare. (1980). *Research Monograph #1: Alcohol and women*. Rockville, MD: NIAAA.

United States Department of Health and Human Services. (1980). *The Health Consequences of Smoking for Women*, a report of the Surgeon General. Rockville, MD: USDHHS.

United States Department of Health, Education and Welfare. (1978). *Special report to the US Congress on alcohol and health*. Rockville, MD.

United States Department of Health and Human Services (1988). *The health consequences of smoking: Nicotine addiction*, A report of the Surgeon General. Rockville, MD: USDHHS.

United States Department of Health and Human Services. (1987). *Sixth special report to the U.S. Congress on alcohol and health*. (DHHS Publication No. ADM 87-1519). Rockville, MD: Nutritional Institute on Alcohol Abuse and Alcoholism.

Vaglum, S., Vaglum, P., & Larson, O. (1987). Depression and alcohol consumption in nonalcoholic and alcoholic women. *Acta Psychiatrica Scaninavia, 75*, 577–584.

Vanicelli, M. (1984). Treatment outcome of alcoholic women: The state of the art in relation to sex bias and expectancy effects. In S. Wilsnack & L. Beckman, (Eds.), *Alcohol problems in women: Antecedents, consequences, and intervention*, 369–412. New York: Guilford Press.

West, D. W., Graham, S., Swanson, M., & Wilkinson, G. (1977). Five year follow-up of a smoking withdrawal clinic population. *American Journal of Public Health, 67,* 536–544.

Wilsnack, R. W., Wilsnaek, S. C., & Klassen, A. D. (1984). Women's drinking and drinking problems: Patterns from a 1981 National Survey. *American Journal of Public Health, 77,* 1231–1238.

Wilsnack, S. C. (1982). Alcohol abuse and alcoholism in women. In E. M. Pattison & E. Kaufman, *Encyclopedic handbook of alcoholism* 718–735. Gardner Press: New York.

Chapter 7

Body Image and the Regulation of Weight

April E. Fallon

In modern Western society the issues of body weight and shape are of central importance for most females from adolescence onward. Although weight remains a health issue for all people, body image and attractiveness have particular importance to women. The first part of this chapter focuses on the special place weight and body shape occupy in a woman's life. The second part of this chapter reviews the mechanisms of weight control—both biological and sociocultural—and some of the causes of weight disregulation and the resulting disorders—anorexia nervosa, bulimia nervosa, and obesity. The chapter concludes with directions for future research.

BEAUTY, SELF-CONCEPT, AND BODY IMAGE

Central to an individual's sense of self is the image of his or her body. Body image includes the way individuals perceive themselves and, equally important, the way they think that others see them. Although men and women say that appearance is not that important to them, their choices and actions run counter to their articulated statements (R. Hill, 1945; Hudson & Hoyt, 1981; McGinnis,

Acknowledgment: Thanks to Finy Hansen and Ted Fallon for their valuable comments on an earlier draft and to Lori Herman for her considerable effort in the technical production of the manuscript.

1959). That is, attractive individuals are thought by others to have distinct advantages: to live happier and more successful lives; to have better personalities; to possess greater intelligence; and to be professionally more successful (Berscheid & Walster, 1974; Hatfield & Sprecher, 1986). In fact, they have a better chance of getting jobs and starting at higher salaries (Cann, Siegfried, & Pearce, 1981; Dipboye, Fromkin, & Wiback, 1975), and they are more likely to receive help and elicit cooperation (Wilson, 1978), and to experience more satisfying interpersonal relationships (Reis, Nezlek, & Wheeler, 1980).

While attractiveness appears to be important for most, it counts more for women (Freedman, 1986; Kalick, 1978). Men admit that they care more about appearance in a woman than women admit that they care about it in men (R. Hill, 1945; Hudson & Hoyt, 1981; McGinnis, 1959). Compared to a man's, a woman's attractiveness is more closely linked to her dating popularity (Berschied, Dion, Walster, & Walster, 1971) and even to her eventual social class in marriage (Goldblatt, Moore, & Stunkard, 1965). Both sexes perceive that for a woman, femininity and good character are linked with beauty (Brownmiller, 1984). The pursuit of and preoccupation with beauty are central features of the female sex role stereotype (Rodin, L. R. Silberstein, & Striegel-Moore, 1985) now and probably throughout time. Because beauty is linked with femininity, the influence of body image on self-concept is greater for girls and women than for boys and men. Both adolescent girls and women are more likely than adolescent boys and men to equate themselves (and their self-concept) with what they believe they look like or what they perceive others think they look like. Beginning in adolescence, girls' degree of happiness, self-concept, and self-esteem are positively correlated with their own perceptions of their attractiveness (Lerner, Karabenick, & Stuart, 1973; Wadden, Brown, Foster, & Linowitz, 1991), whereas there is no such relationship for boys and men (Mathes & Kahn, 1975). Men's self-concepts and worries are more closely related to perceptions of their effectiveness and their physical fitness (Ben-Tovim, Walker, Murray, & Chin, 1990; Lerner, Iwawaki, Chihara, & Sorell, 1980; Wadden, Brown, Fostert, & Linowitz, 1991). Men judge themselves in terms of what they can do, whereas women equate self-worth with attractiveness. For a woman, appearance, not accomplishment or deeds, is essential to desirability and self-worth (Brownmiller, 1984; Freedman, 1986).

Tracing the aesthetic preferences for beauty across time and between cultures reveals no single or absolute standard of beauty. However, Ford and Beach's study of 191 societies suggested that beauty is more often than not synonymous with good looks and a good body (Ford & Beach, 1951). Historically, the majority of societies have associated plumpness in females with desirable social status and beauty (Mazur, 1986). Despite the tremendous differences in the shapes of women, our society as well as nearly every civilization has sought to impose a uniform shape upon the female body and thereby denied the natural state of most female bodies, rearranging, accentuating, or drastically reducing some portion of the female anatomy in an attempt to achieve a "nicely proportioned" body (Fallon, 1990). For example, late in the 19th century beauty was portrayed through art images of matronly plumpness with pendulous, nurturant breasts. It was reported that even doctors encouraged plumpness as a sign of good health, much the way they encouraged diet a century later (Freedman, 1986). In contrast, in the late 1970s Twiggy, the 91-pound English model, was considered to be one of the most attractive figures in the Western world (Garfinkel & Garner, 1982).

The definition of a beautiful body can change in less than a year's time, depending on fashion, politics, and technology. These rapidly changing aesthetic preferences have to do with the ideals of the upper classes as well as the beliefs of the scientific community (to be discussed later in this chapter). Such ideals assume that body size and shape are almost totally under volitional control and that the places that fat cells are distributed, namely the breasts, hips, stomach, and thighs, will expand and contract in uniform and in the desired proportion for all women (Dyrenforth, Wooley, & Wooley, 1980; Freedman, 1986).

Today, women in our society consider thinness an essential and basic element of physical attractiveness (Freedman, 1986). The ideal standard has become considerably thinner over the last 20 years. This is in contrast to actuarial data from the 1979 Build and Blood Pressure Study, which found that the average female under age 30 had actually become heavier by 5–6 pounds over the last 20 years (Garner & Garfinkel, 1980). Concomitant with sociocultural fads of shape and size, the medical community and insurance companies have changed their standards a number of times recently, adding further confusion to the standard of "ideal" weight. For example, in the 1950s insurance companies had standards for women that suggested that most middle-aged women were overweight (Freedman, 1986). Recently medical statistics suggest that individuals who are 5–15% above the "ideal" weight may actually live longer than the average or thin individual, provided there are not complicating medical conditions (A. E. Anderson, 1985). Thus, depending on how obesity is defined, the estimates of differential incidence between men and women who are obese range from 5 to 33% for men and 12 to 40% for women (Domangue, 1987; Gilbert, 1986).

What effect does this pressure have on the women and men in our culture? How happy are people with their bodies and what is their perception of the ideal? A 1972 nationwide survey revealed that more than half the people were quite satisfied with their looks, with men being somewhat more satisfied (55%) than women (45%). Only 4% of the men and 7% of the women were extremely dissatisfied. A larger percentage of women were more dissatisfied than men with each body part except for genitals and height. Women were also considerably more dissatisfied with their buttocks and hips than men. These dissatisfactions occurred as frequently with young adult as with middle age (21–44 years and over 45 years) (Berscheid, Walster, & Bohrnstedt, 1973).

Fifteen years later, a similar survey revealed an increasing number of men (24%) and women (31%) rating their appearance negatively. An even greater number of both men (41%) and women (55%) were dissatisfied with their weight (Cash, Winstead, & Janda, 1986). Indeed, many studies have replicated the finding that females are more dissatisfied (Fallon & Rozin, 1985; Gray, 1977; Rozin & Fallon, 1988; Thompson, 1991; Thompson & Psaltis, 1988) with their weight and shape than males. Thus the pressures for women to be slim have resulted in many women's feeling that they are overweight.[1]

Given the large number of women who feel dissatisfied with their weight, it is not surprising that so many women engage in weight watching activities. Rozin and Fallon (1988) found that 67% of the college women surveyed were dieting at least some of the time, whereas only 25% of the college men were doing so. It is hardly surprising that women are much more likely than men to engage in weight-related behaviors such as weighing themselves more often, being concerned about being overweight, counting calories and holding back at meal times, feeling guilty and depressed when they overeat, and seeking medical help for weight-related problems (Dwyer, Feldman, Seltzer, & Mayer, 1969; Gray, 1977; Rozin & Fallon, 1988; Waldron, 1983). Thus women tend to see themselves as overweight even if they are not; they are more dissatisfied with their body shape, and they diet more often than men to achieve the thin ideal.

Freedman (1986) notes that 90% of the participants in diet programs are female. In one recent year, more than 200 diet books were published, a dozen of which became best sellers (Freedman, 1986). Simonson reported that there are 28,096 weight-reducing methods and gadgets, of which not more than 6% have been demonstrated to be safe and effective in the short term (Haber, 1981). In follow-up studies, most programs have some success, but except for surgery less than 10–20% of those who enter a treatment program will solve their weight problems (Haber, 1981).

Perhaps the most serious consequences of this concern and obsession for a slim shape are the almost epidemic increase in the eating disorders of anorexia nervosa[2] and bulimia nervosa.[3] About 90–95% of the individuals who suffer from these disorders are women (Bushnell, Wells, Hornblow, Oakley-Browne, & Joyce, 1990; Cooper, Charnock, & Taylor, 1987; Halmi, Falk, & Schwartz, 1981; Pope, Hudson, Yurgelen-Todd, & Hudson, 1984).[4] Most studies suggest

[1] It has been postulated that pressure for most women to reach an ideal (in this case to be thin) is related to heterosexual desirability. However, those women with anorectic (restrictive) disturbances in their eating patterns tend to desire an ideal that they recognize as being thinner than what they know the opposite sex would consider desirable (Zellner, Harner, & Adler, 1989).

[2] Anorexia nervosa is a psychiatric disorder characterized by a conscious, relentless preoccupation and pursuit of thinness that results in maintaining a weight at least 15% below what is expected. It is characterized by an intense fear of gaining weight and a distorted body image.

[3] Bulimia nervosa is a psychiatric disorder characterized by recurrent episodes of binge eating often followed by purging (vomiting, laxative, diuretics) and guilt. There is a persistent overconcern with body shape and weight.

[4] Recovery from these disorders is related to the acceptance of one's current physique as the

that even with psychological and/or pharmacological intervention, less than half will recover (Herzog, Deter & Vandereycken, 1992; Keller, Herzog, Lavori, Bradburn & Mahoney, 1992).

An understanding of the etiology and course of these disorders requires a comprehension of the various mechanisms of weight control. A review of the factors involved in maintenance and regulation of weight for both men and women is presented in this next section.

REGULATION OF INTAKE AND WEIGHT

The Remarkable Stability of Weight

Humans are confronted with many variations in type and amount of food available and seasonal temperature changes, which make them potentially susceptible to wide fluctuations in body weight; yet the body maintains amazingly stable temperatures, blood levels of oxygen, pH, and glucose, and weight. Although there is tremendous variation in the height/weight ratio among organisms of the same species, both humans and other animals are able to sustain a relatively constant weight throughout their lifetime. Longitudinal population studies such as the Framingham study suggest that as a group adult human beings maintain remarkably stable weight in the short term and vary only about 10 kilograms in the long term (Dawber, 1980). At age 60, the average white, American male is only 4 to 5 pounds heavier than when he was 30 (Domangue, 1987). In fact, even under circumstances of semistarvation that reduce the body's weight by 25%, when the food restrictions are removed weight will return to its previous level (Keys, Brozek, Henschel, Mickelson, & Taylor, 1950). Conversely, individuals induced to gain another 15–25% of their weight will return to their former weight when those conditions have been terminated (Sims, 1976).

Overview of Weight Regulation

Several different theories have been posited in an attempt to tease out how weight and intake are regulated and maintained. Multiple factors appear to be involved in the control of weight. The degree to which each factor influences the homeostasis of the body in the management and regulation of weight is unknown; nonetheless, it is very clear that all factors influence and are influenced by each of the other factors. The regulation of weight begins with the process of eating—

---

desirable one. Conversely for an individual diagnosed with an eating disorder, continued desire to maintain a thinner physique than one is currently able is associated with continued symptomatology (Channon, deSilva, Hemsley, & Mukherjee, 1990).

the decision to eat or not to eat. The decisions to eat or to stop eating and the intermeal interval are based on the individual's internal biological state, the immediate environmental events, the sociocultural context, and the individual's personality characteristics. A general overview of each of these factors is presented, followed by a more detailed description of the research and current status of each factor's contribution. It is important to note that all these factors overlap and that the separation is an artificial one used only to help understand the contribution that each makes to weight regulation.

The individual's internal state includes the perception of hunger (conscious sensations linked to the desire to eat food), satiation (the willingness to stop eating based on the feeling of being full), and satiety (the maintenance of inhibition of further eating as a result of prior food ingestion). Blundell, A. J. Hill, and Lawton (1989) fully discuss these three concepts. Weight regulation is also dependent upon the way in which the body processes the food (including gastric distension and rate of emptying, release of hormones such as cholecystokinin from the duodenum, and stimulation of the chemically specific receptors along the gastrointestinal tract). Related to this is the extent to which the energy acquired through food intake is equivalent to energy expenditure. The ratio of energy intake/expenditure in turn can affect perception of hunger, satiation, and satiety and thus affect further eating as well as other homeostatic systems such as temperature regulation.

The immediate environmental event can include the social context in which eating takes place as well as the anticipated stimulus properties of the food to be ingested (e.g., palatability and variety of the available foods). The psychobiological system for the regulation of weight has the capacity to form associations between sensory and post-absorptive properties of the foods (Booth, 1977). The sight of food also triggers cephalic phase responses (which include the mouth, stomach and duodenum, lower intestine, and related endocrine glands). Thus sensory properties of foods can provoke physiological responses that anticipate ingestion and may facilitate appetite. These physiological responses differ among people; for example, food smells trigger a cephalic insulin response that is four times greater in obese subjects than in lean ones (Blundell et al., 1989).

The sociocultural context includes the individual's perception of the ideal body image based on mass media impressions as well as the influence of one's subgroup such as sex, social class or cultural group. To date, personality characteristics affecting weight regulation have not been easily articulated. This chapter includes only those aspects that are affected by the individual perception of the discordance between the cultural ideal and one's own body image and the concomitant intentional behaviors (such as dieting and restraint) that the individual employs to decrease the disparity between the ideal and the perception of the self.

Brain Mechanisms and the Role of Neurotransmitters in the Regulation of Weight

Attempts to understand the regulation of intake and weight initially began with efforts to locate a single mechanism for hunger and satiety. The stomach is perhaps the most obvious possibility (Cannon, 1932); it is consistent with the popular view of hunger. Although the amount of sugar, the caloric value of the food, and the process of passing food through the stomach (and stomach distention) all appear to have an effect on the amount eaten, even complete removal of stomach innervation has little effect on the experience of hunger and on the control of food intake (Garg & Singh, 1983). In the 1950s and 1960s this peripheral theory lost favor to a dual center hypothesis in which intake was regulated centrally by a feeding center, the lateral hypothalamus, and a satiety center, the ventromedial hypothalamus. Evidence supporting this included studies showing that lesions in the ventromedial hypothalamus resulted in overeating and that electrical stimulation led to a cessation of eating. Conversely, lesions in the lateral hypothalamus led to cessation of eating, and electrical stimulation led to overeating. Recently this view has been modified by evidence that the lesions may cause visceral, metabolic, and endocrine changes and result in general apathetic behavior or sensory enhancement or neglect. Now it is believed that satiety is influenced by the hedonic value of the food in addition to pure physiological factors. Thus these "centers" in the hypothalamus may not be "turn on-turn off" eating centers, but may influence eating and weight regulation in more indirect ways. That is, the medial hypothalamus may be an *integrator* of satiety signals and the lateral hypothalamus more of an *organizer* for initiating food seeking behavior. The two regions may interact reciprocally to integrate sensory and metabolic factors and thus play an essential role in balancing intake and energy expenditure as well as modulating nutrient balances (Stellar, 1989).[5]

Recently, many researchers have come to believe that specific chemicals, called neurotransmitters, released at the nerve endings in the hypothalamus may play a role in some aspects of weight regulation such as control of food intake, appetite for specific macronutrients, and the timing of meals. These neurotransmitters include the monoamines, (norepinephrine, epinephrine, dopamine and serotonin); the amino acid, gamma-aminobutyric acid (GABA); and the neuropeptides, such as pancreatic polypeptides, opioid peptides, hormone-releasing factors, and various gut-brain peptides (Leibowitz, 1987a). The hypothalamus, rich in neurotransmitters and neurohormones, functions as part of a whole-brain circuitry. It influences and is influenced by the peripheral autonomic and endocrine systems, which may be essential in providing the neurological, metabolic,

[5]Other parts of the brain are also involved in the processing of information having to do with food acceptance and rejection such as the caudal medulla. Possibly peripheral-neural and direct central nervous system effects are involved simultaneously. Neural pathways in the brain connect the vagus nerve, which terminates in the hind brain, to the hypothalamus, amygdala, and the rest of the limbic system.

and hormonal information required for energy and nutritional homeostasis (Leibowitz, 1987a). Thus it is thought that neurotransmitters within the hypothalamus respond to signals from the blood as well as the nervous system, and that the hypothalamus then serves to integrate this information to promote appropriate adjustment in both the quality and quantity of eating behaviors. That is, it is hypothesized that neurotransmitters within the hypothalamus tell us what, when, and how much to eat as well as determine, through the action of hormones, how and when the body metabolizes its nutrients (Leibowitz, 1987a).[6] Most research to date has attempted to study this by injecting neurotransmitters, their precursors, or metabolites and/or drugs that act to release neurotransmitters into various brain sites in animals in an effort to map the sites and the neurotransmitters most central in the regulation of weight. The researcher finds the drug that exerts a specific behavioral action in the animal by altering the concentration or turnover of a specific transmitter (Blundell et al., 1989). Investigation in humans then usually involves the administration of the drug. If the drug alters the same class of behavior in humans that it has previously been found to alter in other animals, then it is assumed that the previously identified neurotransmitter and/or pathway is responsible. Research efforts have focused on the identification of the neurotransmitters involved as well as the nature of their interactions and the specific brain sites where these neurotransmitters are acting to produce their behavioral effects.

The hypothalamus, in contrast to extrahypothalamic forebrain structure, is found to be particularly responsive to injections. Injections of the neurotransmitter norepinephrine, neuropeptide Y,[7] galanin, GABA, and the opiates (at least three families of opioid peptides) in the medial hypothalamus (e.g., paraventricular nucleus) are effective in stimulating food intake (Leibowitz, 1987a). In the same brain area, the injection of the monamine serotonin reduces food intake, probably by reducing serotonin availability at the presynaptic terminals and thereby enhancing serotonergic functioning (Garattini, Bizzi, Caccia, Mennini, & Samanin, 1988).[8] An injection of the peptide cholecystokinin also has been found to have an inhibitory effect on food intake (Leibowitz, 1986).[9] In

[6]The neurotransmitters are probably involved in the neurochemistry of reward and aversion. They may be important in the positive reinforcement of ingestive behavior as well as self-stimulation and in facilitating the satiety inhibition of the feeding reward (Hoebel, Hernandez, Schwartz, Mark, & Hunter, 1989).

[7]Unlike norepinephrine and galanin, which are effective primarily in the paraventricular nucleus area, neuropeptide Y has been found to be effective in multiple areas of the hypothalamus (Leibowitz, 1989).

[8]Activation of central $5\text{-HT}_{1B,A1}$ and $5\text{-HT}_{1C,A1}$ receptors inhibits food intake whereas the opposite effect is obtained by activating central $5\text{-HT}_{1A,A1}$ receptors (Samanin & Garattini, 1989). To date most studies have been done in animals; there is some evidence that receptor subtypes may differ in humans (Garattini, Bizzi, Caccia, Mennini, & Samanin, 1988).

[9]The release of cholecystokinin, its action receptors in the stomach wall, and then the relay of neural information to the brain via the vagus nerve is one of the likely mechanisms for the mediation of satiety.

contrast, these same neurotransmitters injected into the lateral part of the hypo-thalamus do not have the same influence on eating behavior, whereas injections of other neurotransmitters, such as dopamine, norepinephrine, and GABA, into the perifornical region suppress eating behavior (Leibowitz, 1987a). It is believed that when drugs are injected peripherally they influence eating behavior by causing a release of neurotransmitters in the medial or lateral hypothalamus. Consistent with this notion is the finding that damage to specific hypothalamic neurons, or disruption of neurotransmitter-synthesizing capability, obliterates the usual effect of the peripherally administered drugs on eating behavior (Leibowitz, 1987a).

Hypothalamic neurotransmitters may also influence and perhaps determine the temporal patterns of food intake (Leibowitz, 1987b, 1989). Norepinephrine injected into the medial hypothalamus increases food consumption by increasing meal size, duration, and rate of eating rather than by increasing meal frequency (Leibowitz, 1987a). This increased food intake may occur because norepineph-rine acts to delay the onset of satiety rather than to stimulate hunger (Leibowitz, 1987a). A similar response occurs with the administration of neuropeptide Y (Leibowitz, 1989).

The opposite occurs with serotonin. The administration of fenfluramine, a serotonergic agonist, reduces food intake by suppressing the rate of eating, reducing meal size, and prematurely terminating a meal, but does not reduce meal frequency (Garattini et al., 1988). The administration of fenfluramine has been found to be effective in a variety of experimental conditions of hyperphagia (obesity) by reducing the meal size (Garattini et al., 1988). Amphetamines also reduce intake, but appear to do so by causing a delay in the onset of a meal rather than by terminating the meal prematurely (Leibowitz, 1987a).

In addition to controlling the amount of food consumed and temporal pat-terns of eating, specific neurotransmitters also may play a significant role in an appetite for particular macronutrients such as carbohydrates. Injecting norepi-nephrine into the medial hypothalamus of rats causes normally satiated animals to eat additional large amounts of food in a short time period (Leibowitz, 1986). When permitted the choice of separate sources of macronutrients, the norepi-nephrine-injected animals showed a strong preference for carbohydrate at the expense of protein intake (Leibowitz, 1987b).[10] Consistent with these findings are those studies in which the chronic administration of a drug that blocks the brain's synthesis of norepinephrine decreases carbohydrate intake and increases protein preference. Conversely, repeated administration of neuropeptide Y to the hypothalamus produced a marked increase in daily food intake and body weight gain by selectively stimulating carbohydrate ingestion with little effect on protein

[10]Clonidine, the antihypertensive agent, stimulates the same receptors as norepinephrine does; it produces a similar effect when administered orally inducing the ingestion of a large carbohydrate meal (Leibowitz, 1987a). The antidepressant drug amitriptyline similarly has been associated with a "craving" for carbohydrate (Johnson, Stuckey, & Mitchell, 1983).

or fat ingestion (Leibowitz, 1989). Although some of the other neuropeptides (e.g., opiates) appear to have some impact on carbohydrate preference (Czirr & Reid, 1986), opiates generally stimulate increased consumption through an increase of fat intake (Levine & Billington, 1989).

In contrast, administration of the monoamine serotonin (believed to inhibit the action of norepinephrine in the paraventricular nucleus) suppresses carbohydrate ingestion while not affecting protein intake (Leibowitz 1987a; 1989; Rogacki, Weiss, Rueg, Suh, Pal, Stanley, Wong, & Leibowitz, 1989). Peripherally injected drugs such as fenfluramine and fluoxetine produce similar results,[11] probably affecting food intake through the release of endogenous serotonin and a dopamine metabolite in the lateral hypothalamus (Hoebel, Hernandez, Schwartz, Mark, & Hunter, 1989).

These studies suggest that these neurotransmitters can provide critical signals for weight regulation and potentially override the normal signals of energy and nutrient balance. It is important to note that these neurotransmitters may be affected by what we eat and by the products of metabolism (Blundell & A. J. Hill, 1989).

Neurotransmitter animal research supports the following model (Leibowitz, 1987a, 1987b, 1989; Marano, 1993). When the animal is food deprived, there are changes in the neurotransmitters and their receptor sites. The brain attempts to activate the noradrenergic system to increase food-seeking behavior. When the organism is most hungry, norepinephrine and perhaps galanin (through an independent receptor site) in the medial hypothalamus are activated (Hoebel et al., 1989). With norepinephrine activated, the organism searches for carbohydrate. With the ingestion of carbohydrate, there is an increase in circulating levels of tryptophan (a precursor in the synthesis of serotonin). As serotonin synthesis increases, norepinephrine activity is inhibited and satiation for carbohydrate develops. In animals, an injection of serotonin during the first meal after sleep will inhibit the ingestion of carbohydrate, whereas an injection later in the cycle affects carbohydrate ingestion minimally; this suggests that carbohydrate meals that occur later in the active cycle are probably controlled by other neurotransmitters. Although carbohydrate is the macronutrient of choice early in the active phase, protein and fat are preferred later in the cycle. Opiate peptides in the lateral hypothalamus stimulate ingestion of protein and fat. The protein meal affects the synthesis of brain catecholamines, particularly dopamine in the perifornical region of the lateral hypothalamus. The enhanced dopamine synthesis controls the termination of protein meals. (Amphetamines are believed to act in part through the release of dopamine in the lateral hypothalamus to cause a suppression in appetite.) Just prior to the last meal, galanin stimulates preferences

---

[11]Recently, these conclusions have been debated since in humans these effects seem to be true for snacks, but when *total* pattern of food intake is measured, fenfluramine administration has only slight effect upon overall nutrition (Blundell & A. J. Hill, 1987, cited in Blundell, A. J. Hill, & Lawton, 1989).

for fat. Concomitant with neurotransmitter activity changes are fluctuations of nutrients and hormones in the blood that interact with the brain neurotransmitters to influence behavior (Fernstrom & Fernstrom, 1987; Leibowitz, 1986, 1987a, 1987b; Wurtman & Wurtman, 1984). Exactly how these neurotransmitters are regulated is unclear. Challenging this model is some evidence that suggests that carbohydrates are not tightly regulated and that in humans there are no carbohydrate requirements as there are requirements for protein or total calories (Fernstrom & Fernstrom, 1987).

Neurotransmitter Disturbances as an Explanation of Eating Disorders

Obesity in animals is associated with abnormal brain neurotransmitter profiles. For example, genetically obese animals often have elevated plasma and pituitary levels of the endogenous opioid, beta-endorphin. The endogenous opioid may affect obesity by increasing food intake and increasing energy retention (Marks-Kaufman & Kanarek, 1987).[12] Obese animals also have altered responses to injections of neurotransmitters. For example, the neuropeptide Y is differentially effective in stimulating eating behavior in genetically obese rats as compared to nonobese rats (Leibowitz, 1989). However, it is unclear whether these neurochemical abnormalities are the cause or a product of the obesity. Some of the abnormalities found in obese patients may be the result of intermittent dieting and not the consequence of overeating (Pudel, Paul, & Maus, 1988).

In bulimic patients, the search for a primary hypothalamic defect has revealed a large variety of deviant neuroendocrine responses. Many have suggested that the whole system of regulating food intake and storage is severely disturbed in bulimia nervosa (Pirke & Vandereycken, 1988). The disturbances of hunger and satiety appear to have not only a subjective basis, but a physiological basis (Halmi, 1988). Bulimia has been associated with a disturbed release of serotonin in the brain (Brewerton, Brandt, Lessem, Murphy, & Jimerson, 1990; Brewerton, Muller, Brandt, Lesem, Hegg, Murphy, & Jimerson, 1989; Jimerson, Brandt, & Brewerton, 1988; Marano, 1993). Reduced levels of serotonin in the cerebrospinal fluid are consistent with increased carbohydrate intake and increased rate of eating. An increase in serotonin during binging and vomiting has been associated with the termination of those activities (Kaye, Gwirtsman, Brewerton, George, & Wurtman, 1988). However, it is noted that the bulimics did not show exaggerated carbohydrate consumption and that carbohydrate consumption was not correlated with relief of anxiety, so that binge eating for bulimics may not be neurochemically mediated via serotonin.

[12]Unfortunately, not all obese animals have elevated levels of beta-endorphins. Furthermore, the introduction of opioid antagonists has sometimes resulted in decreased food intake rather than increases. Marks-Kaufman and Kanarek (1987) completely review this area.

The autonomic nervous system (specifically, the peripheral noradrenergic system) may also be important in the problems that bulimics have with the regulation of food intake and energy expenditure (Pirke & Vandereycken, 1988). Impaired gonadal function found in bulimics could be responsible for reduced prolactin and impaired peripheral activity of the sympathetic nervous system (Schweiger, Laessle, Fichter, & Pirke, 1988). However, many of these differences can be the result of intermittent eating (Schweiger et al., 1988) and can be recreated in healthy fasting subjects (Fichter, Pirke, Pollinger, Wolfram, & Brunner, 1988). Interestingly, moderate dieting reduces brain serotonin functioning in women, but not men (I.M. Anderson, Parry-Billings, Newsholme, Fairburn, & Cowen 1990). This reduction has been linked to impaired satiety and a tendency to binge and thus may predispose women, but not men, to eating disorders. The questions are, why do some dieters develop bulimia and some not, and could it emerge in an otherwise healthy adult? Further study of the effect of some the symptomatic behaviors that characterize bulimia nervosa will improve understanding of the neurotransmitters and endocrine changes that occur in the syndrome. As Pirke and Vandereycken (1988) have noted, bulimia nervosa is a disorder whose etiology and pathogenesis (predisposition, precipitant, and perpetuation) cannot be explained by a single factor (such as neurotransmitter disturbance) in a linear causal way.

Disturbances in neurotransmitter release exist in patients with anorexia nervosa. Low norepinephrine levels in the cerebrospinal fluid have been found in these patients independent of body weight (Kaye, Gwirtsman, Lake, Siever, Jimerson, Ebert, & Murphy, 1985). In some cases there has been elevated activity of central opiates; this is consistent with the eating habits of anorectics, who often ingest primarily protein while attempting to avoid carbohydrates (Leibowitz, 1987b). There are disturbances in neuropeptide Y functioning in anorectic patients and abstaining bulimic patients. Any disturbances of hormones or nutrients (e.g., glucose) have the potential to alter peptide activity in the brain. The relationship found between hypothalamic neuropeptide Y and onset of puberty in females has led to the postulation that abnormal peptide activity around puberty, as a consequence of either malnutrition or other dysfunction, may lead to anorexia nervosa. The study of amino acid concentration patterns after intake of carbohydrate or protein meals in anorectics may provide additional information regarding the etiology of the disorder (Wurtman & Wurtman, 1983). The biochemical effects of starvation pose special problems in trying to tease out whether neurotransmitter disturbances are the cause or effect of anorexia. Pirke and Ploog (1983) review these biochemical disturbances.

The ability of drugs to decrease eating disorder symptomatology and to have a specific effect on neurotransmitter functioning has been used as evidence of the possible role of neurotransmitter dysfunction in the etiology of eating disorders. For example, there is some evidence that Naloxone and naltrexone (opiate antagonists) decrease frequency of binging in bulimics but do not appear to help in weight loss in obese individuals (Levine & Billington, 1989; Mitchell, Morley, Laine, Pyle, Eckert, & Zollman, 1987). This line of reasoning requires some "leap of faith."

Peripheral Signals Involved in Intake and Weight Control

Peripheral signals must also play some role in the regulation of nutrient balance in that it is likely that they provide the hypothalamus with information about the level of nutrient stores. Certainly placing glucose, amino acids, or fats in the stomach or intestine will decrease food intake. Conversely, decreasing circulating glucose or blocking liver glucose metabolism also stimulates eating (Bray, 1988).

When ingesting food, the gastrointestinal tract secretes a variety of peptides as part of the digestive process. It is believed that some of these, such as cholecystokinin (found in both the gut and brain), act as hormonal or local signals and relay information to the central nervous system, causing a cessation of eating and producing satiation (Woods & Gibbs, 1989). Support for this comes from studies that demonstrate that injection of cholecystokinin into the peritoneum reduces food intake. This peptide hormone seems to play at least an intermediary role in the regulation of satiety (Bray, 1988).

Most of the other hormones appear to be involved in determining body fat. When hypopituitary organisms are injected with growth hormone, body fat is reduced and lean body mass is increased; this body composition change occurs concomitantly with an increase in metabolic rate (Bray, 1988). During adulthood, secretion of the growth hormone declines at the same time there is a gradual increase in body fat, even if weight does not change. One conclusion from this finding might be that this fall in growth hormone may play a role in increasing body fat during aging (Bray, 1988).

Thyroid hormone, secreted by the thyroid gland, also affects metabolic rate. Reduced metabolic rate and an increase in body fat occurs with hypothyroidism; conversely, hyperthyroidism is associated with increased metabolic rate and decreased body fat (Bray, 1988).

Adrenal glucocorticoids are important in the regulation of body fat too. Decreased levels are associated with weight loss and body fat decrease (Addison's disease), and increased levels are associated with increased proportions of fat to protein storage, particularly in the abdomen and facial regions (Cushing's disease). Research with genetically obese animals has revealed the importance of gluococorticoids; obese animals given adrenalectomies lower their food intake and increase energy expenditure. It is hypothesized that the effect of the gluococorticoids is modulated through the paraventricular nucleus of the medial hypothalamus by influencing consumption and changing sympathetic nervous system activities. Thus it is believed that glucocorticoids may reciprocally influence energy intake and expenditure, with high levels promoting positive energy balance and low levels facilitating negative energy balance (Bray, 1988).

Insulin is also believed to be involved in the regulation of weight since there is a direct correlation between adiposity and plasma insulin levels (Woods & Gibbs, 1989). The hypothesis is that insulin provides information to the brain concerning the degree of adiposity in the body. The fatter a person is, the higher the plasma insulin levels and the greater the magnitude of the signal that reaches the brain (Woods & Gibbs, 1989). A peripheral injection of insulin will be followed by a proportionate increase in food intake (Bray, 1988). Injections of insulin directly into the brain (which the brain interprets as an increase in adiposity) reduce eating and encourage weight loss (Woods & Gibbs, 1989). Insulin may work in conjunction with other peptides, such that if a person is underweight a reduction in brain insulin diminishes the perception or response to meal-generated satiety (Wood & Gibbs, 1989).

Energy Regulation

In order to appreciate how weight is lost, gained, or maintained, it is important to understand a few fundamentals of energy regulation. In the maintenance of stable body weight, energy intake (in the form of food) must be balanced by energy expenditure. Energy expenditure can be divided into three categories (Keesey, 1986). The first is basal energy expenditure. This includes thermogenesis (regulation of the body temperature), maintenance of the cell structure, the making of the cell products, and specialized activities of the cells and organs. The second is diet-induced thermogenesis, energy associated with the ingestion and processing of food or ingested energy; that is, body temperature regulation has an effect on metabolism. The body increases its heat production beginning about 20 minutes after eating (Garrow, 1986). In fact, heat production normally increases in proportion to the size of the meal ingested. The third category is energy expended by the somatic musculature; exercise and general activity level falls into this category. The majority of energy is expended with basal metabolism (Keesey, 1986). Energy expended on ingestion and resting metabolism changes with the organism's nutritional status. The larger the body surface, the more energy is required to maintain its basic activities (such as involuntary muscle movements of heart, diaphragm, and gut); that is, more tissue must be maintained in a steady state. Thus, if conditions remain constant, bigger (or heavier) people have a higher basal energy expenditure than smaller (or thinner) people. A higher basal metabolism enables men to burn up calories and expend physical energy at a faster rate than women. Not only do men have a larger frame to fill out, but their dimorphic muscle mass enables them to consume greater amounts of energy without it turning to fat. A man can eat up to 50% more calories than a woman in the course of a day without gaining weight (Brownmiller, 1984). Metabolic differences do not taper off until old age. Energy comes from the intake of food, which is chemically broken down and stored in various forms in several places throughout the body. If it takes less energy than has been ingested to keep the body functioning, the food taken in will be stored as fat or glycogen, and the individual will gain weight. If the energy required is more than the stored energy, the body breaks down its own tissues (e.g., muscles). The standard unit of energy measurement is kilocalories, more commonly known as "calories."

Energy expenditure or exchange takes place in the cells. Therefore, the measurement of this overall exchange throughout the human body is somewhat indirect. There are many methods for attempting to measure energy expenditure or "metabolism," each with its disadvantages and inaccuracies (Garrow, 1986; Nicolaidis & Even, 1989). The most fundamental way to measure energy expenditure can be calculated by measuring the heat that the body generates over a period of time. Since this is not easy to do, more indirect methods involving the measurement of the amount of oxygen the patient consumes during a certain body state are often used. A frequently used measure of energy expenditure is basal metabolism rate (BMR); it is the resting, or "basal energy expenditure," defined as the energy expenditure of a subject in bed at rest in a neutral thermal environment and before breakfast (Garrow, 1986). It is believed that intracellular energy expenditure affects and is affected by hormonal (e.g., growth hormones) and neural input (neurotransmitters), although the precise mechanisms are not clear. Nicholaidis and Even (1989) discuss the influences of metabolism on consumption. Other homeostatic systems within the body also affect the body's metabolic rate. Thermoregulation is an example.

It has long been thought that food intake affects metabolic rate. Nicholaidis and Even (1989) have proposed that metabolic rate directly affects the onset of feeding behavior. That is, hunger is induced by a decrease in metabolic rate (this is known as the ischymetric hypothesis). It is the authors' belief that brain cells monitor body states and detect background metabolism ("metabolisme de fond"). Thus a decrease of background metabolism is transduced into a signal of hunger and facilitates the onset of a meal. A symmetrical phenomenon occurs with satiety (Nicholaidis & Even, 1989). This onset of satiety is better predicted by the background metabolism than by blood glucose. The metabolic signal of hunger is the result of the integration of the level of utilization of carbohydrates, lipids, and amino acids.

Obesity: A Simple Imbalance of Intake and Expenditure?

A common notion is that obesity is the result of eating too much. Research, however, indicates that between people of the same weight, height, and age with similar activity levels, there is much individual variation in the quantity of food consumed (Gilbert, 1986). With a few exceptions (e.g., obese individuals eat more palatable food than normal weight people), there is little evidence that obese individuals eat more than normal weight individuals either in natural settings or in the laboratory (Meyers, Stunkard, & Coll, 1980; Spitzer & Rodin, 1981).

If intake is not different for the obese, then perhaps energy expenditure is. Epidemiological data suggest a positive relationship between inactivity and obesity. The increase in incidence of obesity in the United States is higher than it was in the early part of the 20th century, yet per capita caloric intake is approximately 5% less (Stern, 1984). Perhaps, this is due solely to the decrease in physical activity. For example, Illinois Bell Telephone Company has estimated that in the course of one year an extension phone saves the individual approximately 70 miles of walking, which may be the equivalent of 2–3 pounds of fat (Stern, 1984).

In general, although obese people are not always less active than those of normal weight, inactivity is often associated with obesity (Stern, 1984). A review of the findings suggests that obese men and women are less active than those of normal weight; this finding is somewhat more pronounced for women than men (Stern, 1984). However, it is possible that this may be the result rather than cause of obesity.

The relation of exercise to food intake is more unclear; research suggests that exercise has been known to decrease, increase, or have no affect on food intake (Thompson, Jarvie, Lahey, & Cureton, 1982). Food intake decreases immediately after exercise. Some have found that for moderately active people, exercise promotes increased consumption in the long term. In contrast, in a naturalistic study in West Bengal, sedentary men (within the normal weight range) ate more and weighed more than those engaged in light activity (Mayer, Roy, & Mitra, 1956).

The amount of exercise does contribute to regulating the fat content of the body. When obese individuals are on a standard weight reduction program, they lose lean tissue as well as fat. When exercise is added, lean body mass is preserved or increased. It is believed that exercise contributes to caloric deficit in two ways: first through the caloric cost of the exercise, and second (somewhat more controversially) through increased basal metabolism that occurs for several hours after the exercise has ceased, thus allowing for the continued expenditure of calories. For obese, dieting individuals, exercise can prevent the basal metabolic rate from being lowered (Thompson et al., 1982).

In the past it was felt that changes in food intake resulted in a straightforward loss or gain of adipose tissue and that weight stability was achieved when food consumption and energy expenditure were equal. Thus, if a woman were to eat her usual standard meals but consistently take in 150 kcal (an English muffin with 1 pat of butter) over the daily requirements (energy expenditure), she would gain 15 pounds in 1 year and 150 pounds in 10 years, clearly making her morbidly obese. This calculation assumes 100% food conversion efficiency. However, many reports suggest that this may not happen. For example, in the Sims (1976) study of weight gain, one man who consumed almost double his usual daily caloric intake initially gained weight but then proceeded to lose some of the weight he gained without changing his food intake (Sims, 1976). Not only does body weight sometimes fail to reflect intake, but body weight can change even if intake does not. That is, one can gain weight without overeating or lose weight without dieting. Furthermore, despite earnest efforts to develop efficacious weight reduction programs, weight loss has been modest and transient (Brownell, 1982). These observations have led to the development and popularity of the set point theory.

Set Point Theory

Set point theory postulates that organisms have a biologically based set point for weight that is tenaciously defended when challenged. According to the theory, the body physiologically responds by slowing weight loss when the individual is below set point or by slowing weight gain when the individual is above set point. If weight is lost, metabolic rate drops, and if weight is gained, metabolic rate goes up. This theory has generated much research. Both animal and human studies have been used to support it (Keesey, 1986; Lowe, 1987).

To support this theory investigators have created obese rats by force feeding (Cohn & Joseph., 1962) and thin rats by reducing their normal food allocation (Brooks & Lambert, 1946). When returned to unrestricted feeding, both groups of rats restore their body weights to "normal levels" (Lowe, 1987).[13] A second line of research that supports the theory are studies of animals lesioned in the lateral hypothalamus (Powley & Keesey, 1970). Although lesioned animals gain weight by force feeding, they return to their (reduced) initial post lesion weight when they resume unrestricted feeding (Keesey, 1986). These results suggest that even abnormal weights (produced via lesions) are defended when challenged. Lateral hypothalamic lesioned rats have a resting metabolism appropriate for their reduced mass. Weight-reduced (nonlesioned) rats are hypometabolic, displaying a reduced resting energy expenditure exceeding what would be expected on the basis of their reduced mass (Keesey, 1986). It is postulated that this defense is mediated by the same set point mechanism that regulates weight stability and defense in nonlesioned animals.

A third type of support for set point theory involves the study of three types of obese rats (Keesey, 1986; Lowe, 1987). Genetically obese Zucker rats defend their normally maintained obesity when they are challenged, by means including consuming enough calories of calorically diluted food or even sufficient quan-

[13]The noted exception is that rats placed on high fat diets for several months do not return to their normal weight when restored to a regular diet. Corbett, Stern, and Keesey (1986) found that fat cell number increased in these animals. Thus, long-term maintenance on high fat diets may cause anatomic and/or physiologic changes that cause the set point to be regulated higher.

tities of quinine-contaminated food to maintain their initial weight; a reduced resting metabolism contributes to their obesity. Normal weight rats put on a highly palatable diet (to achieve what is known as diet-induced obesity) increase their consumption and initially show an increase in metabolic rate that slows the rate of weight gain, but continued feeding on a high fat diet results in substantial weight gain and eventually an adjustment of the now-obese rats' metabolic rate to a level appropriate for their increased body mass. If they are calorically restricted, their metabolic rate will fall (Keesey, 1986). Obese rats made heavy by ventromedial hypothalamus lesions also defend their obese body weights when subjected to over- or underfeeding (Hoebel & Teitelbaum, 1966). However, such obesity may be due to an exaggerated response to palatable diets (Keesey, 1986).[14] Thus it may be a failure in regulation rather than an elevated set point.

With the one above-noted exception, normal and abnormal weight rats successfully defend their weight when subjected to forced weight gain or weight loss. The mechanism by which this maintenance occurs is thought to be changes in resting metabolism. Resting metabolism goes up when animals are forced to gain weight and goes down when they are forced to lose weight; this adjustment in metabolic rate is greater than what would be expected on the basis of body mass change alone (Keesey, 1986).

The first type of human evidence to support the set point theory is the studies mentioned earlier. Men persuaded to undergo semistarvation diet and reduce their weights by 25% returned to their original weight when then given unrestricted access to food (Keys et al., 1950). Individuals showed a weight gain of approximately 15–25% when induced to overconsume for a long time period, but restored their weight to their initial level when they were no longer induced to overeat (Sims, 1976). In addition, it appears that the body adjusts its metabolic rate when weight is lost or gained in an attempt to compensate for the increase or decrease in energy consumption. That is, the metabolic rate of humans increases by as much as 28% (even after corrected for body weight) when weight is increased, making weight gains difficult to maintain; conversely weight loss decreases metabolic rate, making weight losses also hard to maintain (Apfelbaum, 1978). This reduced metabolic rate may continue for 6 years or longer after the initial weight loss (Leibel & Hirsch, 1984).

The second type of evidence to support set point theory is the change in preference for sweetness with weight loss (Lowe, 1987). Normally, if glucose is given first, it reduces the pleasantness of most concentrations of sucrose presented following it. However, after weight loss, glucose preload does not decrease liking for sweets (Cabanac & Duclaux, 1970; Cabanac, Duclaux, & Spector, 1971). On the contrary, *increased* liking of sweet substances can occur

---

[14]If ventromedial hypothalamic lesioned rats have their diets adulterated with quinine, they do not become obese and they reduce their intake until their weight is comparable to the nonlesioned animals (Keesey, 1986).

with weight loss (Rodin, Moskowitz, & Bray, 1976). The third type of evidence to support set point theory is the close parallel between hungry individuals' behavior and characteristics often associated with obesity (Nisbett, 1972). That is, obese persons, relative to normal-weight persons, have been found to be more responsive to hedonic differences in the taste of food, to be more emotional, and to be less physically active. Nisbett (1972) argued that obese individuals behave similarly to hungry organisms because they, compared to normal weight ones, often diet and thus are in a chronic state of energy deprivation. Nisbett postulated that the remarkable similarity in behavior associated with both starving organisms and obese persons was due to their both having reduced their weight below set point.

It seems there is not a one-to-one correspondence between changes in metabolic rate and changes in food intake. With mild caloric restriction, rats' weight declined by 9%, but resting metabolism declined by 17% compared to that of unrestricted rats (Keesey, 1986). Similarly, changes occurred in the basal metabolism of the men in Keys et al.'s (1950) study; even after adjusting for lost tissue, resting metabolism was below the expected level by 16%. Similarly, the increase in heat production following a meal reflects more than just the cost of processing the ingested nutrients. Organisms expend greater than expected energy rates when food consumption increases and body weight goes above the normally maintained level. This energy expenditure adjustment contributes to stable weight. By increasing or decreasing the rate of energy expended, one can mute the effects of overconsumption or conserve when underconsuming. This could account for why most dieters only lose a limited number of pounds before even the reduced quantity that they now consume is sufficient to sustain their weight (Keesey, 1986).

The mechanism for set point determination is not known at present. There are two popular sites suggested: the fat cells and the hypothalamus. It has been postulated that fat cell size may partially determine one's set point by giving off the appropriate signal in some form of biochemical message (Bjorntorp, 1986). This view is based on the investigation into the development of adipose tissue in young animals and the cell structure of obese and thin animals (Sjostrom, 1980). There is evidence that suggests that the number of fat cells is determined by genes as well as by environmental experiences (Garrow, 1986).

It was previously thought that adult weight gains were associated only with increase in fat cell size (hypertrophy) since it was believed that fat cell multiplication could occur only during early periods of development prior to adulthood. However, this notion has been reevaluated (Sjostrom, 1980). Bjorntorp (1986) now suggests that when increased consumption occurs the extra nutrients are stored in the existing fat cells. The fat cells (adipocytes) already in existence will increase in volume to a certain critical size. However, before fat cells reach their maximum capacity, an increase of cells to support the fat cells and a multiplication of nondetermined adipocyte precursor cells (which could become either fat cells or some other type of cell) begin. When existing fat cells are full, the previously undetermined precursor cells are ready to make an irreversible change into fat cells. The signal for fat cell multiplication probably circulates in the blood plasma or serum, but the nature of the triggering of the change from precursors to fat cells is unknown (Domangue, 1987). Thus any shift in energy balance that causes fat cell size to change physiologically may be resisted at first, then followed by an increase in fat cell size, and lastly followed by an increase in fat cell number.[15] In support of this theory, there is evidence that fat tissue surgically removed from a groups of rats results in their eating less and also weighing less with no change in the size of the fat cells despite being fed a fattening diet. A second source of support for the theory comes from the finding that obese females on a weight reduction regimen lost weight only until their fat cell size returned to "normal"; the number of cells does not change (Bjorntorp, 1986). In opposition to the fat cell notion is the argument that persons with hypertrophic obesity (enlarged fat cells) should be more successful at weight loss than those with hyperplastic obesity (increased number of fat cells), and that there is no evidence to support this (Lowe, 1987). In addition, if fat cell size determines set point, it should have some association with eating. However, there is little evidence to suggest that fat cell size has a direct effect on eating (Booth, 1980).

The hypothalamus certainly plays a role in determining the set point. Lesions in the ventromedial hypothalamus lead a rat to overeat, and lesions in the lateral hypothalamus lead a rat to become anorectic. These weight changes are defended when challenged (Keesey, 1986). For lesions in the ventromedial hypothalamus, the larger the lesion the more ravenous the eating. Following brain surgery, animals exhibit behavior very similar to bulimia: eating large quantities of food, appearing unable to stop, and manifesting agitation if prevented from eating. However, once some new weight has been established, meal patterns are only slightly different from the normal pattern. If the lesioned animals are induced to lose weight, when given the opportunity, they will eat excessively until their new postlesion weight is reached again. Lateral hypothalamus lesioned rats, although initially anorectic, eventually ingest food and maintain a below-normal body weight. These lateral hypothalamus lesioned rats metabolically defend a reduced body weight. If induced to gain weight by a palatable diet, their resting metabolic rate increases and they show the anticipated decline in metabolic rate. If their intake is restricted again, they lose weight (Keesey, 1986). Observations that may be inconsistent with neural set point are that: (1) most obesity begins

---

[15]Obese men have many more medical complications than women of similar degree of obesity. These sex differences lie partly in the distribution of body fat. The female type of fat distribution enlargement of the femoral gluteal regions is only weakly associated with medical complications of obesity. The male type of fat distribution is with enlarged abdominal fat. Obesity characterized by female fat distribution corresponds to hyperplastic obesity. There are more fat cells in the large femoral-gluteal fat deposit. The male distribution corresponds to the hypertrophic obesity (Bjorntorp, 1986).

in adulthood; (2) weight changes are often precipitated by environmental stresses (e.g., getting a new job, going to college, marrying); and (3) weight is strongly influenced by variety and palatability of food available (Lowe, 1987).

Set Point as an Explanation of Obesity   A number of studies have examined environmental versus genetic contributions to weight. Stunkard et al. (1986), using 540 adult adoptees and their biological and adoptive parents, found that there was a significant relationship between body mass index of the biological parents and weight class of their biological children and that there was no relationship between adoptee weight class and the body mass index of adoptive parents. Although this finding does not explain the recent increases in the prevalence of obesity in the population, the genetic contribution is consistent with a biological mechanism of weight regulation.

Set point theory offers an explanation for differences in weight and obesity that is consistent with the above finding. It also offers a parsimonious explanation for the difficulties dieters encounter in attempting to lose weight. Using the rat obesity models, one could postulate that human obesity is either the result of regulatory failure (the ventromedial hypothalamus lesioned rats being the prototype) or the result of an elevated set point (the genetically fat Zucker rats being the prototype) (Keesey, 1986). Consider the hypothesis that obesity is the result of an elevated set point. The Zucker rats display metabolic resistance to change in weight such that increased consumption results in an increase in metabolic rate and a decreased intake leads to a decrease in metabolic rate. Similarly, in humans, the majority of obese patients a) do display a large decline in metabolic rate with even modest weight loss, b) show diet-induced thermogenesis (James & Trayhurn, 1981), and c) continue to display reduced metabolic rates even after 6 years if they continue to maintain reduced weight (Domangue, 1987; Keesey, 1986; Keesey & Corbett, 1984; Leibel & Hirsch, 1984). However, there are a small but significant number of obese patients who do not make adjustments in resting metabolism when confronted with changes in intake, heat production, and so forth. Keesey (1986) suggests that perhaps these may be more similar to the ventromedial hypothalamus lesioned rats, who also do not display normal metabolic resistance to weight gain but who may display regulatory failure. Thus it is possible that there may be at least two distinct types of obesity (Keesey, 1986).

Problems with Set Point Theory   Set point theory posits that weight remains relatively stable because of the set point that the body maintains (whether via neural mechanisms or fat cell mechanisms). Factors recently discovered that have been shown to reduce or increase weight must be accounted for by formulating a mechanism by which the set point changes. For instance, it is postulated that exercise can alter set point since it has been reported that metabolic rate is elevated for many hours after exercise in trained athletes (Garrow, 1986).

The fact that obese individuals on diets have a decrease in metabolism is another example which requires postulating a change in set point. However, the addition of exercise restores metabolism to preexisting, dieting levels (Stern, 1984). Stopping the exercise returns body weight and metabolism to pre-exercise level. Caution must be taken when generalizing these results to normal weight individuals since the study concentrated on overweight individuals. Changes in body weight also accompany shifts in the ovarian hormones, cessation of smoking, and aging, and thus may involve shifts in set point (Klesges, Meyers, Klesges, & LaVasque, 1989). In addition, when animals are put through repeated cycles of weight loss and gain, the reduction in metabolic rate during weight reduction becomes more pronounced with each weight loss (Garrow, 1986). Further research would be helpful in determining whether reductions in metabolic rate occur because energy intake or expenditure is directly influenced or because the set point has changed.

There are other problems with the set point theory. Some have viewed it as tautological (Lowe, 1987). Without a direct measure of set point, it must be inferred from its behavioral or metabolic effects (e.g., resting metabolism). Weight stability is the most frequently used indicator. Set point is assumed to be that level at which an organism feeds on an unrestricted schedule to maintain its weight. Although this may be reasonable for animal work, it is unacceptable for human beings since many people, especially woman, probably restrict their caloric intake to some extent (Rozin & Fallon, 1988) and weight stability could be influenced by a variety of developmental and social factors other than set point (Lowe, 1987). In humans, it is difficult to discern whether people maintain a high body weight because they are prewired to do so by way of a set point or because they are ingesting more than others in response to increased variety and palatability. Additionally, set point theory would predict that increasing hunger would be the result of continued caloric restriction. However, there is evidence that prolonged caloric restriction *decreases* hunger (Wooley, Wooley, & Dyrenforth, 1979). Third, the effects of some drugs (such as amphetamines and fenfluramine) thought to produce anorectic effects by lowering the set point should be dose related. However, there is no relationship between the drug dose and body weight reduction. Related to this, substitution of one anorectic drug for a second equipotent one produces additional weight losses even though the effect of the two drugs on set point should be the same (Lowe, 1987). To explain this effect without abandoning the set point, it must be postulated that drugs appear to induce weight loss by influencing appetite (reducing the size of the meal), not by altering set point (Blundell & A. J. Hill, 1989).

The postulation of and belief in a set point have additional hazards. The belief in and concretization of this concept may create a "cognitive set point" that discourages individuals from weight loss efforts: efforts to change weight have considerable physiological and psychological consequences without attributing these to a set point mechanism which "implies an unchangeable biological entity" (Lowe, 1987, p.32).

The Effects of Food Palatability and Variety on Weight

One of the biggest problems with set point theory comes in trying to account for the individual environmental influences on individual weight regulation, namely palatability and variety. Unrestricted availability of a variety of highly palatable (high fat and/or sugar content) foods results in significant weight gain both during development and in the mature organism (Sclafani, 1980). Animals maintain body weights that are in direct proportion to the palatability of their diets (Peck, 1978). Conversely, switching from a palatable diet to a normal diet results in a discontinuation of behaviorally defending the higher weight by adjusting intake amount. However, if animals are maintained on this palatable diet for months, they may fail to return to normal weight even when placed back on a regular diet, perhaps due to an increased fat cell number (Keesey, 1986). For humans in the short run, the more palatable the food, the more people will eat (S. W. Hill & McCutcheon, 1975) and the more quickly they will eat it (Bellisle & LeMagnen, 1981).

Similarly, increasing variety has been shown to enhance food intake in the short term and potentially contribute to the development of obesity (Rolls & Hetherington, 1989). The more varied the foods are in terms of both sensory properties (e.g., taste, smell, texture, appearance) and cognitive properties or categories (e.g., soups can be seen as similar even if their sensory properties are very different), the greater the food intake will be (Rolls & Hetherington, 1989). This effect is more noticeable if the foods are also palatable (Pliner, Polivy, Herman, & Zakalusny, 1980). In addition, there seems to be little relationship between the degree of hunger that subjects claim to have had and their consumption (Rolls, Rowe, Rolls, Kingston, Megson, & Gunary, 1981).

In the short run the findings of increased intake at a single sitting with increased palatability and variety cannot be explained by the effects of postabsorption changes in the sensory processing of the responses to food. What does seem to change over the course of ingestion is the perceived pleasantness of the food; that is, the reward or hedonic value of the food changes in response to continued eating of the food. This decrease in pleasantness in a food with continued eating is known as sensory-specific satiety and seems to be associated with changes in the lateral hypothalamus and gustatory cortex (Rolls & Hetherington, 1989). There is some evidence, however, that post-ingestive factors in the long term may be more important than orosensory factors in determining the intake of different types and forms of dietary fat (Sclafani, 1989).

Interestingly, bulimics seem to display little sensory-specific satiety, even when they have consumed great quantities of food (Hetherington & Rolls, 1987). This failure to experience sensory-specific satiety may in part explain how bulimics are able to consume large amounts of food during single episodes.

There are fewer studies to assess the effects of variety on long-term weight regulation. In rats the greater the available variety of foods during development, the more obese they become (Rolls, Van Duijvenvoorde, & Rowe, 1983). Obesity resulting from the presentation of a variety of palatable foods has been termed "dietary obesity" (Sclafani & Springer, 1976). Although there are no long-term controlled studies in humans, the presentation of a monotonous (and probably not very palatable) liquid diet led both obese and normal weight individuals to restrict intake and lose weight (Cabanac & Rabe, 1976). Conversely, a varied and palatable diet led to overeating and weight gain in less than a week for both normal and obese people (Rolls & Hetherington, 1989).

Dietary Restraint and the Boundary Model

If a set point exists, then a woman whose weight is below her set point will have to persistently make an effort to maintain her weight. Thus continual efforts to avoid eating and gaining weight might indicate that she is below her set point. The construct of "restraint" (Herman & Mack, 1975) was originally developed to explain the differences in eating patterns between obese and normal weight people. In restraint theory, dieting is assumed to be a key factor in food regulation (Herman & Polivy, 1988). It is consistent with Nisbett's formulation (1972) that obese individuals' set points were higher than the average set point and that many "obese characteristics" were the result of obese persons' chronic efforts to attain normal weight. That is, they are characteristics of existing in a state of semistarvation, not of being obese. Herman and Polivy proposed that eating patterns are determined by a balance between the physiological factors of hunger and satiety and conscious efforts to resist the desire for food. This cognitively mediated effort to resist eating they called "restraint." They developed a restraint scale to differentiate between those individuals who worry about food intake and attempt to restrain themselves from eating and those who do not (Herman & Mack, 1975). Their assumption was that people who were below their set point would need to maintain a careful watch over their intake.

Two basic hypotheses are at the heart of this theory. The first states that restrained eaters develop eating patterns characterized by periods of restraint (dieting)[16] and overindulgence (Herman & Polivy, 1980). That is, self-control

---

[16]In this chapter the terms "dieting" and "restraint" have been used interchangeably as Herman and Polivy presented them in their boundary model. However, they are not functionally equivalent in that a high score on the restraint scale reflects a history of dieting but does not necessarily reflect current dieting. Weight loss due to dieting affects current eating differently than restraint. Restrained eaters eat more than unrestrained eaters in a preload condition but less without a preload. Restrained

of the restrained eater may be temporarily interfered with by certain circumstances called "disinhibitors." When this happens, the restrained eater may ingest large quantities of food. Herman and Polivy's basic empirical finding was that restrained and unrestrained eaters respond differently to food depending on whether they have had prior food (a "preloading"). Unrestrained eaters regulated their eating (i.e., ate a substantial amount of ice cream with no preload, but decreased their ice cream consumption after a preload of a milkshake) (Herman & Mack, 1975). Restrained eaters ate less ice cream than unrestrained eaters with no preload, but ate more ice cream than unrestrained eaters following a preload. The finding that unrestrained eaters regulate (eat less) and restrained eaters "counterregulate" (eat more) following a preload has been replicated many times (Ruderman, 1986). A preload, Herman and Polivy argued, was restraint releasing or disinhibiting. They proposed that any disinhibition, such as alcohol, anxiety, fear, or depression (Herman & Polivy, 1975; Ruderman, 1986), disrupted the restrained eaters and unleashed "deprivation-motivated eating behavior" (Herman & Polivy, 1975, p. 672).

Origins of Restraint: Cognitive versus Biological   When actual weight loss produces physiological effects that permit overeating to occur, the caloric deficit is not of sufficient magnitude to account for the amount consumed. In fact, restrained eaters are less sensitive than unrestrained eaters to the caloric deprivation effects (Herman & Polivy, 1984; 1988). Yet they are more likely than unrestrained eaters to overestimate caloric content (Stanton & Tips, 1990). Herman and Polivy propose that the initiation of counterregulation occurs for cognitive reasons. Restraint theory emphasized conscious attempts to restrict food intake rather than deviation from the set point; dieters are characterized by their attempts to lose weight rather than by their weight loss per se because in fact they do not lose much weight (Herman & Polivy, 1984). To support this cognitive notion, investigators (Huon & Wooton, 1991; Polivy 1976; Spencer & Fremouw, 1979; Woody, Constanzo, Liefer, & Conger, 1981) found that persons' beliefs about the caloric content of the preloads influenced their subsequent ingestion. Restrained people counterregulated after they ingested a preload they believed to be high in calories, whether the preload was actually high or low in calories. That is, restrained eaters ingested more (counterregulated) and unrestrained eaters ingested less (regulated) after preloads described as high in caloric value than after preloads portrayed as low in caloric value. Similar results were found when there were anticipated dietary violations; both restrained and unrestrained eaters' responses to anticipating preloads were similar to actual preloads (Ruderman, Belzer, & Halperin, 1985). Forcing subjects to be aware of their

---

eaters eat more than unrestrained eaters in a preload condition but less without a preload. Weight loss (i.e., dieting) increases eating independently of preload status (Lowe, Witlow, & Bellwoar, 1991).

behavior decreases the counterregulatory behavior of restrained eaters (Polivy, Herman, Hackett, & Kuleshnyk, 1986). Similarly, the consumption of restrained eaters after preloads can be decreased by the perceived presence of others (Ruderman, 1986) and by being induced to perceive themselves as "good dieters" (Polivy & Herman, 1991). These findings suggest that altering the caloric value of a preload has little effect on how many calories are eaten subsequently; in other words, people do not necessarily respond to the nutritive value of what they have just eaten by adjusting their intake immediately. There is some evidence that people do modulate their eating over time to adjust for the effects of varying preloads, but that change in the amount does not necessarily match the preload differences (Garrow, 1986).

Counterregulation Polivy and Herman (1985) have abandoned their initial idea that restrained eaters are below set point and now argue that the commencement and extent of counterregulatory eating by restrained eaters originates from their cognitive make-up and conditioning history (Lowe, 1987). Polivy and Herman (1985) acknowledge a number of physiological and hormonal differences between restrained and unrestrained eaters: restrained eaters seem to salivate more than unrestrained eaters in response to palatable food and have elevated motilin (associated with gastric emptying) and depressed insulin levels and pancreatic polypeptide responses. These differences suggest that restrained eaters are physiologically hungrier than nonrestrained eaters. Both physiological responses and hormonal differences may permit excessive eating to occur. However, Polivy and Herman (1985) think that physiological and possibly hormonal variations may contribute to or modulate eating of the dieter by affecting the disposition of whatever food is ingested (e.g., food is more likely to be retained as stored energy), rather than to affect eating behavior (e.g., amount, type) at a single setting. Thus in the absence of situational or cognitive inhibition these hormonal and physiological differences remain latent.

Herman and Polivy acknowledge that the origin of diminished satiety responses among restrained eaters may in part be the physiological consequences of weight loss. However, their belief is that reduced sensitivity to hunger and satiety is mostly due to either an unwillingness or an inability to perceive internal states and/or conditioning history (Herman & Polivy, 1988). With satiety signals ignored or not perceived, the individual can eat greater amounts. That is, dieting, which substitutes cognitive for physiological controls over ingestion contributes or may even lead to muting of satiety signals. There are at least two possible explanations of the mechanism for counterregulation. The assumption of restraint theory is that *restraint* (e.g., going on a diet or concern about weight) is the primary defect. Rodin (1981) postulated that *external responsiveness* is the central mechanism that leads to conscious food restraint for some people. This is supported by the finding that weight loss itself produces an increase in taste responsiveness (Rodin et al., 1976). Furthermore, the obese were more responsive to taste cues than normal-weight individuals even before their weight loss. This sensitivity to environmental cues creates additional pressures on dieting and perhaps increases the pressure of restraint contributing to counterregulation. A major difference between set point theory and restraint theory, then, is that set point theory explains diet-induced appetitive adjustments without reference to cognition, whereas restraint theory explains those behaviors in terms of cognition (Lowe, 1987).

A second hypothesis of the restraint model concerns differences between normal-weight and obese people. Obese people are expected to show higher levels of restraint. Differences between obese and normal weight people are the result of conscious restraint rather than deprivation (Nisbett, 1972) or obesity. There is considerable evidence that restraint in normal weight persons is associated with many characteristics once thought to be a reflection of obesity "syndrome" (Herman & Polivy, 1980). For example, obese subjects eat more (although not significantly) following a preload and less with no preload than normal-weight subjects do (Schachter, Goldman, & Gordon, 1968). Both restrained normal-weight persons and obese persons are "hyperemotional" (Polivy, Herman, & Warsh, 1978). Both obese subjects and restrained eaters salivate more than normal-weight and unrestrained eaters when exposed to palatable foods (Klajner, Herman, Polivy, & Chhabra, 1981). There is little evidence that obese people counterregulate (see Lowe, 1992 for an exception). To the contrary, some studies show that overweight people regulate their intake better than normal-weight people (Ruderman, 1986).

Herman and Polivy (1984) have incorporated these hypotheses into a model they refer to as the boundary model. They propose that biological pressures attempt to maintain intake within a range: hunger keeps intake above a certain level, and satiety works to keep intake below some maximum level. The zone between the boundaries is known as a zone of "biological indifference." Within this zone, psychological factors have their greatest impact on consumption. The zone of biological indifference is wider for dieters than nondieters (requiring a greater deprivation for them to report hunger and greater intake of food for them to report satiety). In addition, restrained eaters have a self-imposed boundary indicating their maximum desired intake. Once restrained eaters have transgressed the self-imposed boundaries, they continue to eat until they reach the satiety boundary (Herman & Polivy, 1984).

Restraint as a Cause of Bulimia   The many similarities between dieting and bulimia can potentially aid in the understanding of bulimia (Herman & Polivy, 1987). Bulimia begins by dieting.[17] Chronic dieting results in hunger, frustration, and impaired ability to judge satiety (Herman & Polivy, 1988). Once

---

[17]Bulimia is almost always preceded by dieting, although dieting does not inevitably lead to bulimia (Polivy & Herman, 1985).

disinhibited, dieters and bulimics eat excessively compared to normal eaters and also compared to what is physiologically needed. Dieting leads to an all-or-none pattern of eating; dieters and bulimics go for longer periods of time without eating and eat more when they finally do eat than normal eaters. Both also seem to forget what has been ingested and experience guilt afterwards. Both are hyperemotional. Additional research on the extent to which dieting resembles eating disorders would be fruitful (Herman & Polivy, 1987, 1988).

Although dieting seems to be a precondition for binging, dieting and/or inadequate satiety signals are not the proximal causes of binging. While more women (20.7%) than men (8.9%) are restrained eaters, not all restrained eaters have bulimia nervosa (Rand & Kuldan, 1991). Herman and Polivy (1988) believe it is the emotional distress and loss of control that are the proximal cause of binging. Frustration plus the lack of strongly conditioned satiety signals means that once inhibitions are broken, greater ingestion will occur and override normal satiety pressures (potentially prolonging the binge).

Herman and Polivy (1987, 1988) acknowledge differences between the dieter's behavior and the bulimic's behavior. Bulimics and normal dieters differ in the quantity that they ingest. Dieters will stop eating with a sufficient preload (Herman, Polivy, & Esses, 1990). Bulimics seem to stop because they are physically unable to hold more, the situation does not permit it, or emotional exhaustion occurs. For normal dieters, the palatability has profound effects on the amount eaten. If the food is unpalatable, the eating will be squelched for the dieter (Herman & Polivy, 1988). Bulimics seem relatively unaware of external cues: they exhibit preferences for certain types of foods (Rosen, Letenberg, Fisher, & Khazan, 1986), but will eat almost anything once a binge has begun. Whereas nondieters are relatively unaffected by the possible scrutiny of others, dieters and restrained eaters will regulate intake in the presence of others. Bulimics are even more profoundly affected by the presence of others in that their binges occur only in private.

For a dieter, a preload may be conceived of as distressing. Distress then interferes with self-control or restraint. For the bulimic, however, emotions are more central. Bulimics interpret their emotional turmoil in terms of hunger; distress is reinterpreted as an urge to binge. Binging can serve further as a distraction from anxiety. Binging permits the refocusing of anxiety onto a source that is more psychologically manageable and that masks the real, more vague, less controlable source. Although mainly anecdotal, there is some evidence that binging results in a temporary decrease in anxiety (Kaye, Gwirtsman, George, Weis, & Jimerson, 1986; S. Steinberg, Tobin, & Johnson, 1990). The central role that eating and purging occupy in the emotional life of an individual may be in part caused by "the diet culture" of today (Herman & Polivy, 1988).

Problems with Restraint Theory   Both set point theory and restraint theory suggest that permanent weight loss should be difficult to attain and next to impossible to sustain. However, there is evidence to the contrary. Schachter (1982) interviewed 40 previously obese subjects who had tried to lose weight on their own. Approximately two-thirds were less than 10% overweight. Another large-scale interview found that approximately one-third of the overweight individuals were now within the normal weight range (Lowe, 1987). Although Polivy and Herman (1985) suggest that dieting and weight loss predispose individuals to counterregulation, successful dieters seem to be an exception. That is, those individuals who successfully maintained a weight loss scored lower on the restraint scale, were less responsive to negative emotions, thought less about food, and engaged in less binging than those who had lost and regained weight (Lowe, 1987). It may be the case that many of the restraint studies have not captured that part of the sample that does not show counterregulation. For example, Lowe (1992) found that overweight dieters when asked to go off their diets ate less in the taste test situation than overweight dieters who remained on their diets. Long-term studies are needed to explore the psychological, physiological (fat cell and metabolic), and sensory (taste responsiveness) factors that predict who is most likely to show a positive long-term response to weight reduction.

SOCIOCULTURAL PRESSURES

Although individual biology may constrain the limits of an individuals's weight loss or gain, culturally bound and socially shared definitions of appropriate or ideal weight play a very important part in the development of body image and the maintenance of weight. In fact the primary predictor of weight loss behaviors and binging in adolescents is the desire for a thinner body size (Wertheim, Paxton, Maude, Szmukler, Gibbons, & Hiller, 1992). As argued elsewhere (Fallon, 1990), a woman's body image includes her perception of the cultural standards,[18] her perception of the extent to which she matches the standard, and the perception of the relative importance that she and members of her cultural group place on that match. It is culture, not nature, that determines that the pear-shaped, well-rounded, and fleshed-out portrait of Botticelli's Venus (in the *Birth of Venus*) was the ideal, or that Jayne Mansfield, Mae West, or Marilyn Monroe are the ideal and not the cachectic look of 91-pound Leslie Hornby Armstrong (known as "Twiggy"). Membership in or identification with a particular group can have a powerful influence on one's judgments of one's own attributes. With respect to body image and attractiveness, at least four types of groupings deserve special attention: social class, culture, sex, and occupation. The focus on these particular groupings is the result of the differences in prevalence rates of the

---

[18]One must differentiate between individual. Perception of the ideal rather than the actual ideal held by the rest of the culture is important. Research has shown that an individual or subgroup of individuals can have different perceptions as to what is ideal (Fallon & Rozin, 1985).

eating disorders between these groups. In this section, differences and similarities in each of these groups' conceptions of attractiveness and body image will be explored. The culture and class differences in standards of body shape attractiveness and attitudes toward dieting have been considered as major mediating factors in the concomitant (though correlational) prevalence differences in the eating disorders. In addition, the burgeoning mass media industry has played a crucial role in creating more awareness of standards of the ideal body.

Social Class

Beauty and wealth have been associated with each other throughout history and in various cultures. The most powerful members of the group are able to obtain that which is most valued by the particular group. Their power and wealth have made them targets for emulation. In this way they have the power to dictate trends in fashion. Trends tend to filter down from the "haves" to the "have nots" and discontinue when they become attainable by the "have nots." Weight and shape are particularly poignant examples of this. In past centuries in the Orient, a visibly well-fed woman brought honor to her husband; her abundance confirmed his affluence. There are reports that powerful chieftains may force-feed their wives as testimony to their wealth. A century ago in Western culture a curvy bosomed woman signified luxury. When resources are scarce, weight is associated with prosperity, and plump men and women are admired. In developing countries (where food resources may still be scarce), obesity is more prevalent in the higher social classes than in the lower classes for men, women, and children (Sobal & Stunkard, 1987). However, when resources are plentiful, the weight ideal reverses.

Today, in countries where the fear of starvation has disappeared the rounded belly has lost its ostentatious grandness and has become a symbol of self-indulgence. Upper-class aristocratic women were formerly fat and well fed, then thin and delicate, now firm and fit. It is still mainly upper-middle-class women who have the resources (time and money) to pursue the current fashion trend. Both the pursuit of thinness and the firm, fit look in late 20th century Western society (in which food is plentiful) may have begun as a visible upper-class repudiation of the "common" shape. The Duchess of Windsor is reported is to have said, "A woman can never be too rich or too thin." The connection between thinness and upper-class membership may even be responsible for a favorable stereotype being applied to anorexia nervosa ("Golden Girl Disease"). As the rich become thin and fit, the body becomes a form of "inconspicuous consumption" that distinguishes the upper classes from the lower classes.

The overrepresentation of anorexia and bulimia among upper-social-class women has been observed repeatedly (Garfinkel & Garner, 1982; Garner, Garfinkel, & Olmstead, 1983; Gowers & McMahon, 1989) in the United States and Britain. Conversely, obesity occurs seven times more frequently in American women in the lower socioeconomic classes than in the highest socioeconomic class. No consistent relationship between obesity and social class has been found for men or children (Sobal & Stunkard, 1987).

From these examples, it is clear that women of the upper classes have idealized images that require the pursuit of thinness and most recently of fitness. Although such a goal is ostensibly available to all those that abstain (or can purge), which would include all social classes, it requires considerable time, effort, self-discipline, and social and financial support that are actually only available to the social class with leisure time. Thus the attainment of desirable weight and/or shape is essential for those desiring social admiration and power.

Culture

Every culture or subculture[19] has its unique definition of beauty. A complementary greeting for the Punjab (East) Indians translates into "You look fresh and fat today" (reported in Garner, Garfinkel, & Oimstead, 1983). Although anthropological reports offer detailed impressions of beauty for a multitude of cultures (Fallon, 1990; Liggett, 1974; Morris, 1985), there have been few systematic attempts to study perceptions of the cultural body ideal. Because methodology in measuring body image is so diverse, unless the study makes a direct comparison of two different cultures, it is difficult to draw cross cultural conclusions. It is clear that the United States, Britain, and parts of Europe share a desire for a thin female figure as the ideal (Fallon & Rozin, 1985; Nylander, 1971). For the most part, it is unclear whether any differences exist between these groups in terms of degree of thinness because of the lack of comparative studies.

A study investigating attitudes about body weight and appearance in undergraduate psychology students was conducted at the Flinders University of South Australia and at the University of Vermont (Tiggemann & Rothblum, 1988). Half the subjects thought themselves to be overweight to some degree, although only one-fifth of the sample was actually overweight. Weight was a much greater issue for all women, who felt more overweight, dieted more, expressed more body consciousness, and reported that weight had interfered more with social activities than did men. Vermont students reported greater frequency of dieting, more concern about weight, and more body consciousness than did Australian students. Men and women in both cultures stereotyped obese bodies significantly more negatively than they did nonobese bodies. The negative stereotypes were more prevalent for the fat female body, and women tended to rate thin and fat bodies more discrepantly than did the men. The results indicate excessive and

---

[19]The initial research suggested that eating disorders (anorexia and bulimia) were confined to white upper-middle-class females. However, more recently, an increasing number of studies have suggested that the prevalence in minorities in the United States has been underreported. Although still somewhat controversial, there is increasing evidence that the prevalence rates are similarly high for minorities such as Hispanics and Native Americans (Smith & Krejci, 1991).

maladaptive concerns with weight among women and American students in particular. If this study is representative of other comparisons between the United States and other Western countries, then we may conclude that the United States has an even greater preference for a thin ideal than many other Western cultures. Indeed incidences of symptoms of eating disorders even in parts of Western Europe such as Spain (Raich, Rosen, Deus, Perez, Requena, & Gross, 1992) and France (Ledoux, Choquet, & Flament, 1991) have been shown to be lower than the United States and Canada.

Little systematic work has been conducted on historical or current aspects of body image in nonwestern countries. Some has suggested that there is a positive correlation between body weight and social status and that obesity may be valued as a symbol of success and economic security (Sobal & Stunkard, 1987). Conversely, anorexia nervosa and bulimia nervosa appear to be relatively uncommon in developing countries (Dolan, 1990; Dolan & Ford, 1991; Garner et al., 1983; Lacey & Dolan, 1988; McCarthy, 1990; Nasser, 1986). Surveys have indicated that while eating disorders do exist in countries such as China (Chun, Mitchell, Li, Yu, Lan, Rong, Huan, Filice, Pomeroy & Pyle, 1992) and Pakistan (Choudry & Mumford, 1992; Mumford, Whitehouse & Choudry, 1992) there is a lower incidence of anorexia and bulimia nervosa. Mumford and his colleagues conducted surveys of eating disorders in the United Kingdom and two towns in Pakistan (Choudry & Mumford, 1992; Mumford & Whitehouse, 1988; Mumford, Whitehouse & Choudry, 1992). They found fewer eating disorders among school girls in Pakistan than their Asian counterparts growing up in the United Kingdom. There was also evidence that within the Pakistan group, those girls coming from more "westernized" families had a higher prevalence of eating disorders than those girls whose families were less westernized (Thumford, Whitehouse & Choudry, 1992).

To date, only two non-western/western cross-cultural studies have been published. The first compared preferences of Kenyan Asian, Kenyan British, and British females for various body shapes. There was relatively little disagreement between the groups on the most attractive figures. What was different was the judgment of the obese figures. The British females judged and described the obese figures more negatively than the Kenyan Asians (Furnham & Alibhai, 1983). This study is of interest for two reasons. First, there is no difference in what any of the three groups find most attractive. What does separate the groups is how negatively they view the heavier figures. This finding potentially contradicts the view expressed earlier that third world countries *prefer* a plump figure. Secondly, this study, similar to the studies mentioned above (British-Asians and Native-Asians) suggests that although the foundation of the formulation of ideal body image may be one's intrapsychic life or one's native culture, residence in another culture can cause a change in one's perception of what is ideal in the direction of the "adopted" culture. This study does not compare the extent to which each individual matches the "ideal." In an unpublished study designed to explore just that, Indian and United States male and female college students were asked to indicate their perception of their current and ideal shape. The study concluded that Indian women are similar to Indian and American men, with their ideal being not much different than their current figure. It is only American women for whom there is a significant discrepancy between their current and ideal shapes (Fallon, Rozin, Gogineni, & Desai, 1993).

The several studies of the relations between body weight (and obesity) to socioeconomic status in third world countries have led to the inference that a plump figure is the ideal. Since a great deal of evidence has accrued that the increase in eating disorders is in part the result of sociocultural pressures (Garner et al., 1983), we may hypothesize that the reverse inference may also be true; those cultures that have a higher incidence of bulimia and anorexia nervosa have a thinner ideal. McCarthy (1990) found that for those countries that have a thin ideal there is an increased rate of eating disorders and a higher rate of depression among women.[20]

Identification with one's cultural group (whether it be native or adopted) is important in the individual's perception of what is ideal. It also plays a role in the importance that the individual places on the match of his or her own body with the ideal. It follows that the more pressure an individual feels to conform to a shape that is different than his or her own, the more steps he or she will take to reduce this difference, whether by gorging or by dieting, purging, or surgery.

The Social Stigma of Obesity   Many have written about the discrimination, social isolation, and resulting low self-esteem that have been the result of even moderate obesity (A. E. Anderson, 1985; Chernin, 1981; Freedman, 1986). Children as young as 5 years of age in this culture can discriminate body types and discriminate against overweight children. The overweight child is regarded as responsible for the condition by both children and adults; failure to ameliorate the "problem" is regarded as a personal weakness (Dyrenforth, Wooley, & Wooley, 1980). Overweight children and their silhouettes are less liked than normal weight or thin figures (Lerner & Gellert, 1969). Both normal weight and overweight children themselves describe obese children and silhouettes in pejorative terms such as stupid, lazy, dirty, sloppy, mean, and ugly (Staffieri, 1967,

---

[20]McCarthy (1990) postulates that a cultural ideal of thinness that is below the average weight of women in that culture increases the risk of depression by the way of increasing the amount of body dissatisfaction and importance attached to weight. When cultural expectations set up impossible standards, failure contributes to depression. This notion is supported by the fact that females outnumber males 3:1 in incidence of clinical depression in the United States. Furthermore, women distort their bodies in a negative way, just as depressed people do (Noles, Cash, & Winstead, 1985). Men distort their bodies in a more positive way, just as nondepressed people do. People who se themselves as less attractive than they really are seem to be more prone to depression.

1972). The obese individual is considered even more deviant than someone with physical deformities (Richardson, Goodman, Hastorf, & Dornbusch, 1961).[21]

Although not as openly straightforward, the prejudices against obese adults are similar. For example, obese adults are considered less attractive, competent, productive, industrious, and influential and more disorganized (Chetwynd, Stewart, & Powell, 1975; Dyrenforth et al., 1980). These attitudes are reflected in the way people behave towards the obese. For instance, people are less likely to agree to assist a heavy person than his or her thin counterpart (C. L. Steinberg & Birk, 1983), and heavy executives often earn less than do their thin counterparts (McClean & Moon, 1980).

Both students and professionals think of the obese as consuming more food than average weight people and as having "no will power" (Maiman, Wang, Becker, Finlay, & Simonson, 1979). Even physicians share this belief; for example, a majority of physicians at a public outpatient medical clinic described their obese patients as "ugly" and "weak-willed" (Maddox & Liederman, 1969). Thus obese people are viewed by others, including the obese themselves, as less worthy of respect than are other people. They are assumed to have brought the condition upon themselves through overeating. Our culture has provided not only a thin ideal for emulation, but ostracism for those who do not conform. Thus the avoidance of obesity for fear of social ostracism is probably a strong motivation for many dieters. The culture has provided norms (a thin ideal), the motive (ostracism for nonconformity), and a method (a myriad of diets) to give nature a gentle prod if needed. People are told directly and indirectly that if they cared they would be successful with weight loss. Those who ignore their "potential" are considered lazy and bothersome and have only themselves to blame. This negative attitude toward the obese is particularly strong in relation to women. For example, analysis of admission practices at prestigious colleges in the 1960s showed a rejection rate three times higher for overweight girls than for overweight boys with similar academic records (Canning & Mayer, 1966).

Psychologists have attempted to capture statistically the trends of the decreasing weight ideal by looking at some of the beautiful women over the past several decades. Madame Tussard's London Wax Museum every year polls their 3,500 visitors as to who is the most beautiful of all the figures. Until 1970 Elizabeth Taylor was the most admired figure. By 1976 Twiggy (all 91 pounds of her) had reached the number one position (Garfinkel & Garner, 1982).

Another idealized group of women is the pristine beauties—the Miss America contestants and winners. Researchers (Garner, Garfinkel, Schwartz, & Thompson, 1980; Wiseman, Gray, Mosimann & Aherns, 1992) in two separate

---

[21]Not all researchers believe that the social stigma of obesity is as pervasive as it has been portrayed by the popular press. Jarvie, Lahey, Graziano, & Framer (1983) in a critical review of the empirical evidence suggest that studies have not shown a negative stereotype toward the obese and that facial attractiveness, situational contexts, and the degree of obesity are all potential moderators.

studies collecting data over three decades found that Miss America winners have significantly decreased in their weight to height ratio. For example, compare Venus Ramey, Miss America of 1944, who was 5'7" and weighed 125 pounds, to Susan Atkins, Miss America of 1986, 5'9" at 114 pounds. The same researchers also explored *Playboy's* centerfolds, the voluptuous, sultry, sexy beauty queens who have traditionally maintained a little heavier look. They, too, however, have changed their appearance and have had the same weight to height ratio decrease that their pristine counterparts have undergone. Misses America and Playboy centerfolds as well as actresses and models have reflected a shift in what is desirable.

Sex It is likely that females experience more pressure to conform to a cultural ideal than males, in part due to the potential differential of discrimination against women who are heavy (at least in Western culture). Other factors may play a role in the female attitude toward her body and weight: differences in each gender's perceptions of the cultural ideal and their perception of the extent to which they match it. Adolescent boys judge their ideal to be heavier than their current physique; thus they are more interested in gaining or maintaining weight (Lerner & Karabenick, 1974). In contrast, girls' desire for a thinner physique results in pressures to lose weight beginning as young as age six or seven (Collins, 1991) and accelerating through adolescence (Nylander, 1971; Rolls, Fedoroff & Guthrie, 1991). While initially this trend was thought to exist predominantly in Caucasians, there is increasing evidence that similar rates of minorities including Native Americans and Hispanics also experience pressures (Smith & Krejci, 1991; Snow & Harris, 1989).[22] This general thinning in ideal form is in direct opposition to the general increase in body weight over the last 20 years. It is likely that the resulting tension as well as fear of social ostracism will lead to increased effort on the part of women to conform and to increased beliefs in the discrepancy between what the ideal and their current figure weight. College females judge their current figure to be significantly heavier than their ideal figure. In contrast, male college students (as a group) feel themselves to be close to their ideal in weight.[22] (Actually males were as likely to want to gain weight as to lose weight). Both men and women in their forties and fifties share a similar dissatisfaction with body shape; both judge their ideal to be significantly thinner than their current shape (Rozin & Fallon, 1988). The change in men's attitudes appears to result from ideals that remain almost identical to those of their younger male counterparts, even as their actual figure becomes heavier with age. But despite this discrepancy between current and ideal weights, these older men are similar in behavior to younger men with regard to their weight (i.e.,

---

[22]The exception seems to be the Afro-American group who appear to have less thin ideals and ideals that are more congruent with their perceptions of their own size (Rucker & Cash, 1992), less stringent diet tendencies (Thomas & James, 1988), and have concomitant lower prevalence of anorexia and bulimia nervosa (Dolan, 1991; Gray, Ford & Kelley, 1987; Gross & Rosen, 1988).

they are less concerned than women about dieting and weight). Women not only show greater concern about weight, they also engage in many more weight-related activities, as noted in the first section of this chapter.

The female body has more fat than the male body. A women's body has about 25% fat content, whereas 15% is normal for males; this difference is not caused primarily by exercise and strenuous labor. If a thin muscular body is the ideal, women deviate from it.[23] Women may distort further the extent of the overall lack of congruence between their shape and ideal (Fallon & Rozin, 1985) by misjudging themselves as heavier than they are. Men are more accurate than woman in assessing their proper weight; women feel overweight even when they are not. The number of women who consider themselves "too fat" has doubled in the past decade. In addition, women may misjudge what is most attractive to men. They may feel that men like a thinner woman—thinner than a man actually prefers (Fallon & Rozin, 1985). In contrast, men judge their relative weight more accurately and generally feel that their current body shape is very close to what women want in an ideal man. Thus men's perceptions help to keep them satisfied with their bodies, whereas women's perceptions motivate them toward weight obsession and dieting (Fallon & Rozin, 1985). If dieting behavior indicates the degree of concern for achieving the cultural ideal, woman are far more concerned about matching that ideal than are men.[24]

However, many of the large differences between men's and women's ideals may be the result of stereotypical misconceptions of the genders that are more disparaging distortions of women than of men (Cash & Brown, 1989). Females place more cognitive and behavioral emphasis on managing their appearance and on handling physical illness, while being somewhat less oriented toward fitness than men. It may be that women are not as worried and dissatisfied as we are led to think and apparently have come to believe (Cash & Brown, 1989).

Occupation   One's occupation can be thought of as an important subculture to which one belongs. Garner and Garfinkel (1978, 1980) found that students in occupations in which there are intense pressures to maintain low body weight (e.g., dance and modeling) have a higher rate of eating disorders and their milder variants than students of music (Garner & Garfield, 1978; 1980; Steinhausen, Nevmarker, Vollrath, & Newmarker, 1992; Button & Whitehead, 1981; Crago, Yates, Beutler, & Arizmendi, 1985). Even among college women, those who were less "traditionally feminine" preferred smaller breasts, buttocks, and over-

---

[23]The distribution of fat may be of more concern to a woman than simply attaining a thin physique. There is evidence that women with the greatest distribution of their fat in their hips and buttocks relative to the abdomen and waist had more eating disorder symptoms.

[24]Recently, however, several studies have found that men and women did not differ on several *global* measures of body dissatisfaction yet sometimes differed on the specific focus of their discontent. Females generally wanted to be thinner, whereas males were likely to desire to be heavier (L. R. Silberstein, Striegel-Moore, Timko, & Rodin, 1988).

all shape than those women who were more traditionally feminine (Beck, Ward-Hull, & McLear, 1976; Silverstein, Peterson, & Perdue, 1986).

The Role of Mass Media in Promoting a Thin Standard

Twentieth-century technology has had an extremely important impact on self-image and particularly on the body image of women. Throughout history ideal-ized models of feminine beauty have been created and worshiped. However, the romanticized Venus figures of Botticelli's Venus, for example, although glorified were also unattainable. The artist's creations were impressions and not perfect replications of a woman's body. Today, the visual media "perfectly" reproduce the image. The perfect model profile is captured and magnified by the camera in a *seemingly* natural and everyday pose. In this way modern technology may blur the boundaries between romanticism and realism. "Film creates the optical illusions that encourage Ms. Main Street to aspire to Miss Universe" (Freedman, 1986, p. 43).

Whatever geographic variability in beauty standards may have existed in earlier times, the rise in mass media in this century is likely to create more uniform standards of body weight and image throughout the world than have existed previously. Since the turn of the century, ladies' magazines and cinema have become a part of every middle-class lifestyle. In the fifties television was added to the repertoire and then, in the eighties, video.

Television and the print media emphasize physical appearance to a greater extent for women than for men (Anderson & DiDomerico, 1992; Freedman, 1986). The media convey that women should be and do want to be thinner and more attractive than in earlier times (Garner, Garfinkel, Schwartz & Thompson, 1980; Silverstein, Peterson, & Perdue, 1986). This emphasis on increasing thin-ness and a less curvaceous look is present in men's magazines (e.g., *Playboy*) as well as women's magazines (e.g., *Ladies Home Journal* and *Vogue*). The role of woman as depicted in ladies' magazines has certainly changed over time. Since the turn of the century these same magazines present "before" and "after" pictures along with testimonials from "ordinary" womenfolk that "prove" that nature needs only a gentle push (Freedman, 1986; Hatfield & Sprecher, 1986).

Unlike the cinema and print media, television injects "a potent dose of beauty imagery into the mainstream of life" (Freedman, 1986, p. 43) because it is experienced as part of the daily routine of chores, playing, working, and eating. Even by the late 1970s, 96% of American households had at least one television. Watching television consumes 40% of adult leisure time, and by the time a girl is 15 years old she has on the average watched more hours of television than she has spent in the classroom (Dyrenforth et al., 1980). This suggests that TV is a major source of information for girls and women; it provides a way of understanding themselves, an identity, and a consensual validation for their ideas and beliefs. On television, 69% of the women are thin compared to 18% of the men, and only 5% of the women are heavy compared to 25.5% of the men (Silverstein et al., 1986). The few female characters that are overweight are older, are more likely to belong to a minority group, and have vocations of low status (Dyrenforth et al., 1980).

Concomitant with the preference change toward thinner women, there has been the inundation and manifold increase of materials on dieting and food in the popular written press (Morris, Cooper & Cooper, 1989; Silverstein, Purdue, Peterson & Kelley, 1986; Wiseman, Gray, Mosimann, & Ahrens, 1992). Most of these are directed toward females; the female to male ratio of articles and ads pertaining to diet foods, body shape, and figure enhancement in one study was shown to be more than 10:1 (Anderson & DiDomenico, 1992; Silverstein, Peterson, Purdue, & Kelley, 1986). Interestingly, there also has been an equally large increase in overall advertisement of food products (Schutz & Diaz-Knauf, 1989).

Thus when a women opens a magazine, watches a movie, or turns on the television or home video she is likely to be given further evidence of her own flaws. When a woman compares herself to the models before her visual field, she becomes painfully aware that her attractiveness is less than the model and is likely to give herself and others around her a low evaluation of attractiveness (Cash, Cash, & Butters, 1983; Freedman, 1986). These "natural looking" characters can create unrealistic expectations for men as well. In fact, one study showed that men gave lower ratings of attractiveness to average women after watching an episode of *Charlie's Angels* (Kenrich & Gutierres, 1980).

Some have blamed the media for the increased pressure that women feel to conform to these unrealistic ideal standards; they feel it may have led to an increase in eating disorders such as bulimia and anorexia nervosa (Chernin, 1981; Orbach, 1978). However, the media influence is probably more of a dynamic interaction; commercial images both reflect and then further influence weight trends and the ideal figure. Although it is difficult to prove that the media actually cause women to be obsessed and dissatisfied with their bodies, women do report that they feel more pressure from the media to conform to an ideal than they feel from peers or family, and this is particularly true for those who have bulimic symptoms (Irving, 1990).

The Glorified Thin Ideal: An Important Recruitment for Eating Disorders

In this age of mass communication, television, and other mass media, the idealized thin female role model has been rapidly assimilated throughout the culture. The media have sensationalized and glorified anorexia nervosa, beginning with its identification as "The Golden Girl Disease," an enviable state characteristic of princesses like Princess Diana of Wales, actresses like Jane Fonda, and

Olympic athletes like Cathy Rigby. Karen Carpenter, the late well-known singer, died of complications from bulimia nervosa.

Increases in incidence of eating problems among females in the United States (Cooper & Fairburn, 1983; Pope, Hudson, Yurgelen-Todd, & Hudson, 1984) have paralleled an evolution toward a thinner standard of beauty for American women (Silverstein, Perdue, Peterson, Vogel, & Pantini, 1986). Although the evidence is correlational, some believe that these cultural changes are linked in a causal way, suggesting that women have been socialized in a culture that places intense pressure on women to reduce and diet in spite of the possible adverse physical and psychological effects. These disorders in part are an overcommitment or overadaption to the cultural ideal that is in vogue (Mazur, 1986).

Against a backdrop of increased exposure to high caloric foods and cultural prescription for a slender body ideal, the avoidance of obesity and pursuit of thinness by dieting and other weight-related activities have emerged as concrete activities through which young women may gain favorable social responses and thus enhance self-esteem. Thus the upper and middle classes share the emphasis on slimness as a mark of success. More subjective distress is caused by a few hip bulges, ripples in the thighs, and a convex abdomen than by real medical weight problems. The mixed message that our society gives, inviting consumption of a variety of savory foods high in caloric content while at the same time demanding control of eating and slimness, creates several problems in many, especially those destined to be above average weight (A. E. Anderson, 1985). Obsessive concerns about inhibiting one's consumption and satisfying one's cravings arise directly from the cultural pressures to limit one's intake of appealing foods. Restraint makes the domain of eating vulnerable to distortion (e.g., impaired satiety) and/or psychopathologies imported from elsewhere (Herman & Polivy, 1988). Although anorexia and bulimia have occurred through history (Bromberg, 1988), increased social pressure towards slimness creates a "recruitment" phenomenon in the more vulnerable individuals so that increased numbers of individuals are affected and the kind of individual affected changes (A. E. Anderson, 1985). That is, as sociocultural pressures increase, individuals less predisposed to illness are added to the group becoming ill; individual personality factors may then play a role in the kind of individual who develops symptoms of the disorder (Kishchuk, Gagnon, Belisle, & Laurendean, 1992; Strigel-Moore, Connor-Greene & Shine, 1991). A major part of our dilemma is in establishing a definition of where the disease ends and a phenomenon of culture and modern society begins (Gilbert, 1986).

FUTURE DIRECTIONS OF RESEARCH

It is clear that the regulation of appetite and maintenance of weight involves a multitude of highly complex interactions among various factors, including neural factors, gastrointestinal factors, the peripheral autonomic system, humoral factors such as blood glucose, sensory factors such as palatability and variety, sociocultural factors such as the stigma of obesity and the importance of obtaining the body ideal, individual attitudinal factors toward such things as dieting and restraint, and personality factors including individual conditioning history and degree of emotionality. The relative importance of each of these factors and the nature of their interaction remains unclear. We lack a unifying hypothesis or theory tying these factors together. Several lines of investigation look promising, however. Each of them will be briefly mentioned.

The past decade of work on neurochemistry of appetite regulation, the peripheral autonomic nervous system and endocrine system, and feeding behavior in animals demonstrates complex and reductant regulatory mechanisms with multiple feedback loops. This includes the research on neurotransmitters (e.g., serotonin, norepinephrine, endogenous opiate system) and the ways in which they directly or indirectly mediate immediate food consumption and the long-term process of body weight regulation. The studies of neurochemistry and biology of eating disorders suggest that aberrations in neurobiologic mechanisms may be induced by the initial deviation in eating behavior and may come into play in chronic eating disorders. Investigations involving primary or secondary adaptive changes in several neurotransmitter systems (noradrenergic, serotonergic, and opioid) that are involved in affective state, appetite regulation, food consumption, and neuroendocrine function may yield fruitful information (Ebert, 1986).

Drugs can be used as tools to explore the mechanisms underlying the control of food intake, subjective hunger, and processes of satiety. There is some evidence that the biological system underlying appetite control is vulnerable to the influence of chemicals. The administration of drugs may produce unexpected and desirable effects on food intake and the suppression of appetite. It is important to study the potential ways that various classes of drugs undermine or corrupt the psychobiological control of appetite. Many drugs act upon or change the neurochemicals (biogenic amines and neuropeptides) and are therefore likely to influence hunger, eating, and body weight. Administration of these drugs could precipitate or even directly cause eating problems by impeding the regulation of appetite. Or they could exacerbate the course of eating disorders by making it difficult to regain appetite control (Blundell et al., 1989). Blundell et al. (1989) suggest a model for investigating drugs and satiety that involves giving subject test meals with bodily sensation rating scales, food preferences checklists, and forced-choice preferences. Subjects can be trained to keep accurate diet records. The action of the drug can be measured during the meal, the period between meals, and the following meal. Use of this paradigm to study the effect of drugs and environmental events will provide more information than just a single laboratory session can.

Learning processes such as long-term habituation and physiological and social reinforcement of preferences, appetite, satiety, and aversions all play a role in the control of a person's eating behavior by a personal set to stimulus configurations (Booth, 1989). The extent to which these learning processes play a role is somewhat dependent on the choices of food available and the degree to which these foods are similar to ones with which the organism has had previous experience. It is possible that these learned associations may be sufficient to explain the regulation of body energy and protein observed (Booth, 1989). These learning processes should be further studied since the evidence for both protein intake and energy regulation in humans is limited (Booth, 1989). Related to this, it is not clear how stimulus properties such as palatability and variety and the resulting satiety are influenced by history with specific foods. For example, does a sweetener trigger neurotransmitter changes, cellular glucose deficit, or expectations of prolonged satiation (Booth, 1989)? It seems possible to design studies that measure the relative strength of the alterative mechanisms and/or factors or discover the extent of the interaction. For example, it may be possible to separate externality from restraint; that is, to discover whether externality leads to counterregulation (Rodin, 1981) or restraints lead to counterregulation (Herman & Polivy, 1984).

The influence of social class and culture in the regulation of appetite seems particularly important for women. There are notable differences in the incidence of the different eating disorders between the genders and for women between the social classes and among the different cultures. For example, although there is probably some validity to a downward drift hypothesis for obese women, it is likely that some unspecified social pressures create some of the difference in prevalence. More cross-cultural work on attitudes toward weight, attitudes toward deviation from ideal weight, and differences in parental attitudes toward men, women, and children is needed.

Most of the work to date has focused on a slice of time involving one experimental session or interview. We have precious little information in humans about the potential regulation of ingestion over time. A longitudinal study tracking females and males from adolescence through middle age would be helpful in understanding the natural history of weight regulation, with more detailed study of peripheral factors, neurochemical factors, restraint, measures of metabolism, exercise, dieting, and so forth. It may aid in elucidating some potential hypotheses about what things protect one from developing an eating disorder or enhance one's chances of acquiring an eating disorder. In addition, it would be important to follow successful dieters versus unsuccessful dieters over time with measures that would include biochemistry, food diaries, restraint, and externality. Long-term studies are needed to explore the psychological, physiological, and sensory (taste responsiveness) factors as predictors of who is more likely to show a positive long-term response to weight reduction.

The study of eating disorders is important in that the study of aspects of dysfunction can often yield information about function. To date, however, many of the biochemical studies on eating disorders have yielded information suggesting that many of the biochemical differences are due to the effects of eating, overeating, intermitting eating, or purging. Why some dieters and restrainers do not develop anorexia or bulimia is an important question worth pursuit. Are there factors that spare or predispose the individual to the development of eating disorders in a society that is oriented toward a thin ideal?

Each person has through his or her biology and conditioning history an individual set of circumstances that may create a unique configuration that protects or makes the individual vulnerable to any of the eating disorders. Each of the eating disorders may be a final common behavioral pathway that results from one or several causes. The search for a universal "cause" for anorexia, bulimia, or obesity may eliminate factors that could potentiate the development of the disorder. Although the strength of a particular stimulus may not produce similar behavioral results in all people, it remains extremely important to elucidate each variable and determine the factors affecting its potency for the individual.

We are quite capable of acquiring new information and facts, mapping brain sites and neurotransmitters involved in the regulation of weight, and then linking specific environmental circumstances that affect brain function with peripheral and neurochemical events in animals. Several hypotheses and theories have been of heuristic value in furthering the knowledge of the field. However, no comprehensive theory exists that permits real understanding and transfer to the human condition. For this we need additional facts to understand that physiological, social, and environmental stimuli and aspects of individual personality are involved in the control of food intake and the eating disorders. Even more than that, we need to construct a multifactorial scheme that would show how social and environmental factors, translated into peripheral-central interactions involving immediate metabolic and visceral inputs to the brain, are integrated with past learning (conditioning) history to yield an output that controls metabolism, visceral function, and eating behavior. This comprehensive scheme or theory must then be testable and applicable to dysfunctional eating behavior.

REFERENCES

Anderson, A. E., & DiDomenico, L. (1992). Diet vs. shape content of popular male and female magazines: A dose-response of eating disorders? *International Journal of Eating Disorders*, 11(3), 283–287.

Anderson, A. E. (1985). *Practical comprehensive treatment of anorexia nervosa and bulimia.* Baltimore, MD: Johns Hopkins University Press.

Anderson, I. M., Parry-Billings, M., Newsholme, E. A., Fairburn, C. G., & Cowen, P. J. (1990). Dieting reduces plasma tryptophan and alters brain 5-HT function in women. *Psychological Medicine, 20,* 785–791.

Apfelbaum, M. (1978). Adaptation to changes in caloric intake. *Progress in Food and Nutrition Science, 2,* 543–559.

Beck, S. B., Ward-Hull, C. I., & McLear, P. M. (1976). Variables related to women's somatic preferences of the male and female body. *Journal of Personality and Social Psychology, 34,* 1200–1210.

Bellisle, F., & LeMagnen, J. (1981). The structure of meals in humans: Eating and drinking patterns in lean and obese subjects. *Physiology and Behavior, 27,* 649–658.

Ben-Tovim, D. I., Walker, M. K., Murray, H., & Chin, G. (1990). Body size estimates: Body image or body attitude measures? *International Journal of Eating Disorders, 9,* 57–67.

Berscheid, E., Dion, K., Walster, W., & Walster, W. (1971). Physical attractiveness and dating choice: A test of the matching hypothesis. *Journal of Experimental Social Psychology, 7,* 173–189.

Berscheid, E., & Walster, E. (1974). Physical attractiveness. In Berkowitz, L. (Ed.), *Advances in experimental social psychology* (Vol. 7, pp. 157–215). New York: Academic Press.

Berscheid, E., Walster, E., & Bohrnstedt, G. (1973). The happy American body: A survey report. *Psychology Today, 1,* 119–131.

Bjorntorp, P. (1986). Fat cells and obesity. In K. D. Brownell & J. P. Foreyt (Eds.), *Handbook of eating disorders: Physiology, psychology and treatment of obesity, anorexia and bulimia* (pp. 88–98). New York: Basic Books.

Blundell, J. E., & Hill, A. J. (1989). Serotoninergic drug potentiates the satiating capacity of food: Action of d-fenfluramine in obese subjects. *Annals of the New York Academy of Sciences, 575,* 529–531.

Blundell, J. E., Hill, A. J., & Lawton, C. (1989). Neurochemical factors involved in normal and abnormal eating in humans. In R. Shepard (Ed.), *Handbook of psychophysiology of human eating* (pp. 85–112). New York: John Wiley.

Booth, D. A. (1977). Satiety and appetite are conditioned reactions. *Psychomatic Medicine, 39,* 76–81.

Booth, D. A. (1980). Acquired behavior controlling energy intake and output. In A. J. Stunkard (Ed.), *Obesity* (pp. 101–143). Philadelphia: W. B. Saunders.

Booth, D. A. (1989). Implications of eating research for disease prevention. In R. Shepard (Ed.), *Handbook of psychophysiology of human eating* (pp. 342–358). New York: John Wiley.

Bray, G. A. (1988). Metabolic and endocrine factors in regulation of nutrient balance. In K. M. Pirke, W. Vandereycken, & D. Ploog (Eds.), *The psychobiology of bulimia nervosa* (pp. 59–73). New York: Springer-Verlag.

Brewerton, T., Brandt, H., Lesem, D., & Jimerson, D. (1990). Serotonin in eating disorders. In E. Coccaro & D. Murphy (Eds.), *Serotonin in Major Psychiatric Disorders* (pp. 153–184). Washington, DC: American Psychiatric Press.

Brewerton, T., Muller, E., Brandt, H., Lesem, M., Hegg, A., Murphy, D., & Jimerson, D. (1989). Dysregulation of 5-HT function in bulimia nervosa. *Annals of the New York Academy of Sciences, 575,* 500–502.

Bromberg, J. J. (1988). *Fasting girls.* Cambridge, MA: Harvard University Press.

Brooks, C., Lambert, E. F. (1946). A study of the effect of limitation of food intake and method of feeding on the rate of weight gain during hypothalamic obesity in the albino rat. *American Journal of Physiology, 147,* 695–707.

Brownell, K. D. (1982). Obesity: Understanding and treating a serious, prevalent and refractory disorder. *Journal of Consulting and Clinical Psychology, 50,* 820–840.

Brownmiller, S. (1984). *Femininity.* New York: Ballentine Books.

Bushnell, J. A., Wells, E., Hornblow, A., Oakley-Browne, M., & Joyce, P. (1990). Prevalence of three bulimia syndromes in the general population. *Psychological Medicine, 20,* 671–680.

Button, E. J., & Whitehead, A. (1981). Subclinical anorexia nervosa. *Psychological Medicine, 11,* 509–516. Cabanac, M., & Duclaux, R. (1970). Obesity: Absence of satiety aversion to sucrose. *Science, 168,* 496–497.

Cabanac, M., Duclaux, R., & Spector, N. H. (1971). Sensory feedback regulation of body weight: Is there a ponderostat? *Nature, 229,* 125–127.

Cabanac, M., & Rabe, E. F. (1976). Influence of monotonous diet on body weight regulation in humans. *Psychology and Behavior, 17,* 675–678.

Cann, A., Siegfried, W. D., & Pearce, L. (1981). Forced attention to specific applicant qualifications: Impact of physical attractiveness and sex on applicant biases. *Personnel Psychology, 34,* 65–75.

Canning, H., & Mayer, J. (1966). Obesity: Its possible effect on college acceptance. *New England Journal of Medicine, 275,* 1172–1174.

Cannon, W. B. (1932). *The wisdom of the body.* New York: W. W. Norton.

Cash, T. F., & Brown, T. A. (1989). Gender and body images: Stereotypes and realities. *Sex Roles, 21(5-6),* 357–369.

Cash, T., Cash, D., & Butters, J. (1983). Mirror, mirror on the wall . . . ? Contrast effects and self evaluations of physical attractiveness. *Personality and Social Psychology Bulletin, 9,* 351–358.

Cash, T. F., Winstead, B. A., & Janda, L. H. (1986). The great American shape-up. *Psychology Today, 20(3),* 30–37.

Channon, S., de Silva, P., Hemsley, D., & Mukherjee, K. (1990). Body-size perception and preferences in stable-weight anoretic patients. *International Journal of Eating Disorders, 9,* 403–408.

Chernin, K. (1981). *The obsession: Reflections on the tyranny of slenderness.* New York: Harper and Row.

Chetwynd, S. J., Stewart, R. A., & Powell, G. E. (1975). Social attitudes toward the obese physique. In A. Howard (Ed.), *Recent advances in obesity research* (Vol. 1, pp. 223–226). London: Newman.

Cohn, C., & Joseph, D. (1962). Influence of body weight and body fat on appetite of "normal" lean and obese rats. *Yale Journal of Biological Medicine, 34,* 598–607.

Collins, M. E. (1991). Body figure perceptions and preferences among preadolescent children. *International Journal of Eating Disorders, 10,* 199–208.

Cooper, P. J., Charnock, D. J., & Taylor, M. J. (1987). The prevalence of bulimia nervosa: A replication study. *British Journal of Psychiatry, 151,* 684–686.

Cooper, P. J., & Fairburn, C. G. (1983). Binge-eating and self-induced vomiting in the community. A preliminary study. *British Journal of Psychiatry, 142,* 139–144.

Corbett, S. W., Stern, J. S., & Keesey, R. E. (1986). Energy expenditure of rats with diet-induced obesity. *American Journal of Clinical Nutrition, 44(2),* 173–180.

Crago, M., Yates, A., Beutler, L. E., & Arizmendi, T. G. (1985). Height-weight ratios among female athletes: Are collegiate athletics the precursors to an anoretic syndrome? *International Journal of Eating Disorders, 4*, 79–87.

Czirr, S. A., & Reid, L. D. (1986). Demonstrating morphine's potentiating effects on sucrose-intake. *Brain Research Bulletin, 17*, 639–642.

Dawber, T. B. (1980). *The Framingham study: The epidemiology of atherosclerotic disease.* Cambridge, MA: Harvard University Press.

Dipboye, R. L., Fromkin, H. L., & Wibeck, K. (1975). Relative importance of applicant sex, attractiveness and scholastic standing in evaluations of job applicant resumes. *Journal of Applied Psychology, 60*, 39–43.

Dolan, B. (1990). Cross cultural aspects of anorexia nervosa and bulimia nervosa: A review. *International Journal of Eating Disorders, 10*, 67–78.

Dolan, B., & Ford, K. (1991). Binge eating and dietary restraint: A cross-cultural analysis. *International Journal of Eating Disorders, 10*, 345–353.

Domangue, B. B. (1987). Biological considerations in the treatment of adult obesity. In H. Field & B. Domangue, Eds. *Eating disorders throughout the life span* (pp. 71–89). New York: Praeger.

Dwyer, J. T., Feldman, J. J., Seltzer, C. C., & Mayer, J. (1969). Body image in adolescents: Attitudes toward weight and perception of appearance. *American Journal of Clinical Nutrition, 20*, 1045–1056.

Dyrenforth, S. R., Wooley, O. W., & Wooley, S. C. (1980). A woman's body in a man's world: A review of findings on body image and weight control. In R. Kaplan (Ed.), *A woman's conflict: The special relationship between women and food* (pp. 30–57). New Jersey: Prentice-Hall.

Ebert, M. H. (1986). Neurobiology research in bulimia. In J. I. Hudson & H. G. Pope (Eds.), *The psychobiology of bulimia* (pp. 241–249). Washington, DC: American Psychiatric Press.

Fallon, A. E. (1990). Culture in the mirror: Sociocultural determinants of body image. In T. Cash & T. Pruzinsky (Eds.), *Body images: Development deviance and change* (pp. 80–109). New York: Guilford Press.

Fallon, A., & Rozin, P. (1985). Sex differences in perception of desirable body shape. *Journal of Abnormal Psychology, 94*, 102–105.

Fallon, A., Rozin, P., Gogineni, R., & Desai, K. (1993). *Body image and eating disorders: A cross cultural comparison between Indians and Americans.* Unpublished manuscript.

Fernstrom, M. H., & Fernstrom, J. D. (1987). Diet, brain neurotransmitters, and food selection. In B. T. Walsh (Ed.), *Eating behavior in eating disorders* (pp. 37–50). Washington, DC: American Psychiatric Press.

Fichter, M. M., Pirke, K. M., Pollinger, J., Wolfram, G., & Brunner, E. (1988). Restricted caloric intake causes neuroendocrine disturbances in bulimia. In K. M. Pirke, W. Vandereycken, & D. Ploog (Eds.), *The psychobiology of bulimia nervosa* (pp. 42–58). New York: Springer-Verlag.

Ford, C., & Beach, R. (1951). *Patterns of sexual behavior.* New Haven: Harper and Brothers Publishers and Paul B. Hoeber, Inc. Medical Books.

Freedman, R. (1986). *Beauty bound.* Lexington, MA: Lexington Books.

Furnham, A., & Alibhai, N. (1983). Cross cultural differences in the perception of female body shapes. *Psychological Medicine, 13*, 829–837.

Garattini, S., Bizzi, A., Caccia, S., Mennini, T., & Samanin, R. (1988). Progress in assessing the role of serotonin in the control of food intake. *Clinical Neuropharmacology, 11*, S8–S32.

Garfinkel, E., & Garner, D. M. (1982). *Anorexia nervosa: A multidimensional perspective*. New York: Brunner/Mazel.

Garg, S. K., & Singh, S. (1983). Physiological basis of feeding behavior. *Personality Study and Group Behavior*, Garner, D. M., & Garfinkel, P. E. (1978). Sociocultural factors in anorexia nervosa. *Lancet, 2*, 674.

Garner, D. M., & Garfinkel, P. E. (1980). Socio-cultural factors in the development of anorexia nervosa. *Psychological Medicine, 10*, 647–656.

Garner, D. M., Garfinkel, P. E., & Olmsted, M. (1983). An overview of sociocultural factors in the development of anorexia nervosa. In: P. L. Darby, P. E. Garfinkel, D. M. Garner, & D. V. Coscina (Eds.), *Anorexia nervosa: Recent developments* (pp. 65–82). New York: Allan R. Liss.

Garner, D. M., Garfinkel, P. E., Schwartz, D., & Thompson, M. (1980). Cultural expectations of thinness in women. *Psychological Reports, 47*, 483–491.

Garrow, J. S. (1986). Physiological aspects of obesity. In K. D. Brownell & J. P. Foreyt (Eds.), *Handbook of eating disorders* (pp. 45–62). New York: Basic Books.

Gilbert, S. (1986). *Pathology of eating: Psychology and treatment*. New York: Routledge and Kegan Paul.

Goldblatt, P. E., Moore, M. E., & Stunkard, A. J. (1965). Social factors in obesity. *Journal of the American Medical Association, 192*, 1039–1044.

Gowers, S., & McMahon, J. B. (1989). Social class and prognosis in anorexia nervosa. *International Journal of Eating Disorders, 8*, 105–109.

Gray, S. (1977). Social aspects of body image: Perception of normalcy of weight and affect of college undergraduates. *Perceptual and Motor Skills, 47*, 483–491.

Haber, S. (1981). Obesity: The psychology of a multifaced volitional disorder. In J. S. Mule (Ed.), *Excess: An examination of the volitional disorders* (pp. 209–220). New York: Free Press.

Halmi, K. A. (1988). Cognitive and metabolic responses to eating in anorexia nervosa and bulimia. In K. M. Pirke, W. Vandereycken, & D. Ploog (Eds.), *The psychobiology of bulimia nervosa*. New York: Springer-Verlag.

Halmi, K. A., Falk, J. R., & Schwartz, E. (1981). Binge eating and vomiting: A survey of a college population. *Psychological Medicine, 11*, 697–706. Hatfield, E., & Sprecher, S. (1986). *Mirror mirror: The importance of looks in everyday life*. New York: SUNY Press.

Herman, C. P., & Mack, D. (1975). Restrained and unrestrained eating. *Journal of Personality, 43*, 647–660.

Herman, C. P., & Polivy, J. (1975). Anxiety, restraint, and eating behavior. *Journal of Abnormal Psychology, 84*, 662–672.

Herman, C. P., & Polivy, J. (1980). Restrained eating. In A. J. Stunkard (Ed.), *Obesity* (pp. 208–225). Philadelphia: W.B. Saunders.

Herman, C. P., & Polivy, J. (1984). A boundary model for the regulation of eating. In

A. J. Stunkard & E. Stellar (Eds.), *Eating and its disorders* (pp. 141–156). New York: Raven Press.

Herman, C. P., & Polivy, J. (1987). Studies in eating in normal dieters. In B. Walsh (Ed.), *Eating behavior in eating disorders* (pp. 95–112). New York: American Psychiatric Press.

Herman, C. P., & Polivy J. (1988). Restraint and excess in dieters and bulimics. In K. M. Pirke, W. Vandereycken, & D. Ploog (Eds.), *The psychobiology of bulimia nervosa* (pp. 33–41). New York: Springer-Verlag.

Herman, C. P., Polivy, J., & Esses, V. (1987). The illusion of counter-regulation. *Appetite, 9*, 161–169.

Hetherington, M., & Rolls, B. J. (1987). Sensory-specific satiety and food intake in eating disorders. In B. T. Walsh (Ed.), *Eating behavior in eating disorders* (pp. 141–160). Washington, DC: American Psychiatric Press.

Hill, A. J., & Blundell, J. E. (1989). Comparison of the action of macronutrients on the expression of appetite in lean and obese human subjects. *Annals of the New York Academy of Sciences, 575*, 529–531.

Hill, R. (1945). Campus values in mate selection. *Journal of Home Economics, 37*, 554–558.

Hill, S. W., & McCutcheon, N. B. (1975). Eating responses of obese and non-obese humans during dinner meals. *Psychosomatic Medicine, 37*, 395–401.

Hoebel, B. G., Hernandez, L., Schwartz, D. L., Mark, G. P., & Hunter, G. A. (1989). Microdialysis studies of brain norepinephrine, serotonin, and dopamine release during ingestive behavior: Theoretical and clinical implications. *Annals of New York Academy of Sciences, 575*, 171–193.

Hoebel, B. G., & Teitelbaum, P. (1966). Weight regulation in normal and hypothalamic hyperphagic rats. *Journal of Comparative and Physiological Psychology, 61*, 189–193.

Hudson, J. W., & Hoyt, L. L. (1981). Personal characteristics important in mate preference among college students. *Social Behavior and Personality, 9*, 93–96.

Huon, G. F., & Wootton, M. (1991). The role of dietary carbohydrate and of knowledge of having eaten it in the urge to eat more. *International Journal of Eating Disorders, 10*(1), 31–42.

Irving, L. (1990). Mirror images: Effects of the social standard of beauty on women's self and body esteem. *Journal of Social and Clinical Psychology*, James, W. P. T., and Trayhurn, P. (1981). Thermogenesis and obesity. *British Medical Bulletin, 37*, 43–48.

Jarvie, G. J. (1983). Childhood obesity and social stigma: What we know and what we don't know. *Developmental Review, 3*, 237–273.

Jimerson, D. C., Brandt, H. A., & Brewerton, T. D. (1988). Evidence for altered serotonin function in bulimia and anorexia nervosa: Behavioral implications. In K. M. Pirke, W. Vandereycken, & D. Ploog (Eds.), *The psychobiology of bulimia nervosa* (pp. 83–89). New York: Springer-Verlag.

Johnson, C., Stuckey, M., & Mitchell, J. (1983). Psychopharmacological treatment of anorexia nervosa and bulimia. *Journal of Nervous and Mental Diseases, 171*, 524–534.

Johnson, W. G. (Ed.). (1987). *Advances in eating disorders.* Greenwich, CT: JAI Press.

Jonas, J. M., & Gold, M. S. (1986). Treatment of antidepressant-resistant bulimia with naltrexone. *International Journal of Psychiatry in Medicine, 16,* 305–309.

Kalik, S. (1979). Toward an interdisciplinary psychology of appearance. *Psychiatry, 41,* 243–253.

Kaye, W. H., Gwirtsman, H. E., Brewerton, T. D., George, D., & Wurtman, R. (1988). Binging behavior and plasma amino acids: A possible involvement of brain serotonin in bulimia nervosa. *Psychiatry Research, 23,* 31–43.

Kaye, W. H., Gwirtsman, H. E., George, D. T., Weis, S. R., & Jimerson, D. C. (1986). Relationship of mood alterations to binging behavior in bulimia. *British Journal of Psychiatry, 149,* 479–485.

Kaye, W. H., Gwirtsman, H. E., Lake, R., Siever, L., Jimerson, D., Ebert, M., & Murphy, D. (1985). Disturbances of norepinephrine metabolism and 2-adrenergic? receptor activity in anorexia nervosa: Relationship to nutritional state. *Psychopharmacology Bulletin, 21,* 419–423.

Keesey, R. E. (1986). A set-point theory of obesity. In K. D. Brownell & J. P. Foreyt (Eds.), *Handbook of eating disorders* (pp. 63–87). New York: Basic Books.

Keesey, R. E., & Corbett, S. W. (1984). Metabolic defense of the body weight set-point. In A. J. Stunkard & E. Stellar (Eds.), *Eating and its disorders* (pp. 87–96). New York: Raven Press.

Kenrich, D., & Gutierres, S. (1980). Contrast effects and judgement of physical attractiveness: When beauty become a social problem. *Journal of Personality and Social Psychology, 38,* 131–140.

Keys, A., Brozek, J., Henschel, A., Mickelson, 0., & Taylor, H. L. (1950). *The biology of human starvation.* Minneapolis: University of Minnesota Press.

Kishchuk, N., Gagnon, G., Belisle, D., & Laurendeau, M. C. (1992). Sociodemographic and psychological correlates of actual and desired weight insufficiency in the general population. *International Journal of Eating Disorders, 12*(1), 73–81.

Klajner, F., Herman, C. P., Polivy, J., & Chhabra, R. (1981). Human obesity, dieting and the anticipatory salivation to food. *Physiology and Behavior, 27,* 195–198.

Klesges, R. C., Meyers, A. W., Klesges, L. M., & La Vasque, M. E. (1989). Smoking, body weight, and their effects on smoking behavior: A comprehensive review of the literature. *Psychological Bulletin, 106*(2), 204–230.

Lacey, J., & Dolan, B. (1988). Bulimia in British Blacks and Asians: A catchment area study. *British Journal of Psychiatry, 152,* 73–77.

Ledoux, S., Choquet, M., & Flament, M. (1991). Eating disorders among adolescents in an unselected French population. *International Journal of Eating Disorders, 10*(1), 81–89.

Leibel, R. L., & Hirsch, J. (1984). Diminished energy requirement in reduced obese patients. *Metabolism, 33,* 164–179.

Leibowitz, S. F. (1986). Brain monoamines and peptides: Role in the control of eating behavior. *Federal Proceedings, 45,* 1396–1403.

Leibowitz, S. F. (1987a). Hypothalamic neurotransmitters in relation to normal and disturbed eating patterns. *Annals of the New York Academy of Science, 499,* 137–143.

Leibowitz, S. F. (1987b). Brain neurotransmitters and drug effects on food intake and appetite: Implications for eating disorders. In B. T. Walsh (Ed.), *Eating behavior in eating disorders* (pp. 19–36). Washington, DC: American Psychiatric Press.

Leibowitz, S. F. (1989). Hypothalamic neuropeptide Y, galanin, and amines: Concepts of coexistence in relation to feeding behavior. *Annals of the New York Academy of Sciences. 575,* 221–235.

Lerner, R. M., & Gellert, E. (1969). Body build identifications, preference, and aversion in children. *Developmental Psychology, 1,* 456–462.

Lerner, R. M., Iwawaki, S., Chihara, T., & Sorell, G. T. (1980). Self-concept, self-esteem, and body attitudes among Japanese male and female adolescents. *Child Development, 51,* 847–855.

Lerner, R. M., & Karabenick, S. A. (1974). Physical attractiveness, body attitudes and self concept in late adolescents. *Journal of Youth and Adolescence, 3,* 307–316.

Lerner, R. M., Karabenick, S. A., & Stuart, J. L. (1973). Relations among physical attractiveness, body attitudes, and self concept in male and female college students. *Journal of Psychology, 85,* 119–129.

Levine, A. S., & Billington, C. J. (1989). Opioids: Are they regulators of feeding? *Annals of the New York Academy of Sciences. 575,* 209–215.

Liggett, J. (1974). *The human face.* New York: Stein and Day.

Lowe, M. (1992). Staying on versus going off a diet: Effects in normal weight and overweight individuals. *International Journal of Eating Disorders, 12*(4), 417–424.

Lowe, M. (1987). Set point, restraint, and the limits of weight loss: A critical analysis. In W. G. Johnson (Ed.), *Advances in eating disorders* (Vol 1) (pp. 1–38). Greenwich, CT: JAI Press.

Lowe, M. R., Whitlow, J. W., & Bellwoar, V. (1991). Eating regulation: The role of restraint, dieting, and weight. *International Journal of Eating Disorders, 10*(4), 461–471.

Maddox, G. L., & Liederman, U. (1969). Overweight as a social disability with medical implications. *Journal of Medical Education, 44,* 210–220.

Maiman, L. A., Wang, V. L., Becker, M. H., Finlay, J., & Simonson, M. (1979). Attitudes towards obesity and the obese among professionals. *Journal of the American Dietetic Association, 74,* 331–336.

Marks-Kaufman, R., & Kanarek, R. B. (1987). The endogenous opioid peptides: Relationship to food intake, obesity and sweet tastes. In B. T. Walsh (Ed.), *Eating behavior in eating disorders* (pp. 51–68). Washington, DC: American Psychiatric Press.

Marano, H. E. (1993). Chemistry and craving. *Psychology Today, Jan/Feb,* 30–74.

Mathes, E. W., & Kahn, A. (1975). Physical attractiveness, happiness, neuroticism, and self esteem. *Journal of Psychology, 90,* 27–30.

Mayer, J., Roy, P., & Mitra, K. P. (1956). Relation between caloric intake, body weight, and physical work: Studies in an industrial male population in west Bengal. *American Journal of Clinical Nutrition, 4,* 169–175.

Mazur, A. (1986). U.S. trends in feminine beauty and overadaptation. *Journal of Sex Role Research, 22,* 281–303.

McCarthy, M. (1990). The thin ideal. Depression and eating disorders in women. *Behaviour Research and Therapy, 28,* 205–215.

McGinnis, R. (1959). Campus values in mate selection: A repeat study. *Social Forces, 36*, 368–373.

McLean, T., & Moon, M. (1980). Health, obesity and earnings. *American Journal of Public Health, 70*, 1006–1009.

Meyers, A. W., Stunkard, A. J., & Coll, M. (1980). Food accessibility and food choice: Test of Schachter's externality hypothesis. *Archives of General Psychiatry, 37*, 1133–1135.

Millman, M. (1980). (Ed.) *Such a pretty face: Being fat in America.* New York. W. W. Norton.

Mitchell, J. E., Morley, J., Laine, D., Pyle, R, Eckert, E., & Zollman, M. (1987). 12 monitored eating behavior in women with bulimia nervosa. In B. T. Walsh (Ed.), *Eating behavior in eating disorders* (pp. 187–198). Washington, DC: American Psychiatric Press.

Morris, D. (1985). *Bodywatching. A field guide to the human species.* New York: Crown.

Mumford, D. B., Whitehouse, A. M., & Choudry, I. Y. (1992). Survey of eating disorders in English-medium school in Lahore, Pakistan. *International Journal of Eating Disorders, 11*(2), 173–184.

Nasser, M. (1986). Comparative study of the prevalence of abnormal eating attitudes among Arab female students of both London and Cairo Universities. *Psychological Medicine, 16*, 621–625.

Nicolaidis, S., & Even, P. (1989). Metabolic rate and feeding behavior. *Annals of the New York Academy of Sciences, 575*, 86–105.

Nisbett, R. E. (1972). Hunger, obesity, and the ventromedial hypothalamus. *Psychological Review, 79*, 433–453.

Noles, S., Cash, T., & Winstead, B. (1985). Body image, physical attractiveness, and depression. *Journal of Consulting and Clinical Psychology, 53*, 88–94.

Nylander, I. (1971). The feeling of being fat and dieting in a school population. *Acta Socio-Medica Scandinavica, 1*, 7–26.

Orbach, S. (1978). *Fat is a feminist issue: The anti-diet guide to weight loss.* New York: Paddington Press.

Peck, J. W. (1978). Rats defend different body weight depending on palatability and accessibility of their food. *Journal of Comparative and Physiological Psychology, 92*, 555–570.

Pirke, K. M., & Ploog, D. (1983). Are all somatic symptoms of anorexia nervosa a consequence of malnutrition? In K. M. Pirke & D. Ploog (Eds.), *The psychobiology of anorexia nervosa* (pp. 179–181). New York: Springer-Verlag.

Pirke, K. M., & Vandereycken, W. (1988). Summary: Research and treatment in the psychology of bulimia nervosa. In K. M. Pirke, W. Vandereycken, & D. Ploog (Eds.), *The psychobiology of bulimia nervosa* (pp. 179–181). New York: Springer-Verlag.

Pliner, P., Polivy, J., Herman, C. P., & Zakalusny, J. (1980). Short-term intake of overweight individuals and normal weight dieters and non-dieters with and without choice among a variety of foods. *Appetite, 1*, 203–213.

Polivy, J. (1976). Perception of calories and regulation of intake in restrained and unrestrained subjects. *Addictive Behavior, 1*, 237–243.

Polivy, J., & Herman, C. P. (1991). Good and bad dieters: Self-perception and reaction to a dietary challenge. *International Journal of Eating Disorders, 10*(1), 91–99.

Polivy, J., & Herman, C. P. (1985). Dieting and binging: A causal analysis. *American Psychologist, 40*, 193–201.

Polivy, J., Herman, C. P., Hackett, R., & Kuleshnyk, I. (1986). The effects of self-attention and public attention on eating in restrained and unrestrained subjects. *Journal of Personality and Social Psychology, 50*, 1253–1260.

Polivy, J., Herman, C. P., & Warsh, S. (1978). Internal and external components of emotionality in restrained and unrestrained eaters. *Journal of Abnormal Psychology, 87*, 497–504.

Pope, H. G., Hudson, J. I., Yurgelen-Todd, D., & Hudson, M. (1984). Prevalence of anorexia and bulimia in three student populations. *International Journal of Eating Disorders, 3*, 45–51.

Powley, T. L., & Keesey, R. E. (1970). Relationship of body weight to the lateral hypothalamic feeding syndrome. *Journal of Comparative and Physiological Psychology, 70*, 25–36.

Pudel, V., Paul, T., & Maus, N. (1988). Regulation of eating in obesity and bulimia nervosa. In K. M. Pirke, W. Vandereycken, & D. Ploog (Eds.), *The psychobiology of bulimia nervosa* (pp. 109–119). New York: Springer-Verlag.

Rogacki, N., Weiss, G. F., Fueg, A., Suh, J. S., Pal, S., Stanley, B. G., Wong, D. T., & Leibowitz, S. F. (1989). Impact of hypothalamic serotonin on macronutrient intake. In: L. Schneider, S. Cooper & K. Halmi (Eds.), *The psychobiology of human eating disorders: Preclinical and clinical perspectives. Annals of the New York Academy of Sciences, 575*, 619–621, New York.

Raich, R. M., Rosen, J. C., Deus, J., Perez, O., Requena, A., & Gross, J. (1992). Eating disorder symptoms among adolescents in the United States and Spain: A comparative study. *International Journal of Eating Disorders, 11*(1), 63–72.

Rand, C. S. W., & Kuldau, J. M. (1991). Restrained eating (weight concerns) in the general population and among students. *International Journal of Eating Disorders, 10*(6), 699–708.

Reis, H. T., Nezlek, K. K. J., & Wheeler, L. (1980). Physical attractiveness in social interaction. *Journal of Personality and Social Psychology, 38*, 604–617.

Richardson, A. H., Goodman, N., Hastorf, S. A., & Dornbush, S.M. (1961). Cultural uniformity in reaction to physical disabilities. *American Sociological Review, 26*, 241–247.

Rodin, J. (1981). Current status of the internal-external hypothesis for obesity: What went wrong? *American Psychologist, 36*, 361–372.

Rodin, J., Moskowitz, H. R., & Bray, G. A. (1976). Relationship between obesity, weight loss, and taste responsiveness on weight. *Physiology and Behavior, 17*, 591–597.

Rodin, J., Silberstein, L. R., & Striegel-Moore, R. (1985). Women and weight: A normative discontent. In T. B. Sonderegger (Ed.), *Nebraska symposium on motivation, 1984: Psychology and gender* (pp. 267–307). Lincoln: University of Nebraska Press.

Rolls, B. J., Fedoroff, I. C., & Guthrie, J. F. (1991). Gender differences in eating behavior and body weight regulation. *Health Psychology, 10*(2), 133–142.

Rolls, B. J., & Hetherington, M. (1989). The role of variety in eating and body weight regulation. In R. Shepard (Ed.), *Handbook of psychophysiology of human eating.* New York: John Wiley.

Rolls, B. J., Rowe, E. A., Rolls, E. T., Kingston, B., Megson, A., & Gunary, R. (1981). Variety in meal enhances food intake in man. *Physiology and Behavior, 26,* 215–221.

Rolls, B. J., Van Duijvenvoorde, P. M., & Rowe, E. A. (1983). Variety in the diet enhances intake in a meal and contributes to the development of obesity in the rat. *Physiology and Behavior, 31,* 21–27.

Rosen, J. C., Letenberg, H., Fisher, C., & Khazan, N. C. (1986). Binge eating episodes in bulimia nervosa: The amount and type of food consumed. *International Journal of Eating Disorders, 5,* 255–267.

Rozin, P., & Fallon, A. E. (1988). Body image, attitudes to weight and misperceptions of figure preferences of the opposite sex: A comparison of men and women in two generations. *Journal of Abnormal Psychology, 97,* 342–345.

Rucker, C., & Cash, T. F. (1992). Body images, body-size perceptions, and eating disorders among African-American and white college women. *International Journal of Eating Disorders, 12*(3), 291–299.

Ruderman, A. J. (1986). Dietary restraint: A theoretical and empirical review. *Psychological Bulletin, 99,* 247–262.

Ruderman, A. J., Belzer, L. J., & Halperin, A. (1985). Restraint, anticipated consumption, and overeating. *Journal of Abnormal Psychology, 94,* 547–555.

Schachter, S. (1982). Recidivism and self-cure of smoking and obesity. *American Psychologist, 37,* 436–444.

Schachter, S., Goldman, R., & Gordon, A. (1968). Effects of fear, food, deprivation, and obesity on eating. *Journal of Personality and Social Psychology, 10,* 91–97.

Sclafani, A. (1980). Dietary obesity. In A. J. Stunkard (Ed.), *Obesity* (pp. 166–181). Philadelphia: W. B. Saunders.

Sclafani, A. (1989). Dietary-induced overeating. *Annals of the New York Academy of Sciences, 575,* 281–291.

Sclafani, A., & Springer, D. (1976). Dietary obesity in adult rats: Similarities to hypothalamic and human obesity syndrome. *Physiology and Behavior, 17,* 461–471.

Schutz, H. G., & Diaz-Knauf, K. V. (1989). The role of mass media in influencing eating. In R. Shepard (Ed.), *Handbook of the psychophysiology of human eating* (pp. 141–154). New York: John Wiley.

Schweiger, U., Laessle, R. G., Fichter, M. M., & Pirke, K. M. (1988). Consequences of dieting at normal weight: Implications for the understanding and treatment of bulimia. In K. M. Pirke, W. Vandereycken, & D. Ploog (Eds.), *The psychobiology of bulimia nervosa* (pp. 74–82). New York: Springer-Verlag.

Silberstein, L. R., Striegel-Moore, R. H., Timko, C., & Rodin, J. (1988). Behavioral and psychological implication of body dissatisfaction: Do men and women differ. *Sex Roles, 19,* 219–232.

Silverstein, B., Perdue, L., Peterson, B., Vogel, L., & Pantini, D. A. (1986). Possible causes of the thin standard bodily attractiveness for women. *International Journal of Eating Disorders, 5,* 907–916.

Silverstein, B., Peterson, B., & Perdue, L. (1986). Some correlates of the thin standard of bodily attractiveness for women. *International Journal of Eating Disorders, 5,* 895–905.

Sims, E. A. H. (1976). Experimental obesity, dietary-induced thermogenesis, and their clinical implications. *Clinics in Endocrinology and Metabolism, 5,* 377–395.

Sjostrom, L. (1980). Fat cells and body weight. In A. J. Stunkard (Ed.), *Obesity* (pp. 72–100). Philadelphia: W. B. Saunders.

Smith, J. E., & Krejci, J. (1991). Minorities join the majority: Eating disturbances among Hispanic and Native American youth. *International Journal of Eating Disorders, 10,* 179–186.

Sobel, J., & Stunkard, A. J. (1987). Socioeconomic status and obesity: A review of the literature. *Psychological Bulletin, 105,* 260–275.

Spencer, J. A., & Fremouw, W. J. (1979). Binge-eating as a function of weight and restraint classification. *Journal of Abnormal Psychology, 88,* 262–267.

Spitzer, L., & Rodin, J. (1981). Human eating behavior: A critical review of studies in normal weight and overweight individuals. *Appetite: Journal for Intake Research, 2,* 293–329.

Staffieri, J. R. (1967). A study of social stereotype of body image in children. *Journal of Personality and Social Psychology, 7,* 101–104.

Staffieri, J. R. (1972). Body build and behavioral expectations in young females. *Developmental Psychology, 6,* 125–127.

Stanton, A. L., & Tips, T. A. (1990). Accuracy of calorie estimation by females as a function of eating habits and body mass. *International Journal of Eating Disorders, 9,* 387–393.

Steinberg, C. L., & Birk, J. M. (1983). Weight and compliance: Male-female differences. *Journal of General Psychology, 109,* 95–102.

Steinberg, S., Tobin, D., & Johnson, C. (1990). The role of bulimic behaviors in affect regulation: Different functions for different patient subgroups? *International Journal of Eating Disorders, 9,* 51–55.

Stellar, E. (1989). Long-term perspectives on the study of eating behavior. *Annals of the New York Academy of Sciences, 575,* 478–486.

Steinhausen, H. C., Neumarker, K. J., Vollrath, M., Dudeck, R., & Neumarker, U. (1992). A transcultural comparison of the eating disorder inventory in former East and West Berlin. *International Journal of Eating Disorders, 12*(4), 407–416.

Stern, J. S. (1984). Is obesity a disease of inactivity? In A. J. Stunkard & E. Stellar (Eds.), *Eating and its disorders* (pp. 131–140). New York: Raven Press.

Stunkard, A. J., Sorensen, T. I. A., Harris, C., Teasdale, T. W., Chakraborty, R., Schull, W. J., & Schulsinger, F. An adoption study of human obesity. *New England Journal of Medicine, 324,* 193–198.

Thompson, J. K. (1991). Body shape preferences: Effects of instructional protocol and level of eating disturbance. *International Journal of Eating Disorders, 10,* 193–198.

Thompson, J. K., Jarvie, G. J., Lahey, B. B., & Cureton, K. J. (1982). Exercise and obesity: Etiology, physiology, and intervention. *Psychological Bulletin, 1,* 55–79.

Thompson, J. K., & Psaltis, K. (1988). Multiple aspects and correlates of body figure ratings: A replication and extension of Fallon and Rozin (1985). *International Journal of Eating Disorders, 7,* 813–817.

Tiggemann, M., & Rothblum, E. D. (1988). Gender differences in social consequences of perceived overweight in the United States and Australia. *Sex Roles, 18,* 75–86.

Wadden, T. A., Brown, G., Foster, G. D., & Linowitz, J. R. (1991). Salience of weight-related worries in adolescent males and females. *International Journal of Eating Disorders, 10*(4), 407–414.

Waldron, I. (1983). Sex differences in illness incidence prognosis and mortality: Issues and evidence. *Social Science and Medicine, 17,* 1107–1123.

Wertheim, E. H., Paxton, S. J., Maude, D., Szmukler, G. E., Gibbons, K., & Hiller, L. (1992). Psychosocial predictors of weight loss behaviors and binge eating in adolescent girls and boys. *International Journal of Eating Disorders, 12*(2), 151–160.

Wilson, D. W. (1978). Helping behavior and physical attractiveness. *Journal of Social Psychology, 104,* 313–314.

Wiseman, C. V., Gray, J. J., Mosimann, J. E., & Aherns, A. H. (1992). Cultural expectations of thinness in women: An update. *International Journal of Eating Disorders, 11*(1), 85–89.

Woods, S. C., & Gibbs, J. (1989). The regulation of food intake by peptides. *Annals of the New York Academy of Sciences, 575,* 236–243.

Woody, E. Z., Constanzo, P. R., Liefer, H., & Conger, J. (1981). The effects of taste and caloric perceptions on the eating behavior of restrained and unrestrained subjects. *Cognitive Research and Therapy, 5,* 381–390.

Wooley, S. C., Wooley, O. W., & Dyrenforth, S. M. (1979). Theoretical, practical, and social issues in behavior treatment of obesity. *Journal of Applied Behavior Analysis, 12,* 3–25.

Wurtman, R. J., & Wurtman, J. (1984). Nutrients, neurotransmitter synthesis, and the control of food intake. In A. J. Stunkard & E. Stellar (Eds.), *Eating and its disorders.* New York: Raven Press.

Zellner, D., Harner, D., & Adler, R. (1989). Effects of eating abnormalities and gender on perceptions of desirable body shape. *Journal of Abnormal Psychology, 98,* 93–96.

Zielinski, J. (1978). Depressive symptomatology: Deviations form a personal norm. *Journal of Community Psychology, 6,* 163–167.

Part Four

Menstruation and Pain

The authors in Part Four of this volume address women's experience of menstrual symptoms and women's experience of pain, focusing, in particular, on pain arising from the female reproductive organs. While pain and other symptoms (e.g., irritability, tension) commonly associated with the menstrual cycle represent, in part, learned cultural beliefs, menstrual pain is the only "menstrual-related" symptom that has been shown to relate directly to physiologic/hormonal factors (i.e., prostaglandin levels).[1] Pain (like infertility, which is discussed in the next section of this book) also sometimes is related to pelvic disease (e.g., endometriosis). Moreover, few "menstrual-related" symptoms other than dysmenorrhea (menstrual pain) are described by women as severe or reported cross-culturally. Consequently, the first chapter in this section (Kato Klebanov and Ruble) critically reviews research on women's experience of menstrual cycle symptoms, and the second chapter (Reading) covers broad issues related to the experience of chronic pain in women (in particular, pelvic pain) and its assessment and management.

Pamela Kato Klebanov and Diane Ruble's review of the research on menstrual cycle-related changes represents a significant contribution to our understanding of women's experience of menstrual symptoms. The authors present convincing evi-

[1]Although water retention has been linked to hormone changes, the hormonal link for water retention is weaker than that for pain.

dence showing that women's experience of menstrual symptoms is best understood as an interaction of physiological/hormonal and sociocultural factors.

The approach and onset of menstruation have often been thought to have a debilitating effect on women's physical and mental health, academic, athletic, and work performance, and decision-making capabilities. Remarks that a woman president might impulsively "push the button" and initiate global nuclear warfare during her "period" and admonishments to avoid physical activity during menstruation reflect these assumptions. In their review of the literature Kato Klebanov and Ruble demonstrate that these assumptions are unfounded and present critical evidence to challenge these assumptions point by point. They reveal that there is little empirical evidence to support the notion of menstrual cycle-related performance decrements (or enhancements), that only a small minority of women experience cycle-related somatic or affective symptoms, and that women's reports of moods across the month do not differ from men's. Further, as indicated above, researchers have been unable to relate any "menstrual-related" symptoms directly to cyclic changes in hormones, with the notable exception of pain. Thus a direct hormonal basis for the purported debilitating effects of the menstrual cycle remains unsubstantiated. Yet as Kato Klebanov and Ruble note, progesterone therapy continues to be the most popular "treatment" for premenstrual symptomatology even though double-blind studies show it to have no greater therapeutic effectiveness than placebo administration. Finally, Kato Klebanov and Ruble marshall ample evidence to demonstrate the crucial role of cultural beliefs in menstrual symptom reports.

Anthony Reading's chapter on pain represents a unique contribution to the literature on women's health in that it specifically focuses on pain arising from the female reproductive organs. Reading discusses both acute pain associated with normal functions and events such as menstruation and childbirth and chronic pain associated with disorders such as dysmenorrhea and endometriosis. A substantial body of research on chronic pain patients suggests that chronic pain can contribute to disturbances in many areas of health and functioning. Reading carefully examines the many factors that place individuals at risk for the development of chronic pain. These risk factors include not only organic pathology but also a host of personality and overall adjustment factors. The absence of longitudinal research makes a full understanding of the connections among these factors obscure at present. Reading also summarizes a fascinating line of research that indicates a connection between childhood abuse, both physical and sexual, and chronic pelvic pain. This research suggests the importance of understanding the role not only of the biologic but also of the environmental and learning factors in the development and treatment of the experience of pain. Indeed, Reading asserts that "it is necessary to embrace the twofold reality that pain is always real, never imagined and that it always has both physiologic and psychosocial components."

Chapter 8

Toward an Understanding of Women's Experience of Menstrual Cycle Symptoms

Pamela Kato Klebanov
Diane N. Ruble

Menstruation has often been viewed as a "curse" to women (Delaney, Lupton, & Toth, 1976). The menstruating woman has been commonly thought of as unclean, impure, irrational, and even dangerous. Although much of women's suffering can be attributed to the stigma surrounding menstruation, women's claims of both unpleasant physical symptoms and psychological changes associated with the approach of menstruation have been documented by medical journals and in 1953 formally proposed as the premenstrual syndrome (Greene & Dalton, 1953).

The primary research question concerning the premenstrual syndrome has been whether underlying hormonal changes are responsible for the reported psychological, somatic, and behavioral effects. This question has remained unanswered despite over 30 years of research and a resurgence of interest in the issue over the last 10 to 15 years. Research findings have been inconclusive: evidence of cycle-related changes is reported in some studies and not in others. Curiously, there appear to be negative implications for women whatever the findings. Research supporting an association between cycle phase and the experience of symptoms has often led to statements that women are unstable, controlled by their biology. On the other hand, an inability to find an association has often led to suggestions that cycle-related changes are "all in a woman's head" (Bird, 1987).

The intent of this chapter is to provide a critical review of menstrual research, from the past research tendency to examine cycle-related changes as a result of either physiological/hormonal changes or psychological factors to the more recent efforts towards considering their interaction. The chapter will begin with a brief overview of the hormonal events underlying the menstrual cycle, followed by a discussion of the physiological, psychological, and behavioral effects associated with the menstrual cycle. Methodological issues will be examined before an evaluation of the findings is offered. Finally, promising directions for future research will be discussed.

HORMONAL EVENTS AND PHYSIOLOGICAL CORRELATES OF THE MENSTRUAL CYCLE

Menstruation, or the monthly shedding of the endometrial blood, is a natural cyclic process regulated by changes in hormone levels that are controlled by the hypothalamus and the pituitary gland. Menstruation occurs in women between the ages of 10–14 and 40–50 years (Linkie, 1982), and the average menstrual cycle is 28 days long. Many women, however, have either longer or shorter cycles than the 28 days and also experience some variability in their cycle from month to month. Along with the hormonal changes during each menstrual cycle, the ovaries develop and release an ovum, and the uterus is prepared for possible implantation of the ovum if it is fertilized. If fertilization does not occur, the decline of estrogen and progesterone levels results in the shedding of the endometrial lining, or the start of menstrual flow.

The menstrual cycle begins with the first day of (blood) flow. During the menstrual phase, which lasts an average of 3 to 5 days, approximately 2–3 ounces of menstrual blood and uterine tissue are lost. As menstruation begins on Day 1, one of the many immature ova begins to mature in one of the two ovaries. In addition, once the uterine lining is shed, a new lining begins to develop. An increase in estrogen thickens the endometrial lining of the uterus. The ovary is now in the follicular phase, the stage that follows menstrual flow and ends with ovulation, and the hypothalamus signals the production of more estrogen.

During the next two weeks of the menstrual cycle, estrogen levels continue to rise and the follicle grows and matures. By approximately Day 16, estrogen has reached its highest point of the cycle and the ovary releases the follicle, which is now fully mature. During ovulation, the ovum lives for about 2 days in the woman's reproductive system and can be fertilized by sperm at this time.

After Day 17, estrogen levels decline slightly, and the empty follicle develops into the corpus luteum. The corpus luteum produces both estrogen and progesterone, and as a result, the ovary enters the luteal phase. The luteal phase is approximately 14 days long and spans the interval between ovulation and the onset of menstruation (Gannon, 1985; Hatcher et al., 1982). The increased levels of progesterone from the ovaries now stimulate glands in the endometrium to secrete a mucus-like substance that prepares the uterus for a fertilized egg. Joint levels of estrogen and progesterone peak on or around Day 24; if fertilization has not occurred, the corpus luteum begins to atrophy and levels of both estrogen and progesterone decline. This rapid decline of hormones is often designated as the late luteal or premenstrual phase and signals the end of the cycle. The uterus prepares to shed the lining developed during that cycle and to initiate a new menstrual cycle (e.g., Hongladarom, McCorkle, & Woods, 1985).

PSYCHOLOGICAL, PHYSICAL, AND BEHAVIORAL CORRELATES OF THE MENSTRUAL CYCLE

It is widely believed that underlying hormonal changes throughout the menstrual cycle are responsible for a variety of negative psychological, physical, and behavioral effects. Symptoms occurring in the premenstrual phase often have been referred to as the premenstrual syndrome, though other terms have also been used: premenstrual tension syndrome (Haskett, Steiner, Osmun, & Carroll, 1980), premenstrual distress (Moos, 1968b, 1985), and premenstrual changes (Halbreich & Endicott, 1985a,b). In addition, a distinction between the premenstrual syndrome and premenstrual symptoms was made by Brooks-Gunn (1986). The term ''premenstrual syndrome'' refers to a specific cluster of severe and time-limited symptoms, whereas the term ''premenstrual symptoms'' refers to a mild to moderate experience of symptoms not strictly demarcated in time. Although this distinction is useful, until very recently few studies have designated specific criteria for such a syndrome. Thus, in the present chapter, the less restrictive term ''premenstrual symptoms'' will be used. The term ''perimenstrual symptoms'' will refer to symptoms experienced during both the premenstrual and menstrual phases. In addition, the term ''dysmenorrhea'' will refer to primary dysmenorrhea, or the experience of severe spasmodic pain during menstruation in the absence of pelvic pathology. Secondary dysmenorrhea, or the experience of severe menstrual pain associated with diseases of the pelvis, will not be discussed (Fuchs, 1982).

Many women report experiencing more negative affective states such as depression, irritability, and tension, as well as physical discomfort from water retention and cramps, during the perimenstrual phase of their cycle (Logue & Moos, 1986; Moos, 1985). Estimates of prevalence vary widely. By some recent accounts, approximately 30–50% of all women experience some degree of perimenstrual symptoms (Logue & Moos, 1986; Woods, Most, & Dery, 1982). Although such prevalence statistics imply that a substantial percentage of women experience cycle-related symptoms, these reports are deceiving. When such reports assess symptom severity, it appears that relatively few of these women experience strong symptoms (Fuchs, 1982). According to Woods et al. (1982), for example, with the exception of cramps (17%) and irritability (12%), less than 8% of the women reported intense perimenstrual symptoms.

Although much of the focus of recent scientific and popular concern has involved affective fluctuations, actual evidence of a link between cycle phase and affective symptoms such as negative mood changes has been weak. Some studies have found increases in stress and self-reported negative moods during the perimenstrual phase (Collins, Eneroth, & Landgren, 1985; Golub, 1976a,b; Sanders, Warner, Backstrom, & Bancroft, 1983), and others have not (Abplanalp, Rose, Donnelly, & Livingston-Vaughn, 1979; Cockrill, Appell, & Carson, 1988; Laessle, Tuschl, Schweiger, & Pirke, 1990; Little & Zahn, 1974; C. McFarland, Ross, & DeCourville, 1989). One early review found that about half of the studies examining mood changes prospectively failed to show even marginally significant differences across cycle phase (Ruble & Brooks-Gunn, 1979). In a more recent review, of the 20 studies examined, 9 failed to find significant effects, 6 reported significant effects, and 5 reported equivocal findings (Gannon, 1985).

Among possible physical changes (pain, water retention, weight gain), increased pain and water retention during the perimenstrual phase have received more consistent support (Biro & Stukovsky, 1985; Englander-Golden, Whitmore, & Dienstbier, 1978; Laessle et al., 1990; C. McFarland et al., 1989; Rouse, 1978; Ruble & Brooks-Gunn, 1979; Sampson & Jenner, 1977; Wilcoxon, Schrader, & Sherif, 1976). However, most significant findings are based on self-reports of symptoms. In some cases, studies that have relied on more objective measures of water retention (i.e., the potassium-sodium ratio or actual weight gain) have not found significant effects for water retention. Gannon (1985) reviews these studies.

As for actual behavior change, the consensus after years of research (Golub, 1976a; Jensen, 1982; Sommer, 1982, 1983) suggests there is no significant decrement in cognitive functioning or motor performance over the menstrual cycle. This conclusion holds for a range of cognitive, visual-spatial, perceptual-motor, and psychophysiological measures as well as for studies of work and academic performance. However, recent highly publicized findings of performance decrements on selected tasks, which will be discussed later in the chapter, have reopened this question (Hampson, 1990; Hampson & Kimura, 1988).

In sum, actual support for the existence of perimenstrual symptoms is weak. Although stronger evidence exists in support of certain physical symptoms, pain and water retention, the results for mood changes and for actual behavioral changes are tenuous. We turn now to a more detailed discussion of methodological problems with the research linking psychological changes to the menstrual cycle.

METHODOLOGICAL PROBLEMS IN RELATING HORMONAL EVENTS TO PSYCHOSOMATIC CHANGES

The Determination of Menstrual Cycle Phases

Because researchers are often interested in assessing women's reports of symptoms at discrete points in time, accurate determination of a woman's cycle phase is highly important. Although the onset of menses is salient, other phases of the menstrual cycle are not in any way distinct. Hormonal assays provide the most direct and accurate means of assessing cycle phase because they detect levels of estrogen and progesterone that fluctuate throughout the menstrual cycle. Many researchers (Halbreich & Endicott, 1985a; Osborn, 1981) have specifically relied on levels of progesterone as an indicator of menstrual cycle phase. Progesterone levels increase during the start of the luteal phase, reach a peak during the middle, and decline sharply immediately before the onset of menstruation. There is even evidence that biweekly measurements of progesterone can predict menstrual onset to within 1 day with 98% accuracy (Osborn, 1981). Despite the greater accuracy in determining menstrual cycle phase, few studies have employed hormonal assays. Practical considerations are one obvious influencing factor, because the use of hormonal assays is both time consuming and expensive (Gannon, 1985). There are, however, some unresolved methodological issues associated with the use of hormonal assays (Paikoff, Buchanan, & Brooks-Gunn, 1991). Three commonly cited factors that may influence the results of hormonal assays are the time of day assays are drawn, the frequency of measurement, and the method of measurement (urine, blood plasma, or saliva). To date, however, the actual significance of each of these factors in contributing to the variability of hormone levels obtained has not been fully assessed.

Recently, a few investigators have used physiological indicators of phases, but this methodological refinement in itself does not ensure consistency of results across studies when other systematic methodological differences exist between studies. For example, in two studies that agreed on the designation of phases based on regular hormonal assays of blood plasma and that studied cycle-related mood changes, quite discrepant results were found (Abplanalp et al., 1979; Sanders et al., 1983). The study by Abplanalp et al. (1979) did not find a significant relationship between mood states and cycle phase or a significant correlation between levels of estrogen and progesterone and mood states. In contrast, Sanders et al. (1983) found, for women claiming to experience premenstrual symptoms, that mood was highest during ovulation and decreased in the luteal phase. All women, however, reported an increase in physical distress that peaked in the premenstrual phase.

Although the two studies employed similar methodologies, there are several differences between them that may account for the discrepant results: (a) In

Sanders et al. (1983), a distinction was made between women who reported experiencing premenstrual symptoms and women who reported being asymptomatic. Because it was found that only women who claimed to experience premenstrual symptoms reported significant mood changes, this difference may in part explain the results; (b) as noted by Sanders et al. (1983), who solicited the participation of 55 women, the Abplanalp et al. (1979) study was based on a much smaller sample of 14 women. For this reason, there may not have been sufficient statistical power for the study by Abplanalp et al. to have obtained significant results; (c) Abplanalp's subjects were prescreened for neuroticism, whereas Sanders et al.'s subjects were not, creating possibly important differences in subject groups; and (d) the women in the Sanders et al. study were informed about the purpose of the study, whereas those in the Abplanalp et al. study were not. To some extent women in the Sanders et al. study may have responded in a manner consistent with the expectation of the experimenter. Although the results of Sanders et al. and Abplanalp et al. demonstrate that accurate phase designations do not guarantee comparable results, studies that rely on indirect assessment of menstrual cycle phase have additional problems.

At best, a majority of studies have relied on an indirect assessment of menstrual cycle phases. Many researchers have relied upon a simple division of the menstrual cycle into four phases of equal length (Sommer, 1983). Others have fixed the designated phases of interest, namely, the premenstrual and menstrual phases, and have designated the remainder of the cycle as the intermenstrual phase (Gannon, 1985). Although the menstrual phase is commonly designated as the first 3 to 4 days of menstrual flow, some researchers have designated the premenstrual phase as anywhere between 1 day prior to menstruation to 14 days prior, or the entire length of the luteal phase (Halbreich, Endicott, & Lesser, 1985). Such variation is one possible reason for inconsistent findings across studies. Recently, there has been a trend toward specifying the premenstrual phase as 4 days prior to menstruation, the time when both estrogen and progesterone drop markedly (Asso, 1978; Asso & Beech, 1975; Golub, 1976a,b; Haskett & Abplanalp, 1983; Moos, 1985; Villa & Beech, 1977; Wilcoxon et al., 1976).

To determine a woman's menstrual phase, most studies rely on counting reverse cycle days, that is, counting backwards from the onset of menstrual flow (Adesso & Freitag, 1989; Englander-Golden, Willis, & Dienstbier, 1977; Kato, 1989; Klebanov & Jemmott, 1992; Ruble, 1977). Women's predictions of onset are thought to be inaccurate because the length of a woman's menstrual cycle varies from month to month, so that a woman may actually be either closer or farther from her period than she thinks. A recent study (Adesso & Freitag, 1989) revealed that a woman's accuracy for her predicted onset of menstruation depends on her actual phase of the menstrual cycle. Women more accurately predicted the onset of menstruation when they were in their ovulatory phase than when they were in their menstrual phase. This result is explained in terms of the length of time from a woman's last period. Menstruating women, who are further from their last period than ovulatory women, have a greater difficulty remembering when their last period started. Because of this, menstruating women are not able to determine the amount of intercycle variability and should have greater difficulty accurately predicting the onset of their next period than ovulatory women.

Although the use of reverse cycle days and the attempt to control the variation in premenstrual phase designation permit comparability between studies, they do not necessarily lead to consistent findings. In two studies designating the premenstrual phase as 4 days prior to menstruation and employing the same mood measure, the State-Trait Anxiety Inventory (STAI), contradictory findings were obtained. In one study (Golub, 1976a), significant increases in self-reported premenstrual depression and anxiety were found, though no significant differences were found for cognitive performance. In the other study (Cockrill et al., 1988), no significant results were found for either mood or cognitive performance.

In summary, there are two issues to consider: the consistency of the day designation itself and the problem of linking designated days to actual hormonal events. The failure to have a common definition of the timing of the premenstrual phase makes it difficult to interpret inconsistencies across studies. At an even more basic level, however, the reliance on indirect measures of phase as an indicator of hormonal status may result in misleading conclusions. Even if cycle phase differences are found in such studies, the hormonal basis of these differences cannot be distinguished from more social psychological aspects of a woman's perceptions of her cycle phase, an issue to be discussed in greater detail in subsequent sections.

Self-Reports as Measures of Psychosomatic Change

One inherent problem facing menstrual cycle research is its reliance on self-reports of menstrual symptomatology. The most widely used measure to gather information about the nature, severity, and prevalence of symptoms experienced throughout the menstrual cycle has been the Moos Menstrual Distress Questionnaire (MDQ; Moos, 1968b). The MDQ is composed of 47 symptoms representing eight symptom scales (pain, water retention, negative affect, autonomic reactions, arousal, behavior change, concentration, and control). Symptom reports are assessed either prospectively or retrospectively. Women are either asked to keep a daily record of their symptom experience over a period of one or more menstrual cycles or asked to recall their previous experience of symptoms during their menstrual and premenstrual phases. Of the two measures of assessment, retrospective reports are often preferred because they expedite data collection. Ratings of symptoms for all phases of the menstrual cycle are gathered at once, rather than over the entire cycle. In general, studies that have employed retrospective reports reveal larger symptom changes across the menstrual cycle than studies that have employed prospective reports (Cook et al., 1990; May, 1976;

Parlee, 1974, 1982; Ruble & Brooks-Gunn, 1979; Sommer, 1983). Moreover, retrospective and daily self-reports may even show completely different patterns of symptoms (Englander-Golden, Sonleitner, Whitmore, & Corbley, 1985).

Prospective reports have consistently shown small or nonsignificant symptom changes (Englander-Golden et al., 1978; Swandby, 1981; Wilcoxon et al., 1976). In one study (Parlee, 1982) women's daily reports of symptoms were measured over a 90-day period. A significant increase in *positive* mood was found during the premenstrual phase. At the end of the study, these same women retrospectively reported experiencing an increase in *negative* mood during the premenstrual phase. A recent study by J. McFarland, Martins, and Williams (1988) obtained similar results. In this study, subjects made daily ratings of mood over 70 days and then provided retrospective ratings at the end of the study. Although prospective reports revealed nonsignificant changes over the menstrual cycle, these women recalled the premenstrual phase as significantly less pleasant than the follicular phase. These studies elegantly demonstrate that when subjects fill out retrospective reports and are aware that menstrual-cycle symptoms are being researched, they may be simply responding in accordance with widely held beliefs about the association between symptomatology and the menstrual cycle (Brooks-Gunn & Ruble, 1980b; Parlee, 1974).

In addition to the problems of demand characteristics, retrospective reports rely on a woman's memory for a past cycle and may be easily distorted because of difficulties in recalling past events. Prospective reports minimize the problem of vagaries in memory and also often avoid problems of demand characteristics. Studies employing prospective reports often disguise the purpose of such reports (Parlee, 1982; Wilcoxon et al., 1976), though subjects in some prospective studies are told that menstrual symptoms are of interest to the researcher (Sanders et al., 1983).

Generally, studies investigating the effect of demand characteristics on prospective reports have found that disguised reports result in smaller cycle phase changes than studies in which subjects are told that menstrual symptoms are of interest to the researcher (AuBuchon & Calhoun, 1985; Englander-Golden et al., 1978; for exceptions see Gallant, Popiel, Hoffman, Chakraborty, & Hamilton, 1992a). Such findings have led some researchers to question the validity of self-reports as representing women's direct experience of symptoms and the clinical significance or magnitude of cycle-related changes (Parlee, 1974, 1982; Ruble, 1977; Ruble & Brooks-Gunn, 1979. Richardson, 1990 has recently reviewed these issues).

Assessing the Clinical Significance of Women's Reports: Proper Comparison Groups and Measures

A third kind of problem in menstrual cycle research is what constitutes a proper baseline or comparison for reported changes in psychosomatic symptoms. In order to argue that cycling hormones lead to cycling patterns of symptoms, it is important to show that symptom cyclicity does not occur in individuals without such hormone variation. Moreover, in order to argue that symptom cyclicity is of clinical significance, it is important to show that the magnitude of negative changes is greater than comparison reports that are not considered to be of clinical significance.

One way these concerns have been addressed is to compare women's reports with those of men because the hormone levels of men are stable and noncyclic in contrast with the hormonal fluctuations characteristic of the menstrual cycle. The overall conclusion from these studies has been that women's reports of symptoms are not significantly greater or different than those of men's (Au-Buchon & Calhoun, 1985; J. McFarland et al., 1988; Parlee, 1980; Rogers & Harding, 1981; Swandby, 1981; Weidner & Helmig, 1990). There is, however, some evidence that women's reports of increased pain and water retention are linked to hormone changes. Whereas men reported stable levels of pain and water retention, women reported increases in pain and water retention only during the perimenstrual phase. In contrast, an association between negative mood and hormone changes was not supported (Cox, 1983; Wilcoxon et al., 1976).

Other studies have relied upon comparisons between women on oral contraceptives and normally cycling women to assess the effect of differing hormone levels on symptom patterns and severity. Unlike the hormone levels of normally cycling women, the hormone levels of women on oral contraceptives are regulated by the dosage of progestin and estrogen, which suppress ovulation and thereby maintain relatively stable hormone levels throughout the menstrual cycle. Although a few studies cite an attenuation of perimenstrual symptoms for women on birth control pills (Englander-Golden et al., 1977; Moos, 1968a), most studies have not (Brooks, Ruble, & Clarke, 1977; Glick & Bennett, 1982; Morris & Udry, 1972; Silbergeld, Brast, & Noble, 1971; Sampson & Jenner, 1977; Swandby, 1981; Wilcoxon et al., 1976). Similarly, a recent prospective symptom report study by J. McFarland et al. (1988) found that neither women on birth control pills nor normally cycling women reported significant changes in symptoms throughout the menstrual cycle.

Further attempts to assess the clinical significance of actual cycle-related changes have compared the magnitude and experience of these changes with those of stressful daily life events. One study (Wilcoxon et al., 1976) found that daily stressors accounted for more of the overall statistical variance in women's negative mood than did actual cycle phase. Similarly, other studies (J. McFarland et al., 1988; Rossi & Rossi, 1980) have found mood to be significantly related to day of the week, with greatest arousal and pleasantness reported for weekends and lowest ratings at the start of the week. The study by J. McFarland et al. (1988) even found that women's moods fluctuate less over the menstrual cycle than they do over days of the week. This pattern for day of the week was also found for men, and the pattern was more pronounced when assessed by retrospective reports. One recent study (Beck, Gevirtz & Mortola, 1990), however, found that for women with prospectively confirmed severe PMS, daily stress did not significantly account for their report of mood or physical symptoms.

In summary, the bulk of research does not support the claim that women's experience of perimenstrual symptoms is either qualitatively or quantitatively different from what is experienced by men or by women on birth control pills, or from what is experienced during other phases of the menstrual cycle. These results thus seriously question assumptions that women's reports of menstrual symptoms are necessarily hormone related and that they are of clinical significance, at least when comparisons are made across group averages. However, these findings do not negate the possibility that a subset of women experience clinically significant symptoms that are hormone related.

INTERPRETATIONS OF THE FINDINGS

Methodological problems, from a lack of consensus about the definition of cycle phases to problems with the method of assessment, have impeded research efforts. It is often not clear whether significant results are methodological artifacts or meaningful findings. In this section, we consider the various ways that finding menstrual-related psychosomatic changes (or lack thereof) may be interpreted.

Proposed Hormonal Basis for Premenstrual Symptoms

Because the timing or onset of symptoms is crucial to defining premenstrual symptoms, the fluctuations of the ovarian hormones estrogen and progesterone have been implicated as possible underlying causes. Hypotheses have emerged as to a progesterone deficit, an estrogen excess, the ratio between estrogen and progesterone, or more recently, to women's sensitivity to hormonal levels or fluctuations during the menstrual cycle (Schechter, Bachmann, Vaitukaitis, Phillips, & Saperstein, 1989). Although further research is necessary to evaluate the merits of the last hypothesis, all of the other hypotheses have met with, at best, modest explanatory success (Abplanalp, 1983; Clare, 1985; Gannon, 1985; Green, 1982; Janowsky, 1985; Rubinow & Roy-Byrne, 1984). Hormonal differences between asymptomatic women and women experiencing premenstrual symptoms have not been found (Rubinow et al., 1987; Sondheimer, Freeman, Scharlop, & Rickels, 1985; for exceptions see Dennerstein, Spencer-Gardner, Brown, Smith, & Burrows, 1984). One study by Collins et al. (1985), however, found that women with high levels of estrogen in the luteal phase reported greater fatigue, egotism, and affection than women with low levels of estrogen. No significant relationship between estrogen and eight other mood variables was found. This finding is discrepant with women's self-reports of consistently negative perimenstrual mood. There was no significant relationship between levels of progesterone, LH (luteinizing hormone), FSH (follicle stimulating hormone), and catecholamine excretion and self-reported mood. Despite scant support for the relationship between fluctuation of the ovarian hormones estrogen and progesterone and premenstrual symptoms, none of the alternative hypotheses proposed in recent years has garnered much support. A detailed discussion of each hypothesis is beyond the scope of this chapter, and many reviews of the literature exist (Abplanalp, 1983; Alberts & Alberts, 1990; Clare, 1985; Gannon, 1985; Green, 1982; Janowsky, 1985).

Most of these hypothesized mechanisms attempt to explain specific symptoms associated with the premenstrual phase, such as mood or water retention (Gannon, 1985; Rubinow & Roy-Byrne, 1984). Increases in prolactin and aldosterone have been implicated because of their purported effects on water retention and weight gain, though the results for each are mixed (Gannon, 1985; Rausch & Janowsky, 1982; Rubinow & Roy-Byrne, 1984). Most studies have not supported increases in aldosterone and prolactin during the luteal phase or a significant difference in the levels of prolactin or aldosterone between women experiencing premenstrual symptoms and asymptomatic women (Janowsky, 1985; Rubinow et al., 1987; Rubinow & Roy-Byrne, 1984).

Other hypothesized mechanisms have related levels of serum cortisol, melatonin, and monoamine oxidase (MAO) to negative affective states such as depression. Elevated levels of serum cortisol have been purported to exist in women reporting premenstrual symptoms, though the actual evidence is inconsistent (Gannon, 1985; Rubinow et al., 1987). Similarly, though there is some evidence that melatonin can improve mood in normal subjects, evidence linking levels of melatonin to premenstrual negative affect is nonexistent (Rausch & Janowsky, 1982). Elevated levels of MAO also have been proposed as a mediator between ovarian hormones and depression. Although the evidence for elevated levels of MAO is mixed, there is some evidence for higher levels in depressed women than in normal women (Gannon, 1985). Some researchers have recently even postulated that carbohydrate metabolism, because of the similarity between hypoglycemia symptoms and premenstrual symptoms, and endogenous opiates, because of their purported physiological effects, are important mediators of premenstrual symptoms. Actual evidence in support of either carbohydrate metabolism or endogenous opiates is scant. As a whole, support for any of the proposed physiological mechanisms is unconvincing.

These conclusions have important implications for current forms of treatment. Despite the lack of support for a hormonal basis of premenstrual symptoms, progesterone therapy is currently the most popular method of treatment. There have been several specific attempts to evaluate the initial claims that premenstrual symptoms improve as a result of progesterone therapy (Dalton, 1984; Freeman, Sondheimer, Rickels, & Weinbaum, 1985), but such claims have not been substantiated by studies employing proper standards of control—

i.e., a double-blind administration of progesterone and placebo. Two of the most commonly cited studies, Smith (1976) and Sampson (1979), both failed to find any difference in treatment effects between progesterone and placebo. More recent studies by Andersch and Hahn (1985) and Freeman, Rickels, Sondheimer, and Polansky (1990) that employed a double-blind administration of progesterone and placebo reported an improvement in symptoms for both treatments but no difference in the effectiveness of the two. Similarly, Vander Meer, Benedek-Jaszmann and Van Loenen (1983) and Richter, Hattvick, and Shapiro (1984) report no difference in treatment effectiveness between progesterone and placebo treatments.

One treatment study (Metcalf & Hudson, 1985), however, presents some interesting qualifications to the findings in support of the placebo effect. Reports of mood and physical premenstrual symptoms during regular cycles were compared with reports during cycles where a placebo treatment was introduced. The results revealed that the placebo treatment had a significant effect on reports of premenstrual *mood* symptoms. There was a decrease in both the incidence (number of women who met the experimenters' criteria for premenstrual mood symptoms) and the overall severity of reported premenstrual mood symptoms. The results for *physical* symptoms, however, revealed that the placebo treatment did not affect the incidence of reported premenstrual physical symptoms, but did significantly attenuate the severity of physical symptoms reported. Overall, the placebo treatment affected 26% of the women. These women reported significantly less severe cycle-related changes during placebo cycles than during regular cycles. For 67% of the women, however, there were no differences between the severity of symptom ratings for regular cycles versus placebo cycles. The remaining 7% of the women reported no sign of premenstrual symptoms during both regular and placebo cycles. This study suggests that affective symptoms may be somewhat more susceptible to suggestion than physical symptoms and that the placebo effect may be limited to certain subtypes of women.

Other treatments have addressed the alleviation of specific symptoms. Diuretic therapy was found to be no more effective than placebo in alleviating water retention (Green, 1982). The use of bromocriptine, a dopamine agonist which suppresses the secretion of prolactin and purportedly eases water retention, has met with some success, though the presence of side effects limit its uses as a treatment (Gannon, 1985; Rausch & Janowsky, 1982; Rubinow & Roy-Byrne, 1984). Similarly, lithium carbonate and pyridoxine were no more effective than placebo in treating mood symptoms (Green, 1982; Rubinow & Roy-Byrne, 1984).

In sum, most reviews of the literature have not supported the hypothesis that menstrual-related symptom changes are associated with fluctuations in estrogen and progesterone (Green, 1982; Gannon, 1985; Keye, 1985) or that progesterone therapy is more effective than a placebo, at least for most women reporting premenstrual symptoms. Whether women who report more premenstrual and menstrual symptoms differ from other women in their sensitivity to hormones remains to be seen. However, other proposed physiological mechanisms have not received substantiation, and the treatment of symptoms has remained unsuccessful. Although a robust placebo effect does not rule out physiological explanations, it underscores the importance of psychological mediators.

Proposed Hormonal Basis for Dysmenorrhea

Unlike premenstrual symptoms, primary dysmenorrhea, or painful menstruation in the absence of pelvic pathology (Fuchs, 1982), has been linked empirically to physiological factors. Compelling evidence exists for the link between dysmenorrhea and prostaglandins. Prostaglandins, or naturally occurring unsaturated fatty acids, are present in menstrual fluid and bodily tissues. The immediate cause of pain has been traced to myometrial contractions, and women with dysmenorrhea have experienced cramps of even greater severity than those experienced by women at the height of labor (Friederich, 1983). Studies have shown that reports of pain coincide with contractions and, conversely, that as contractions decrease, pain levels subside (Gannon, 1985). In addition, it has been found that the administration of prostaglandins produces myometrial contractions and other dysmenorrheic symptoms, whereas prostaglandin inhibitors provide relief of such symptoms. The mere presence of prostaglandin, however, is not the cause of dysmenorrhea since prostaglandins normally increase during the luteal and menstrual phases. Rather, it is the level of prostaglandins that is important. Most studies have found that women with dysmenorrhea have higher levels of prostaglandins in menstrual fluid than asymptomatic women (an exception being Chan, Dawood, & Fuchs, 1979). Although it is not known why dysmenorrheic women have higher levels of prostaglandins, many hypotheses have been proposed: increased prostaglandin production, excess or abnormal release of prostaglandin, and hypersensitivity to prostaglandins (Friederich, 1983; Gannon, 1985). Others have even hypothesized that high levels of prostaglandins may be the result, rather than the cause, of increased contractions since prostaglandin is often released in response to the stretching of muscle (Gannon, 1985). In this case the contractions are brought on by an obstruction of the cervix, either because of a small cervical exit or because of large endometrial fragments that need to be expelled. Prostaglandins are thus released as a result of the contractions. However, the question of the mechanism that triggers the contraction is left unanswered (Gannon, 1985).

Other methods of treating dysmenorrhea have dealt mainly with the experience of pain through behavioral treatments such as systematic desensitization techniques or relaxation techniques (Gannon, 1985). Methodological problems such as the absence of control groups and differences between studies in amount of training and method of administration make comparability of results difficult. Overall, treatment results have been equivocal (Calhoun & Burnette, 1984).

Still, the effectiveness of methods such as heating pads, exercise regimens, and diet changes, cannot be assessed (Fuchs, 1982).

Proposed Psychological Basis for Perimenstrual Symptoms

The social psychological literature abounds with demonstrations that personal expectations or social cues are important in the perception and labeling of undifferentiated physical states (Nisbett & Schachter, 1966; Pennebaker, 1983; Rodin, 1976; Ross & Olson, 1981; Schachter & Singer, 1962; Zillman, 1983). Because the psychosomatic symptoms associated with the menstrual cycle represent subjective, ambiguous states and because they occur in a social context with known beliefs about what menstruating women are supposed to experience or be like, such social psychological processes may be quite important in interpreting the results of menstrual cycle research.

In the past 10 to 15 years, there have been several accounts of how social psychological processes may influence perceptions of menstrual symptoms. Empirical and theoretical analyses by Koeske (1980), for example, indicate the significance of labeling and misattribution effects. In one study, Koeske and Koeske (1975) found that men and women, in making judgments about another woman's mood, tend to attribute her negative moods to the menstrual cycle if they are aware that the woman was in her premenstrual phase, even when other negative situational factors are present and may account for her actions. A recent replication of the study by Bains and Slade (1988) also supports the tendency of women to attribute negative moods to the premenstrual phase of the menstrual cycle rather than to personality and environmental factors. Thus knowledge that a woman is premenstrual may serve as a salient though possibly incomplete or erroneous explanation for negative moods or behaviors. Consequently, it is difficult to determine the extent to which changes in a woman's behavior, either reported by herself or perceived by others, are products of cyclic hormonal influences or labeling effects.

Ruble and Brooks-Gunn (1979) have described how perceptions of cyclicity may be acquired and maintained by common biases and errors in the way people process information when making judgments (e.g., Ross, 1977; Tversky & Kahneman, 1974). For example, the tendency or bias to remember instances of the co-occurrence of two events and not instances of their nonoccurrence may result in an "illusory correlation"—an overestimation of the degree of relation between the approach of menstruation and the experience of symptoms, occasioned by the pairing of two distinctive events (Chapman & Chapman, 1967; Hamilton & Gifford, 1976). In this view, the premenstrual phase is distinctive because of its limited temporal interval relative to the entire cycle marked by the onset of menstruation. Symptoms, too, are distinctive because they draw attention and because they occur relatively infrequently. Thus, even if symptoms occurred with equal frequency in all phases of the menstrual cycle, the co-occurrence of symptoms and the premenstrual phase would constitute paired distinctiveness (Chapman & Chapman, 1967; Hamilton & Gifford, 1976). Once a set of symptoms is labeled as menstrual related, an individual may continue to perceive an association between these symptoms and phases of the cycle even in the absence of a true relationship because the evidence can be distorted to be consistent with preexisting beliefs (e.g., the same abdominal discomfort may be labeled and perceived differently—cramps vs. indigestion—depending on the time of the month it occurs).

Biases in the recall of symptom experience may also serve to confirm or further reinforce women's beliefs of menstrual cyclicity. Recent work by C. McFarland et al. (1989) has found that women's beliefs about cyclicity—that symptoms occur during the premenstrual and menstrual phases and not during the intermenstrual phase of the menstrual cycle—guide the recall of symptom experience. Specifically, women who are in one phase of their cycle may recall the experience of symptoms in another phase of the cycle as qualitatively different. Pilot data collected by C. McFarland et al. showed that menstruating women recall the intermenstrual phase much more positively than women who are not menstruating at the time. Further research by the authors using a repeated measures design found that nonmenstruating women (i.e., women in their intermenstrual phase) recall the menstrual phase as worse than what they themselves had reported earlier when they were menstruating. In addition, the more a woman believes that the menstrual phase is associated with negative effects, the more negative symptoms she recalls. Thus encoding biases and memory biases may operate to exaggerate the association between symptoms and cycle phase and thereby help to maintain women's beliefs in cyclicity.

One of the most prevalent social-psychological accounts of menstrual symptoms involves the effects of social stereotypes or expectations. A considerable number of studies now support Parlee's (1974) suggestion that there is a set of clear cultural beliefs about cyclic changes and that direct experience of menstrual and premenstrual symptoms cannot fully account for reports of cyclic fluctuations. Two lines of research provide indirect evidence for the role of expectations: research on cross-cultural differences and research comparing individuals' beliefs within a culture. First, the shaping of our expectations by the culture in which we are socialized is evident in the differences in the pattern and severity of symptoms reported cross-culturally. Although the symptoms commonly experienced by Western women (cramps, aches and pains, irritability, and depression) are also experienced by women in third world countries (Ericksen, 1987) and there is some similarity in the incidence of physical symptoms in women across a wide range of cultures, reports of mood changes vary (Ericksen, 1987; Maluf & Ruble, 1993; Woods et al., 1982). Reports of premenstrual negative mood swings are more common among Anglo-Saxon Western women than among women in third world countries, who tend to report shifts in mood associated with the onset of menstruation or to report mood changes throughout the menstrual cycle (Ericksen, 1987; Snowden & Christian, 1983). In addition, other cultural variables related to lower socioeconomic standing and to traditional values and beliefs have also been associated with greater reports of menstrual-related symptoms (Ericksen, 1987; Woods et al., 1982). These relations are probably due either to greater stress associated with lower socioeconomic status or to cultural attitudes and practices associated with, for example, traditional religious beliefs (see Delaney et al., 1976, for a discussion of menstrual rituals and taboos associated with different religions). Delaney et al. also suggest that more traditional women may be more likely to think about and notice minor physical discomforts and emotional changes because they are more often home-bound than women who are working outside the home. Whatever the explanation, such findings clearly support a sociocultural view of symptom reporting.

Second, reports of symptoms that can only involve cultural beliefs are difficult to distinguish from self-reports of real symptoms. Results remarkably similar to women's retrospective accounts of their own symptoms are found, for example, when men and boys are asked to report what women experience (Brooks-Gunn & Ruble, 1986; Clarke & Ruble, 1978; Parlee, 1974) and when women are asked to respond "as if" they were menstrual or premenstrual (Ruble, Brooks-Gunn, & Clarke, 1980). Moreover, as described above, such accounts of cyclic changes in psychosomatic symptoms, especially mood, are often not supported by daily ratings, reports that should have greater validity because they occur much closer in time to the actual events. Of course, problems in the data base per se do not necessarily indicate the existence of biased beliefs, only that assumptions regarding cyclic changes are not yet justified by the data. Moreover, comparisons of retrospective and prospective accounts confound the effects of awareness that the study is concerned with menstrual changes with the effects of type of measure employed (prospective/retrospective). Thus such studies do not provide unequivocal evidence concerning the impact of expectations.

Recent experimental studies have avoided this problem, however, and provided more direct evidence concerning the effects of expectations. These studies employ a between-subjects design in which the same measure is used (prospective). Some subjects are explicitly informed that the study is concerned with menstrual cycle effects, and other subjects are not given any information that the study concerns the menstrual cycle. A study by AuBuchon and Calhoun (1985) found that women who were explicitly informed that the study's purpose was to examine the extent of menstrual-related changes reported greater perimenstrual psychological and somatic symptoms than women who were informed that the study addressed psychological and physiological changes over time. In a similar study (Rogers & Harding, 1981), women who were aware that the questionnaire assessed reports of menstrual cycle symptoms reported a more uniform pattern of symptoms than women who were not aware of the questionnaire's intent. However, in this study, women who were not aware reported greater overall symptoms than women who were aware.

Symptom reports by women who are aware that the menstrual cycle is of interest to the experimenter may be influenced by both personal expectations for menstrual symptoms and the experimental demands of the experiment. Subjects who do not believe in the association between the menstrual cycle and symptoms may provide stereotypical responses simply because they are aware that the experimenter is interested in menstrual cycle symptoms. In this sense, personal expectations and experimental expectations may be confounded.

A study by Ruble (1977) managed to overcome these methodological difficulties. Ruble manipulated a woman's perception of the timing of menstruation, quite apart from her actual menstrual cycle phase, while disguising the fact that the study was concerned with menstrual symptoms. It was hypothesized that if women's reports of menstrual symptoms were colored by expectations, manipulating a woman's perception of her phase would affect her report of symptoms regardless of her actual phase in the cycle. If, however, women's reports of symptoms were based on their experience of tangible cycle-related changes, reports of symptoms would not be affected. Volunteers for a study on contraception were told that a new technique using electroencephalogram readings would predict the onset of menstruation. The readings were engineered so that when women were informed of the results, some women were told their period would start in 1 to 2 days (''premenstrual'') and others were told their period would start in 7 to 10 days (''intermenstrual''). Although all the women were actually 6 to 7 days away from their period, women who were led to believe they were ''premenstrual'' reported experiencing greater pain and water retention on the previous few days than women led to believe they were ''intermenstrual.'' Thus women who labeled themselves as ''premenstrual'' responded as if they were premenstrual, though they may not have been symptomatic at this time.

A similar recent study by Klebanov and Jemmott (1992) also manipulated a woman's perception of the timing of menstruation, quite apart from her actual menstrual cycle phase. However, unlike the study by Ruble, a woman's report of premenstrual symptoms was assessed during either of two phases of her menstrual cycle (i.e., either premenstrual or intermenstrual) and her past history of premenstrual distress was assessed prior to her participation in the experiment. Individual differences in premenstrual distress were based on responses to the retrospective version of the Moos MDQ (1985) discretely administered prior to their participation in the experiment. As in the study by Ruble (1977), women were kept blind to the purpose of the experiment by being told that they were participating in a health study. The women were asked to try a new hormonal assay test designed to predict ovulation. In reality, the test was fictitious and was used to manipulate a woman's perception of her menstrual phase. Half of the women were told they were 3 to 4 days away from menstruation (''premenstrual'') and half were told they were 8 to 9 days away (''intermenstrual''). In fact, independent of perceived menstrual phase, approximately half the women were 1 to 7 days away from their period (premenstrual) and half were 8 or more days away (intermenstrual).

It was hypothesized that if women's retrospective reports of symptoms simply measure their expectations for symptoms rather than their experience of symptoms, as many researchers have claimed, then retrospective reports of higher distress should be more strongly associated with symptom reports in the lab when women are led to believe they are ''premenstrual,'' than when they are led to believe they are ''intermenstrual.'' If, however, retrospective reports reflect women's symptom experience, then the higher the woman's retrospective reports of premenstrual distress, the more symptoms she would report in the lab during her premenstrual phase or time of purported distress, regardless of whether the test indicated she was ''premenstrual'' or ''intermenstrual.'' Finally, it may be that all women respond to the expectation of being premenstrual by selectively attending to symptoms (Ruble, 1977). Thus, women led to believe they were ''premenstrual'' should report more symptoms during the lab session than women led to believe they were ''intermenstrual.''

Contrary to the hypothesis that women who report more premenstrual distress are doing so because of their expectancies for symptoms, the higher the woman's retrospective report of premenstrual distress, the more symptoms she reported in the lab during her premenstrual phase, regardless of what the test indicated. However, women who were told they were ''premenstrual'' reported greater symptoms than women who were told they were ''intermenstrual.'' Thus, this study, like Ruble's, found that expectations influence women's reports of premenstrual symptoms. Women respond to the label ''premenstrual'' as if they were premenstrual. However, this study also supports women's claims of a general worsening of symptoms during the premenstrual phase and suggests that future research focus on individual differences in premenstrual symptom reports.

Other recent studies have demonstrated that women report fewer premenstrual symptoms if they are told that the premenstrual syndrome has a psychological basis as opposed to a physiological basis (Fradkin & Firestone, 1986). However, a study that told women that menstrual cycle phase was unrelated to negative mood affected beliefs about premenstrual symptoms but failed to affect actual premenstrual symptom reports (Olasov & Jackson, 1987). Together, both studies suggest that women's premenstrual expectations/beliefs may not be firmly based upon their actual experience of symptoms, but rather upon what women are socialized to believe about the nature of symptoms.

In short, numerous studies have demonstrated that expectations can affect women's reports of symptoms. A further question is whether such expectations actually have a self-fulfilling effect on women's behavior. The self-fulfilling prophecy—that the expectations people hold often translate into behavior consistent and confirming of the initial expectation—is a well-documented social-psychological phenomenon (Rosenthal & Jacobson, 1968). If a woman believes that women become irritable with the approach of menstruation, she may not only report experiencing irritability, but may also behave in a more irritable manner. An actual change in mood and behavior may be evidenced premenstrually because of a woman's initial expectation and not necessarily because of a woman's actual cycle phase.

Actual evidence showing such a self-fulfilling prophecy effect is scarce, however (Ruble & Brooks-Gunn, 1982b). As described earlier, for example, women do not actually perform worse during the premenstrual and menstrual phases of their cycles even though they believe they do. Moreover, studies varying expectations show similar null effects. Although women perceive their performance differently according to expectations and/or cycle phase, no actual differences in performance are observed. As Ruble and Brooks-Gunn (1982b) argue, it may be that in general beliefs about menstrual-related behavior changes are not strong enough to affect actual performance.

A recent study by Kato (1989) offered support for this argument. In this study, women who retrospectively reported greater premenstrual distress, who also more strongly held beliefs that menstruation was debilitating, bothersome, and behaviorally relevant performed significantly worse on a perceptual memory task than women who retrospectively reported less premenstrual distress, but only when they were led to believe they were "premenstrual." Retrospective reports of premenstrual distress were not associated with performance when they thought they were "intermenstrual," nor were there differences in performance when the women were actually in their premenstrual phase. The fact that behavioral confirmation was only found for women holding strong negative expectations provides initial evidence that behavioral effects are evidenced under limited conditions.

In addition to this study, there have been only two other documented studies supporting a self-fulfilling prophecy effect. First, a longitudinal study of adolescent girls examined the association between premenarcheal girls' expectations for perimenstrual symptoms and their actual experience of symptoms once they reached menarche (i.e., had their first menstrual period). In this study, premenarcheal girls between the ages of 11 and 12 first reported their expectations for perimenstrual symptoms. The girls were then phoned every 2 months to determine whether they had started to menstruate. Once a girl had two to three menstrual periods, she was asked to rate her experience of perimenstrual symptoms. Also at this time, a girl who had remained premenarcheal, but was of the same age and from the same school as the menstruating girl, was questioned. The premenarcheal girl, however, was asked once again to report her expectations for perimenstrual symptoms. Thus at the initial assessment all girls were premenarcheal. By the second assessment, half the girls had begun to menstruate while half were still premenarcheal. The study found that premenarcheal girls' expectations for menstrual symptoms were significantly correlated with their later reports of actual symptom experiences once they began to menstruate (Brooks-Gunn & Ruble, 1982a). Moreover, additional analyses suggested that these correlations were not simply a response bias. A matched set of premenarcheal girls who remained premenarcheal over the past few months showed no such correlations in their expectations. Thus it is as if expectations present at the time a girl begins to menstruate provide the definition of that experience, whereas expectations of premenarcheal girls continually change, presumably in response to age-related changes in the information available.

Second, women's performance sometimes shows an *improvement* at the menstrual versus the intermenstrual phase. Specifically, Rodin (1976) found that high-symptom menstruating women performed better under conditions of high arousal on some cognitive measures (anagrams, digit/symbol substitution tasks) than did asymptomatic women or women tested at midcycle. Such data have been interpreted in terms of menstrual beliefs in two ways. First, Rodin (1976) suggested that the high-symptom women may have misattributed their task-related arousal to their menstrual symptoms and thereby performed more effectively than women who did not have this salient alternative attribution. Second, Ruble and Brooks-Gunn (1982b) interpreted the findings in terms of individuals' attempts to regain control under conditions of threat (e.g., Wortman & Brehm, 1975). Among women who believe that their cycles affect their performance (and thus that menstruation signals a possible loss of control), factors in the task situation, such as importance, may determine the extent to which they respond "actively" (with reactance) or "passively" (with learned helplessness). Since reactance tends to be the initial response to threatened loss of control, high-symptom women would be expected to respond actively, especially in situations of high importance. Thus, Rodin's (1976) finding of superior performance by the high-symptom women during the menstrual phase is consistent with this analysis.

In summary, many diverse types of studies suggest that reports of menstrual-related psychosomatic changes are, at least in part, a function of sociocultural factors—labeling, biased information processing, and cultural beliefs and expectations. Although there is limited evidence that such processes lead to impaired performance, as would be predicted by a self-fulfilling prophecy analysis, further studies are needed to address the self-fulfilling effect of strong negative expectations on women's level of cognitive-motor performance. Moreover, such negative beliefs may have important consequences for a woman's self-esteem, both because she believes she is impaired and because others' evaluations of her are affected by menstrual-related beliefs (Koeske & Koeske, 1975; Ruble, Boggiano, & Brooks-Gunn, 1982).

Proposed Psychophysiological Interactions

Although a hormonal basis for premenstrual symptoms has not been supported, a psychological basis also has not fully accounted for the existence and nature of symptoms experienced. Because premenstrual symptoms include both physical and psychological effects, some researchers have supported a biopsychosocial model that considers the existence and interaction of many variables (Logue & Moos, 1986; Miota, Yahle, & Bartz, 1991; Paige, 1971; Ruble, Brooks-Gunn, & Clarke, 1980).

Although menstrual cycle research has only described the correlation of variables, causal directionality has often been implied. The direction of causality has often depended on the researcher's orientation. Early research, most of which was physiologically based, often assumed the unidirectionality of physiological changes that led to psychological and/or behavioral outcomes. More recently, the consideration of psychological and behavioral changes leading to physiological outcomes has been emphasized in menstrual cycle research. Early studies suggesting the existence of a premenstrual phase decrement in academic performance (Dalton, 1969), for example, have been reinterpreted. That is, it has been posited that the stress of the exams, rather than cycle phase, may have been the cause of premenstrual decrements. This is because in Dalton's study not only were more women than expected menstruating during the examination period, but Dalton herself (as noted in Sommer, 1982) reported that exam stress lengthened the cycles of 42% of the school girls. This result suggests that if stress lengthened or otherwise disrupted the girls' menstrual cycles, stress may have also negatively affected cognitive performance (Sommer, 1982). It also has been proposed that premenstrual symptoms may be a stress reaction to the approach of menstruation (Paige, 1971; Ruble, Brooks-Gunn, & Clarke, 1980). If women perceive menstruation as a stressful event, they may become more anxious, depressed, or irritable because of the expectation that symptoms (bloating, breast tenderness, cramping, acne, weight gain, headache) are soon to occur once menstruation begins. Paige (1971) even suggested that some premenstrual symptoms may be a socially mediated response to the onset of menstruation rather than a result of biochemical changes. Thus irritability and anxiety may result from concern over preparation for menstruation, which is commonly viewed by women as an inconvenience or an embarrassment. Alternatively, some women may become increasingly anxious as menstruation approaches because of concern over the possibility of pregnancy.

In summary, even when psychological changes are linked to the underlying hormonal fluctuations of estrogen and progesterone during the premenstrual phase of the menstrual cycle, it may be in a way different from normally envisioned. Rather than hormonal changes directly causing psychological changes, there are at least two alternative direction of effects that appear quite reasonable. These are represented in Figure 8.1. First, the psychological changes may represent responses to hormonally induced physical changes, so that, for example, physical discomforts, inconvenience, or even weight gain may elicit negative affective responses. Second, other variables, such as stress, may affect hormone levels, physical responses, and affective responses simultaneously. From these

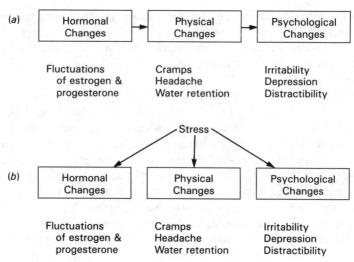

Figure 8.1 Directions of physiological and psychological effects.

perspectives, menstrual cycle variation is most reasonably considered in terms of interactions of social and physiological variables.

CURRENT AND FUTURE RESEARCH DIRECTIONS

Although the increased interest in menstrual cycle research in the past 10 to 15 years has contributed several innovative theoretical directions and addressed several hypotheses concerning the etiology of menstrual distress, many of the fundamental questions remain open. As recently as 1987, a volume presenting the results of a conference including major physicians, psychiatrists, psychologists, and neuroscientists in the field concluded that the exact nature and prevalence of the premenstrual syndrome remains unclear (Ginsburg & Carter, 1987). To address this issue, current research is attempting to answer the following questions: (a) Is there a subgroup of women that can be shown in prospective observations to exhibit a set of symptoms closely linked to a particular phase of the menstrual cycle; (b) can the symptoms of this subgroup or subgroups be demonstrated by more objective measures than self-reports, and can they be linked to hormone levels or hormone changes; and (c) why do some women believe they have menstrual-related problems, such as premenstrual syndrome, when prospective assessments fail to support their beliefs? In this section, we present the recent efforts to confront these issues and to reassess the validity of basic assumptions. Directions for future research are also suggested, based upon these considerations.

Redefinition of Perimenstrual Symptoms and Reassessment of Assumptions

There are two issues crucial to the definition of a premenstrual syndrome, the severity of symptoms and the time-limited nature of symptoms, that have not yet been resolved (Mitchell, Woods, & Lentz, 1991; Rubinow, Hoban, Roy-Byrne, Grover, & Post, 1985). Most studies have overlooked the fact that any-where between one-half to two-thirds of all women do not experience perimen-strual symptoms (Laube, 1986; Logue & Moos, 1986; Moos, 1968b) and have considered the symptom experience of all women as similar. Menstrual research is in need of standard diagnostic criteria that distinguish women who experience severe and time-limited perimenstrual symptoms from women who are asymp-tomatic and women who experience intermittent symptoms.

Recently, a few researchers (Halbreich & Endicott, 1985b; Haskett et al., 1980; Parry & Wehr, 1987) have established their own diagnostic criteria in the selection of subjects. Each criterion considers the number, severity, and onset of symptoms. The process involves a prescreening interview during which a psychiatric history is taken, a confirmation of retrospective reports with daily ratings, and clinical interviews during a woman's actual follicular and premen-strual phases. The use of such criteria very much affects estimates of the prev-alence of the premenstrual syndrome. Only a very small percentage of the women, 12% (Haskett & Abplanalp, 1983) and 16% (Haskett et al., 1980), who claimed to experience the premenstrual syndrome actually met the experimental criteria for diagnosis of premenstrual tension syndrome. In addition, a study by McMillan and Pihl (1987) revealed that of the 28 women categorized as suffering from premenstrual depression by retrospective reports, the vast majority (61%) failed to meet the criteria when prospective measures were assessed. Although the establishment of such criteria demonstrates the existence of a small subgroup of women who experience relatively severe and time-limited symptoms, defini-tional agreement among researchers is necessary.

In the recently revised edition of the *Diagnostic and Statistical Manual of Mental Disorders* (*DSM IIIR*), the primary guidebook for clinical psychologists and psychiatrists, diagnostic criteria for what has been termed the late luteal (e.g., premenstrual) phase dysphoric disorder (American Psychiatric Association [APA], 1987) have been proposed in the section on categories needing further study. According to the *DSM IIIR*, a diagnosis of a late luteal phase dysphoric disorder (LLPDD) is made if the experience of premenstrual symptoms is severe enough to cause "marked impairment in social or occupational functioning" (APA, 1987, p. 367), occurs during a majority of menstrual cycles, and only occurs the week before the period and remits shortly after the period. As yet, few researchers have adopted these criteria (for exceptions see Gallant, Popiel, Hoffman, Chakraborty, & Hamilton, 1992a,b; Hurt et al., 1992; Rivera-Tovar & Frank, 1990), though such criteria may help to standardize menstrual cycle research. However, as cautioned by the APA's DSM-IV Work Group on LLPDD who conducted a recent analysis of existing prospective data, without a standard method for assessing symptom change, the number of women diagnosed as having LLPDD could range from 14–45% (Hurt et al., 1992). Thus, the establishment of a single method of assessing change is necessary so that the results of studies utilizing these criteria can be compared and the issue of the existence and incidence of such a disorder (e.g., a premenstrual syndrome) can be assessed.

With this understanding, future research can more fruitfully address other theoretical issues such as whether the premenstrual syndrome/LLPDD is in fact a single syndrome or whether a consideration of subtypes or different syndromes is necessary (Halbreich & Endicott, 1985a; Steiner, Haskett, & Carroll, 1980). In recent years, some researchers have thought that the premenstrual syndrome may coexist with other psychiatric affective disorders (Chisholm, Jurg, Cumming, Fox, et al., 1990; Clare, 1983; Harrison, Rabkin, & Endicott, 1985; Ofosky & Blumenthal, 1985; Van Der Ploeg, 1986). Affective disorders have been considered a useful model to study premenstrual depression. Studies have found that the percentage of women who experience perimenstrual symptoms, specifically premenstrual depressive syndrome, is higher than expected among women with an affective disorder. Conversely, a greater percentage of women than expected who report perimenstrual symptoms also meet the criteria for a depressive disorder (Logue & Moos, 1986; Ofosky & Blumenthal, 1985). Nevertheless, on the average, women experiencing premenstrual symptoms report substantially less premenstrual depression than psychiatric patients (Golub, 1976b).

More recently, researchers have speculated that there may be a link between the experience of the premenstrual syndrome and other cyclic disorders (Parry, 1989; Wurtman & Wurtman, 1989). According to Wurtman and Wurtman (1989), for example, premenstrual syndrome, seasonal affective disorder (SAD) and carbohydrate-craving obesity (CCO) all share similar symptoms (depression, lethargy, increased carbohydrate consumption), and the hormone melatonin and the neurotransmitter serotonin are thought to play a role in each of the disorders. Although this research is intriguing, further research is needed to evaluate the basis for such claims.

Once definitional issues surrounding the premenstrual syndrome/LLPDD are resolved and it is possible to identify an appropriate subgroup of women to study, two further steps are necessary: (1) attempting to verify self-report measures with more objective assessments and (2) attempting to link these to underlying physiological events.

Alternative Measures of Assessment

As discussed earlier, self-report measures are affected by women's expectations for symptoms and may not be veridical reports of symptom experience. For this reason, measures of autonomic arousal—that is, skin conductance response (SCR) and heart rate (HR)—could be used to address psychological changes rather than self-reports of mood. To our knowledge, relatively few studies have obtained direct measures of arousal. These studies have not offered consistent support for a premenstrual increase in arousal (Asso, 1978; Little & Zahn, 1974). For example, even studies employing the same measures of arousal have obtained discrepant results. Although one study reported a follicular phase increase in skin conductance response (Little & Zahn, 1974), another reported no significant phase effect (Slade & Jenner, 1980), and a third reported a premenstrual increase in skin conductance response (Asso & Braier, 1982). Finally, no study has attempted to directly link hormone changes to physiological changes in different subgroups of women.

One recent study (Kirsch & Geer, 1988) employed direct measures of autonomic arousal for disaggregated groups of women, though it relied on day designations of menstrual phase. Using cut-off scores of their retrospective and prospective premenstrual symptom reports, it categorized women as experiencing premenstrual distress or as not experiencing premenstrual distress. Measures of physiological change (skin conductance response, heart rate) were taken during the premenstrual and ovulatory phases to assess the overall nature of cycle changes and any possible differences between groups. Although the premenstrual symptom group initially reported severe premenstrual distress, they actually experienced significantly *less* arousal (SCR) during the premenstrual phase and *greater* arousal postmenstrually than did the asymptomatic group. No significant phase effects were obtained for heart rate. Thus these results show a difference between groups, but in a direction that would appear to contradict the premenstrual symptom group's claims of greater distress. In contrast, a similar study that disaggregated women into either a premenstrual symptom group or an asymptomatic group found a significant premenstrual *increase* in arousal (HR) for the premenstrual symptom group. This result, however, was evidenced only when both groups were exposed to a pain stimulus during the premenstrual phase (Kuczmierczyk & Adams, 1985).

In summary, only a few studies have considered the possible differences between women who claim to experience premenstrual symptoms and women who do not, using objective measures of arousal during different phases of the menstrual cycle. The results of these studies suggest that this differentiation across groups may be productive, though the differences found in high-symptom women by use of objective measures may deviate from what these women report experiencing or may occur only under limited conditions. These findings also indicate that cycle-related physiological changes may be subtle and evidenced under stressful conditions. Because measures of heart rate and skin conductance response provide information only on the magnitude of arousal and not on the actual direction of arousal, physiological indicators of stress (e.g., catecholamine excretions) may provide promising measures for further research. However, as argued earlier, it is also important to couple such attempts at objective measurement with an analysis of subgroups of women.

Studies including objective measures of perceptual-motor and cognitive function may also need to improve their assessment measures, in addition to assessing the subgroups of women throughout the menstrual cycle. Some of the cognitive tasks previously employed, such as simple reaction time experiments, have been criticized as requiring little effort or attention (Jensen, 1982). Thus more challenging or effortful tasks should be employed. There is some evidence that different levels of cognitive demand have an effect on performance. In a study by Slade and Jenner (1980), women who claimed to experience an increase in negative affect during the perimenstrual phase simultaneously engaged in primary and secondary reaction time and detection tasks that competed for their attention. The experimenters, who were interested in creating a situation of mental overload, paired the secondary task with each of four levels of difficulty of the primary task. Although no phase differences in reaction time or detection were found when the secondary task was paired with easier primary tasks, a perimenstrual decrement of fewer correct detections was evidenced when the secondary task was paired with the most difficult primary task.

Similarly, another study (Jensen, 1982) did not find a significant premenstrual decrement in performance for simple reaction time, though a significant premenstrual decrement was found for the more complex task of pursuit tracking. Because the effects of premenstrual debilitation may be masked by compensatory effort from women (Sommer, 1982), cognitive tasks also may be made more demanding by requiring a longer period of sustained performance. Finally, because cognitive decrements may be evident on certain tasks and not others (Parlee, 1982), some researchers have proposed the administration of a series of tasks (Jensen, 1982).

Recent research suggests that a woman's level of performance on cognitive tasks may depend not only on the phase of the menstrual cycle she is in, but on whether the task is one in which either men or women excel (Hampson, 1990; Hampson & Kimura, 1988). In Hampson & Kimura (1988), women were asked to take a series of cognitive and motor tests during their midluteal and menstrual phase. The tests chosen were ones on which previous research had reported that either males or females tended to excel. The Rod-and-Frame test (a test of perceptual-spatial skill) was chosen to represent a task favoring males, and a series of manual coordination tasks were chosen to represent tasks favoring females. Performance on these tasks was compared during the woman's midluteal and menstrual phases to assess whether high levels of female hormones (estrogen and progesterone) during the midluteal phase would be associated with differential performance on the cognitive versus motor tasks. The results revealed that relative to their performance during menstruation, women who were in their midluteal phase generally performed better on the manual coordination tasks but worse on the cognitive task. These findings recently have been extended to a wider range of tasks (Hampson, 1990). Although these results are intriguing and suggest that cognitive performance during the midluteal phase should be examined and evaluated separately from performance during the premenstrual (e.g., late-luteal) or menstrual phases, they cannot be used to support claims that levels of hormones enhance or suppress certain cognitive or motor processes. These results are based on indirect assessments of a woman's menstrual cycle phase, determined by counting reverse cycle days, and therefore cannot be specifically linked to fluctuating levels of female hormones.

Even if cognitively demanding lab studies were designed that linked fluctuating levels of female hormones with a perimenstrual decrement, it would still be difficult to assess whether these situations were in any way comparable to practical situations and therefore had direct bearing on a woman's everyday life. There is relatively little information relevant to this issue. Two recent studies (Asso, 1986; Richardson, 1989) examined women's performance on academic examinations and found no significant premenstrual decrement in performance. Another study (Gruber & Wildman, 1987) revealed only minor disruptions to daily life. Although 71% of the women in the study reported bothersome menstrual pain, less than 1% of the 36% of the women who were employed actually reported missing work during menstruation. No other daily disruptions were reported by these women, though interestingly, 50% reported spending more time in bed and 60% reported more time spent resting during their period.

In contrast to popular beliefs about menstrual debilitation, women's experience of menstrual symptoms does not generally appear to have a measurable impact on their daily lives. In general, studies that have directly challenged the validity of assumptions by addressing specific hypotheses or have employed objective measures have made headway for further research of the nature and magnitude of perimenstrual symptoms.

The Origin and Maintenance of Women's Beliefs about Menstrual Symptoms

Because retrospective reports of premenstrual symptoms are often not confirmed by prospective reports or by more objective measures, a final issue for research concerns the subjective reality of women's experience of perimenstrual symptoms. As numerous studies have demonstrated, expectations or beliefs have a significant impact on women's perception and report of symptoms and can even affect their level of cognitive performance. For this reason, the role of expectations in symptom perception and reporting merits further research consideration. In this section, we examine recent attempts to address the cognitive and motivational bases for the development and maintenance of women's expectations of menstrual symptoms.

Ruble and Brooks-Gunn have studied the impact of menarche, and the socialization of menstrual attitudes and expectations in defining what it means to be a woman (Brooks-Gunn & Ruble, 1980a; Ruble & Brooks-Gunn, 1987). These researchers have found that premenarcheal girls as young as the fifth grade already expect to experience the same symptoms as those often reported by adult women (Brooks-Gunn & Ruble, 1982; Clarke & Ruble, 1978). Specifically, girls who learned more about menstruation from negative sources, such as male sources (Ruble & Brooks-Gunn, 1987), felt unprepared for menstruation, or started to menstruate early relative to their peers (Rierdan & Koff, 1985; Ruble & Brooks-Gunn, 1987) reported a more negative symptom experience than girls who did not. These findings suggest that an unpleasant first experience can help to define menstruation as a negative event. As a result of this label, a girl may respond to the approach of her next period with heightened arousal and anxiety or may have biased perceptions of the relation between negative feelings and the menstrual cycle, which in turn sustain the initial belief that menstruation is unpleasant (Ruble & Brooks-Gunn, 1982a).

Recently, Ruble (1989) has incorporated this cognitive-informational approach to the development of menstrual attitudes within a broader context. This sociocultural approach posits an interaction between cultural attitudes and situational stressors in determining symptom experience. Ruble hypothesizes that a predominantly negative cultural attitude toward menstruation provides a ready explanation for the experience of physiological arousal or negative affect, even when such arousal may be the result of other stressful events. This hypothesis was supported by a recent study where differences in menstrual attitudes of Anglo-Saxon and Hispanic adolescents from comparable socioeconomic levels in New York City were examined (Maluf & Ruble, 1993). Consistent with the cross-cultural findings, discussed earlier, showing greater reported negative affect among Anglo-Saxon Western women than among other groups (Snowden & Christian, 1983), Anglo-Saxon adolescents were thought to be more likely to link negative affect with menstruation than Hispanic adolescents. The researchers hypothesized that this difference would be due to the former's greater exposure to or cultural acceptance of media that popularize negative aspects of menstruation such as the premenstrual syndrome. As an example, Maluf and Ruble cited the delay of Spanish language media to publicize the use of tampons by adolescent girls until the early 1980s. Consistent with this analysis, the Anglo-Saxon sample more strongly associated the premenstrual phase with affective symptoms for both premenarcheal and postmenarcheal girls.

Maluf and Rubin also hypothesized that even if both groups of adolescents experienced the same social stresses of growing up, Anglo-Saxon adolescents would attribute their negative state to the menstrual cycle, whereas Hispanic adolescents would not. The results also supported this hypothesis. Among Anglo-Saxon girls only, more menstrual-related negative affect was reported for girls who were experiencing stress in their lives—in this case, the transition to junior high school or negative maternal attitudes. These findings suggest that in a culture where negative affect and menstruation are clearly linked (i.e., the popularization of PMS), the experience of negative events can be easily attributed to phase of the menstrual cycle.

Although cognitive and sociocultural factors have been examined as important to the maintenance of women's negative attitudes toward menstruation, researchers have not explored a possible motivational basis for women's negative attitudes. Women's negative attitudes toward menstruation may actually help women cope with anxiety or stressful situations by serving as an explanation for many negative physiological states. Rodin's (1976) finding that menstruating women who believed they experience perimenstrual symptoms performed better under experimental stress than nonmenstruating women and women who did not claim to experience perimenstrual symptoms is a case in point. Rodin suggests that because high-distress menstruating women may have attributed their performance anxiety to the menstrual cycle rather than to their own personal insecurity or instability, they may have tried harder at the task and therefore performed better than women who could not make such attributions. In this way, women's negative attitudes toward menstruation may not be maladaptive as often assumed.

Future research could consider whether women's beliefs of debilitation serve as a self-handicapping strategy (Jones & Berglas, 1978) or an excuse for expected or actual poor performance. Initial evidence from Kato (1989) indicates that women who report experiencing greater levels of premenstrual distress also more strongly endorse self-handicapping strategies (e.g., the internalization of success and the externalization of failure). Thus women who claim to experience greater levels of distress may be able to deal with their experience of symptoms in a strategic, self-presentational way. By adopting this strategy, they can attribute failure to a "legitimate" physical cause rather than to more personally damaging reasons, such as a lack of intelligence or motivation. Such beliefs "save face" (Goffman, 1959) in the eyes of others as well as oneself should failure occur. However, perimenstrual performance decrements have not been found for a range of perceptual-motor and cognitive tasks, so women's expected but unconfirmed excuses for failure may "augment" (Kelley, 1971), or make their success or accomplishment seem all the more impressive because debilitating symptoms have been overcome.

Similarly, beliefs of debilitation may serve as explanations for extreme moods or out-of-role behaviors. Aggressive acts may be attributed to hormonal fluctuations rather than to a nasty disposition, while malaise or listlessness attributed to menstruation may allow women to enter a sick role (Parsons, 1979). Rather than being labeled as a malingerer, a person who takes the sick role is not held responsible for her actions and is granted the legitimacy to rest and relinquish responsibilities. Such beliefs seem to give women not only an explanation for their behavior but also the choice or option to engage in such behaviors. It is estimated that 32% of women believe menstruation is debilitating and

59% that it is bothersome (Brooks et al., 1977). It is possible, then, that the use of menstrual debilitation as an explanation for undesirable behavior may represent a kind of face-saving strategy for some women.

Finally, women who deny the effects of menstruation may be motivated to hold such beliefs because of the similar need for self-esteem maintenance. Women who deny the effects of menstruation may have the need to preserve a positive image of themselves as active, unfettered, or invulnerable. It is estimated that only 12% of women believe that menstruation is an event that does not and should not affect a woman's behavior (Brooks et al., 1977). Although both beliefs may serve the same need, it is not clear what determines whether a woman will believe menstruation is debilitating and use such beliefs as an excuse or whether she will deny its effects. Social learning, or the process of teaching a young girl the appropriate expression of behavior, may be an important factor. What is interesting and novel about this analysis is that it goes beyond simply addressing the self-fulfilling behavioral effects of expectations that imply that women are victims of their expectations or beliefs, but suggests that women may be motivated to hold certain expectations about menstruation because of the outcomes or consequences they foresee for themselves.

In summary, after 30 years of research it is not known whether women's experience of symptoms during the premenstrual phase constitutes a premenstrual syndrome. The existing evidence bearing on this issue has not consistently supported cycle-related physical, psychological, or behavioral effects. Even if an association between symptom experience and menstrual cycle phase is found, researchers will still need to link these changes to hormonal fluctuations and to assess the clinical significance of such changes. To date, there is no support for a hormonal/physiological basis for the premenstrual syndrome, though there is compelling evidence linking the experience of primary dysmenorrhea with higher levels of prostaglandins.

Considerable support exists for a psychological interpretation—that a woman's expectations for symptoms affect her perception and report of menstrual cycle symptoms and may even affect her level of cognitive performance—though this interpretation also has not fully accounted for the existence and nature of symptoms experienced. For this reason, many researchers have now proposed that the premenstrual syndrome can be best understood as the interaction of physiological and psychological factors, and efforts are being made to understand the direction of effects. Current research is also working to establish specific diagnostic criteria for the premenstrual syndrome and to use more objective measures for assessing mood and cognitive performance changes. Finally, research is examining a number of processes that may lead to the development and maintenance of negative beliefs about menstrual and premenstrual symptoms. These include: (1) misattribution and information-processing biases; (2) socialization processes that lead girls experiencing their first menstruation to categorize it in negative terms; and (3) the experience of stress within a cultural context that facilitates the attribution of the resulting distress to the menstrual cycle. In addition, researchers are beginning to consider the possibility that such beliefs may serve certain self-enhancing functions for some women, thereby providing an additional motivation to maintain those beliefs.

REFERENCES

Abplanalp, J. M. (1983). Premenstrual syndrome: A selective review. In S. Golub (Ed.), *Lifting the curse of menstruation: A feminist appraisal of the influence of menstruation on women's lives* (pp. 107–123). New York: Haworth Press.

Abplanalp, J. M., Rose, R. M., Donnelly, A. F., & Livingston-Vaughn, L. (1979). Psychoendocrinology of the menstrual cycle: II. The relationship between enjoyment of activities, moods, and reproductive hormones. *Psychosomatic Medicine, 41*, 605–615.

Adesso, V. J., & Freitag, W. J. (1989). An evaluation of the accuracy of self-reports for predicting menstrual *Psychology and Health, 3*, 217–220.

Alberts, P. S., & Alberts, M. S. (1990). Unvalidated treatment of premenstrual syndrome. *Health, 19*(3), 69–80.

American Psychiatric Association. (1987). *Diagnostic and statistical manual of mental disorders*, (3rd ed., rev.). Washington, DC: APA.

Andersch, B., & Hahn, L. (1985). Progesterone treatment of premenstrual tension—A double blind study. *Journal of Psychosomatic Research, 29*, 489–493.

Asso, D. (1978). Levels of arousal in the premenstrual phase. *British Journal of Social and Clinical Psychology, 17*, 47–55.

Asso, D. (1986). Psychology examinations and the menstrual phase of the menstrual cycle. *Women and Health, 10(4)*, 91–104.

Asso, D., & Beech, H. R. (1975). Susceptibility to the acquisition of a conditioned response in relation to the menstrual cycle. *Journal of Psychosomatic Research, 19*, 337–344.

Asso, D., & Braier, J. R. (1982). Changes with the menstrual cycle in psychophysiological and self-report measures of activation. *Biological Psychology, 15*, 95–107.

AuBuchon, P. G., & Calhoun, K. S. (1985). Menstrual cycle symptomatology: The role of social expectancy and experimental demand characteristics. *Psychosomatic Medicine, 47*, 35–45.

Bains, G. K., & Slade, P. (1988). Attributional patterns, moods, and the menstrual cycle. *Psychosomatic Medicine, 50*, 469–476.

Beck, L. E., Gevirtz, R., & Mortola, J. F. (1990). The predictive role of psychosocial stress on symptom severity in premenstrual syndrome. *Psychosomatic Medicine, 52*, 536–543.

Bird, S. (1987). Neuroscience research and PMS. In B. F. Ginsburg & B. F. Carter (Eds.), *Premenstrual syndrome* (pp. 31–46). New York: Plenum Press.

Biro, V., & Stukovsky, R. (1985). Changed self-ratings of young women during the phases of their cycle. *Studia Psychologica, 27*, 239–244.

Brooks, J., Ruble, D. N., & Clarke, A. (1977). College women's attitudes and expectations concerning menstrual-related changes. *Psychosomatic Medicine, 39,* 288–297.

Brooks-Gunn, J. (1986). Differentiating premenstrual symptoms and syndromes. *Psychosomatic Medicine, 48,* 385–387.

Brooks-Gunn, J., & Ruble, D. N. (1980a). Menarche: The interaction of physiological, cultural, and social factors. In A. J. Dan, E. A. Graham, & C. P. Beecher (Eds.), *The menstrual cycle. Vol. 1. A synthesis of interdisciplinary research* (pp. 141–159). New York: Springer.

Brooks-Gunn, J., & Ruble, D. N. (1980b). The Menstrual Attitude Questionnaire. *Psychosomatic Medicine, 42,* 503–512.

Brooks-Gunn, J., & Ruble, D. N. (1982). The development of menstrual-related beliefs and behaviors during early adolescence. *Child Development, 53,* 1567–1577.

Brooks-Gunn, J., & Ruble, D. N. (1986). Men's and women's attitudes and beliefs about the menstrual cycle. *Sex Roles, 14,* 287–299.

Calhoun, K. S., & Burnette, M. M. (1984). Etiology and treatment of menstrual disorders. *Behavioral Medicine Update, 5(4),* 21–26.

Chan, W. Y., Dawood, M. Y., & Fuchs, F. (1979). Relief of dysmenorrhea with the prostaglandin synthetase inhibitor ibuprofen: Effect on prostaglandin levels in menstrual fluid. *American Journal of Obstetrics and Gynecology, 135,* 102.

Chapman, L. J., & Chapman, J. P. (1967). Illusory correlation in observational report. *Journal of Verbal Learning and Verbal Behavior, 6,* 151–155.

Chisholm, G., Jung, S. O., Cumming, C. E., Fox, E. E., et al. (1990). Premenstrual eanxiety and depression: Comparison of objective psychological tests with a retrospective questionnaire. *Acta Psychiatrica Scandinavica, 8(1),* 52–57.

Clare, A. W. (1983). The relationship between psychopathology and the menstrual cycle. In S. Golub (Ed.), *Lifting the curse of menstruation* (pp. 125–136). New York: Haworth Press.

Clare, A. W. (1985). Premenstrual syndrome: Single or multiple cause? *Canadian Journal of Psychiatry, 30,* 474–482.

Clarke, A. E., & Ruble, D. N. (1978). Young adolescents' beliefs concerning menstruation. *Child Development, 49,* 231–234.

Cockrill, C. L., Appell, M. A., & Carson, R. R. (1988, April). The effect of menstrual cycle on physiological and psychological function. Paper presented at the meeting of the Society of Behavioral Medicine, Boston.

Collins, A., Eneroth, P., & Landgren, B.-M. (1985). Psychoneuroendocrine stress responses and mood as related to the menstrual cycle. *Psychosomatic Medicine, 47,* 512–527.

Cook, B. L., Noyes, R. Jr., Garvey, M. J., Beach, V., Sobotka, J., & Chaudhry, D. (1990). Anxiety and the menstrual cycle in panic disorder. *Journal of Affective Disorders, 19,* 221–226.

Cox, D. J. (1983). Menstrual symptoms in college students: A controlled study. *Journal of Behavioral Medicine, 6,* 335–338.

Dalton, K. (1969). *The menstrual cycle.* London: Penguin Books.

Dalton, K. (1984). *The premenstrual syndrome and progesterone therapy* (2nd ed.). London: William Heinemann.

Delaney, J., Lupton, M. J., & Toth, E. (1976). *The curse: A cultural history of menstruation.* New York: E. P. Dutton & Co.

Dennerstein, L., Spencer-Gardner, C., Brown, J. B., Smith, M. A., & Burrows, G. D. (1984). Premenstrual tension-Hormonal profiles. *Journal of Psychosomatic Obstetrics & Gynecology, 3,* 37–51.

Englander-Golden, P., Sonleitner, F. J., Whitmore, M. R., & Corbley, G. J. M. (1985). Social and menstrual cycles: Methodological and substantive findings. In V. L. Olesen & N. F. Woods (Eds.), *Culture, society, and menstruation* (pp. 77–96). Washington, DC: Hemisphere.

Englander-Golden, P., Whitmore, M., & Dienstbier, R. (1978). Menstrual cycle as a focus of study and self-reports of mood and behaviors. *Motivation and Emotion, 2,* 75–86.

Englander-Golden, P., Willis, K. A., & Dienstbier, R. A. (1977). Stability of perceived tension as a function of the menstrual cycle. *Journal of Human Stress, 3,* 14–21.

Ericksen, K. P. (1987). Menstrual symptoms and menstrual beliefs: National and cross-national patterns. In B. E. Ginsburg & B. F. Carter (Eds.), *Premenstrual syndrome* (pp. 175–188). New York: Plenum Press.

Fradkin, B., & Firestone, P. (1986). Premenstrual tension, expectancy, and mother-child relations. *Journal of Behavioral Medicine, 9,* 245–259.

Freeman, E. W., Rickels, K., Sondheimer, S. J., & Polansky, M. (1990). Ineffectiveness of progesterone suppository treatment for premenstrual syndrome. *JAMA, 264,* 349–353.

Freeman, E. W., Sondheimer, S. J., Rickels, K., & Weinbaum, P. J. (1985). PMS treatment approaches and progesterone therapy. *Psychosomatics, 26*(10). Presented at the 31st Annual Meeting of the Academy of Psychosomatic Medicine on November 11, 1984, Philadelphia, PA.

Friederich, M. A. (1983). Dysmenorrhea. In S. Golub (Ed.), *Lifting the curse of menstruation* (pp. 91–105). New York: Haworth Press.

Fuchs, F. (1982). Dysmenorrhea and dyspareunia. In R. C. Friedman, (Ed.), *Behavior and the menstrual cycle* (pp. 199–216). New York: Marcel Dekker.

Gallant, S. J., Popiel, D. A., Hoffman, D. M., Chakraborty, P. K., & Hamilton, J. A. (1992a). Using daily ratings to confirm premenstrual syndrome/late luteal phase dysphoric disorder. Part I. Effects of demand characteristics and expectations. *Psychosomatic Medicine, 54,* 149–166.

Gallant, S. J., Popiel, D. A., Hoffman, D. M., Chakraborty, P. K., & Hamilton, J. A. (1992b). Using daily ratings to confirm premenstrual syndrome/late luteal phase dysphoric disorder. Part II. What makes a "real" difference? *Psychosomatic Medicine, 54,* 167–181.

Gannon, L. (1985). *Menstrual disorders and menopause: Biological, psychological, and cultural research.* New York: Praeger Press.

Ginsburg, B. E., & Carter, B. F. (1987). *Premenstrual syndrome: Ethical and legal implications in a biomedical perspective.* Based on a Conference on Ethical Issues for Research on Biological Factors Affecting the Capacity for Responsible Behavior, Sept. 17–21, 1984, Philadelphia, PA. New York: Plenum Press.

Glick, I. A., & Bennett, S. E. (1982). Oral contraceptives and the menstrual cycle. In R. C. Friedman (Ed.), *Behavior and the menstrual cycle* (pp. 345–365). New York: Marcel Dekker.

Goffman, E. (1959). *The presentation of self in everyday life*. Garden City, NY: Doubleday.

Golub, S. (1976a). The effect of premenstrual anxiety and depression on cognitive function. *Journal of Personality and Social Psychology, 64*, 99–104.

Golub, S. (1976b). The magnitude of premenstrual anxiety and depression. *Psychosomatic Medicine, 38*, 4–12.

Green, J. (1982). Recent trends in the treatment of premenstrual syndrome: A critical review. In R. C. Friedman (Ed.), *Behavior and the menstrual cycle* (pp. 367–395). New York: Marcel Dekker.

Greene, R., & Dalton, K. (1953). The premenstrual syndrome. *British Medical Journal, i*, 1007–1014.

Gruber, V. A., & Wildman, B. G. (1987). The impact of dysmenorrhea on daily activities. *Behavioral Research and Therapy, 25*, 123–128.

Halbreich, U., & Endicott, J. (1985a). Methodological issues in studies of premenstrual changes. *Psychoneuroendocrinology, 10(1)*, 15–32.

Halbreich, U., & Endicott, J. (1985b). The clinical diagnosis and classification of premenstrual changes. *Canadian Journal of Psychiatry, 30*, 489–497.

Hamilton, D. L., & Gifford, R. K. (1976). Illusory correlation in interpersonal perception: A cognitive basis of stereotypic judgments. *Journal of Experimental Social Psychology, 12*, 392–407.

Hampson, E. (1990). Variations in sex-related cognitive abilities across the menstrual cycle. *Brain and Cognition, 14*, 26–43.

Hampson, E., & Kimura, D. (1988). Reciprocal effects of hormonal fluctuations on human motor and perceptual-spatial skills. *Behavioral Neuroscience, 102*, 456–459.

Harrison, W. M., Rabkin, J. G., & Endicott, J. (1985). Psychiatric evaluation of premenstrual changes. *Psychosomatics*, 789–799. Presented at the 31st Annual Meeting of the Academy of Psychosomatic Medicine on November 11, 1984, Philadelphia, PA.

Haskett, R. F., & Abplanalp, J. M. (1983). Premenstrual Tension Syndrome: Diagnostic criteria and selection of research subjects. *Psychiatric Research, 9*, 125–138.

Haskett, R. F., Steiner, M., Osmun, J., & Carroll, B. J. (1980). Severe premenstrual tension: Delineation of the syndrome. *Biological Psychiatry, 15*, 121–139.

Hatcher, R. A., Stewart, G. K., Stewart, F., Guest, F., Josephs, N., & Dale, J. (1982). *Contraceptive technology 1982–1983*. New York: Irvington.

Hongladarom, G., McCorkle, R., & Woods, N. F. (1985). *The complete book of women's health*. NJ: Prentice-Hall.

Hurt, S. W., Schnurr, P. P., Severino, S. K., Freeman, E. W., Gise, L. H., Rivera-Tovar, A., & Steege, J. F. (1992). Late luteal phase dysphoric disorder in 670 women evaluated for premenstrual complaints. *American Journal of Psychiatry, 149(4)*, 525-530.

Janowsky, D. S. (1985). Biochemical hypotheses of premenstrual tension. *Psychological Medicine, 15*, 3–8.

Jensen, B. K. (1982). Menstrual cycle effects on task performance examined in the context of stress research. *Acta Psychologica, 50*, 159–178.

Jones, E. E., & Berglas, S. (1978). Control of attributions about the self through self-handicapping strategies: The appeal of alcohol and the role of underachievement. *Personality and Social Psychology Bulletin, 4*, 200–206.

Kato, P. S. (1989). The effect of expectations and bodily sensations on women's perceptions of cyclicity. Doctoral dissertation, Princeton University, 1989.

Kelley, H. H. (1971). *Attribution in social interaction.* Morristown, NJ: General Learning Press.

Keye, W. R. (1985). Medical treatment of premenstrual syndrome. *Canadian Journal of Psychiatry, 30,* 483–488.

Kirsch, J. R., & Geer, J. H. (1988). Skin conductance and heart rate in women with premenstrual syndrome. *Psychosomatic Medicine, 50,* 175–182.

Klebanov, P. K., & Jemmott, J. B. III. (1992). Effects of expectations and bodily sensations on self-reports of premenstrual symptoms. *Psychology of Women Quarterly, 16,* 289–310.

Koeske, R. K. (1980). Theoretical perspectives for menstrual cycle research. In A. J. Dan, E. A. Graham, & C. P. Beecher (Eds.), *The menstrual cycle. Vol. 1. A synthesis of interdisciplinary research* (pp. 8–25). New York: Springer.

Koeske, R. K., & Koeske, G. S. (1975). An attributional approach to moods and the menstrual cycle. *Journal of Personality and Social Psychology, 31,* 473–478.

Kuczmierczyk, A. R., & Adams, N. E. (1985). Autonomic arousal and pain sensitivity in women with premenstrual syndrome at different phases of the menstrual cycle. *Journal of Psychosomatic Research, 30,* 421–428.

Laessle, R. G., Tuschl, R. J., Schweiger, U., & Pirke, K. M. (1990). Mood changes and physical complaints during the normal menstrual cycle in healthy young women. *Psychoneuroendocrinology, 15(2),* 131–138.

Laube, D. W. (1986). Premenstrual syndrome. *The Female Patient, 11,* 107–114.

Linkie, D. M. (1982). The physiology of the menstrual cycle. In R. C. Friedman, (Ed.), *Behavior and the menstrual cycle* (pp. 1–21). New York: Marcel Dekker.

Little, B. C., & Zahn, T. P. (1974). Changes in mood and autonomic functioning during the menstrual cycle. *Psychophysiology, 11,* 579–590.

Logue, C. M., & Moos, R. H. (1986). Perimenstrual symptoms: Prevalence and risk factors. *Psychosomatic Medicine, 48,* 388–414.

Maluf, J., & Ruble, D. N. (1993). *Cultural and family influences on adolescent girls' perception of menstrual symptoms.* Manuscript in preparation.

May, R. R. (1976). Mood shifts and the menstrual cycle. *Journal of Psychosomatic Research, 20,* 125–130.

McFarland, C., Ross, M., & DeCourville, N. (1989). Women's theories of menstruation and biases in recall of menstrual symptoms. *Journal of Personality and Social Psychology, 57,* 522–531.

McFarland, J., Martins, C. L., & Williams, T. M. (1988). Mood fluctuations: Women versus men and menstrual versus other cycles. *Psychology of Women Ouarterly, 12,* 201–223.

McMillan, M. J., & Pihl, R. O. (1987). Premenstrual depression: A distinct entity. *Journal of Abnormal Psychology, 96(2),* 149–154.

Metcalf, M. G., & Hudson, S. M. (1985). The premenstrual syndrome: Selection of women for treatment trials. *Journal of Psychosomatic Research, 29,* 631–638.

Miota, P., Yahle, M., & Bartz, C. (1991). Premenstrual syndrome: A bio-psycho-social approach to treatment. In D. L. Taylor & N. F. Woods (Eds.), *Menstruation, health, and illness. Series in health care for women* (pp. 143–152). Hemisphere Publishing Corp.: New York.

Mitchell, E. S., Woods, N. F., & Lentz, M. J., (1991). Recognizing PMS when you see it: Criteria for PMS sample selection. In D. L. Taulor & N. F. Woods (Eds.), *Menstruation, health, and illness. Series in health care for women* (pp. 89–102). Hemisphere Publishing Corp.: New York.

Moos, R. (1968a). Psychological aspects of oral contraceptives. *Archives of General Psychiatry, 19,* 87–94.

Moos, R. (1968b). The development of a Menstrual Distress Questionnaire. *Psychosomatic Medicine, 30,* 853–867.

Moos, R. (1985). *Perimenstrual symptoms: A manual and overview of research with the Menstrual Distress Questionnaire.* Stanford, CA: Stanford University, School of Psychiatry.

Morris, N. M., & Udry, J. R. (1972). Contraceptive pills and day-by-day feelings of well-being. *American Journal of Obstetrics and Gynecology, 113,* 763–765.

Nisbett, R. E., & Schachter, S. (1966). Cognitive manipulation of pain. *Journal of Experimental Social Psychology, 21,* 227–236.

Ofosky, H., & Blumenthal, S. (1985). Menstrually related mood disorders. In H. Ofosky & S. Blumenthal (Eds.), *Premenstrual syndrome: Current findings and future directions* (pp. 27–35). Based on a symposium held during the 137th Annual Meeting of the Psychiatric Association, May 1984, Los Angeles, CA.

Olasov, B., & Jackson, J. (1987). Effects of expectancies on women's reports of moods during the menstrual cycle. *Psychosomatic Medicine, 49,* 65–78.

Osborn, M. (1981). Physical and psychological determinants of premenstrual tension: Research issues and a proposed methodology. *Journal of Psychosomatic Research, 25,* 363–367.

Paige, K. E. (1971). Effects of oral contraceptives on affective fluctuations associated with the menstrual cycle. *Psychosomatic Medicine, 33,* 515–537.

Paikoff, R. L., Buchanan, C. M., & Brooks-Gunn, J. (1991). Methodological issues in the study of hormone-behavior links at puberty. In R. M. Lerner, A. C. Petersen, & J. Brooks-Gunn (Eds.), *The encyclopedia of adolescence* (pp. 508–512). New York: Garland.

Parlee, M. B. (1974). Stereotypic beliefs about menstruation: A methodological note on the Moos Menstrual Distress Questionnaire and some new data. *Psychosomatic Medicine, 36,* 229–240.

Parlee, M. B. (1980). Positive changes in moods and activation levels during the menstrual cycle in experimentally naive subjects. In A. J. Dan, E. A. Graham, & C. P. Beecher (Eds.), *The menstrual cycle. Vol 1. A synthesis of interdisciplinary research* (pp. 247–263). New York: Springer.

Parlee, M. B. (1982). The psychology of the menstrual cycle: Biological and physiological perspectives. In R. C. Friedman (Ed.), *Behavior and the menstrual cycle* (pp. 77–99). New York: Marcel Dekker.

Parry, B. L. (1989). Reproductive factors affecting the course of affective illness in women. *Psychiatric Clinics of North America, 12,* 207–220.

Parry, B. L., & Wehr, T. A. (1987). Therapeutic effects of sleep deprivation in patients with premenstrual syndrome. *American Journal of Psychiatry, 144,* 808–810.

Parsons, T. (1979). Definitions of health and illness in the light of American values and social structure. In E. G. Jaco (Ed.), *Patients, physicians, and illness* (pp. 119–144). New York: Free Press.

Pennebaker, J. W. (1983). Physical symptoms and sensations: Psychological causes and correlates. In J. T. Cacioppo & R. E. Petty (Eds.), *Social psychophysiology: A sourcebook* (pp. 543–564). New York: Guilford Press.

Rausch, J. L., & Janowsky, D. S. (1982). Premenstrual tension: Etiology. In R. C. Friedman (Ed.), *Behavior and the menstrual cycle* (pp. 397–427). New York: Marcel Dekker.

Richardson, J. T. E. (1989). Student learning and the menstrual cycle: Premenstrual symptoms and approaches to studying. *Educational Psychology, 2,* 215–238.

Richter, C. P., Hattvick, M. A., & Shapiro, S. S. (1984). Progesterone treatment of premenstrual syndrome. *Current Therapeutic Research, 36,* 840–850.

Rierdan, J., & Koff, E. (1985). Timing of menarche and initial menstrual experience. *Journal of Youth and Adolescence, 14,* 237–244.

Rivera-Tovar, A. D., & Frank, E. (1990). Late luteal phase dysphoric disorder in young women. *American Journal of Psychiatry, 147*(12), 1634–1636.

Rodin, J. (1976). Menstruation, reattribution, and competence. *Journal of Personality and Social Psychology, 33,* 345–353.

Rogers, M. L., & Harding, S. S. (1981). Retrospective and daily menstrual distress measures in men and women using Moos's instruments (Forms A & T), and modified versions of Moos's instruments. In P. Komnenich, M. McSweeney, J. A. Noack, & N. Elder (Eds.), *The menstrual cycle. Vol. 2. Research and implications for women's health* (pp. 71–81). New York: Springer.

Rosenthal, R., & Jacobson, L. (1968). *Pygmalion in the classroom: Teacher expectation and pupils' intellectual development.* New York: Holt, Rinehart, & Winston.

Ross, L. (1977). The intuitive psychologist and his shortcomings: Distortions in the attribution process. In L. Berkowitz, (Ed.), *Advances in experimental social psychology.* New York: Academic Press.

Ross, M., & Olson, J. M. (1981). An expectancy-attribution model of the effects of placebos. *Psychological Review, 88,* 405–437.

Rossi, A. S., & Rossi, P. E. (1980). Body time and social time: Mood patterns by menstrual cycle phase and day of week. In J. E. Parsons (Ed.), *The psychobiology of sex differences and sex roles* (pp. 269–304). Washington, DC: Hemisphere.

Rouse, P. (1978). Premenstrual tension: A study using the Moos Menstrual Distress Questionnaire. *Journal of Psychosomatic Research, 22,* 215–222.

Rubinow, D. R., Hoban, C., Grover, G. N., Galloway, D. S., Roy-Byrne, P., Anderson, R., & Merriam, G. R. (1987). Changes in plasma hormones across the menstrual cycle in patients with menstrually related mood disorder and in control subjects. *American Journal of Obstetrics and Gynecology, 158,* 5–11.

Rubinow, D. R., Hoban, C., Roy-Byrne, P., Grover, G. N., & Post, R. M. (1985). Premenstrual syndromes: Past and future research strategies. *Canadian Journal of Psychiatry, 30,* 469–473.

Rubinow, D. R., & Roy-Byrne, P. (1984). Premenstrual syndromes: An overview from a methodologic perspective. *American Journal of Psychiatry, 141,* 163–172.

Ruble, D. N. (1977). Premenstrual symptoms: A reinterpretation. *Science, 197,* 291–292.

Ruble, D. N. (1989). Menarche and menstrual symptoms: Psychosocial perspectives. In B. Lerer & S. Gershon (Eds.), *New directions in affective disorders* (pp. 21–26). New York: Springer.

Ruble, D. N., Boggiano, A. K., & Brooks-Gunn, J. (1982). Men's and women's evaluations of menstrual-related excuses. *Sex Roles, 8,* 625–637.

Ruble, D. N., & Brooks-Gunn, J. (1979). Menstrual symptoms: A social cognition analysis. *Journal of Behavioral Medicine, 2,* 171–194.

Ruble, D. N., & Brooks-Gunn, J. (1982a). A developmental analysis of menstrual distress in adolescence. In R. C. Friedman (Ed.), *Behavior and the menstrual cycle* (pp. 177–198). New York: Marcel Dekker.

Ruble, D. N., & Brooks-Gunn, J. (1982b). Expectations regarding menstrual symptoms: Effects on evaluation and behavior of women. In A. M. Voda, M. Dinnerstein, & S. R. O'Donnell (Eds.), *Changing perspectives on menopause* (pp. 208–219). Austin: University of Texas Press.

Ruble, D. N., & Brooks-Gunn, J. (1987). Perceptions of menstrual and premenstrual symptoms: Self-definitional processes at menarche. In B. E. Ginsburg & B. F. Carter (Eds.), *Premenstrual syndrome: Ethics and legal implications in a biomedical perspective* (pp. 237–251). New York: Plenum Press.

Ruble, D. N., Brooks-Gunn, J., & Clarke, A. (1980). Research on menstrual-related psychological changes: Alternative perspectives. In J. E. Parsons (Ed.), *The psychobiology of sex differences and sex roles* (pp. 227–243). Washington, DC: Hemisphere.

Sampson, G. A. (1979). Premenstrual syndrome: A double-blind controlled trial of progesterone and placebo. *British Journal of Psychiatry, 135,* 209–215.

Sampson, G. A., & Jenner, F. A. (1977). Studies of daily recordings from the Moos Menstrual Distress Questionnaire. *British Journal of Psychiatry, 130,* 265–271.

Sanders, D., Warner, P., Backstrom, T., & Bancroft, J. (1983). Mood, sexuality, hormones, and the menstrual cycle. I. Changes in mood and physical state: Description of subjects and method. *Psychosomatic Medicine, 45,* 487–501.

Schachter, S., & Singer, J. E. (1962). Cognitive, social, and physiological determinants of emotional state. *Psychological Review, 69,* 379–399.

Schechter, D., Bachmann, G. A., Vaitukaitis, J., Phillips, D., & Saperstein, D. (1989). Perimenstrual symptoms: Time course of symptom intensity in relation to endocrinologically defined segments of the menstrual cycle. *Psychosomatic Medicine, 51,* 173–194.

Silbergeld, S., Brast, N., & Noble, E. P. (1971). The menstrual cycle: A double-blind study of symptoms, mood, and behavior, and biochemical variables using Enovid and placebo. *Psychosomatic Medicine, 33,* 411–428.

Slade, P., & Jenner, F. A. (1980). Performance tests in different phases of the menstrual cycle. *Journal of Psychosomatic Reseasch, 24,* 5–8.

Smith, S. L. (1976). The menstrual cycle and mood disturbance. *Clinical Obstetrics and Gynecology, 19,* 391–397.

Snowden, R., & Christian, B. (1983). *Patterns and perceptions of menstruation: A World Health Organization international collaborative study.* New York: St. Martins Press.

Sommer, B. (1982). Cognitive behavior and the menstrual cycle. In R. C. Friedman (Ed.), *Behavior and the menstrual cycle* (pp. 101–127). New York: Marcel Dekker.

Sommer, B. (1983). How does menstruation affect cognitive competence and psychophysiological response. In S. Golub (Ed.), *Lifting the curse of menstruation: A feminist appraisal of the influence of menstruation on women's lives* (pp. 53–89). New York: Haworth Press.

Sondheimer, S. J., Freeman, E. W., Scharlop, B., & Rickels, K. (1985). Hormonal changes in the premenstrual syndrome, *Psychosomatics, 26(10)*. Presented at the 31st Annual Meeting of the Academy of Psychosomatic Medicine, November 11, 1984, Philadelphia, PA.

Steiner, M., Haskett, R. F., & Carroll, B. J. (1980). Premenstrual Tension Syndrome: The development of research diagnostic criteria and new rating scales. *Acta Psychiatrica Scandinavica, 62*, 177–190.

Swandby, J. R. (1981). A longitudinal study of daily mood self-reports and their relationship to the menstrual cycle. In P. Komnenich, M. McSweeney, J. A. Noack, & N. Elder (Eds.), *The menstrual cycle. Vol. 2. Research and implications for women's health* (pp. 93–103). New York: Springer.

Tversky, A., & Kahneman, D. (1974). Judgment under uncertainty: Heuristics and biases. *Science, 185*, 1124–1131.

Vander Meer, Y. G, Benedek-Jaszman, L. J., & Van Loenen, A. C. (1983). Effect of high-dose progesterone on the premenstrual syndrome: A double-blind cross-over trial. *Journal of Psychosomatic Obstetrics and Gynecology, 2(4)*, 220–222.

Van Der Ploeg, H. M. (1986). Emotional states and the premenstrual syndrome. *Personality and Individual Differences, 8(1)*, 95–100.

Villa, J., & Beech, H. R. (1977). Vulnerability and conditioning in relation to the menstrual cycle. *British Journal of Social and Clinical Psychology, 16*, 69–75.

Weidner, G., & Helmig, L. (1990). Cardiovascular stress reactivity and mood during the menstrual cycle. *Women & Health, 16(3–4)*, 5–21.

Wilcoxon, L., Schrader, S., & Sherif, C. (1976). Daily self-reports on activities, life events, moods and somatic changes during the menstrual cycle. *Psychosomatic Medicine, 38*, 399–417.

Woods, N. F., Most, A., & Dery, G. (1982). Prevalence of perimenstrual symptoms. *American Journal of Public Health, 72*, 1257–1264.

Wortman, C. B., & Brehm, J. W. (1975). Responses to uncontrollable outcomes: An integration of reactance theory and the learned helplessness model. In L. Berkowitz (Ed.), *Advances in experimental social psychology* (Vol. 8, pp. 277–336). New York: Academic Press.

Wurtman, R. J., & Wurtman, J. J. (1989). Carbohydrates and depression. *Scientific American, 260*, 68–75.

Zillman, D. (1983). Transfer of excitation in emotional behavior. In J. T. Caccioppo & R. E. Petty (Eds.), *Social psychophysiology: A sourcebook* (pp. 215–242). New York: Guilford Press.

Pain

Anthony E. Reading

DEFINITION

Pain is defined by the individual experiencing it. There are no biochemical markers that establish the degree of pain, and so reliance is placed upon the individual to convey the type and severity of her or his pain, whether verbally or by behaviors such as moaning, avoiding activities, or taking steps to seek relief. Scaling showing that subjects can reliably discriminate between pain descriptors (Melzack & Torgerson, 1971) has led to attempts to distinguish between different pain conditions on the basis of the language used to describe the sensations, and these endeavors have resulted in a pain adjective checklist known as the McGill Pain Questionnaire (Melzack, 1975). Early studies suggested that different pain conditions could be distinguished by the profiles of adjectives checked (e.g., Dubuisson & Melzack, 1976). Subsequent studies suggest there may be less specificity than originally thought, with individuals varying on the dimensions of intensity and the relevance of affect-laden words (Reading, Hand, & Sledmere, 1983), but less reliably on sensory descriptors.

The last two decades have witnessed an exponential growth of specialist pain centers, paralleled by the emergence of psychological treatment methods as a core component of pain programs. Clinical practice has been reflected in

Acknowledgment: I am grateful to Hazel Myers for her expert preparation of this manuscript.

theoretical shifts from biomedical models of pain as a direct response to trauma, to approaches that embrace psychosocial factors in shaping both the experience and the expression of pain. Pain for women occupies a special place both because it may be a sign of aberrant processes and because it accompanies normal reproductive events such as menstruation, childbirth, and, to a lesser extent, ovulation. Women can be subject to chronic pain originating from the reproductive organs, as well as pain arising from sexual intercourse (dyspareunia), which may be more prevalent when estrogen levels are depleted postmenopausally. In spite of the high prevalence of chronic pelvic pain, there has been remarkably little study of this subject compared to the attention given to low back pain, predominantly in men. This may reflect the economic bias of addressing a problem with significant implications for productivity and disability payments. It may also reflect the cultural stereotype of attributing women's pains to psychological or emotional factors, illustrated by past psychological theories in the sixties that attributed dysmenorrhea to conflicts over the female role (Reading, 1982).

In addition to those types of pain that are specific to females, there are types of pain that are not confined to women, yet from which women suffer disproportionately. These may arise from acute illness or trauma, and may be exacerbated by reproductive hormones. A random survey of a sample of 500 households found both temporary and persistent pain to be reported more frequently by women, with 16% of women falling into either of these categories (Crook, Rideout, & Browne, 1984). For example, women seem to be more prone to musculoskeletal disorders, which give rise to pain; only gout and work-related back injuries are more prevalent among men. Osteoarthritis occurs at a rate of 3 to 2 in women compared to men. Rheumatoid arthritis and lupus are five times more common in women. Fibromyalgia and myofascial pain syndrome are also more common in women. Women make up 60–75% of migraine and tension headache sufferers. Although migraine prevalence is equal prior to puberty, from age 10 on, the prevalence increases for females and is eight times more prevalent by age 15 (Andrasik & Kabela, 1988).

Pelvic pain is a common complaint in women. Epidemiologic data on the prevalence, associated morbidity, and socioeconomic impact of this problem are not available. Its frequency is illustrated by the number of diagnostic laparoscopies carried out for pelvic pain. Estimates published in the United Kingdom in the seventies indicated that over 10,000 women annually underwent this procedure for the diagnosis of pelvic pain (Royal College of Obstetricians & Gynecologists, 1978).

Persistent pain usually necessitates diagnostic procedures of this kind because the etiology and anatomic site are difficult to establish by history and physical alone. The differential diagnosis for pelvic pain includes acute salpingitis, ectopic pregnancy, ovarian cysts, uterine myoma, genital tumors, adhesions, and endometriosis. In addition, pain originating from pelvic organs may be referred to the skin areas supplied by the somatic afferent fibers of the same spinal segment. Other causes of pelvic pain may originate in the gastrointestinal, urologic, or skeletal systems. According to Beard and Pearce (1989), "the sensory innervation of all the pelvic organs makes it difficult to localize the site of gynecologic pain." There is both a sympathetic and a parasympathetic nerve supply. The taxonomy of chronic pain published by the International Association for the Study of Pain (Merskey, 1986) included an additional category of chronic pelvic pain without obvious pathology to describe the patient who complains of pain in the absence of positive findings. Estimates suggest pathophysiology will not be found in up to 20% of women complaining of pain. Even in cases when no clear pathology can be identified, this does not mean it does not exist. Some investigators have ascribed the pain to circulatory factors such as pelvic congestion or pelvic varicosities (Beard, Highman, Pearce, & Reginald, 1984).

Laparoscopic studies of women with pain have failed to find a clear relationship between organic findings and degree of pain. For example, although endometriosis may be found in 15–20% of women, in 30–40% of these there will be no discomfort (Merskey, 1986). Rapkin (1986) compared the laparoscopic results of 100 pelvic pain patients and 97 infertile controls. Adhesions were present as the only abnormality in 26% of pain patients and 39% of controls. There was no difference between groups in the density or the location of the adhesions. Similarly, a study of 24 women with pain associated with endometriosis found no relationship between laparoscopic classification of the degree of disease and pain complaints or functioning (Reading, Chang, Randle, Meldrum, & Judd, 1987). These findings refute a simple linear relationship between nociceptive input and pain sensation.

This chapter will focus on pain arising from the female reproductive organs. No other form of pain is unique to women. In spite of the prevalence of various types of pelvic pain, there has been a comparative neglect of this topic compared to the volume of research devoted to other chronic pain conditions. Although the interdisciplinary approach to pain understanding and management is legion, pelvic pain in women, with notable exceptions (e.g., Rapkin & Kames, 1987), has tended to be conceptualized dichotomously as either organic or psychogenic and treated accordingly. This chapter will review what is known about pelvic pain and draw upon our understanding of pain mechanisms to guide the assessment and management enterprise.

THEORIES OF PAIN

Traditionally, pain was thought of as a sensory process that occurred in response to aversive stimulation and was registered cortically. One theory suggested the presence of specific sensory receptors for pain; another (pattern theory) emphasized the importance of patterns of sensory stimulation. Neither of these models has been able to accommodate the role of higher processes in modulating pain experience, yet everyday experience, as well as empirical study, demonstrates the influence of attention, distraction, anxiety, depression, and the meaning attached to the sensation on the sensory processing. Both specificity and pattern theories have also failed to account for the failure of therapeutic procedures, such as nerve blocks, which disconnect nerve impulses from the source, to abolish centrally experienced pain.

It is now accepted that pain is the product of the interaction between nociceptive input and input from the cortex. Pain activation and inhibition may occur at the periphery, at the spinal column, or centrally in the cortex. Two major groups of nerve fibers are involved in nociception. The term "pain receptors" has given way to "nociceptors" in order to avoid the connotation that these sensory units create the pain. These nociceptors are found in the skin, deep somatic tissues, and the viscera. A-delta fibers are small, myelinated fibers representing immediate or sharp pain. C fibers are unmyelinated and generate dull, diffuse, or aching pain. Fibers may be activated by mechanical, temperature, or biochemical stimulation.

These peripheral nerve fibers enter the spinal cord through the dorsal horn, where they undergo modulation both within the dorsal horn and within descending brain centers. In 1965, Melzack and Wall proposed the gate control theory to reflect these formulations and give explicit recognition to the role of psychological processes. The theory proposed a gate mechanism that could be closed or opened according to the balance between A-delta fibers, C fibers, and descending influences from the brain. The more recent discovery and characterization of the endorphin system (Fields & Basbaum, 1989) has helped to clarify at least some of the ways in which the brain can "close" the pain gate.

Endorphins are naturally occurring opiate or analgesic substances produced by the brain. They seem to be triggered by stress and pain and have multiple functions. They may help to explain the placebo effect. Studies of drugs consistently find about one-third of individuals achieve pain relief by placebo. The question then becomes, "Is this as a result of endorphin release?" Levine, Gordon, and Fields (1979) performed an elegant study where, in addition to giving a placebo, they administered a second drug, naloxone, which is known to block the effects of opiates. They hypothesized that if the pain relief was caused by the placebo's triggering of endorphins, these effects would be lost when the naloxone was subsequently administered. In those displaying pain relief following placebo, the effect was blocked by naloxone, confirming at least one way in which placebos change neurochemistry and so pain experience.

A variety of psychological factors have been shown to influence the pain response (Sternbach, 1978). The meaning of the situation in which the pain occurs, the anxiety engendered, the individual's ability to redirect her or his attention, her or his mood, past experience (direct and vicarious), and the prevailing reinforcement contingencies have all been demonstrated to exert an effect. For example, Taenzer, Melzack, and Jeans (1986) studied pain reports following surgery. Half the variability in the postoperative indices studied (pain, mood, and analgesic use) was predicted by anxiety, mood, educational level, prior pain history, and attitudes towards pain medication. Studies also show a learning component to pain. Both respondent and operant processes have been implicated. Operant approaches to pain understanding have given rise to treatment methods based on operant principles (Fordyce, 1976). These studies have demonstrated that pain complaints and behavior respond to shifts in reinforcement contingencies.

A PAIN MODEL

In the background of studies on physiologic and psychologic processes has been the enterprise of mapping the respective contributions of psyche and soma. This has involved determining the relative contributions of organic versus psychosocial factors. The dichotomous model of pain as real or imagined has largely been discarded. It is too simplistic, and a wealth of clinical and experimental findings refute it. Thus the clinical enterprise of deciding whether pain is real or imagined is not only impossible but also counterproductive.

An example of the outmoded view of pain as real or psychogenic can be found in past writings on dysmenorrhea. (Chapter 10 of this volume contains additional information on dysmenorrhea.) In the sixties, psychiatric textbooks described the woman with painful periods as exhibiting conflicts over her female role. Such a formulation arose from two lines of thought. First was the failure to find a "real" or organic cause for dysmenorrhea. Clearly, some women experienced little or no menstrual pain and others were disabled. Second, a psychological explanation reflected the prevailing psychosomatic disease model, which matched disease to specific psychic conflicts or personality types (Alexander, 1952). Just as hypertension was seen as a response to suppressed hostility, so dysmenorrhea was viewed as a rejection of the female reproductive role. With the discovery of the role of prostaglandins in causing menstrual pain and the use of antiprostaglandins as an effective treatment (Ylikorkala & Dawood, 1978), the psychosomatic model was discarded. Yet it lingers on for conditions where uncertainty remains about etiology and pathophysiology.

Rather than construct opposing psychologic models in cases where the etiology for pain remains obscure, it is necessary to embrace the twofold reality that pain is always real, never imagined, and that it always has both physiologic and psychosocial components. Pain comes about in response to noxious stimulation, with sensations transmitted across nerve cells to the spinal cord and then to the brain. These messages may be blocked, superseded, or occasionally lost before reaching the brain. In some conditions, pain is experienced without peripheral input, and in others, pain stimuli are fired without being registered cortically. As a result, models of pain as a sensation have been discarded because pain,

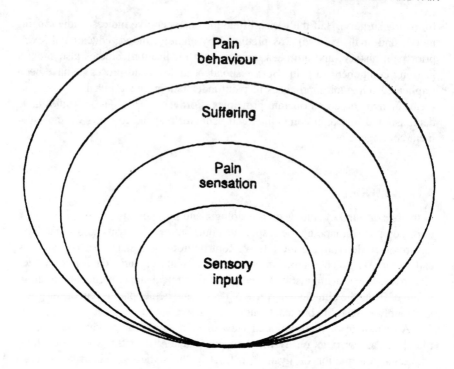

Figure 9.1 Loeser's hierarchical model of pain.

whether acute or chronic, is a complex experience influenced by a variety of extrinsic and intrinsic stimuli.

Biomedical models of pain have given way to models that acknowledge the complex interactions among psychological, social, and physiologic factors. Loeser (1980) has provided a hierarchical model that assists in both understanding and managing the pain patient. This model, depicted in Figure 9.1, shows four levels of pain expression: nociception, sensation, suffering and behavior. The pain experience may reflect input from all or some of these levels. Extensive modulation occurs between the level of nociception and pain expression. Modulation is physiologic in terms of the firing of pain-inhibiting fibers and the release of endorphins, but is also influenced by psychological factors such as attention, mood, anxiety, personal meaning, and the prevailing reinforcement contingencies. As pain endures and becomes chronic, pain and functioning have a reciprocal relationship, thereby implicating the individual's social and family milieu.

There may be cases when nociceptive input is absent and yet pain continues to be reported. This pain is no less real or worthy of management. Alternatively, there may be cases demonstrating attenuated input at the suffering or behavioral levels. Although it is commonly assumed that the greater the pain, the greater the suffering, there are exceptions. Less suffering may arise from pains known to be shortlived, such as pain associated with childbirth, which, as will be seen, may be intense from a sensory standpoint. Conversely, pains associated with dire consequences, those accompanied by uncertainty as to cause or by fear of not being controllable are likely to give rise to increased suffering. It follows, therefore, that under certain circumstances suffering may be relieved despite continued sensory input.

Loeser's model directs us to map the relative contributions of each component to the overall pain experience. To return to the earlier example of dysmenorrhea, the model would accommodate physiologic findings of the action of prostaglandins, as well as explain individual differences in processing of sensations, behavioral reactions, and emotional impact of sensations. From a treatment standpoint, it endorses parallel interventions at whatever level is predominant or most accessible. In selecting a treatment strategy, consideration needs to be given to the individual's life circumstances. An effective treatment for pelvic pain may be radical surgery, in which the reproductive organs are removed. This may not be acceptable if the patient also wishes to preserve her fertility. Neither will it be effective if there are significant psychosocial forces maintaining the level of complaint and disability.

ACUTE VERSUS CHRONIC PAIN

An additional distinction can be drawn between acute and chronic pain. This distinction is important because, as will be seen, it influences management. Acute pain arises in response to an event or trauma or sometimes for unknown reasons. However, within a discrete period of time, usually 3 to 6 months, the pain responds to treatment. Treatment typically consists of symptomatic relief combined with management of underlying pathology. Usually this involves rest, withdrawal, and reassurance, in addition to medical and surgical remedies. Chronic pain by definition is not shortlived. It may be continuous or episodic, controlled by endogenous factors in the case of pain with menstruation, triggered by external conditions (such as activity), or intermittently occurring without obvious precipitants. Usually pain persisting longer than 3 to 6 months is acknowledged as chronic. Pelvic pain arising from an acute infection, ectopic pregnancy, or tumor will respond to treatment of the underlying cause. Pain associated with adhesions or endometriosis is more variable and likely to be ongoing.

Different management principles apply to chronic pain conditions. It is not well understood why some individuals with pain respond well to treatment whereas for others the pain becomes chronic. Similarly, it is not understood why some individuals with chronic pain lead a relatively full life, attempting to minimize the toll of the pain, whereas others become disabled by it. The variability in response to pain has led to a further distinction between chronic pain and chronic pain syndrome, sometimes referred to as "chronic benign pain syndrome." The latter refers to pain that persists beyond a reasonable time and exerts a disproportionate effect on life circumstances and for which there is a lack of objective laboratory or clinical evidence commensurate with the level of pain complaint or lack of treatment response.

Where pain is managed without consideration to this multifaceted model, the problem may become intractable, evoking frustration for caregivers as patients fail to respond to somatic interventions. Pain and suffering tend to evoke comparable behaviors, making it difficult to differentiate pain behaviors from suffering. Similarly, as pain persists, its potential to influence behavior increases. Pain behaviors may then be influenced by factors other than nociceptive input and possibly be maintained by reinforcement contingencies. The search for the cause of the pain may involve a succession of diagnostic and therapeutic surgeries. During this time the acute model of managment may be in force, whereby the patient is encouraged to use pain killing medication as needed, withdraw from obligations and activities, and remain in a passive role awaiting the discovery and remediation of the cause. If there is pathology, it may be treated. If there is not, the patient may be left to feel the pain is imaginary. Both approaches are inadequate because the patient treated symptomatically may not have a good prognosis if there are other factors maintaining the pain behavior. As Loeser's model indicates, pain behavior can be maintained even when nociceptive input has been blocked. Similarly, the absence of demonstrable pathology does not signify that none exists. Presented with pain and suffering, the physician may gravitate toward corrective surgery. This may have a poor prognosis if the contribution of the patient's mood and reinforcement contingencies is not recognized.

The chronic model of pain indicates that the patient should be encouraged not to withdraw from activities because such withdrawal precludes the beneficial distracting effects of activity and leads to greater focus on pain and disability, intensifying depressed affect. Pain-contingent, or "prn," medication should be avoided and replaced by time-contingent administration in order to achieve a steady blood level of the drug and avoid the unwanted reinforcement contingencies associated with pain regimens applied on demand.

METHODOLOGICAL TECHNIQUES USED TO STUDY PAIN

There is no direct test of pain. Indirect assessments encompass functional evaluations, tissue examination, and clinical evaluation. From a psychological standpoint, assessment has involved extensive psychometric evaluation. At one point it was driven by the object of identifying the contribution of psychological factors and whether there was a pain-prone or predisposed personality. The Minnesota

Multiphasic Personality Inventory (MMPI) has been used most extensively in this respect. Most of this testing has been carried out on chronic patients. There is a high prevalence of elevated MMPI score profiles among pain patients. Typically, chronic pain has been associated with a conversion "V" profile, consisting of elevated scores on Scales 1 and 3 (hypochondriasis and hysteria), with lower but elevated scores on Scale 2 (depression) (Love & Peck, 1987). Attempts to distinguish between "functional" and "organic" paients on the basis of MMPI scores have largely been discarded, owing to their large overlap (McCreary, Turner, & Dawson, 1977). Pain patients with and without physical findings produce roughly comparable MMPI scores (Fordyce, Brena, Holcomb, DeLateau, & Loeser, 1978). The elevations on Scales 1 and 2 may derive from the item relevance of the symptoms rather than hypochondriacal dispositions (Watson, 1982).

MMPI profiles have been subjected to cluster analysis in an attempt to discriminate between groups (Bradley, Prokop, Margolis, & Gentry, 1978). Subsequent studies have examined scale elevations and their implications for treatment (Bradley, Prieto, Hopson, & Prokop, 1978). The drawback of such studies is their failure to determine whether the profiles predate or result from the pain. The MMPI profiles thought to be characteristic of chronic pain have been shown to be a reflection of chronic disability rather than unique to pain, since other patient groups achieve comparable profiles (Naliboff, Cohen, & Yellen, 1982). Taken together, these findings are consistent with Loeser's pain model, which indicates the importance of charting the input from each of the four levels rather than assuming homogeneity with respect to etiology. It appears that MMPI profiles become disturbed by chronic illness and are not specific to chronic pain. This does not mean chronic illness with disability inevitably gives rise to psychological symptoms. Clearly these will vary in both type and degree.

The relationship between MMPI score elevations and pain may also be dubious in that it may be a function of the population under study. Most reports are based on pain clinic patients, that is, subjects who not only experience chronic pain but also attend chronic pain clinics. Psychologieal disturbance or a certain personality profile may influence whether a patient is likely to be treated at a pain clinic. A comparison of women with pain associated with endometriosis showed significantly greater psychopathology, as indexed by MMPI scores, among the group attending a chronic pain clinic than among the group receiving treatment from gynecologists (Rapkin, Kames, & Reading, 1989). Since the pain reports of the pain clinic group were also higher, it remains unclear whether patients who attend pain clinics have more severe pain or whether other characteristics are important.

Pain improvement leads to an improvement in MMPI profiles and overall functioning. This has been demonstrated for chronic pain patients by Naliboff, McCreary, McArthur, Cohen, and Gottlieb (1988) who reported MMPI profiles before and after treatment for chronic low back pain. Patients entered treatment with high levels of pain and disability and improved following treatment. There was a general normalization of MMPI scores. Although pretreatment MMPI scores were elevated, they were closer to normal at the end of treatment. Similar findings emerged from a study of women with chronic pain arising from endometriosis (Reading et al., 1987). Although none of the MMPI scale scores were elevated above a T-score of 60 prior to treatment with a gonadotrophin releasing hormone (GnRH) analogue, scores were lower following effective treatment of the disease, as indexed by both symptom reports and laparoscopic findings.

MMPI profiles have also been examined in terms of predicting treatment response. High scores on Scales 1 and 3 have been associated with poor response to surgery, although this has not applied to response to nerve blocks, or anesthesiological procedures (Love & Peck, 1987). In contrast, MMPI profiles have not been shown to be predictive of response to pain management programs (e.g., Keefe & Block, 1982).

It has been suggested that elevations on Scales 1, 2 and 3 (hypochondrias, depression, and hysteria), which are thought to reflect reaction to pain and disability, may respond to traditional medical treatment but that elevations on other scales may signify complex and longstanding psychological issues, thereby suggesting a poor prognosis even in multidisciplinary pain clinic approaches (Love & Peck, 1987). In contrast, Naliboff et al. (1988) found change across all scales, suggesting for chronic pain patients at least, the entire range of psychological symptoms (as measured by the MMPI clinical scales) can be associated with chronic illness.

ACUTE PELVIC PAIN

Acute Pain Dysmenorrhea

Less attention has been given to the study of dysmenorrhea since the discovery of prostaglandins and the subsequent effective use of antiprostagladin medication. A survey of 265 menstruating women selected at random revealed 57% reported painful periods (Gath, Osborn, Bungay, Ileg, Day, Bond, & Passingham, 1987). A random survey of 19-year-old women showed that 72% described dysmenorrhea (Andersch & Milsom, 1982). Studies have shown prostagladins regulate myometrial contractility, leading to ischemia (Ylikorkala & Dawood, 1978). Women with dysmenorrhea have increased levels of prostaglandins in their menstrual flow (Chen & Hill, 1978). Walker and Katz (1981) described the use of electrical stimulation of the peripheral nerves for the treatment of menstrual cramps. The resulting analgesia was not reversed by administration of naloxone, suggesting that nonopioid mechanisms were responsible.

Labor Pain

There has been extensive study of childbirth pain. Assessments using the Maudsley Personality Questionnaire (MPQ) have shown that women report this in extreme terms (Reading & Cox, 1985). Melzack, Taenzer, Feldman, and Kinch (1981) have reviewed studies of labor pain and found wide variability. Primiparae have higher scores than women undergoing a repeat delivery. Comparing MPQ profiles with other pain conditions, Melzack et al. showed pain report to exceed most other types of pain, confirming its intensity. A positive correlation emerged between childbirth pain and menstrual difficulties, suggesting a common pathology in the form of excessive release of prostaglandins.

Dyspareunia

Pain associated with sexual activity is extremely rare in men but relatively common for women. A survey of gynecology patients revealed 20% experienced pain with intercourse (Bachmann, Leiblum, & Grill, 1989). This may reflect pelvic structure in the form of mechanical stimulation activating nociceptive input or be secondary to a lack of sexual arousal, possibly due to anticipatory anxiety over the prospect of pain. It may coexist with ongoing pain or be the only problem.

Pain History and Pain Thresholds

Given the ubiquitous presence of pain during a woman's life, there has been interest in pain thresholds and tolerance among women. Are women more or less sensitive to pain as a result of their past experience? Studies have shown that pain reactions vary according to menstrual cycle phase, although whether women are more or less sensitive during menstruation has varied across studies. The adaptation level model (Rollman, 1979) states that the chronic pain patients, because of prior experience with pain, may judge experimentally induced pain more conservatively and have higher thresholds than pain-free individuals (Naliboff, Cohen, Scandler, & Heinrich, 1981). Hapidou and Catanzaro (1988) found a lower pain threshold during the luteal phase for women with dysmenorrhea, supporting the adaptation model. Cogan and Spinnato (1986) found that the discomfort threshold of pregnant women responding to a painful stimulus increased before the onset of labor, whereas that of nonpregnant women was unchanged, suggesting reduced sensitivity to pain prior to parturition. However, using a signal detection paradigm, Goolkasian and Rimer (1984) found no differences in discrimination of sensations across pregnancy for pregnant women or controls. There was an increase in pain report in the last two weeks of pregnancy but no change over time for controls. Others have suggested that pain thresholds do increase during pregnancy (e.g., Goland, Wardlaw, Blum, Tropper, & Stark, 1988). Whipple and Komisaruk (1985) studied the effects of stimulation of the anterior vaginal wall on pain perception. Sensation was rated less aversive when occurring in the presence of vaginal stimulation. The authors suggested that such reduced sensitivity to pain may occur in childbirth or sexual intercourse, either by changing dorsal transmission of sensations or by release of central neurotransmitters.

Does prior experience of pelvic pain affect the reaction to subsequent episodes? For example, do women with menstrual pain cope better or worse in the event of ongoing pelvic pain? The influence of past pain experience was studied by Melzack and Belanger (1989). Their hypothesis was that prior experience of pain may be associated with more intense pain in labor. Drawing upon previous work showing the variability that exists with labor pain, with about 15% of women reporting intense pain and a small proportion relatively little (Melzack et al., 1981), they studied the influence of past experience of low back pain and menstrual pain on pain during labor. The results were inconsistent. There was a relationship between labor pain and menstrual pain experienced in the back region but not the front. This relationship emerges for women with heavier babies. Melzack and Belanger (1989) suggested parallel physiologic mechanisms, with an extensive production of prostaglandins giving rise to more intense menstrual contractions, resulting in referred pain to the back. During labor, more intense contractions would be expected with a larger baby, creating increased pressure on abdominal structures and leading to diffuse abdominal and low back pain. It would be interesting to study prior history of pain with women experiencing chronic pain.

CHRONIC PELVIC PAIN

Research

Research on chronic pelvic pain has employed two strategies. One has been to compare women with pathology with those without obvious pathology. Degree of pathology has been established on the basis of laparoscopic study. Groups derived in this way have been compared on psychometric testing. Alternatively, women with pelvic pain have been compared to nonpain control groups. Most of these studies have been cross-sectional and have relied upon samples available in the clinics where they were conducted. Clearly the nature of the clinic (gynecology, psychiatry, or pain clinic) will influence the findings obtained. For example, Rapkin et al. (1989) showed significant differences on psychological testing among women with pain associated with endometriosis as a function of whether they were recruited from a pain clinic or a gynecology service.

Comparisons of women with chronic pelvic pain according to diagnosis, drawing a distinction between women with and without demonstrable pathology, have shown a high prevalence of psychopathology in women with chronic pain. For example, Castelnuova-Tedesco and Krout (1970) administered the MMPI to 40 women with pelvic pain and a comparison group with pathology and no pain. Within the pelvic pain group, 15 had no demonstrable pathology. There was no relationship between pathology and psychopathology, though the group with pain showed significantly more disturbed MMPI profiles. Beard, Bedsey, Lieberman, and Wilkinson (1977) studied 18 women with pain and negative findings on laparoscopy and compared their psychological test scores with 17 women with comparable complaints and clear pathology. The neuroticism score on the Eysenck Personality Inventory was higher for the laparoscopy negative group than for the gynecology nonpain control group. Gross, Doerr, Caldirola, Guzinski, and Ripley (1980/1981) also reported high levels of psychopathology in women with pelvic pain, as well as a past exposure to childhood sexual abuse in 90% of their sample.

Unfortunately, although these studies describe the level of distress and disturbance associated with chronic pain, they do not disentangle cause and effect. In other words, is pelvic pain an expression and concomitant of psychopathology or does chronic pain lead to emotional disturbance? Renaer, Vertomme, Nijs, Wagemans, and Vanhemel (1979) clarified these issues by comparing MMPI profiles for women with chronic pain without obvious pathology, women with pain arising from endometriosis, and controls. They found the two pain groups differed from controls but not from each other. The authors concluded that chronic pain of whatever etiology can lead to a neurotic reaction.

More recent approaches have attempted to identify specific psychological mechanisms or processes rather than to describe overall psychologic disturbance. For example, Magni, Salmi, Leo, and Cecola (1984) studied the role of depression. They found higher depression scores for women with chronic pelvic pain without pathology compared to women with pain and identifiable pathology on laparoscopic evaluation. In addition, a higher frequency of depressive disorders was found in the family histories of women with pain and no identifiable pathology. Magni et al. (1984) suggested that pelvic pain under these circumstances may reflect a masked depression, and drew upon evidence showing the involvement of serotoninergic, adrenergic, and endorphinergic systems in both depression and chronic pain (Terenius, 1980). Pain may be improved by antidepressant medication (Feinman, 1985). This result may be due not only to the medication's mood-elevating properties, but also to the medication's direct operation on central mechanisms, with increased availability of norepinephrine changing the pain experience. These studies demonstrate the close relationship between pain and depression. Pre-existing or coexisting depression may influence the processing of pain sensations. Depression is known to change information processing, creating a selective bias toward negative information (Clark & Teasdale, 1985). Such a bias would lead to the amplification of pain sensations. Depression also leads to withdrawal from activities that paradoxically, if engaged in, might have an antidepressant effect. In this respect, at both cognitive and behavioral levels, the effects of pain and depression are similar and additive.

The relationship between chronic pelvic pain and prior history of childhood sexual abuse has also been studied. Gross et al. (1980/1981) reported a high prevalence (90%) of sexual abuse in their sample of women with chronic pelvic pain. Harrop-Griffiths, Katon, Walker, Holm, Russo, and Hickok (1988) described a series of 25 women with chronic pelvic pain. No differences emerged between women with pathology identified by laparoscopy and those with pain but negative laparoscopic findings on any of the psychosocial measures. Comparing the pain patients with a gynecologic control group, the researchers found that women with pain had a greater likelihood of a prior major depressive episode. In 12 of the 16 patients with a positive history for depression, the depression preceded the onset of the pain. There was also a higher prevalence of prior substance abuse, functional dyspareunia, inhibited sexual desire, higher scores on the Symptom Checklist-90 (SCL 90), and a history of sexual abuse, both prior to age 14 and in adulthood. Being sexually abused as a child and having a past history of depression were strongly related to the development of pelvic pain.

Walker, Katon, Harrop-Griffiths, Holm, Russo, and Hickok (1988) suggested that chronic pelvic pain may be a metaphorical way of describing chronic psychological pain and coping with painful memories. They emphasized the adaptive function of the symptoms in legitimizing avoidance of sexual contact. Women with a history of childhood sexual abuse are likely to have poor adult sexual adjustment, more depressive symptoms, and lower self-esteem, and to suffer from a greater number of psychological symptoms (Gold, 1986). Thus there may not be a high cost to avoiding sexual behavior through pain. Avoidance may be reinforcing because the pelvic pain may result from intrapsychic conflicts about sexuality that remain repressed until sexual activity commences. It would be premature to make such generalizations, and such a formulation has connotations of the psychosomatic model criticized earlier in this chapter. An alternative consideration is that the sexual and physical abuse coexist with a chaotic home environment, with women coming from families with multiple problems. Whether previous exposure to sexual abuse predisposes to chronicity by increasing vulnerability to depression and helplessness in the face of pain or whether pelvic pain triggers specific flashbacks to the sexual abuse remains to be determined. There may have been a lack of care and protection, predisposing to abuse, with recurrent episodes of drug abuse and depression in adult life. There may be role models for pain as a means of avoiding obligations. Studies on family mechanisms have demonstrated the role of learning by selective reinforcement (Turk, Flor, & Rudy, 1987) and observation (Craig, 1978). Unfortunately, studies on prior exposure to abuse lack appropriate controls.

Although an association between pain and a prior history of abuse has emerged, the mechanism of effect is unclear. First, it is necessary to define the nature of the abuse. Is it confined to sexual abuse, or does it encompass all forms of abuse? Rapkin, Kames, Darke, Stampler, and Naliboff (1990) compared the prevalence of sexual and physical abuse in women with pelvic pain, women with pain from other sites, and a gynecology control group. The prevalence of childhood sexual abuse did not differ among groups although a difference did emerge for physical abuse. Second, is there a critical developmental time, such as before puberty, that confers increased risk, or is sexual abuse a risk factor throughout life? Third, why is a prior history of abuse linked to pain, and is this effect confined to women or is it also present for men? Fourth, are the effects of abuse direct, or are they mediated via increased vulnerability to depression, which in turn predisposes toward chronic pain?

There are few answers to these questions, so a consideration of mechanisms remains speculative. Sexual abuse involves trauma, distress, and possibly pain. The experience of pelvic pain in adult life may reactivate such memories or associations, thereby causing increased distress in women experiencing pelvic pain against a background of previous sexual abuse (Brewin, 1989). This may be amplified further if the cognitive appraisal interprets the pain as retribution for past behavior or as an ongoing pattern in the form of yet another inevitable problem. Such an explanatory style of seeing negative events as stable and global is identified as a risk factor for depression by the reformulated learned helplessness model (Seligman, Abramson, Semmel, & Von Baeyer, 1979). The pain can be seen as a further violation of a woman's belief and trust in the world. Such an attributional framework, if transferred to the pain, will construe pain as uncontrollable, stable, and global.

Assessment

Management of the woman with chronic pelvic pain is no different in principle from that of any other chronic pain patient. The assumption has to be that a simple remedial cause will not be found. Even if one originally existed, the chances are that the pain is now being maintained by additional factors. Management needs to commence with a comprehensive evaluation of the pain problem from a multidimensional standpoint. Such an evaluation imposes the challenge of integrating the resultant information. A full physical evaluation should be accompanied by a review of psychosocial factors. Pain is commonly accompanied by depression and anxiety, so these need to be carefully assessed by standard methods (Tyrer, Capon, Peterson, Charlton, & Thompson, 1989). The impact of the pain on the patient's life circumstances should also be evaluated, drawing upon an operant model, in order to identify reinforcement contingencies.

In addition to objective findings, assessment should include examining the woman's understanding of the pain and the personal meaning she attaches to it.

Pain   By its very nature, pain precludes direct assessment. Its presence and severity is inferred from subject report. This can be systematized by using rating scales of one form or another to quantify dimensions of the pain experience. Traditionally a distinction has been drawn between ratings of pain sensation and the accompanying distress (Gracely, 1986). Subjective report has also been studied in terms of the language used to describe the pain. The McGill Pain Questionnaire (Melzack, 1975) consists of 78 pain adjectives, arranged in clusters according to meaning, which yield intensity scores on the dimensions of sensation, affective reaction, and overall evaluation. More recently, consideration has been given to deriving more representative scoring protocols by using weighted scores (Melzack, Katz, & Jeans, 1985) or the square root function of the weighted scores (Harkins, Price, & Braith, 1989).

Subjective report can also be assessed via the use of diary ratings carried out over a specified time period. These can give information on the frequency of pain, its intensity and duration, and concomitant events or activities, which may suggest controlling factors. A diary format introduces the possibility of parallel monitoring events or experiences that may have a bearing on the pain. It is insufficient to rely solely upon self-report instruments. In addition to subjective report, pain has a behavioral component that is amenable to observation and therefore measurement. Behavior needs to be assessed in terms of overall functioning and use of health agencies and possibly by time sampling observations of pain behaviors. Fordyce (1976) suggested a fourfold classification consisting of: (1) verbal complaints of pain and suffering; (2) body postures and gestures; (3) nonverbal expressions of pain and suffering; and (4) functional limitations or disability in the form of avoiding activities or downtime. Behaviors may be observed directly and their frequency rated, or patients may record activities in a behavioral diary. Alternatively, the examiner may observe the patient's behavior while requiring him or her to engage in a standard series of tasks (Keefe & Block, 1982).

Psychological State   In conjunction with assessments of pain report, an evaluation of the patient's emotional state should be conducted. This should include a determination of coexisting depression, anxiety, or other psychopathology, not because there is necessarily a causal relationship between mood and pain, but because psychological factors may affect the management plan.

Psychosocial Functioning   Measures of psychosocial functioning evaluate the impact of the pain on the woman's lifestyle. Pelvic pain is likely to affect sexual functioning, and this development may have additional repercussions in terms of the quality of the relationship and self-esteem. It is important to ascertain whether sexual problems predated the pain or developed subsequently. Similarly, the way in which the pain affects work and nonwork activities and opportunities should be addressed. Previous experience of sexual or physical abuse can be recorded, given the prevalence of this in women with unremitting pain.

Physiologic Factors   In addition to a careful medical history and physical, laparoscopic examination may be necessary to identify treatable conditions. As has been stated, for a substantial number of patients the pathophysiology will remain unclear, and even where disease is identified, it may not correlate well with pain complaint. Biomedical markers are also imprecise. Even though there may be increased prostaglandin concentrations in the menstrual flow of women with dysmenorrhea (Chen & Hill, 1978), the finding of such concentrations does not constitute a diagnostic evaluation. Use of short-acting epidural blocks may assist in determining the contribution of nociceptive input.

Management Considerations

The goal of treatment for the pain patient is pain relief. In the case of chronic pain, by definition this has been an elusive goal. Once the pain has become refractory to initial treatment, additional management considerations apply. The goal of pain relief subsumes the additional objectives of reduced dependence on pain medication, increasing activity, and reducing the toll of the pain and associated disability on the patient's lifestyle.

To date, pelvic pain has tended to be managed traditionally and not to benefit from the interdisciplinary approaches found in specialist pain centers (Rapkin & Kames, 1987). Surgical management is often unsuccessful. Indications for poor surgical prognosis include a disproportionate degree of pain and/or disability, excessive withdrawal from activities, unwillingness to acknowledge stress or depression, drug dependence, family disorganization, and evidence of depression. Paradoxically, the depressed patient may be more likely to become a candidate for surgery. The depression may amplify her suffering, making her pain less tolerable and thereby increasing her complaint. The gynecologist may construe the depression as a sign of intolerable pain and may more aggressively recommend radical surgery, to which the patient in a depressed state may agree. If the patient's depression predated the pain, the surgery is unlikely to help her mood, and the loss of reproductive functioning and/or the failure of surgery to remedy the pain may further compound the problem.

Where pain persists, a pain management model of pain is most appropriate. This model embraces the philosophy of maximizing overall functioning and minimizing suffering and disability but is not focused on pain relief per se. Such an approach is not constrained by the prescription of pain-relieving medication or surgery. The initial contract with the patient is twofold: both parties agree that the pain is real and distressing and that the goal is now to achieve pain control rather than abolition of pain. If pain abolition occurs, it is a bonus and will only happen by the systematic application of pain control principles. Such application involves refraining from further doctor shopping in the quest for the magic bullet, whether in the form of surgery or drugs. It may involve attending a specialist pain clinic or at least working with a group of professionals from different backgrounds.

Treatment modalities include both physiologic and psychosocial interventions. Treatment usually follows baseline behavioral records. These serve as a yardstick by which to measure subsequent progress, as well as identify controlling features. They also serve to assess motivation to participate in a treatment program that requires active participation on the patient's part. Physiologic modalities include trigger point injections, nerve blocks, and physical therapy. Walker and Katz (1981) demonstrated the benefits of electrical stimulation of the peripheral nerves for women complaining of menstrual cramps. The analgesic effects were not naloxone reversible and so were nonopioid mediated. Typically, the patient will be weaned off pain medication, which after all has not been helping and may be fostering a passive, helpless role. When pain medication is used, this is administered on a time-contingent rather than pain-contingent basis. Antidepressant medication may be used. This may be targeted at any concomitant depression or may be used as a direct intervention for pain. There is evidence that antidepressant medication has benefits in terms of both mood elevation and and specific analgesic properties (Magni, 1987).

From a psychological standpoint, treatment may include use of hypnosis or relaxation techniques as well as biofeedback. These may be used to decrease physical arousal, reduce associated emotional distress, or serve as coping techniques that the patient can use to redirect attention from the pain, thereby engendering a feeling of control and self-efficacy (e.g., Pearce, Knight, & Beard, 1982). Cognitive behavioral approaches may be used to change self-defeating cognitions and exchange counterproductive pain behaviors for more constructive activities. Cognitive approaches have the dual benefit of attempting to change cognitions that may increase both depression and pain. Marital and sexual therapy may also be necessary in order to deal with issues that have arisen. There may be a fear of sexual activity because this has been associated with pain in the past, leading to avoidance, which may create further strain on the relationship. Therapy may focus on reintroducing sexual activity in a graduated way, allowing the woman to become comfortable with each step and to cope with pain, should it occur, by changing the focus of what the partners are doing rather than stopping altogether.

DIRECTIONS FOR FUTURE RESEARCH

Pain is woven into the fabric of a woman's life. Normal reproductive events such as menstruation and childbirth give rise to pain. In addition, women are more prone than men to other kinds of pains, such as headache and joint pains. Women are also more prone to depressive disorders, at least during their reproductive years. The prevalence of chronic pelvic pain is unknown. Pain in this location will affect sexual functioning and so may create conditions for marital instability. Management has tended to be approached from a traditional medical standpoint, with resort to surgery, which may impose the additional burden for the woman of the loss of her fertility potential and, when the ovaries are not spared, all of the additional health consequences of early menopause. Early attention to the multifactorial nature of pain and risk factors for chronicity will help to ensure more satisfactory management.

The traditional acute model of pain has also been thought to predispose toward chronicity when the pain does not respond and the acute care is prolonged (Fordyce, 1976). The acute model leads to a passive lifestyle. Fordyce (1987) has suggested that pain from acute tissue injuries becomes chronic because health care approaches are not based on what is known about healing and the adverse effects of disuse. The health care system reinforces pain behaviors of all description, whether in the form of medication use, complaints, rest, or avoidance of activities. Secondary prevention is aimed at overcoming these tendencies in an attempt to prevent pain from becoming both chronic and disabling (Fordyce, Brockway, Bergman, & Spengler, 1986; Linton, Bradley, Jensen, Spangfort, & Sundell, 1989).

The question then becomes, why does pain persist in some individuals and what determines the role it occupies? Answering this question involves considering risk factors for chronicity as well as the adequacy of functioning in the face of chronic pain. Acute pelvic pain, whether in the form of dysmenorrhea, midcycle pain, dyspareunia, or pain arising from infection or endometriosis, is common. What in addition to organic pathology determines why it persists? Risk factors identified in the field of chronic pain include protracted treatment based on an acute pain model, prior history of substance abuse, prior history of depression, a low overall psychosocial cost to being disabled, social reinforcement, personality factors, and possibly favorable economic contingencies. It is evident that many of these risk factors are related and associated with generally poor adjustment. None of these are specific, because individuals can be exposed to these, experience pain, and not have it become chronic.

Personality may be a risk factor for chronicity. Certain kinds of personality types may lead individuals to gravitate to less effective ways of coping and be more susceptible to conditioning effects, which may serve to entrench them even further in the sick role. Personality influences both the processing of sensory information in terms of threshold levels (Harkins et al., 1989) and suffering and behavior. Individuals displaying a repressive coping style typically report lower levels of negative emotions, more somatic symptoms, greater tolerance of nociceptive stimulation, and low affective reaction to aversive stimulation. Jamner and Schwartz (1986) suggested endogeneous opioids may account for these effects. A repressive personality style may be paralleled by greater central endogeneous opioid activity (Jamner, Schwartz, & Leigh, 1988). Further investigation of this model is called for, assessing coping styles as well as response to noxious stimulation across the menstrual cycle.

Of interest is the relationship between chronic pain and depression. Haley, Turner, and Romano (1985) reported gender differences in the associations between depression, activity, and chronic pain. For women, depression was significantly associated with self-reported pain severity. No such relationship emerged for males, although the associations between activity levels and depression were consistently stronger for men than women. Chronic pain may trigger depression, as a result of its aversive nature, the lack of control, and the loss of functioning. Depression has been shown to be associated with systematic shifts in information processing (e.g., Williams, Watts, MacLeod, & Matthews, 1988). Such changes in cognitive structures are thought to increase vulnerability to recurrence and influence treatment response. Longitudinal studies of pain patients could investigate whether shifts of this kind occur shortly after the onset of pain and so predispose towards chronicity, by measuring cognitive processing during pain-free and painful times in women with periodic chronic pain, such as endometriosis pain that flares up around menstruation. Further investigations of coping styles (e.g., Fernandez, 1986) may shed light on individual differences that may mediate disability levels.

REFERENCES

Alexander, F. (1952). *Psychosomatic medicine: Its principles and applications*. London: Allen & Urwin.

Andersch, B., & Milsom I. (1982). An epidemiologic study of young women with dismenorrhea. *American Journal of Obstetrics and Gynecology, 144*, 655–660.

Andrasik, F., & Kabela, E. (1988). Headaches. In E. A. Blechman & K. D. Brownell (Eds.), *Handbook of behavioral medicine for women* (pp. 206–221). New York: Pergamon Press.

Bachmann, G. A., Leiblum, S. R. & Grill, J. (1989). Brief sexual inquiry in gynecologic practice. *Obstetrics and Gyneology, 73*, 425–427.

Beard, R. W., Belsey, E. M., Lieberman, B. A., & Wilkinson, J. C. M. (1977). Pelvic pain in women. *American Journal of Obstetrics and Gynecology, 128*, 566–570.

Beard, R. W., Highman, J. H., Pearce, S., & Reginald, P. W. (1984). Diagnosis of pelvic varicosities in women with chronic pelvic pain. *Lancet*, 946–949.

Beard, R. W., & Pearce, S. (1989). Gynecological pain. In P. D. Wall & R. Melzack (Eds.), *Textbook of pain* (pp. 466–481). New York: Churchill Livingstone.

Bradley, L. A., Prieto, E. J., Hopson, L., & Prokop, C. K. (1978). Comment on "Personality organization as an aspect of back pain in a medical setting." *Journal of Personality Assessment, 42*, 573–578.

Bradley, L. A., Prokop, C. K., Margolis, R., & Gentry, W. D. (1978). Multivariate analyses of the MMPI profiles of low back pain patients. *Journal of Behavioral Medicine, 3*, 253–272.

Brewin, C. R. (1989). Cognitive change processes in psychotherapy. *Psychological Review, 96*, 379–394.

Castelnuovo-Tedesco, P., & Krout, B. M. (1970). Psychosomatic aspects of chronic pelvic pain. *Psychiatry in Medicine, 1*, 109–126.

Chen, W. Y., & Hill, J. C. (1978). Determination of menstrual prostaglandin levels in nondysmenorrheic and dysmenorrheic subjects. *Prostaglandins, 15*, 365–375.

Clark, D. M., & Teasdale, J. D. (1985). Constraints on the effects of mood in memory. *Journal of Personality and Social Psychology, 48*, 1595–1608.

Cogan, R., & Spinnato, J. A. (1986). Pain and discomfort thresholds in late pregnancy. *Pain, 27*, 63–68.

Craig, K. (1978). Social modeling influences on pain. In R. Sternback (Ed.), *The psychology of pain* (pp. 73–110). New York: Raven Press.

Crook, J., Rideout, E., & Browne, G. (1984). The prevalence of pain complaints in a general population. *Pain, 18*, 299–314.

Dubuisson, D., & Melzak, R. (1976). Classification of clinical pain descriptions by multiple group discriminant analysis. *Experimental Neurology, 51*, 480–487.

Feinmann, C. 1985). Pain relief by antidepressants: Possible modes of action. *Pain, 23*, 1–8.

Fernandez, E. (1986). A classification system of cognitive coping strategies for pain. *Pain, 26*, 141–151.

Fields, H. L., & Basbaum, A.I. (1989). Endogenous pain control mechanisms. In P. D. Wall & R. Melzack (Eds.), *Textbook of pain* (pp. 206–217). New York: Churchill Livingstone.

Fordyce, W. E. (1976). *Behavioral methods for chronic pain and illness*. St. Louis, MO: C. V. Mosby.

Fordyce, W. E. (1987). Prevention of reinjury. *Ergonomics, 30*, 457–462.

Fordyce, W. E., Brena, S. F., Holcomb, R. J., DeLateau, B. J., & Loeser, J. D. (1978). Relationship of patient semantic pain descriptions to physician diagnostic judgements, activity level measures and MMPI. *Pain, 5*, 293–303.

Fordyce, W. E., Brockway, J., Bergman, J. A., & Spengler, D. (1986). Acute back pain: A control group comparison of behavioral vs. traditional management methods. *Journal of Behavioral Medicine, 9*, 127–140.

Gath, D., Osborn, M., Bungay, G., Ileg, S., Day, A., Bond, A., & Passingham, C. (1987). Psychiatric disorder and gynecological symptoms in middle-aged women: A community survey. *British Medical Journal, 294*, 213–218.

Golard, R. S., Wardlaw, S. L., Blum, M., Tropper, P. J., & Stark, R. I. (1988). Biologically active corticotropin-releasing hormone in maternal and fetal plasma during pregnancy. *American Journal of Obstetrics and Gynecology, 159*, 884–890.

Gold, E. R. (1986). Long-term effects of sexual victimization in childhood: An attributional approach. *Journal of Consulting and Clinical Psychology, 54*, 471–475.

Goolkasian, P., & Rimer, B. A. (1984). Pain reactions in pregnant women. *Pain, 20*, 87–95.

Gracely, R. H. (1986). New approaches to the assessment of experimental and clinical pain. *Journal of Dental Research, 65*, 164.

Gross, R. J., Doerr, H., Caldirola, D., Guzinski, G. M., & Ripley, H. S. (1980/1981). Borderline syndrome and incest in chronic pelvic pain patients. *International Journal of Psychiatry and Medicine, 10*, 79–96.

Haley, W. E., Turner, J. A., & Romano, J. M. (1985). Depression in chronic pain patients: Relation to pain, activity and sex differences. *Pain, 23*, 337–343.

Hapidou, E. G., & Catanzaro, D. D. (1988). Sensitivity to cold pressor pain in dysmenorrheic and non-dysmenorrheic women as a function of menstrual cycle phase. *Pain, 34*, 277–283.

Harkins, S. W., Price, D. D., & Braith, J. (1989). Effects of extraversion and neuroticism on experimental pain, clinical pain, and illness behavior. *Pain, 36*, 209–218.

Harrop-Griffiths, J., Katon, W., Walker, E., Holm, L., Russo, J., & Hickok, L. (1988). The association between chronic pelvic pain, psychiatric diagnoses and childhood sexual abuse. *Obstetrics and Gynecology, 71*, 589–594.

Jamner, L. D., & Schwarz, G. E. (1986). Self-deception predicts self-report and endurance of pain. *Psychosomatic Medicine, 48*, 223.

Jamner, L. D., Schwartz, G. E., & Leigh, H. (1988). The relationship between repressive and defensive coping styles and monocyte, eosinophile, and serum glucose levels: Support for the opioid peptide hypothesis of repression. *Psychosomatic Medicine, 50*, 567–575.

Jeffcoate, T. N. A. (1975). *Principles of gynecology* (4th ed.). London: Butterworths.

Keefe, F. J., & Block, A. R. (1982). Development of an observation method for assessing pain behavior in chronic low back pain patients. *Behavior Therapy, 4*, 93–103.

Levine, J. D., Gordon, N. C., & Fields, H. L. (1979). Naloxone dose dependently produces analgesia and hyperalgesia in postoperative pain. *Nature, 278*, 740–741.

Linton, S. J., Bradley, L. A., Jensen, I., Spangfort, E., & Sundell, L. (1989). The secondary prevention of low back pain: A controlled study with follow-up. *Pain, 36*, 197–207.

Loeser, J. D. (1980). Perspectives on pain. In *Proceedings of First World Conference on Clinical Pharmacology and Therapeutics* (313–316). London: Milton Publications.

Love, A. W., & Peck, C. L. (1987). The MMPI and psychological factors in chronic low back pain: A review. *Pain, 28*, 1–12.

Magni, G. (1987). On the relationship between chronic pain and depression when there is no organic lesion. *Pain, 31*, 1–21.

Magni, G., Salmi, A., Leo, D., & Ceola, A. (1984). Chronic pelvic pain and depression. *Psychopathology, 17*, 132–136.

McCreary, C., Turner, J., & Dawson, E. (1977). Differences between functional versus organic low back pain patients. *Pain, 4*, 73–78.

Melzack, R. (1975). The McGill Pain Questionnaire: Major properties and scoring methods. *Pain, 1*, 277–299.

Melzack, R., & Belanger, E. (1989). Labour pain: Correlations with menstrual pain and acute low-back pain before and during pregnancy. *Pain, 36*, 225–229.

Melzak, R., Katz, J., & Jeans, M. E. (1985). The role of compensation in chronic pain: Analysis using a new method of scoring the McGill Pain Questionnaire. *Pain, 23*, 101–112.

Melzack, R., Taenzer, P., Feldman, P., & Kinch, R.A. (1981). Labour is still painful after prepared childbirth training. *Canadian Medical Association Journal, 125,* 357–363.

Melzak, R., & Torgerson, W. S. (1971). On the language of pain. *Anesthesiology, 34,* 50–59.

Melzak, R., & Wall, P. D. (1965). Pain mechanisms: A new theory. *Science, 150,* 971–979.

Merskey, H. (1986). Classification of chronic pain: Descriptions of chronic pain syndromes and definitions of pain terms. International Association for the Study of Pain, Subcommittee on Taxonomy. *Pain, 3.*

Naliboff, B. D., Cohen, M. J., Scandler, S. L., & Heinrich, R.L. (1981). Signal detection and threshold measures for chronic low back pain patients, chronic illness patients, and cohort controls to radiant heart stimuli. *Journal of Abnormal Psychology, 90,* 271–274.

Naliboff, B. D., Cohen, M. J., & Yellen, A. N. (1982). Does the MMPI differentiate chronic illness from chronic pain? *Pain, 13,* 333–361.

Naliboff, B. D., McCreary, C. P., McArthur, D. L., Cohen, M. J., & Gottlieb, H. J. (1988). MMPI changes following behavioral treatment of chronic low back pain. *Pain, 35,* 271–277.

Pearce, S., Knight, C., & Beard, R. W. (1982). Pelvic pain: A common gynaecological problem. *Journal of Psychosomatics, Obstetrics, & Gynecology, 1-1,* 12–17.

Rapkin, A. J. (1986). Adhesions and pelvic pain: A retrospective study. *Obstetrics and Gynecology, 68,* 13.

Rapkin, A. J., & Kames, L. D. (1987). The pain management approach to chronic pelvic pain. *Journal of Reproductive Medicine, 32,* 323–327.

Rapkin, A. J., Kames, L. D., Darke, L. L., Stampler, F. M., & Naliboff, B. D. (1990). History of physical and sexual abuse in women with chronic pelvic pain. *Obstetrics and Gynecology, 76,* 92–96.

Rapkin, A. T., Kames, L. D., & Reading, A. E. (1989). A comparison of cohorts of women with pain associated with endometriosis attending a pain clinic or gynecologic treatment. American Pain Society Annual Meeting, Phoenix, AZ.

Reading, A. E. (1982). The management of pain in gynecology. In J. Barber & C. Adrien (Eds.), *Psychological management of chronic pain* (pp. 137–149). New York: Brunner/Mazel.

Reading, A. E., Chang, L. C., Randle, D., Meldrum, D. R., & Judd, H. C. (1987). Psychosocial correlates of pain associated with endometriosis. World Congress on Pain, Hamburg.

Reading, A. E., & Cox, D. N. (1985). Psychosocial predictors of labor pain. *Pain, 22,* 309–315.

Reading, A. E., Hand, D., & Sledmere, C. M. (1983). A comparison of the McGill Pain Questionnaire and a random checklist in the evaluation of clinical pain. *Pain, 16,* 375–383.

Renaer, M., Vertomme, H., Nijs, P., Wagemans, L., & Vanhemel, T. (1979). Psychological aspects of chronic pelvic pain in women. *American Journal of Obstetrics and Gynecology, 134,* 75–80.

Rollman, G. B. (1979). Signal detection theory pain measures: Empirical validation studies and adaptation-level effects. *Pain, 6,* 9–21.

Royal College of Obstetricians and Gynecologists. (1978). Gynecological Laparoscopy. In G. Chamberlain & J. C. Brown (Eds.), Report of the Working Party of the Confidential Enquiry into Gynecological Laparoscopy. London: Author.

Seligman, M. E. P., Abramson, L. Y., Semmel, A., & Von Baeyer, C. (1979). Depressive attributional style. *Journal of Abnormal Psychology, 88,* 242–247.

Sternbach, R. A. (1978). *The psychology of pain.* New York: Raven Press.

Taenzer, P., Melzack, R., & Jeans, M. E. (1986). Influence of psychological factors on postoperative pain, mood and analgesic requirements. *Pain, 24,* 331–342.

Terenius, L. Y. (1980). Biochemical assessment of chronic pain. In Kosterlitz & L. Y. Terenius, *Pain and society.* Weinheim: Verlag Chemie.

Turk, D. C., Flor, H., & Rudy, T. E. (1987). Pain and families. I. Etiology, maintenance, and psychosocial impact. *Pain, 30,* 3–27.

Tyrer, S. P., Capon, M., Peterson, D. M., Charlton, J. E., & Thompson, J. W. (1989). The detection of psychiatric illness and psychological handicaps in a British pain clinic population. *Pain, 36,* 63–74.

Walker, E., Katon, W., Harrop-Griffiths, J., Holm, L., Russo, J., & Hickok, L. R. (1988). Relationship of chronic pelvic pain to psychiatric diagnoses and childhood sexual abuse. *American Journal of Psychiatry, 145,* 75–80.

Walker, J. B., and Katz, R. L. (1981). Peripheral nerve stimulation in the managment of dysmenorrhea. *Pain, 11,* 355–361.

Watson, D. (1982). Neurotic tendencies among chronic pain patients: An MMPI item analysis. *Pain,* 365–385.

Whipple, B., & Komisaruk, B. R. (1985). Elevation of pain threshold by vaginal stimulation in women. *Pain, 21,* 357–367.

Williams, J. M. G., Watts, F. N., MacLeod, C., & Matthews, A. (1988). *Cognitive psychology and emotional disorders.* London: Wiley.

Ylikorkala, O., & Daywood, M. Y. (1978). New concepts in dysmenorrhea. *American Journal of Obstetrics and Gynecology, 130,* 833–847.

Part Five

Sexuality and Infertility and AIDS

This section reviews research on three burgeoning theoretical, empirical, and applied areas of women's health that have frequently been neglected in other books on women's health. The first chapter in this section (Morokoff and Calderone) discusses research on women's sexuality within a framework of heterosexuality and the experience of infertility in women. Although sexuality and infertility are separate topics, they are considered together in one chapter because as Morokoff and Calderone note they are inextricably linked. Conception is sometimes a goal of the sexual act, and repeated failure to conceive can result in sexual difficulties. Moreover, as discussed in Morokoff and Calderone's chapter, sexual behavior can affect the hormonal milieu necessary for conception. Finally, as societal expectations for female sexuality have become less restrictive, frequency of sexual relations has increased and so has the incidence of sexually transmitted diseases. The increased incidence of sexually transmitted diseases is thought to account partially for the dramatic increase in infertility observed in the United States in the last 25 years. As discussed in the second chapter (Murphy and Kelly) in this section, concurrent infection with sexually transmitted diseases (e.g., syphilis) is also thought to increase the probability of human immunodeficiency virus (HIV) transmission. Given that heterosexual contact currently accounts for about 60% of worldwide HIV transmission, and that heterosexual contact is projected to become an even more significant mode of viral transmission in the future, the impact of the AIDS/HIV epidemic on women is also covered in this section.

Patricia Morokoff and Karen Calderone begin their thoughtful chapter by discussing female sexual behaviors and important factors affecting these behaviors within the context of heterosexual relationships. They argue that societal expectations markedly restrict a woman's sexuality. She must wait for him to initiate sex. She must give in to her husband's sexual overtures. She must act demurely to avoid being considered promiscuous. At the same time she must be sexually responsive to him. Their analysis of findings related to women's sexual behavior and sexual decisions significantly contributes to our understanding of the culturally derived constraints on women's sexual fulfillment. The sexuality portion of their chapter ends with an interesting discussion of the effects of stress and moods on sexual functioning.

The second half of Morokoff and Calderone's chapter deals with infertility. The authors systematically discuss definitions of infertility, incidence and prevalence figures, diagnosis and treatment, factors contributing to infertility, and psychological consequences of infertility treatment.

Increased understanding of reproductive endocrinology has led to significant changes in the treatment of women with fertility problems. Fewer cases of infertility are now thought to be due to stress than in the past. Consequently, it is likely that fewer women are being told today to "just relax and you'll get pregnant." The inclusion of a woman's male partner in the infertility workup in the last 20 years is another sign of progress. Women are no longer thought to be exclusively responsible for fertility problems. Despite this progress, mention of in vitro fertilization and cryopreservation of embryos often evokes uncomfortableness and even fear among people in the general public. Images of frozen babies and babies growing in test tubes abound. Alarmed reactions from well-meaning relatives and friends may add to the emotional toll that infertility and its diagnosis and treatment exact in those involved.

Finally, although diagnosis of infertility is often paid for by health insurance companies, treatment of infertility is typically not covered. As Morokoff and Calderone point out, costs for a single in vitro cycle are estimated at $4,000 to $5,000. In some cases the costs are even higher. Obviously, the financial cost involved precludes many women and men from taking advantage of the technology that could possibly allow them to have the child they so desire. Health insurance companies that do pay expenses incurred in fertilization procedures have not seen sharp rises in their costs. This is because only a minority of women and their partners elect to undergo these arduous procedures even when they are paid for. Nonetheless, thousands of children have been conceived in the last 14 years through in vitro fertilization and related procedures.

In the concluding chapter in this section, Debra Murphy and Jeffrey Kelly provide convincing evidence that AIDS should be considered a major health threat in women and men and that the problem of HIV infection in women can no longer be neglected. Their timely, detailed review not only discusses the projected scope of HIV infection among women, but also covers HIV transmission, progression, and psychological complications in women. Issues related to pediatric AIDS and the prevention and psychological treatment of HIV infection in women are also discussed.

It is clear from this chapter that HIV infection in women poses many challenges for psychologists. For example, current behavior change efforts focusing on condom use may be ineffective in women. As Murphy and Kelly note, few women are willing to initiate condom use. Perhaps women do not want to risk being considered promiscuous by appearing too ready or prepared for sexual intercourse in a new relationship. Researchers must not only create new primary prevention strategies appropriate to women, but also develop treatment interventions for the unique psychological sequelae that HIV-infected women may experience (e.g., severe guilt associated with knowing that one has transmitted a fatal disease to one's offspring).

Chapter 10

Sexuality and Infertility

Patricia J. Morokoff
Karen L. Calderone

The purpose of this chapter is to address issues in women's sexuality and infertility. Although in some ways these areas represent separate topics, fertility/infertility and sexuality are inextricably linked. Present-day contraceptives have allowed for a potential disassociation between sexuality and conception, but a significant meaning of the sexual act remains a reproductive one. Sexual behaviors may affect the hormonal environment required for conception, and infertility may have strong consequences for the couple's sexual functioning. In the section on sexuality, we begin by discussing sexual behaviors and factors affecting these behaviors within the context of the relationship. We then discuss the effects of stress and moods on sexual functioning, an area that bridges the gap between psychological and physiological factors affecting sexuality. The section on infertility begins with the definition of incidence and prevalence of infertility. We then summarize factors contributing to infertility, both physiologically based and behavioral, including nutrition, exercise, stress, smoking, and sexual dysfunctions. Medical treatment of infertility is a rapidly changing field, and the most common procedures are discussed, including psychological effects of participation in infertility treatment. Finally, directions for research in the fields of sex-

Karen Calderone passed away December 24, 1991. The first author expresses her appreciation in memoriam for Karen's contributions to their work together.

uality and the psychological/behavioral causes and consequences of infertility are presented.

WOMEN'S SEXUALITY

Women's sexuality exists within the contexts of cultural expectation, individual experience, and biological potential. Current cultural values present a mixed message to women: be sexually responsive but within the expected bounds. Over this century expectations have changed dramatically. At the beginning of the century women were assumed to be sexually unresponsive, were not given information about their sexual capabilities, including orgasm, and were considered dysfunctional if they were too sexual. At present, women are considered dysfunctional both if they are too "promiscuous" and if they are not sexual enough, e.g., they lack desire for an appropriate partner or do not become aroused or reach orgasm in lovemaking with that partner. Margaret Mead observed that women have a biological potential for orgasm, a response that may be societally encouraged or discouraged by cultural expectation and information offered (Mead, 1949). In our current culture, women are made aware that they are capable of sexual satisfaction, including orgasm, through sex education and the media, if not parental instruction, and that it is desirable for women to have a sexual relationship characterized by frequent sex and orgasm with their committed partner. Sex with an uncommitted partner is viewed equivocally. It is currently less clear whether it is culturally desirable for a woman to initiate sex in the absence of some sign of encouragement from her committed partner. It is agreed that equal initiation is desirable, and that a woman should try to be receptive if her partner initiates, but should he try to be receptive if she initiates when he was not otherwise in the mood? To the extent that sex is a coerced experience for women, full sexual functioning is quite unlikely to occur. Coercion exists along a continuum which at its mildest consists of guilt induced by a partner's hurt feelings if he is refused and at its most extreme consists of rape. Male sexual coercion of females is endemic in our society, and its effects may be subtle.

Sexual Behaviors/Sexual Decisions

Kinsey et al. (1953) note that the incidence of marital intercourse approaches 100% but that there are a small percentage of marriages that are not consummated. Excluding convenience marriages, there are probably relatively few unions in which no sexual relationship exists. It is certainly possible for the couple to have a sexual relationship that does not usually include intercourse, due to either preference or sexual dysfunction. Contrary to what one might expect, however, intercourse has been found to be a more important part of the sexual relationship for women than for men. Heterosexual men who have intercourse every time they have sex are not happier with their sex lives than those who report less frequent intercourse. Women who have intercourse every time they have sex are more sexually satisfied and happier with their relationships (Blumstein & Schwartz, 1983).

Both age and length of relationship have been found to be significant predictors of frequency of intercourse (Doddridge, Schumm, & Bergen, 1987). Kinsey et al. (1953) report that younger couples in their twenties had intercourse two to four times per week, but that the rate dropped to about once a week by age 40. A considerable variation of rate of coitus was found, but even those couples with the highest frequencies showed age-related declines. Blumstein and Schwartz (1983) used regression analysis to separate effects of age and years together. They report that the modal frequency of sex for couples who had been together for up to two years was three times per week or more (this was the case for 45% in this group). For married couples together 10 years or more, the modal frequency of sex was one to three times per week (this was also the case for 45% in this group). Blumstein and Schwartz found that for married couples the impact of age and length of relationship were approximately equal. For married couples the husband's age may be a more important predictor of intercourse frequency than the wife's age. This conclusion is similar to one drawn by Kinsey et al. (1953), who felt that age-related declines in intercourse were a product of the aging process in men. Kinsey et al. based this conclusion on the fact that masturbation and total sexual outlet rates for women stay relatively constant until after 60 years of age.

These findings raise the general question of how couples make decisions about type and frequency of sexual activities. The fact that coital rates appear to follow the male pattern may be related to the husband's greater power in the relationship as will be discussed further. According to Kinsey et al. (1953), "There is little evidence of any aging in the sexual capacities of the female until late in her life" (p. 353). For couples who are cohabitating rather than married, duration of relationship was a significant predictor of frequency of intercourse, but age was not (Blumstein & Schwartz, 1983).

It is also evident that on average men have greater sexual interest than women. Recent data show that level of rated sexual desire is significantly higher in men than in women (Popeil, Gallant, & Morokoff, 1988; Morokoff & Gilliland, 1993) and that preferred frequency of intercourse is greater for men than for women (Doddridge, Schumm, & Bergen, 1987). An alternative way to look at this question is to examine rates of sexual behavior in the relationships of lesbians and gay men. Gay men in the beginning of their relationships have the highest levels of sex compared to heterosexual and lesbian couples. As the relationship progresses, frequency of sex with the partner declines but interest in sex stays high, reflected in increased sex outside the relationship. Lesbians have the lowest frequency of sex among the three types of couples. Among lesbians who have been together over 10 years, almost half have sex once a month or less (Blumstein & Schwartz, 1983). Blumstein and Schwartz also suggest that the male role, unfettered by the necessity to control sex, permits greater awareness of sexual interests. It seems that if women can control sexual frequency, genital sex will usually be less frequent, whether due to biology, cultural pressure, or both.

It should be noted that these analyses are based on samples of predominantly white men and women. Because there are fewer effective social constraints on black young women, if less frequent desire for intercourse is culturally derived, it might be expected that black women would desire intercourse more frequently than white women. An interesting test would be a comparison of sexual frequency in black and white lesbian women. This comparison would not separate biological or cultural influences, but would separate male-initiated from female-initiated frequencies of sexual behavior. Weinberg and Williams (1988) report that black women have more liberal sexual attitudes and more extramarital sex than white women, but engage in masturbation, oral sex, and foreplay less than white women. These findings are based on archival data collected between 1938 and 1970 and may not reflect current trends, however.

Effects of Power on the Sexual Relationship   The more powerful partner is more likely to refuse sex, according to Blumstein and Schwartz (1983). Among cohabitating couples, if the woman refuses sex more than her partner, she tends to be the more powerful partner. When the man is more powerful, he tends to refuse sex more. This pattern reflects who can control when to have sex. Although greater power may give women the right of refusal, this does not necessarily lead to greater satisfaction. For women, the use of coercion to obtain their way in relationships has been associated with lesser sexual satisfaction and less perceived sexual satisfaction for their partners. Similarly, autonomy in decision making has also been found to be associated with less sexual satisfaction for both the respondent and her partner. The same inverse relationship between decision-making autonomy and sexual satisfaction was found for men, except that the relationship between use of coercion and sexual satisfaction was not statistically significant (Hansen & Morokoff, 1988). These findings appear consistent with the general finding that where wives dominate decision making there is less marital happiness, that highest levels of satisfaction are found in egalitarian relationships, and that coercion control techniques in particular are associated with less marital satisfaction (Gray-Little & Burks, 1983). Explanations offered for these findings are that it is the role incongruency that leads to dissatisfaction, or that husbands in wife-dominated relationships are incapacitated in some way, that is, not taking on the usual responsibilities.

Sexual Satisfaction, Intercourse Frequency, and Relationship Satisfaction   Greater frequency of intercourse has been found to be related to greater sexual satisfaction. Low frequency of sex is also associated with less global relationship satisfaction. Blumstein & Schwartz (1983) found that 88–89% of people who have sex three times per week or more are satisfied with their sex lives, whereas only 30–32% of people who have sex once a month or less are satisfied. It could be that where women in heterosexual couples control decision making about sex, sex is less frequent (due to either biological influences or cultural prescription) and therefore less satisfying. It may be easier for men than for women to supply the motivation to have sex.

Other researchers have found that happy couples engage in sexual inter-course more frequently than unhappy couples (Barnett & Nietzel, 1979; Birchler & Webb, 1977), that marital and sexual satisfaction are related (Barnett & Nietzel, 1977; Morokoff & Gillilland, 1993; Perlman & Abramson, 1982), and that marital happiness is related to greater orgasm frequency (Chesser, 1956; Gebhard, 1966; Morokoff, 1978; Terman, 1938, 1951). A significant relation-ship has been found between frequency of intercourse and marital satisfaction measured by the Locke-Wallace marital adjustment test for both men and women (Morokoff & Gillilland, 1993). In addition, Morokoff and Gillilland (1993) report a significant negative relationship between sexual desire and marital hap-piness for men. This could be because the wives of men with high levels of sexual desire are less happy.

Initiation and Refusal of Sex   Sex role stereotypes prescribe that men initiate sexual activity while women exercise controls. Premaritally, women's controls on sex are sanctioned by societal and religious approval. When women continue to exercise restrictive control over sexual behavior after marriage, they receive less societal support. It is traditionally considered a woman's duty to be sexually available to her husband. Conversely, husbands have had the right and duty to have sex with their wives. As pointed out by Blumstein and Schwartz (1983), this right was even specified in religious and civil law. These situations would seem to result from the dual phenomenon of greater male status/resources and their sex role assignment of greater sexual desires. However, it has special consequences for the process of initiating and refusing sex. Although it seems to be the case that fewer men and women feel rigidly confined by sex roles now than in the past, the role may not be easy to shake off. Fifty-one percent of husbands and 48% of wives indicated that the husband is more likely to initiate sex. Only 12% of women and 16% of men indicated that wives were more likely to be the initiator. Among cohabitors a larger percent (42–46%) reported equal initiation, but followed the same path as married couples (Blumstein & Schwartz, 1983).

Interview data presented by Blumstein and Schwartz indicate that for women, initiation of sex may be a delicate and sensitive matter. Although clinical experience suggests that many men desire their partners to be more sexually aggressive, what they may really want is that their partner be more responsive when they initiate. A women's initiative may overstep what is seen as a male prerogative. Wives expressed concerns about not threatening their husband's need to feel in control and bolstering his view of himself as a man. One woman who had been happily married 5 years said:

> Well, after the initial period of passion started settling down, Larry wasn't quite so sure that women should take the initiative. So we would go back and forth. It is actually kind of funny. I would get the typical excuses . . . "I had too much to drink," "I have a headache"—a couple of those. And I said, "Hmmm, this sounds familiar." . . . I can remember a specific instance. It was when I was traveling. Right before I left I was making advances to Larry. He told me he felt like he was being used before I was going out of town. It is all so classical a situation in reverse! (p. 211)

For women who were cohabitating, older women were just as likely as younger women to be initiators. However, 42% of male partners over age 40 indicated they would be bothered by their partner's initiating sex. When women do initiate, they may find they are turned down. This can be more distressing to the couple than if the woman turns down sex because it goes against sex roles and can be interpreted by the man as his failure or by the woman as a personal rejection of her. Blumstein and Schwartz also report that equality of initiation is related to greater sexual satisfaction. Thus many women may feel in a bind. They wish to be self-actualized in their sexual relationships and not constrained by the traditional roles, yet meet conflict when they attempt initiation.

Contraceptive Choices   An important aspect of the decision to engage in sexual behavior is an awareness of the consequences of sexuality, with respect to both pregnancy and sexually transmitted disease. Data on contraceptive use by women in the United States are available from Cycle IV of the National Survey of Family Growth. Results indicate that 60% of women between the ages of 15 and 44 use contraception. Only 7% of women could be classified as at risk for unintended pregnancy. The leading method of contraception in 1988 was the pill, taken by 19% of women, followed by female sterilization (17%) condom use (9%), male sterilization (7%), and the diaphragm (4%). Periodic abstinence and the IUD were each used by 1% of women, and foam and douche were each used by less than 1%. Among never-married women who were sexually active, only 71% were using contraception. For these women, like the total sample, the pill was the leading method of contraception. In contrast, for married couples, female surgical sterilization was the leading method of contraception. The percentage of never-married couples using condoms remained constant across these years at 14% (Mosher & Pratt, 1990).

A large literature has emerged attempting to explain factors related to use of contraceptives in single women, especially among adolescents (Chilman, 1986; Morrison, 1985). On the whole these attempts at explanation have not been extremely successful, probably because researchers often fail to include variables of importance.

Stress and Moods

How do life stressors, dysphoric moods, and even positive moods affect sexuality? These are questions that surprisingly are only beginning to receive research attention. Despite lack of research documentation, clinicians have noted that major life stressors are common in patients presenting sexual dysfunction (Brecher, 1977; Kaplan, 1974).

Stress and Hormones   There are a variety of ways in which stress might negatively impact sexual functioning, one of which is a direct physiological effect. As discussed in Chapter 2 of this volume, chronic stress leads to elevation of cortisol and catecholamine (stress hormone) output as well as sympathetic nervous system response. Evidence suggests that sexual arousal tends not to occur during periods of stress hormone elevation. For example, Kling, Barowitz, and Cartwright (1972) found that men who reported no arousal in the laboratory during exposure to erotic stimuli had the highest urinary corticosteroid levels. Ismail, Davidson, and Lorraine (1972) found that sexual intercourse tends to occur between episodic bursts of cortisol. It is noteworthy that these studies have not been conducted with women. The relationship between elevation of stress hormones and sexual response, either arousal or initiation of sexual activity, needs to be determined in women before generalization of the findings can be made.

It is interesting to note that catecholamine output has been reported to be higher in the luteal phase than other phases of the menstrual cycle (Feichtinger et al., 1979; Goldstein, Levinson, & Keiser, 1983; Wasilewska, Kobus, & Bargiel, 1980). The luteal phase is a time period during which peaks of sexual activity have rarely been observed (Bancroft, 1987). It is also of interest that acute stress has been shown to lead to increased catecholamine output in the luteal as compared to ovulatory or follicular cycle phase (Collins, Eneroth, & Landgren, 1985) and increased cortisol in the premenstrual (luteal) versus mid-cycle phase (Marinari, Leshner, & Doyle, 1976). Anxiety, which is associated with heightened sympathetic response, and sexual arousal are considered to be reciprocally inhibiting (Wolpe, 1973).

Stress and Sexual Behavior   In addition to effects of stress on hormones, stress may also produce psychological effects that may impact on sexual functioning, such as sleep disturbance, difficulty concentrating, hyperalertness, and mood disturbance (Baum, Singer, & Baum, 1981). The investigation of effects of stress on sexual functioning is a new area that has received little research attention to date. More evidence is available for men than women to support the assumption that stress disrupts sexual functioning. Sexually dysfunctional men showed less penile tumescence while viewing an erotic videotape when given instructions designed to create performance demands than when given low-demand instructions (Heiman & Rowland, 1983). The interactive effects of chronic and acute stress were studied by Morokoff, Baum, McKinnon, and Gillilland (1987). Unemployed men who anticipated giving a speech had less tumescence in response to an erotic videotape than employed men under the same conditions. Morokoff and Gillilland (1993) found a significant relationship between unemployed status and self-reported erectile dysfunction.

No laboratory investigations on effects of stress on sexual arousal have been conducted in women. However, two self-report studies have examined the relationship between stress and sexual behavior. Morokoff and Gillilland (in press) administered questionnaire measures of stress to 73 women, 45 of whom were unemployed. A significant interaction between stress and age in predicting desired frequency of intercourse was found. Although desire for intercourse declined with age for the whole sample, it declined more sharply for unemployed than employed women. Unemployment, however, was not related to measures of overall sexual satisfaction, arousal, or orgasm. Why is unemployment associated with erectile dysfunction in men but no arousal impairment in women? Unemployment may have a different symbolic meaning for men than women. If being employed, and thus able to support one's family, is a component of the masculine sex role, then unemployment may be seen as a failure to fulfill an important sex role expectation. Unemployment certainly creates financial stress for women, but it does not have the same symbolic association with failure to fulfill the feminine sex role ideal. A stressor with symbolic meaning of this type for women might be infertility. Although it is anecdotally reported that infertility causes sexual problems for couples, a careful study of effects on sexual functioning has not been undertaken.

One of the questionnaire measures of stress administered in Morokoff and Gillilland's study was the Hassles scale (Kanner, Coyne, Schaefer, & Lazarus, 1981), designed to tap occurrences of minor stressors that may have a cumulative effect on health or other outcomes. Score on the Hassles scale was positively correlated with both desired frequency of sexual intercourse and level of desire. This finding is counterintuitive but was also observed in males in the same study. Why would people who are more hassled desire sex more? A possible explanation for this finding is that sexual release may be one way of coping with hassles or low levels of stress. It should be noted that actual frequency of intercourse was not significantly related to Hassles score, and thus that this coping strategy may not have been entirely successful. It would be of great interest also to determine hormonal characteristics of these samples.

A significant positive correlation between hassles and frequency of sex was found in another study (Popiel, Gallant, & Morokoff, 1988). In this study women indicated in daily records the examples of stress they had experienced that day.

The stressors were content analyzed into nine categories, including financial stress, hassles/irritants, time pressure, interpersonal, work/achievement, medical, physical sensations, and intrapersonal stress. Hassles and financial stress were positively correlated with desire for sex. The only negative effect of stress for women in this study was an inverse relationship between time pressure and frequency of orgasm in sexual intercourse. It should be noted that results of this study cannot be directly compared to those of Morokoff and Gillilland (1993) because sexual arousal was not measured in this study.

Moods and Sexual Behavior   Bancroft (1987) reports that approximately one-third of the variance in women's sexual feelings is attributable to variations in general well-being. That is, women are more likely to feel sexual when they were feeling good. This relationship appears to be especially pronounced in the late follicular or periovulatory menstrual cycle phases. These observations are based on, but extend findings reported by Sanders, Warner, Backstrom, and Bancroft (1983). They report a peak in well-being in the late follicular phase. Bancroft concludes that this cyclicity of well-being tends to produce a follicular phase increase in sexual feelings.

Data from a study conducted in a "women's" magazine further support the idea: 41% of women indicated peaks in sexual interest and well-being in the postmenstrual week (Warner & Bancroft, 1988). These data are supported by Gallant, Hamilton, Popiel, Morokoff, and Chakraborty (1991), who found a midcycle peak in well-being for both women who were aware and women who were unaware that the purpose of the study was to relate moods to menstrual cycle phase.

The relationship of moods to sexual functioning was directly tested by Popeil, Gallant, and Morokoff (1988). Factor analysis of women's daily mood diaries revealed factors for dysphoric moods, well-being, physical symptoms, depression, and personal space. A significant correlation was found between well-being and sexual desire, supporting Sanders and Bancroft's results. Furthermore, a negative relationship between depressed mood and frequency of sex was found for women.

It is clear that the interrelationship of the hormonal milieu and sexual behavior is extremely complex. The extent to which women are aware of hormonal changes and believe that these changes affect their sexuality is unclear. However, Warner and Bancroft's (1988) report from over 4,000 women indicates that only about 7% felt that their sexual interest did not change across the menstrual cycle, the modal response being the premenstrual week. It seems extremely likely that hormonal factors can be overridden by psychological factors of sufficient magnitude: the follicular increase in well-being will not be enough to outweigh effects of a significant loss or separation. Research needs to address the relative contributions to sexual desire, arousal, and behavior of hormonal changes, mood, stress, and the factors known to influence sexuality, such as relationship satisfaction, age, and direction of relationship.

INFERTILITY

Definition, Incidence, and Prevalence

Infertility is generally defined as the inability of a couple to conceive after 12 months of intercourse without use of contraception. Infertility affects an estimated 2.4 million married couples in the United States (Congressional Report, 1988). This represents 8.5% of married couples with wives of childbearing age and does not include the 12 million couples (42%) who are surgically sterile. The percentage of infertile couples declined from 11.2% in 1965. This decrease in infertility is principally accounted for by a decrease in couples who already have at least one child (secondary infertility) from 2.5 million couples in 1965 to 1.4 million in 1982. However, most importantly, primary infertility (infertility in those who have never had children) doubled from 500,000 in 1965 to 1 million in 1982 (Congressional Report, 1988).

Potential causes for the increase in primary infertility are multiple. The larger number of couples of childbearing age resulting from the baby boom accounts in part for the increase, but not the fact that the percentage of couples with primary infertility increased by 5% between 1965 and 1982. One potential factor in primary infertility is the increase in the number of women who have chosen to delay childbearing, since infertility increases with age (Menken, 1985; Menken, Trussell, & Larsen, 1986). Fourteen percent of married couples with wives aged 30–34 are infertile, whereas 25% of couples with wives aged 35–39 are infertile (Mosher, 1987). The constellation of factors involved in women's changing role is related to choices to delay childbearing. These include women's greater opportunity to attain educational and career goals that may delay both marriage and childbearing as well as the availability of effective contraceptives such as the pill or IUD. Furthermore, couples may be quicker to define themselves as infertile due to the need to condense childbearing into a shorter interval of time. Other possible causes of the increase in primary infertility include lifestyle changes among women that may make conception more difficult, such as increased smoking, strenuous exercise, or exposure to stress. The role of these factors in increasing the incidence of infertility in the population has not been documented. Increased exposures to environmental hazards such as irradiation, lead, chronic loud noise, or physical strain associated with use of video display terminals have also been suggested as causes of infertility but have not been well documented.

The decrease in secondary infertility can be explained by the increase in voluntary surgical sterilization for contraceptive purposes. The percentage of married couples using sterilization as a method of contraception more than doubled in the 15 years between 1973 and 1988 from 16% in 1973 to 36% in 1988. An additional 6% of women are surgically sterile for noncontraceptive reasons, producing a total of 42% of women of childbearing age who are surgically sterile. Female surgical sterilization is the leading contraceptive method among married couples (Mosher & Pratt, 1985). Thus the decrease in secondary infertility is believed to be directly related to the fact that a large number of couples who might otherwise have had difficulty conceiving have prevented that outcome by electing surgical sterilization.

Certain couples are more likely to be infertile than others. The incidence of infertility among black couples is reported as being 1.5 times higher than that among white couples (Congressional Report, 1988). Couples with wives having less than a high school education are also more likely to be infertile (Aral & Cates, 1983; Mosher, 1982). Though there are no presently existing data to explain these higher rates, it has been suggested that demographic characteristics such as education, urban dwelling, socioeconomic status, and accessibility to comprehensive health care, rather than actual racial or ethnic differences, are reflected in the higher incidence of infertility observed in these couples.

The National Survey of Family Growth, conducted in 1965 and 1982, reveals that one age group, married couples with wives age 20 to 24, exhibited an increase in infertility from 3.6% infertile in 1965 to 10.6% infertile in 1982. This particular group is important since one in three births in the United States occurs to women aged 20 to 24 (Mosher & Pratt, 1985). This increase is believed to be linked to the tripled gonorrhea rate of this group between 1960 to 1977 (Mosher, 1987). It is important to note that sexually transmitted diseases account for an estimated 20% of infertility overall (Congressional Report, 1988).

Although there has been little increase in the overall incidence of infertility in the population, the number of office visits to physicians for infertility services rose from approximately 600,000 in 1968 to approximately 1.6 million in 1984 (Congressional Report, 1988). Several factors have contributed to this increased demand for infertility services. They include: (1) The increase in incidence of primary infertility has led to greater demand because the percentage of couples who seek treatment for primary infertility (51%) far exceeds that of couples who seek treatment for secondary infertility (22%) (Congressional Report, 1988); (2) the evolution of new reproductive technologies and the ensuing extensive media coverage of these new technologies have increased public awareness of various treatments available for infertility; (3) an increased proportion of infertile couples seek care because the supply of infants available for adoption has decreased, couples have heightened expectations for their ability to have children, and there are more people in higher income brackets with infertility problems; and (4) there is an increasing number of physicians providing infertility services (Aral & Cates, 1983).

Though the demand for infertility services has more than doubled in the last two decades, not all infertile couples seek treatment. National survey data in

1982 revealed that only 31.4% of infertile married couples had ever sought services for infertility. White couples seek medical evaluation for infertility problems more frequently than black couples even though black couples are more likely to be infertile (Horn & Mosher, 1984). Married women who have higher incomes and higher educational levels report greater use of infertility services than married women with low incomes and/or low levels of education (Horn & Mosher, 1984; Mosher & Pratt, 1985).

An important issue to address in interpreting these data is the affordability of infertility services. There is considerable evidence that infertility services are less available to low- and middle-income couples due to financial barriers to treatment. An analysis of the costs and effectiveness of infertility services reveals that the "average" infertility work-up, usually completed in 4–6 months, costs $2,500–$4,000 (Thorne & Langner, 1987). However, the range of treatment cost is much wider. Not only does the cost of therapy vary widely, but the initial infertility work-up yields a pregnancy rate of only approximately 30% (Congressional Report, 1988). Therapy may require several surgeries of several thousands of dollars each. In vitro fertilization (IVF) costs an average of $4,000–$6,000 per cycle and may require one, two, three, or more cycles to succeed (Stillman, 1987; Thorne & Langner, 1987).

Since many low- to middle-income couples are uninsured or underinsured, the burden of infertility costs may prevent them from seeking treatment even though they desire a child. For couples who have health insurance, the out-of-pocket costs of infertility services can range from 6 to 62% of annual income for married couples with annual incomes under $20,000 and from 2 to 23% of annual income for married couples with annual incomes of $20,000 to $35,000 (Thorne & Langner, 1987). A recent study examining the need, accessibility, and utilization of infertility services in the United States (Guttmacher Institute, 1985) concluded that, in general, people with adequate financial resources, either their own or insurance with infertility coverage, do not have difficulty obtaining infertility services. However, these services are less available to low-income couples, and low-income women face serious financial obstacles to obtaining specialized or complex infertility services.

Factors Contributing to Infertility

An infertility diagnosis can be established in approximately 85–90% of the couples undergoing infertility investigation. Approximately 10–15% of infertile couples are classified as having "infertility of unknown origin" since their infertility investigation reveals no abnormalities and thus no cause or diagnosis can explain their failure to conceive (Stillman, 1987). Of the couples in whom a diagnosis is established, male factors account for approximately 35–40% of infertility and female factors account for approximately 40% of infertility (Stillman, 1987). Thus men and women are equally likely to be infertile. The remaining 25% of couples in whom a diagnosis is established have a combination of factors causing their infertility.

The factors that contribute to infertility are multiple, and thus classification of infertility due to any one condition is misleading. Therefore, the factors that most often contribute to infertility among women are divided among factors that may influence the ability to ovulate; factors affecting tubal function; cervical, uterine, or immunological factors; and a common disorder called endometriosis, characterized by the presence of endometrial tissue (lining of the uterus) outside the uterus. Among men, most cases of infertility are a consequence of factors that contribute to abnormal or too few sperm.

To understand the anatomic and physiologic aspects of infertility, it is important to understand the normal reproductive process. Fertilization and maintenance of pregnancy depend on a series of complex and interrelated events. The male must produce an adequate number of sperm and deposit them in the upper vagina during the time of ovulation. The female must be able to ovulate. Female hormone levels must be adequate to produce cervical mucus around the time of ovulation that allows sperm to pass into the uterus. Adequate hormone levels are also necessary for implantation of the embryo and maintenance of pregnancy. The oviducts must be open, allowing fertilization of the ovum by sperm and transport of the ovum from the ovary to the uterus. Tubal ciliary action must be functioning to assist sperm travel up the fallopian tubes. The uterus must be able to support implantation of the embryo and fetal growth (Talbert, 1981).

A defect at any point in this series of interrelated events can result in infertility or the inability to carry a pregnancy to term. A number of physiological and behavioral factors are known to contribute to infertility. Infections account for an estimated 20% of infertility in the United States (Congressional Report, 1988). Gonorrhea, chlamydial infection, and mycoplasmal infection are most responsible for infertility. Endometriosis impairs fertility through a variety of possible mechanisms. It appears that displaced endometrial tissue may interfere with ovulation, ovum transport, or implantation of the fertilized ovum. Endometriosis may also induce early spontaneous abortion (Hahn, Carraher, Foldsey, & McGuire, 1986; Holtz, Williamson, Mathur, Landgrebe, & Moore, 1985). Hormonal disturbances of various types can also lead to infertility. Such disorders include polycystic ovarian disease (POD), in which the ovaries are clogged with cysts; poor cervical mucus; and hyperprolactinemia, leading to estrogen deficiency and anovulation in women or testosterone deficiency and decreased spermatogenesis in men (Kelley, 1989). Stress may be associated with hyperprolactinemia for which other causes cannot be identified (Bensen, 1978; Kelley, 1989). Stress is also associated with hypothalamic amenorrhea, the absence of menstruation for at least three cycles in a woman with previously established menses and for which no physical pathology can be found (Bensen, 1978; Kelley, 1989).

Cancer of the cervix, uterus, or ovaries causing damage to these organs necessary for reproduction can obviously impair fertility. In addition, however, the treatment of cancer by surgery, chemotherapy, and/or radiation can lead to infertility if not sterility. Finally, the very presence of cancer in the body is known to affect semen quality (Newton, 1987) and is likely to affect the female reproductive process (Congressional Report, 1988). Genetic and chromosomal abnormalities can affect fertility in several ways. Abnormalities in human embryos can lead to early fetal loss or affect the health of the embryo. In addition, chromosomal abnormalities can impair the fertility of an adult.

Nutrition and Eating Disorders   In women, sexual maturation and continuation of cyclic ovulation depend on achieving and maintaining an adequate amount of body fat as a proportion of total body mass (Frisch, 1984; Van Der Spuy, 1985). It has also been suggested that possession of adequate fat stores may serve as a physiologic precondition for conception and pregnancy since completion of pregnancy and lactation requires approximately 50,000 calories, roughly the amount of energy most women possess in body fat (Frisch, 1984). When malnutrition exists and the individual's fatty tissues are depleted, the probability that conception will occur is greatly decreased since estrogen deficiency, associated with hypothalamic suppression, results in anovulation as well as amenorrhea.

Exercise   Regular, strenuous exercise is frequently associated with altered menstrual function, temporarily impairing fertility in women. Research indicates that if women with normal menstrual function begin a program of strenuous exercise, that many will develop some form of menstrual abnormality. A prospective study in which untrained women engaged in strenuous exercise, found that 87% of women who engaged in the exercise regimen developed some menstrual abnormality (Bullen et al., 1985).

Anecdotes are frequently cited indicating that infertile couples will conceive after a reduction in stress, for example when they discontinue infertility treatment or "stop trying." It has similarly been reported that women may become pregnant after scheduling an initial infertility evaluation. Baker, Mathur, Kirk, and Williamson (1981) found that 39% of their sample of women with normal menses prior to running were amenorrheic. The American College of Sports Medicine reports that one-third of competitive female long distance runners aged 12–45 experience menstrual dysfunction (Baker, 1981). Acute exercise has been found to produce an increase in testosterone in women immediately after running (Shangold, Gatz, & Thysen, 1981; Sutton, Coleman, Casey, & Lazarus, 1973). Shangold et al. (1981) observed a greater testosterone increase during the follicular than the luteal cycle phase. Johansson, Laakso, Peder, and Karonen (1988) speculate that increased plasma testosterone during exercise may be caused by decreased hepatic blood flow, resulting in decreased degradation, rather than increased secretion of the hormone, although it is not clear why this would vary across cycle phase. Lack of significant change in testosterone after running has also been reported (Loucks & Horvath, 1984), although hormone means were in the right direction. Inconsistent results for basal testosterone in runners versus controls have been reported. Findings include higher testosterone in runners compared to controls (Dale, Gerlach, & Wilhite, 1979), lower basal testosterone in runners versus controls (Ronkainen, Pakarinen, Kirkinen, & Kauppila, 1985), and no difference (Chang, Richards, Kim, & Malarkey, 1984). One reason for variable results may be failure to control for cycle phase in eumenorrheic runners in light of the cyclicity of testosterone levels. As previously indicated, intensive exercise appears to increase the likelihood of menstrual dysfunction. Predictors for women exercisers who become amenorrheic include prior menstrual dysfunction, older age at menarche, younger current age, nulliparity, mileage run per week, and alteration in percent body fat (Baker, 1981; Baker et al., 1981). Intensive exercise can also cause anovulation. Based on measurement of serum progesterone, Dale et al. (1979) found that while 83% of control subjects showed evidence of ovulation, only 50% of runners (over 30 miles per week) and 67% of joggers (5–30 miles per week) ovulated. Both progesterone and estradiol were low in the amenorrheic women. Another factor impairing fertility in women runners may be prolactin elevations that occur during exercise. Daily exposure to very high prolactin levels even briefly may adversely affect ovarian function (Baker, 1981).

Stress   Evidence suggests that mild to severe emotional stress may lead to impaired fertility in both men and women. For example, 50% of women in concentration camps were reported to be amenorrheic (Mazer & Israel, 1959). Osofsky and Fisher (1967) conducted a longitudinal study of freshman nursing students to look at the effects of the stress of leaving home on amenorrhea. Twelve of 63 students studied became amenorrheic. Furthermore, Tudiver (1983) found that women with dysfunctional uterine bleeding had experienced more life change events in the preceeding 12 months than controls. As previously discussed, stress can impact on sexual behavior in men and women, but appears to be more disruptive for men. Stress can also directly affect reproductive hormones. There is a substantial literature in men demonstrating that stress results in reduced testosterone level with possible interference with spermatogenesis. For example, testosterone may remain suppressed up to seven days following surgery (Ghanadian, Puah, Williams, Shah, & McWhinney, 1981). Psychological stress caused by Army basic training, anticipation of combat duty, parachute jumping, and flying fighter planes results in lower testosterone compared to controls or baseline (Rose, et al., 1969; Kreuz, Rose, & Jennings, 1972; Davidson, Smith, & Levine, 1978; Leedy & Wilson, 1985). Intensive exercise regimens produce lower basal testosterone in men (Wheeler, Wall, Belcastro, & Cumming, 1984). Acute prolonged exercise also leads to reduced testosterone in men (Dessypris, Kuoppasalmi, & Adlercreutz, 1976).

It is not clear whether stress suppresses testosterone in women. Testosterone values in a normal range are important in maintaining women's sexual desire (Sherwin, 1985). There is a shortage of studies examining the effect of stress on testosterone in women; however, those results that have been found are inclusive. Effects of surgical stress on testosterone have not been studied, presumably because testosterone is not considered to have reproductive or other significance. It would be of great interest to know whether the normal midcycle peak in women's testosterone is suppressed during chronic stress, especially as this elevation is correlated with sexual functioning (Morris & Udry, 1987; Persky et al. 1978).

Stress may affect other aspects of reproductive functioning in women. For example, Sandler (1968) provides examples of stress-related tubal blockage, and as previously noted, has been implicated in hypothalamic amenorrhea (Benson, 1978). It is probable that stress may have other more complex effects on human reproductive functioning. It is important to recognize, however, that while in the recent past 40–50% of all infertility was attributed to stress (Siebel & Taynor, 1982), this figure has dropped to 5% or less (Congressional Report, 1988).

Smoking   Evidence from several studies indicates that cigarette smoking has adverse effects on the reproductive system (Congressional Report, 1988). In women, smoking has been associated with menstrual abnormalities and tubal disease (Baird & Wilcox, 1985; Hartz et al., 1987; Stillman, Rosenberg, & Sachs, 1986; Thomford & Mattison, 1986). Smoking has also been associated with primary infertility resulting from cervical factors and impaired tubal function (Phipps, Cramer, & Schiff, 1987). In males, smoking or nicotine consumption has been associated with decreased sperm motility and count, altered sperm morphology, and altered hormone levels (Weisberg, 1985; Wentz, 1986). Experimental evidence suggests that these alterations are caused by changes in hypothalamic/pituitary axis function and possibly impaired motility of cilia in the genital tract (Mattison, 1982).

Sexual Dysfunction   Conception requires that sperm be transmitted to the female reproductive tract. If a couple is unable to have intercourse, sperm transmission may not occur. Thus sexual dysfunction is another etiological factor in infertility. One study of etiological factors in male infertility revealed that sexual problems between the couple were the primary cause of infertility for 64 (5%) of 1294 consecutive cases of male infertility (Dubin & Amelar, 1971). Erectile dysfunction is probably the single most prevalent type of sexual dysfunction producing infertility, and was found to be responsible for 27 (42%) of the cases described above (Dubin & Amelar, 1972). Difficulty attaining an erection may result from a variety of psychogenic as well as organic causes. In some men, conflict surrounding conception may result in lack of erection during the period in which they perceive their wife to be fertile. It is also common for the pressures of "trying to conceive" to result in decreased arousal.

Organic causes of erectile dysfunction may include any condition that impairs the neuromuscular, vascular, or hormonal components of the male sexual response. Neurological conditions that may negatively impact on erection or ejaculation include amyotrophic lateral sclerosis, transection of the cord, multiple sclerosis, or peripheral neuropathies. The most common endocrine condition known to impair erectile functioning is diabetes mellitus, but many other endocrine disorders may also result in erectile dysfunction. Vascular disease is a common cause of impotence. Obstruction of the penile arteries, leading to vascular insufficiency, becomes increasingly more common as a man approaches middle age. In addition, many drugs can produce erectile or ejaculatory dysfunction, including barbiturates, cocaine, alcohol, amphetamines, heroin, and some categories of tranquilizers, antidepressants, and antihypertensive medications (Reckless & Geiger, 1978).

Other sexual dysfunctions may also result in failure to transmit sperm to the female reproductive tract. Premature ejaculation, defined as climaxing involuntarily before a man chooses to (Kaplan, 1989), may affect fertility if the ejaculation occurs prior to or during penile penetration for intercourse. Premature ejaculation was the cause of infertility for 10% of the 69 men who were infertile due to sexual dysfunction in Dubin and Amelar's (1972) sample discussed above. Retrograde ejaculation, in which semen is propelled into the bladder rather than out through the penis, or lack of ejaculation for some other reason is also a cause of infertility.

Sexual dysfunction in women can also affect reproduction. Although it is not necessary for conception that women reach orgasm or even become aroused during sex, lack of desire to have sex or aversion to sexual activity may result in sexual activity too infrequent to make conception likely. Inhibited sexual desire may be present for men or women. Interesting new data support the conclusion that conceptive chances are enhanced by regular sexual activity. Women who have regular weekly heterosexual sex (at least once in every 7-day nonmenstruating week) have more regular cycles than women who have sporadic sex (Cutler, Garcia, & Krieger, 1979). Women whose cycles approach 29 days have the highest likelihood of having fertile cycles. Shorter and longer cycles have a lesser incidence of fertility (Treloar, Boynton, Behn, & Brown, 1967; Vollman, 1977). Furthermore, a fertile menstrual cycle requires both ovulation and an adequately long luteal phase in order to ensure sufficient time and steroid output to prepare the endometrium for implantation (Cutler, Preti, Huggins, Erickson, & Garcia, 1985). Women who had weekly sex were shown to have the highest incidence of fertile type basal body rhythms (90%), compared to women engaging in sporadic sex (55%) and celibate women (44%) (Cutler et al., 1985). Fertile basal body rhythms were defined as a basal body temperature pattern indicating both the presence of ovulation and an adequate length luteal phase. Research indicates that regular weekly sex is associated with higher estrogen levels (Cutler, Garcia, Huggins, & Preti, 1986) and adequate length luteal phases (Cutler et al., 1979). In the latter study, 7 of 8 women attending an infertility clinic who exhibited a luteal phase deficit had sex on a sporadic basis. It has been estimated that 20% of women presenting infertility complaints have an inadequate luteal phase. Other research indicates a relationship between exposure to men and increased incidence of ovulatory cycles (Veith, Buck, Getzlaf, Van Dalfsen, & Slade, 1983). These data suggest that not only frequency but regularity of sexual activity is more important than previously thought for fertility. If desire for sex is impaired in either partner, it is likely that their sexual behavior will not approximate weekly regularity. Many couples in this category may engage in sex only during the ovulatory phase of the menstrual cycle. If these data are correct, this pattern of sexual activity alone might predispose them to impaired fertility.

It is important to note that sexual dysfunction may well be a result of infertility as well as a cause of it. Years of reproductive frustration makes spontaneous sex difficult to maintain. Sexuality is a central source of communication and growth in the development of a couple's relationship. When sexual activity takes on a mechanical or demand type of value, as is often the case when the desired end result is reproduction, couples experiencing impaired fertility may find themselves facing a sexual identity crisis. Women may find themselves initiating sexual activity around the time of ovulation even though they are experiencing decreased or low sexual desire. Men may experience "reactive impotence," or the inability to perform sexually around the time of ovulation, since they are threatened and even resentful of "sex on demand" (Burns, 1987; Levie, 1962).

Thus sexual issues are frequently experienced by both partners, regardless of which partner has been diagnosed as the one responsible for the couple's infertility (Bell, 1981). Unfortunately, the sexual disturbances experienced by the individual or couple are often overlooked or avoided by both the couple and caregivers. Medical personnel may avoid sexual issues due to their own feelings of inadequacy in dealing with the subject. The couple's sexual relationship may thus come to be impaired by a belief that sexual problems are an inevitable concomitant of infertility or that sacrifice of sexual satisfaction will ensure the desired child (Burns, 1987).

To avoid or correct these sexual value dilemmas often faced by infertile couples, it is essential for caregivers to respect the couple's sexual health and to be alert to potential problems. When necessary, caregivers should provide early education, intervention, and treatment or appropriate referral and resources for the couple (Burns, 1987).

It is important for infertility caregivers to be comfortable with sexual issues the couple experiences. Couples would be most helped if caregivers were able to evaluate the sexual relationship to determine presence of sexual dysfunction as well as sexual issues caused by infertility or infertility treatments that may cause concern. The infertility caregiver could then provide information, treatment, or referrals to directly address sexual problems.

MEDICAL TREATMENTS FOR FEMALE INFERTILITY

Fertility Drugs

The most commonly used therapeutic agents for treating ovulatory dysfunction are compounds known as fertility drugs. These include clomiphene citrate (Clomid), human gonadotropins (human menopausal gonadotropin, follicle-stimulating hormone, and human chorionic gonadotropin), bromocriptine, glucocorticoids, and progesterone.

Clomid   Clomid is the most commonly prescribed fertility drug (Congressional Report, 1988). Clomid is a nonsteroidal synthetic, weak estrogen antagonist that stimulates follicular maturation in the ovary. In the anovulatory woman, Clomid binds to estrogenic receptors, causing a false signal to be sent to the hypothalamus and pituitary gland. They respond by increasing secretion of luteinizing hormone (LH) and follicle-stimulating hormone (FSH), which in turn, cause increased secretion of endogenous estrogen and progesterone (Dwyer, 1986). In this environment, the ovarian follicle matures and ovulation occurs.

Clomid is usually given on the fifth day after the onset of menses and continued through day 9 to induce ovulation, which is expected to occur between days 14 to 18 of the cycle. Treatment may be necessary for as long as 6 months. Therapy is not recommended beyond one year. An 8–12% increase in the occurrence of multiple birth accompanies Clomid treatment (Dwyer, 1986).

Human Gonadotropins   Administration of human gonadotropins may be indicated when Clomid is ineffective and pituitary dysfunction is causing ovulatory dysfunction. Either human menopausal gonadotropin (hMG) or human follicle- stimulating hormone (hFSH) may be administered. These gonadotropins are extracted and purified from the urine of postmenopausal women. They act directly on the ovary to promote growth and maturation of the ovarian follicle. However, effects are not sufficient to stimulate ovulation. For ovulation to occur, human chorionic gonadotropin (hCG) must be given after gonadotropins have stimulated the follicle. The high hCG levels resulting from administration mimic the action of the natural LH surge, causing rupture of the follicle and release of the ovum.

These hormones are potent stimulators of ovarian function. Careful monitoring of hMG's potent effects must accompany its administration, necessitating daily blood estrogen levels and ultrasound monitoring to determine growth of the ovarian follicle (O'Herlihy, Evans, Brown, de Crespigny, & Robinson,

1982). Human chorionic gonadotropin may also be used in conjunction with Clomid therapy. Clomid is first administered to induce ovulation. Injections of hCG are then administered for 6 to 8 days after ovulation to stimulate the corpus luteum to produce estrogen and progesterone in order to facilitate implantation of the embryo (Dwyer, 1986). The use of hCG may lead to multiple birth, with the incidence being reported as approximately 20% (Cahill, 1988).

Progesterone   Treatment with progesterone can be an effective treatment for luteal phase defect (Mason, Wentz, & Herbert, 1984). This defect, characterized by a uterine lining that is poorly prepared for implantation of the embryo, is due to inadequate progesterone production in the postovulatory phase of the menstrual cycle (Dwyer, 1986).

Bromocriptine   Bromocriptine is commonly used in cases of infertility associated with oversecretion of prolactin, which results in disruption of regular ovulatory function. Bromocriptine is a synthetic compound that interferes with the pituitary gland's ability to secrete prolactin. Ovulation usually returns after 6 to 12 weeks of daily treatment (Stillman, 1987).

Glucocorticoids   Glucocorticoids are one class of hormones naturally produced by the adrenal glands. Women with adrenal disorders often experience ovulatory dysfunction. Treatment of the adrenal disorder with synthetic glucocorticoids alone or in conjunction with other drugs (e.g., Clomid, human gonadotropins) can result in resumption of ovulatory cycles (Daly, Walters, & Soto-Albers, 1984). This treatment can also be effective for ovulatory dysfunction associated with polycystic disease (Evron, Navot, Laufer, & Diamont, 1983).

Glucocorticoid therapy is also effective in suppressing the production of sperm antibodies in the female. These antibodies are most likely responsible for abnormal sperm and cervical mucus interactions that inhibit or prevent fertilization. Administration of glucocorticoids can improve the quality of the cervical mucus, making it more receptive to sperm survival (Dwyer, 1986).

As previously mentioned, some fertility drugs create a risk of multiple conceptions. Multiple births increase the risk of miscarriage, birth defects, low birth weight, and complications during delivery (Congressional Report, 1988). Side effects associated with some or all of these drugs include weight gain, nausea, acne, hot flashes, and mood swings. Further, fertility drugs are not suitable for all women. They are contraindicated in women who exhibit undiagnosed vaginal bleeding, fibroid tumors, ovarian cysts (in some instances), hepatic dysfunction, or thrombophlebitis (Cahill, 1988). And they should be used cautiously in women with asthma, seizure disorders, or heart disease (Dwyer, 1986).

In Vitro Fertilization (IVF)

In vitro fertilization is a revolutionary infertility treatment that offers the possibility of nearly complete control of reproduction. This treatment is indicated in a number of disorders including irreversible tubal obstruction, azoospermia, endometriosis, and cervical mucus abnormalities.

In most instances, IVF treatment begins with administration of fertility drugs such as Clomid, human menopausal hormone, or gonadotropin releasing hormone, though some women are capable of producing oocytes (eggs) by natural ovulatory cycles. Although protocols for ovulation induction vary among IVF practitioners, development of follicles under the influence of fertility drugs is usually monitored by ultrasound imagery and blood estrogen levels (Congressional Report, 1988).

Once the follicles are mature, oocytes are collected via laparoscopy or nonsurgically with ultrasound-guided aspiration techniques. The aspirated oocytes are placed in a culture dish containing maternal serum and a culture medium, and fertilization is attempted with washed sperm obtained from the woman's husband or a donor. If available, at least 50,000 motile sperm per oocytes are added to the culture dish to achieve fertilization. The oocytes and sperm are then incubated for a 36-hour period, with the oocyte dividing after this period if fertilization has occurred.

If fertilization has occurred, the resulting embryos are transferred back into the uterine cavity using a small catheter. Typically, this procedure causes no cervical dilation or pain. Immediately after the woman receives the embryo, she is given an injection of progesterone to supplement the natural luteal phase hormonal environment. Afterward, she may return home, but will continue to need daily injections of progesterone until implantation of the embryo into the uterine wall has occurred (Cahill, 1988). To date, in most cases, IVF has been considered a last resort treatment. The procedures are costly, time consuming, and laborious. Couples using IVF must accept its relatively low success rate, which is estimated at 25% (Congressional Report, 1988). Further, IVF pregnancies are about two to four times as likely as unaided conception to result in an ectopic pregnancy due to preexisting risk factors in the infertile couple (Thorne & Langner, 1987). Other risks include the side effects associated with the daily intake of hormones and anesthesia during egg retrieval, stress to the uterus, spontaneous abortion, and multiple pregnancies (Congressional Report, 1988).

Total cost of IVF, assuming an average of two IVF treatment cycles, is estimated at $9,000 to $10,000 (Congressional Report, 1988). Couples must also be able to travel to the clinic, bear the expense of lost time at work, travel, and hotel stays, and endure the anxiety of waiting to see whether fertilization occurs. In addition, the majority of IVF programs in the United States have waiting lists of patients as long as 1 to 2 years. According to recent Congressional Surveys (1988), some IVF centers have policies restricting their services to only certain types of patients—for example, refusing to treat individuals without partners, unmarried couples, people under 17 or between the ages of 39 and 50, or homosexuals.

Artificial Insemination

Artificial insemination is one of the oldest forms of infertility treatments and continues to be one of the simplest and most successful infertility procedures. Sperm donation has existed as a therapeutic option in the United States since about 1950 (Congressional Report, 1988). Artificial insemination by donor (AID) refers to the practice of mechanically introducing into a woman's vagina live sperm obtained by masturbation from a man other than her husband (Waltzer, 1982). Artificial insemination homologous (AIH) is a similar procedure, but using the husband's sperm.

The most commonly used procedure is AID, particularly in the treatment of infertility due to abnormal sperm conditions such as azoospermia, oligospermia, and necrospermia (Waltzer, 1982). When AIH procedures are employed, several sperm samples are collected from the husband since in these instances his sperm is usually of poor quality. These samples are frozen and later pooled to increase the sperm count (Cahill, 1988).

The technique of AID or AIH requires prior determination of the expected ovulatory cycle using at least several monthly records of the woman's basal body temperature (BBT). The optimum time for insemination is just prior to or during ovulation, since cervical mucus is most receptive to sperm at this time. Semen collected from the donor or husband is injected into the cervical area by means of a syringe or catheter. The remaining semen is sprayed around the cervix or placed in a cervical cap, bathing the cervix in a pool of semen (Dwyer, 1986). Multiple inseminations during the time of ovulation are usually performed to increase the likelihood of conception. In cases where cervical mucus is hostile to sperm, the intracervical insemination technique is used, which involves depositing the sperm directly into the uterine cavity.

The artificial insemination technique achieves conception in approximately 70% of women when the husband's sperm is used and in approximately 90% of women when donor sperm is used (Cahill, 1988). These figures reflect success rates after multiple treatments, usually 6 months, since correctly timing insemination and ovulation may necessitate multiple trials. The AID or AIH techniques cause few complications, though multiple births are possible (Cahill, 1988). However, the major risk of using donor sperm is transmission of disease from the donor to the recipient, including chlamydia, gonorrhea, cytomegalovirus, hepatitis B virus, and human immunodeficiency virus (HIV) (Holmes, 1987; Scialli, 1987). It should be noted, however, that these risks do not exceed those present in unaided conception. The estimated cost of AIH services ranges from

$30 to $200, and the cost for for AID services ranges from $35 to $350 (Congressional Report, 1988).

Gamete Intrafallopian Transfer (GIFT)

Gamete intrafallopian transfer is an infertility treatment that involves the transfer of ova and sperm directly into the fallopian tubes, where fertilization can take place. In this procedure, oocytes are retrieved via laparoscopy after ovulation induction is accomplished by administration of Clomid or hMG and hCG, and a semen sample is collected. Both sperm and oocytes are directly emptied into one or both fallopian tubes using a catheter guided by laparoscopy. Following sperm and ova transfer, progesterone is administered daily until implantation of the embryo takes place.

Treatment of infertility using the GIFT technique is indicated in instances of endometriosis, premature ovarian failure, unexplained infertility, tubal adhesions, and oligospermia (Asch, Balmaceda, Ellsworth, & Wong, 1985; Guastella, Comparetto, Palermo, Cefalu, Ciriminna, & Cittadini, 1986). Risks associated with this procedure are similar to those associated with the IVF technique. The estimated cost of treatment with GIFT ranges from $2,500 to $6,000 (Congressional Report, 1988). An interesting aspect of the GIFT technique is that both donor sperm and donor eggs can be used. GIFT also simplifies some of the legal and ethical issues raised by noncoital reproduction technologies because it eliminates the presence of the extracorporeal embryo, thus avoiding the possibility of commercial cryobanking of embryos (Congressional Report, 1988).

Embryo Lavage and Transfer (ET)

Embryo lavage and transfer involves the retrieval of a fertilized ovum from a donor woman followed by transfer of the ovum to a waiting recipient (gestational mother) whose menstrual cycle has been synchronized in such a way that the uterine lining is prepared for implantation (Buster et al., 1983; Bustillo et al., 1984). Fertilization of the ovum is achieved by artificial insemination performed on a fertile donor woman. To date, embryo transfer and lavage is quite rare and may remain uncommon (Congressional Report, 1988).

Surgical Treatments

Several different surgical procedures are employed in treatment of various conditions leading to infertility in women. The availability of new and better microsurgical techniques has greatly improved the success rates of tubal surgery (Dwyer, 1986). Adhesions, occlusion, and scarring of one or both fallopian tubes due to infection, pelvic inflammatory disease, endometriosis, and previous surgery can impair fertility by severely restricting movement of the fallopian tubes or occluding the tubes, thus hindering ovum transport and the passage of sperm. The most common tubal microsurgical procedures involve excision and repair of scarring or damage at various points along the fallopian tubes (Congressional Report, 1988). Success rates for these procedures vary, and pregnancy is achieved in approximately 60% of women (Dwyer, 1986).

Salpingostomy, usually performed without magnification, attempts to re-create tubal patency and fimbria function when complete occlusion has occurred. Fimbrioplasty attempts to correct occlusions or adhesions of the finger-like appendages of the fimbria so that normal movement within the tube can resume. Removal of adhesions is accomplished by cauterization, dissection, or lasers. Ovarian resection may improve fertility with endometriosis and resulting cysts of the ovary or in cases of polycystic ovarian disease. Fibroid tumors that may inhibit implantation of the embryo may be removed by uterine myomectomy (Dwyer, 1986), and congenital malformation of the uterus can be repaired through reconstructive surgery, thus creating one uteral cavity. These procedures commonly involve a large incision in the abdominal wall to allow for direct visualization. Success rates for these procedures vary depending upon the type of surgery and on the skill and training of the individual surgeons (Congressional Report, 1988).

Surgical complications such as injury to the bowel, excessive blood loss, and infection, and the complications of general anesthesia, which include drug reactions, cardiac depression, and death, do not appear to be different for infertility surgery than with any intra-abdominal operation (Scialli, 1987). Ironically, however, because surgery may cause scar tissue of its own, adhesions and scarring remain potential consequences of reproductive tract surgery (Congressional Report, 1988). The main complication of tubal surgery is ectopic pregnancy, with ectopic pregnancy rates after tubal surgery reported as ranging from 4% to 38% (Scialli, 1987).

Psychological Consequences of Infertility Treatment

The cause of an individual couple's infertility is important to understand because it determines the type of treatment the couple might undergo and the prognosis for conceiving and delivering a healthy baby. Medical treatment may range from instructing the couple in the relatively simple methods of pinpointing ovulation to more complex treatments involving powerful fertility drugs, artificial insemination, or in vitro fertilization. Whatever the method, the medical investigation and treatment of infertility is often a protracted and time-consuming process (Lalos, Lalos, Jacobsson, & Von Schoultz, 1986).

Despite increasing attention to the diagnosis and treatment of infertility, little attention is paid to the psychological and social consequences of infertility.

The ability to conceive is closely related to self-esteem, identity, sexuality, and body image. Couples involved in fertility investigations are often preoccupied with conceiving, and their daily activities are often focused on pregnancy. Their sexual lives are often planned around a temperature chart, with hope rising each month. The onset of menstruation may be seen as failure that may be accompanied by depression (Batterman, 1985). Thus it seems that the crisis reactions to infertility are often prolonged and repeated. The very nature of the human reproductive cycle produces a sequence of hope, expectation, and despair that is commonly referred to as the ''emotional rollercoaster'' of infertility (Batterman, 1985).

The added apprehension, anticipation, and anxiety associated with testing complicates this effect. Both men and women find the testing procedures to be intrusive and alienating (McEwan, Costello, & Taylor, 1987). Men and women have also been found to have only a vague idea of the function and purpose of the laboratory tests, and feel threatened by what these procedures might reveal, although initially they may not be consciously aware of their fears (McEwan, Costello, & Taylor, 1987). The uncertainty over the length of time necessary to complete treatment further complicates the process. As couples undergo infertility investigation, the social pressure on them intensifies and they may have to make important decisions about the type of treatment they are willing to receive. These decisions may include dealing with the ethical and legal implications of treatment such as artificial insemination by donor (AID) and in vitro fertilization (IVF) and coming to terms with whether they can accept a child conceived in such a manner as ''theirs'' (Matthews & Matthews, 1986). Couples using the AID, IVF, GIFT, and ET techniques must adjust to achieving pregnancy non-coitally and thus succeed in separating sexuality and procreation. These couples may be particularly vulnerable to emotional stress, since in such situations, the semen or ovum of an anonymous donor is introduced to a complex dyadic system (Brand, 1987). Indeed, many social scientists have suggested that a thorough psychological evaluation of couples deciding to make use of these procedures should be a necessary prerequisite.

These emotional reactions have important implications for both physicians and clinicians in regard to their need for increased awareness of the psychological support needed by couples as they undergo fertility investigation and treatment. Psychotherapeutic interventions in cases of infertility usually begin after the individual couple has terminated medical testing and treatment. It has been suggested that the psychotherapeutic intervention begin before or in conjunction with medical intervention (Batterman, 1985). Supportive counseling offered throughout the medical investigation may aid in reducing the couple's anxiety and providing them with an increased sense of control. Supportive counseling should be designed for the couple since inclusion of both partners enhances treatment by keeping each well informed and actively involved in the process.

In conclusion, the major objective of the psychological treatment of the infertile couple is to facilitate a positive resolution of this life crisis, regardless of whether the couple conceives.

DIRECTIONS FOR RESEARCH

The field of sexuality, especially women's sexuality, has suffered from chronic underfunding and lack of serious research attention. There have been no research programs based on national probability samples of adult sexual behavior, even in this era of AIDS. This does not, of course, mean that there are no survey data on adult sexuality, but that the representativeness of the findings cannot be easily assessed and that changes over time cannot be easily examined. Although the National Family Growth Survey supplies information on adolescent sexual behaviors and both adolescent and adult contraception use, adult sexual behaviors are omitted. This is a clearly important gap in our knowledge, especially with respect to behaviors that put men and women at risk for sexually transmitted diseases including AIDS. This information is urgently needed both to predict the course of the AIDS epidemic and to supply the demographic knowledge needed to devise interventions to help women make behavioral changes needed to lower their risk of AIDS and other sexually transmitted diseases.

Perhaps the research area that has received the greatest attention is sexual behaviors and contraceptive choices of adolescent women. A pervasive problem in this literature may be the imposition of male values or male models of sexuality on prediction of female subjects' behavior. Research on contraception largely adheres to the cultural view that contraception is the woman's responsibility because she bears children. Therefore, young women are sought as subjects for studies to determine why they put themselves at risk for pregnancy by engaging in sex and failing to use effective contraception. The resulting knowledge may be limited by a masculine conceptualization of sexual motives. This could be because most researchers are male and/or because most research is based on a masculine model of science.

The male script for sexual motivation is that the individual desires sex to satisfy biological urges and operates autonomously to meet and satisfy this goal (Simon & Gagnon, 1969). Consistent with this conceptualization, many researchers adhere to the theory that if young women have adequate information, they will have positive attitudes and will use contraception. Barriers to use are conceptualized as ways in which contraceptives detract from sexual enjoyment (i.e., interfering with satisfying biological urges). A female script of sexual motivation is that engaging in sex is a way of increasing intimacy and commitment in a relationship (Simon & Gagnon, 1973). A woman thus engages in sex and makes sexual/contraceptive decisions in relation to the interests of her partner and her assessment of how her behavior may be viewed by her partner. This conceptualization is not intended to assert that biological influences occur for men and not women, but that sociocultural values reinforce biological urges for men and act against them for women. From this point of view, to answer the question, "Why does she put herself at risk by engaging in sexual behaviors and not using effective contraception?" one must look at her relationship goals and the barriers she encounters from her partner. The failure to adopt this relational view has often impeded asking appropriate research questions.

Factors affecting sexual desire in women are very poorly understood at present. Research relating feelings of well- being to sexual desire is extremely promising and needs to be pursued. This type of research may be methodologically challenging because it often relies on intrasubject analysis to determine the association across time between specific moods and sexuality variables.

Psychological consequences of infertility are just beginning to receive research attention. Although it is clear that infertility, infertility evaluation, and infertility treatment procedures are extremely stressful, the effects on psychological well-being, marital satisfaction, and sexual functioning have not been adequately studied. The effects of sexual behavior on reproductive hormones and infertility is a relatively new field. Findings showing that regularity of sexual behavior affects fertility need to be replicated and extended. The next step would be a prospective study in which the effects of having sex on a regular weekly basis could be monitored in couples who are infertile due to unknown etiology.

Whether one is studying physiological or psychological influences, women's sexuality cannot be understood outside of a cultural context. Women's social roles and status have a profound effect on both sexual/fertility choices and physiological functioning. Sexual behaviors are affected by power within relationships, just as sexual dysfunctions are shaped by cultural expectations. Women's sexuality, the effects of sexuality on infertility, and the psychological consequences of infertility are important issues. Research on these issues needs to be conducted taking social context into account and deserves to receive the resources of our society.

REFERENCES

Aral, S. O., & Cates, W. (1983). The increasing concern with infertility: Why now? *Journal of the American Medical Association, 250,* 2328–2331.

Asch, R. H., Balmaceda, J. P., Ellsworth, L. R., & Wong, P.C. (1985). Gamete intrafallopian transfer (GIFT): A new treatment for infertility. *International Journal of Fertility, 30,* 41–45.

Baird, D. D., & Wilcox, A. J. (1985). Cigarette smoking associated with delayed conception. *Journal of the American Medical Association, 253,* 2979–2983.

Baker, E. R. (1981). Menstrual dysfunction and hormonal status in athletic women: A review. *Fertility and Sterility, 36,* 692–692.

Baker, E. R., Mathur, R. S., Kirk, R. F., & Williamson, H. O. (1981). Female runners and secondary amenorrhea: Correlation with age, parity, mileage, and plasma hormonal and sex-hormone binding globulin concentrations. *Fertility and Sterility, 36,* 183–187.

Bancroft, J. (1987). Hormones, sexuality and fertility in humans. *Journal of Zoology, 213,* 445–461. Barnett, L. R., & Nietzel, J. T. (1979). Relationship of instrumental and affectional behaviors and self-esteem to marital satisfaction in distressed and nondistressed couples. *Journal of Consulting and Clinical Psychology, 47,* 946–957.

Barnett, L. R., & Nietzel, M. T. (1979). Relationship of instrumental and affectional behaviors and self-esteem to marital satisfaction in distressed and nondistressed couples. *Journal of Consulting and Clinical Psychology, 47,* 946–957.

Batterman, R. (1985). A comprehensive approach to treating infertility. *Health and Social Work, 10,* 46–54.

Baum, A., Singer, J. E., & Baum, C. S. (1981). Stress and the environment. *Journal of Social Issues, 37,* 4–35.

Bell, J. S. (1981). Psychological problems among patients attending an infertility clinic. *Journal of Psychosomatic Research, 25,* 1–3.

Bensen, R. C. (1978). *Current obstetric and gynecologic diagnosis and treatment.* Los Altos, CA: Longe Medical Publications.

Birchler, G. R., & Webb, L. J. (1977). Discriminating interaction behaviors in happy and unhappy marriages. *Journal of Consulting and Clinical Psychology, 45,* 494–495.

Blumstein, P., & Schwartz, P. (1983). *American couples: Money, work, and sex.* New York: William Morrow.

Brand, H. J. (1987). Complexity of motivation for artificial insemination by donor. *Psychological Reports, 60,* 951–955.

Brecher, J. (1977). Sex, stress, and health. *International Journal of Health Services, 7,* 89–101.

Bullen, B. A., Skrinar, G. S., Beitins, I. Z., von Mering, G., Turnbull, B. A., & McArthur, J. W. (1985). Induction of menstrual disorders by strenuous exercise in untrained women. *New England Journal of Medicine, 312,* 1329–1353.

Burns, L. H. (1987). Infertility and the sexual health of the family. *Journal of Sex Education and Therapy, 13,* 30–34.

Buster, J. E., Bustillo, M., Thorneycroft, I. H., Simon, J. A., Boyers, S. P., Marshall, J. R., Louw, J. A., Seed, R. W., & Seed, R. G. (1983). Nonsurgical transfer of in vivo fertilized donated ova to five infertile women: Report of two pregnancies. *Lancet, 2,* 223–226.

Bustillo, M., Buster, J., Cohen, S., Thorneycroft, I. H., Simon, J. A., Bayers, S. P. Marshall, J. R., Seed., R. W., Law, J. A., & Seed, R. G. (1984). Nonsurgical ovum transfer as a treatment in infertile women. *Journal of the American Medical Association, 251,* 1171–1178.

Cahill, M. (Ed.). (1988). *Treating obstetric and gynecological dysfunction.* Springhouse, PA: Springhouse Corp.

Chang, F. E., Richards, S. R., Kim, M. H. & Malarkey, W. B. (1984). Twenty four-hour prolacting profiles and prolactin responses to dopamine in long distance running women. *Journal of Endocrinology and Metabolism, 59,* 631–635.

Chesser, E. (1956). *The sexual, marital, and family relationships of the English woman.* London: Hutchinson's Medical Publications.

Chilman, C. S. (1986). Some psychosocial aspects of adolescent sexual and contraceptive behaviors in a changing American society. In J. B. Lancaster & B. A. Hamburg (Eds.), *School age pregnancy and parenthood: Biosocial dimensions* (pp. 191–217). New York: DeGruyter.

Collins, A., Eneroth, P., & Landgren, B. (1985). Psychoneuroendocrine stress responses and mood as related to the menstrual cycle. *Psychosomatic Medicine, 47,* 512–527.

Congressional Report. (1988). *Infertility: Medical and social choices* (OTA Publication No. BA-358). Washington, D. C.: Office of Technology Assessment.

Cutler, W. B., Garcia, C. R., Huggins, G. R., & Preti, G. (1986). Sexual behavior and steroid levels among gynecologically mature premenopausal women. *Fertility and Sterility, 45,* 496–502.

Cutler, W. B., Garcia, C. R., & Krieger, A. M. (1979). Luteal phase defects: possible relationship between short hyperthermic phase and sporadic sexual behavior in women. *Hormones and Behavior, 13,* 214–218.

Cutler, W. B., Preti, A., Huggins, G. R., Erickson, B., & Garcia, C. R. (1985). Sexual behavior frequency and biphasic ovulatory type menstrual cycles. *Physiology & Behavior, 34,* 805–810.

Dale, E., Gerlach, D. H., & Wilhite, A. L. (1979). Menstrual dysfunction in distance runners. *Obstetrics and Gynecology, 54,* 47.

Daly, D. C., Walters, C. A., Soto-Albors, C. E., et al. (1984). A rendomized study of dexamethasone in ovulation induction with clomiphene citrate. *Fertility and Sterility, 41,* 32.

Davidson, J. M., Smith, E. R., & Levine, S. (1978). Testosterone. In H. Ursin, E. Baade, and S. Levine (Eds.), *Psychology of Stress: A study of coping in man.* New York: Academic Press.

Dessypris, A., Kuoppasalmi, K., & Adlercreutz, H. (1976). Plasma cortisol, testosterone, androstenedione and luteinizing hormone (LH) in a non-competitive marathon run. *Journal of Steroid Biochemistry, 7,* 33–37.

Doddridge, R., Schumm, W. R., & Bergen, M. B. (1987). Factors related to decline in preferred frequency of sexual intercourse among young couples. *Psychological Reports, 60,* 391–395.

Dubin, L., & Amelar, R. D. (1971). Etiologic factors in 1294 consecutive cases of male infertility. *Fertility and Sterility, 22,* 8.

Dubin, L. & Amelar, R. D. (1972). Sexual causes of male infertility. *Fertility and Sterility, 23,* 579–582.

Dwyer, J. M. (1986). *Manual of gynecological nursing.* Boston: Little, Brown.

Evron, S., Navot, D., Laufer, N., & Diamant, Y. Z. (1983). Induction of ovulation with combined human gonadotropins and dexamethasone in women in polycystic ovarian disease. *Fertility and Sterility, 40,* 183–186.

Feichtinger, W., Kemeter, P., Salzer, H., Euller, A., Korn, A., & Fulmek, F. (1979). Daily epinephrine and norepinephrine excretion of normal cyclic women compared with prolactin, LH, FSH, estradiol, progesterone, testosterone and cortisol. In L. Zichella & P. Pancheri (Eds.), *Psychoneuroendocrinology in reproduction* (pp. 215–223). Amsterdam: Elsevier.

Frankenhauser, M. (1975). Sympathetic-adrenomedullary activity, behavior, and the psychosocial environment. In P. H. Venables & M. J. Christie (Eds.), *Research in psychophysiology* (pp. 71–94). New York: John Wiley.

Frisch, R. E. (1984). Body fat, puberty, and fertility. *Biological Review, 59,* 161–188.

Gallant, S. J., Hamilton, J. A., Popiel, D. A., Morokoff, P. J., & Chakraborty, P. K. (1991). Daily moods and symptoms: Effects of awareness of study, focus, gender, menstrual cycle phase, and day of the week. *Health Psychology, 10,* 180–189.

Gebhard, P. H. (1966). Factors in marital orgasm. *Journal of Social Issues, 22,* 88–95.

Ghanadian, R., Puah, C. M., Williams, G., Shah, P. J. R., & McWhinney, N. (1981). Suppressive effects of surgical stress on circulating androgens during and after prostatectomy. *British Journal of Urology, 53,* 147–149.

Goldstein, D. S., Levinson, P., Keiser, H. R. (1983). Plasma and urinary catecholamines during the human ovulatory cycle. *American Journal of Obstetrics and Gynecology, 146,* 824–829.

Gray-Little, B. & Burks, N. (1983). Power and satisfaction in marriage: A review and critique. *Psychological Bulletin, 93,* 513–538.

Guastella, G., Comparetto, G., Palermo, R., Cefalu, E., Ciriminna, R., & Cittadini, E. (1986). Gamete intrafallopian transfer in the treatment of infertility: The first series at the University of Palermo. *Fertility and Sterility, 46,* 417–423.

Guttmacher Institute. (1985). *Infertility services in the United States: Need, accessibility and utilization.* New York: Alan Guttmacher Institute.

Hahn, D. W., Carraher, R. K., Foldsey, R. G., & McGuire, J. L. (1986). Experimental evidence for failure to implant as a mechanism of infertility associated with endometriosis. *American Journal of Obstetrics and Gynecology, 155,* 1109–1113.

Hansen, C., & Morokoff, P. J. (1988). Marital influence strategies: Relationships to marital and sexual satisfaction. Presented at the Annual Meeting of the North American Psychological Association, Atlanta.

Hartz, A. J., Kelber, S., Borkowf, H., Wild, R., Gillis, B. L., & Rimm, A. A. (1987). The association of smoking with clinical indicators of altered sex steroids—A study of 50,145 women. *Public Health Reports, 102,* 254–259.

Heiman, J. R., & Rowland, D. I. (1983). Affective and physiological sexual response patterns: The effects of instructions on sexually functional and dysfunctional men. *Journal of Psychosomatic Research, 27,* 105–116.

Holmes, H. (1987). *Risks of infertility diagnosis and treatment.* Washington, DC: Office of Technology Assessment.

Holtz, G., Williamson, H. O., Mathur, R. S., Landgrebe, S. C., & Moore, E. E. (1985). Unruptured follicle syndrome in mild endometriosis: Assessment with biochemical parameters. *Journal of Reproductive Medicine, 30,* 643–645.

Horn, M. C., & Mosher, W. D. (1984). Use of services for family planning and infertility: United States, 1982. *NCHS: Advance Data, 103,* 1–8.

Ismail, A. A. A., Davidson, D. W., & Lorraine, J. A. (1972). Relationship between plasma cortisol and human sexual activity. *Nature, 237,* 288–289.

Johansson, G. G., Laakso, M. L., Peder, M., & Karonen, S. L. (1988). Examination stress decreases plasma level of luteinizing hormone in male students. *Psychosomatic Medicine, 50,* 286–294.

Kanner, A. D., Cayne, J. C., Schaefer, C., & Lazarus, R. S. (1981). Comparison of two modes of stress measurement: Daily hassles and uplifts versus major life events. *Journal of Behavioral Medicine, 4,* 1–39.

Kaplan, H. S. (1974). *The new sex therapy: Active treatment of sexual dysfunctions.* New York: Brunner/Mazel.

Kaplan, H. S. (1989). How to overcome premature ejaculation. New York: Brunner/ Mazel.

Kelley, W. N. (Ed.) (1989). *Textbook of internal medicine.* Philadelphia: J. B. Lippincott.

Kinsey, A. C., Pomeroy, W. B., Martin, C. E., & Gebhard, P. H. (1953). *Sexual behavior in the human female.* Philadelphia: W. B. Saunders.

Kling, A., Barowitz, G., & Cartwright, R. D. (1972). Plasma levels of 17 hydroxycor-tico-steroids during sexual arousal in man. *Journal of Psychosomatic Research, 16,* 215–221.

Kreuz, L. E., Rose, R. M., & Jennings, J. R. (1972). Suppression of plasma testosterone levels and psychological stress. *Archives of General Psychiatry, 26,* 479–482.

Lalos, A., Lalos, O., Jacobsson, L., & Von Schoultz, B. (1986). Depression, guilt and isolation among infertile women and their partners. *Journal of Psychosomatic Obstetrics and Gynecology, 5,* 197–206.

Levie, L. H. (1962). The indications for homologous artificial insemination. *International Journal of Fertility, 7,* 37–42.

Loucks, A. B., & Horvath, S. M. (1984). Exercise induced stress responses of amenor-rheic and eumenorrheic runners. *Journal of Clinical Endocrinology and Metabolism, 59,* 1109–1120.

Marinari, K. T., Leshner, A. I., & Doyle, M. P. (1976). Menstrual cycle status and adrenocortical reactivity to stress. *Psychoneuroendocrinology, 1,* 213–218.

Mason, J. W. (1968). A review of psychoendocrine research on the sympathetic adrenal medullary system. *Psychosomatic Medicine, 34,* 15.

Mason, W. S., Wentz, A. C., & Herbert, C. M. (1984). Outcome of progesterone therapy of luteal phase inadequacy. *Fertility and Sterility, 41,* 856–862.

Matthews, R., & Matthews, A. M. (1986). Infertility and involuntary childlessness: The transition to nonparenthood. *Journal of Marriage and the Family, 48,* 641–649.

Mattison, D. R. (1982). The effects of smoking on fertility from gametogenesis to implantation. *Environmental Research, 28,* 410–433.

Mazer, C., & Israel, L. (1959). *Diagnosis and treatment of menstrual disorders and sterility.* New York: Hoeber.

McEwan, K. L., Costello, C. G., & Taylor, P. J. (1987). Adjustment to infertility. *Journal of Abnormal Psychology, 96,* 108–116.

Mead, M. (1949). *Male and female.* New York: William Morrow.

Menken, J. (1985). Age and fertility: How late can you wait? *Demography, 22,* 469–483.

Menken, J., Trussell, J., & Larsen, U. (1986). Age and infertility. *Science, 233,* 1389–1394.

Morokoff, P. J. (1978). Determinants of female orgasm. In J. LoPiccolo & L. LoPiccolo (Eds.), *Handbook of sex therapy* (pp. 147–165). New York: Plenum Press.

Morokoff, P. J., Baum, A., McKinnon, W. R., & Gillilland, R. (1987). Effects of chronic unemployment and acute psychological stress on sexual arousal in men. *Health Psychology, 6,* 545–560.

Morokoff, P. J., & Gillilland, R. (1993). Stress, sexual functioning, and marital satisfaction. *The Journal of Sex Research, 30*, 34–44.

Morris, N., Udry, R., Khan-Dawood, F., & Dawood, M. Y. (1987). Marital sex frequency and midcycle female testosterone. *Archives of Sexual Behavior, 16*, 27–37.

Morrison, D. M. (1985). Adolescent contraceptive behavior. *Psychological Bulletin, 98*, 538–568.

Mosher, W. D. (1982). Infertility trends among U.S. couples, 1965–1976. *Family Planning Perspectives, 14*, 22–30.

Mosher, W. D. (1987). Infertility: Why business is booming. *American Demographics, 9*, 42–43.

Mosher, W. D., & Pratt, W. F. (1985). Fecundity and infertility in the United States, 1965–82. *NCHS: Advance Data, 104*, 1–8.

Newton, R. (1986, May). Effect of cancer on semen quality and cryopreservation of sperm. Paper presented at the International Conference on Reproduction and Human Cancer, Bethesda, MD.

O'Herlihy, C., Evans, J. H., Brown, J. B., de Crespigny, L. J., & Robinson, H. P. (1982). Use of ultrasound in monitoring ovulation induction with human pituitary gonadotropin. *Obstetrics and Gynecology, 60*, 577–582.

Osofsky, H. I., & Fisher, S. (1967). Psychological correlates of the development of amenorrhea in a stress situation. *Psychosomatic Medicine, 1*, 15–23.

Perlman, S. D., & Abramson, P. R. (1982). Sexual satisfaction among married and cohabitating individuals. *Journal of Consulting and Clinical Psychology, 50*, 458–460.

Persky, H., Lief, H. I., Strauss, D., Miller, W. R., & O'Brien, C. P. (1978). Plasma testosterone level and sexual behavior of couples. *Archives of Sexual Behavior, 7*, 157–173.

Phipps, W. R., Cramer, D. W., & Schiff, J. (1978). The association between smoking and female infertility as influenced by the cause of the infertility. *Fertility and Sterility, 48*, 377–382.

Popeil, D., Gallant, S. J., & Morokoff, P. J. (1988). The effect of stress and needs on sexual functioning. Paper presented at the Annual Meeting of the Association for Women in Psychology, Bethesda, MD.

Rickless, J., & Geiger, N. (1978). Impotence as a practical problem. In J. LoPiccolo & L. LoPiccolo (Eds.), *Handbook of sex therapy.* New York: Plenum.

Ronkainen, H., Pakarinen, A., Kirkinen, P., & Kauppila, A. (1985). Physical exercise induced changes and season- associated differences in the pituitary-ovarian function of runners and joggers. *Journal of Clinical Endocrinology and Metabolism, 60*, 416–422.

Rose, R. M., Bourne, P. G., Poe, R. O., Mougey, E. H., Collins, D. R., & Mason, J. W. (1969). Androgen responses to stress. II. Excretion of testosterone, epitestosterone, androsterone and etiocholanolone during basic combat training and under threat of attack. *Psychosomatic Medicine, 31*, 418–435.

Sanders, D., Warner, P., Backstrom, T., & Bancroft, J. (1983). Mood and the menstrual cycle. *Psychosomatic Medicine, 45*, 487–502.

Sandler, B. (1969). Emotional stress and infertility. *Journal of Psychosomatic Research, 12*, 51–59.

Scialli, A. R. (1987). *Risks of infertility diagnosis and treatment*. Washington, DC: Office of Technology Assessment.

Shangold, M. M., Gatz, M. L., & Thysen, B. (1981). Acute effects of exercise on plasma concentrations of prolactin and testosterone in recreational women runners. *Fertility and Sterility, 35*, 699–702.

Sherwin, B., Gelfand, M., & Brenner, W. (1985). Androgen enhances sexual motivation in females: A prospective, crossover study of sex steroid administration in the surgical menopause. *Psychosomatic Medicine, 47*, 339–351.

Siebel, M., & Taynor, M. (1982). Emotional aspects of infertility. *Fertility and Sterility, 37*, 137–145.

Simon, W. & Gagnon, J. (1973). Psychosexual development. In E. S. Morrison & V. borosage (Eds.), *Human sexuality: Contemporary Perspectives*. Palo Alto, CA: National Press Books.

Stillman, R. J. (1987). Definitions, statistics, and the human and financial costs of infertility. [Summary] *Alternative reproductive technologies: Implications for children and families*. Washington, DC: U.S. Government Printing Office.

Stillman, R. J., Rosenberg, M. J., & Sachs, B. P. (1986). Smoking and reproduction. *Fertility and Sterility, 46*, 545.

Sutton, J. R., Coleman, M. J., Casey, J., & Lazarus, L. (1973). Androgen responses during physical exercise. *British Medical Journal, 1*, 520.

Talbert, L. M. (1981). Overview of the diagnostic evaluation. In M. G. Hammond & L. M. Talbert (Eds.), *Infertility: A practical guide for the physician*. Chapel Hill, NC: Health Sciences Consortium.

Terman, L. M. (1938). *Psychological factors in marital happiness*. New York: McGraw-Hill.

Terman, L. M. (1951). Correlates of orgasm adequacy in a group of 556 wives. *Journal of Psychology, 32*, 115–172.

Thomford, P. J., & Mattison, D. R. (1986). The effect of cigarette smoking on female reproduction. *Journal of the Arkansas Medical Society, 82*, 597–604.

Thorne, E., & Langner, G. (1987). *Expenditures on infertility treatment*. Washington, DC: Office of Technology Assessment.

Treloar, A. E., Boynton, R. E., Behn, D. G., & Brown, B. W. (1967). Variation of the human menstrual cycle through reproductive life. *International Journal of Fertility, 12*, 77–126.

Tudiver, F. (1983). Dysfunctional uterine bleeding and prior life stress. *The Journal of Family Practice, 17*, 999–1003.

Van Der Spuy, Z. M. (1985). Nutrition and reproduction. *Clinics in Obstetrics and Gynecology, 12*, 579–604.

Veith, J. L., Buck, M., Getzlaf, S., Van Dalfsen, P., & Slade, S. (1983). Exposure to men influences the occurrence of ovulation in women. *Physiology and Behavior, 31*, 313–315.

Vollman, R. F. (1977). The menstrual cycle. In *Major problems in obstetrics and gynecology*. Philadelphia: W. B. Saunders.

Waltzer, H. (1982). Psychological and legal aspects of artificial insemination (A.I.D.): An overview. *American Journal of Psychotherapy, 36*, 91–102.

Warner, P. & Bancroft, J. (1988). Mood, sexuality, oral contraceptives and the menstrual cycle. *Journal of Psychosomatic Research, 32*, 417–427.

Wasilewska, E., Kobus, E., & Bargiel, Z. (1980). Urinary catecholamine excretion and plasma dopamine-beta-hydroxylase activity in mental work performed in two periods of menstrual cycle in women. In E. Usdin, R. Kvetnansky, & I. J. Kopin (Eds.), *Catecholamines and stress: Recent advances* (pp. 549–554). Amsterdam: Elsevier.

Weinberg, M. S., & Williams, C. (1988). Black sexuality: A test of two theories. *Journal of Sex Research, 25,* 197–218.

Weisberg, E. (1985). Smoking and reproductive health. *Clinical Reproduction and Fertility, 3,* 175–186.

Wentz, A. C. (1986). Cigarette smoking and infertility. *Fertility and Sterility, 46,* 365–367.

Wheeler, G. D., Wall, S. R., Belcastro, A. N., & Cumming, D. C. (1984). Reduced serum testosterone and prolactin levels in male distance runners. *Journal of the American Medical Association, 252,* 514–516.

Wolpe, J. (1973). *The Practice of Behavior Therapy*, New York: Pergamon.

Chapter 11

Women's Health: The Impact of the Expanding AIDS Epidemic

Debra A. Murphy
Jeffrey A. Kelly

Many people still view the acquired immune deficiency syndrome (AIDS) crisis as primarily affecting males who are homosexual and/or involved in intravenous drug use. Although it is true that the epidemic of human immunodeficiency virus (HIV) has for the most part affected young men, HIV infection is increasingly becoming a major health threat in women. Cases of AIDS among women in the United States accounted for 10% of all cases reported to the Centers for Disease Control (CDC) as of the end of 1991—more than 20,000 women have been diagnosed with AIDS (CDC, 1991). Further, HIV infection in women of reproductive age is directly linked to AIDS in children. (Oxtoby, 1990). AIDS is now among the 10 leading causes of death in women of reproductive age (Chu, Buehler, & Berkelman, 1990), and women with AIDS or HIV infection are the major source of infection of infants with AIDS.

Due to the long average latency period between infection and the onset of symptoms or illness and the fact that infection with HIV is often asymptomatic, AIDS case reports have typically not reflected the scope of the problem. Therefore, although over 20,000 women have been reported to the CDC as having full-blown AIDS, for each person with AIDS several more have AIDS-related conditions and an even larger number are asymptomatic, yet infected with the virus.

PROJECTED SCOPE OF HIV INFECTION AMONG WOMEN

The World Health Organization (WHO) has estimated that during the first decade of HIV/AIDS there were approximately 500,000 cases of AIDS in women and children worldwide, most of which have been unrecognized. It is anticipated that the pandemic will kill an additional 3 million or more women and children throughout the world in the 1990s. In some areas of the world, AIDS has become the leading cause of death for women aged 20–40 (Chin, 1990). For example, WHO has estimated that in certain areas of Africa, by the end of 1992, there will be more than 600,000 cases of AIDS in women and more than 600,000 in children. Nearly 300,000 AIDS cases in *1 year* in women and children are expected in Africa in 1992 (Chin, 1990).

Though the rates of infection among women in the United States are lower, there is cause for increasing concern. Only recently has there been some study of the seroprevalence of HIV infection among women in the United States. It has been estimated that if current morality trends continue HIV/AIDS will become one of the five leading causes of death in women of reproductive age (Chu et al., 1990). For example, the New York City Department of Health (1989) estimated that 21,000–50,000 women in New York City were HIV infected by December of 1988, and AIDS is the leading cause of death among women aged 25 to 34 in New York City (Weinberg & Murray, 1987). In contrast to the 8:1 male-to-female AIDS case ratio among active duty members of the United States Army reported previously, the HIV seroprevalence ratio is now 2.4:1, and the ratio for black and Hispanic women is 1.6 times higher than that found in white males (Kelley et al., 1990). Between January of 1987 and November of 1991, the number of AIDS cases among women in the United States increased by more than 1,000%. Therefore, although women currently represent a minority of AIDS cases in this country, infections among women are doubling every one to two years—and as noted, these cases will represent just a portion of the people involved in the epidemic.

In addition to viewing HIV infection as a primarily male disease, many also view it as a disease of minorities and the lower socioeconomic class. Although the urban poor are disproportionately overrepresented, the incidence of AIDS is beginning to expand to other populations. In a recent study of heterosexual transmission of HIV among New York City middle-class white females and males with a mean household income of over $40,000, 22% of the women tested seropositive (Glaser, Strange, & Rosati, 1989). Most of the women had few lifetime sexual partners and were involved in a steady relationship. The predominant source of infection was sexual contact with intravenous drug users who did not fit the stereotype of being minority or lower class. Although this was a single, small study, it indicates the need for concern for the spread of the disease to other populations. However, the current epidemic is expanding most rapidly among minority, low-income women.

The impact of the AIDS/HIV epidemic on women—medically, socially, and economically—has been neglected until recently. This has been primarily because during the 1980s men were the focus of study, given that the epidemic was severe in that population. Nevertheless, as noted in the estimated scope of the problem outlined above, there have been some shifts in the percentage of increase of infection within different populations. As the proportion of total AIDS cases among homosexual and bisexual men decreases, it appears that the proportion of AIDS cases among intravenous drug users and their sexual partners increases; thus, the proportion of AIDS cases among women increases. Also of concern is the fact that the increase of infection among women of childbearing age has implications for rates of childhood HIV infection. In addition, women of color are disproportionately affected by AIDS. Of female AIDS patients in the United States, approximately 49% are black, 25% are Hispanic, and 26% are white. Of these women, 80% are of childbearing age (Lambert, 1990). Many HIV seropositive women are poor, with limited education and access to health and other social services (CDC, 1991). In blinded serologic surveys conducted in 1988 and 1989 in the United States and Puerto Rican reproductive health clinics, Sweeney et al. (1992) found that prevalence of HIV was generally low but widely spread throughout the United States, with 83% ofen, adolescents, and African Americans (Quinn et al., 1992). Over the ten years of the Baltimore study, the most dramatic change in epidemiology was the declining male-to-female ratio, which went from 16:1 to 1.01. What accounts for the variation in percentages of HIV infection across race and age? Certain women appear to be at risk for acquiring HIV based on risk behavior related to how the virus is transmitted to women.

MODE OF TRANSMISSION

Guinan and Hardy (1987) and Shapiro, Schulz, Lee, and Dondero (1989) have listed the modes of transmission of HIV to women: (1) those associated with intravenous drug use—estimated to be the most common mode of transmission to women—with approximately 62% of the women with the virus thus far infected in this manner; (2) heterosexual contact with a person with AIDS or at risk for AIDS, with approximately 29% of women infected through this mode of transmission; (3) those associated with transfusion of blood or blood products (11%); (4) those associated with coagulation disorder (0.4%); and (5) undetermined (8%). It should be noted that frequency of infection by mode of transmission has shown certain shifts over time. For example, the percentage of women acquiring AIDS through drug use declined from 1983 to 1986, whereas the percentage of women acquiring AIDS through heterosexual contact increased (Lambert, 1990). As will be seen in the following discussion, each mode of transmission is affected by numerous other factors. In this section, we shall concentrate on the two most common modes of transmission for females: that associated with intravenous drug use and that associated with sexual contact.

Transmission Associated with Intravenous Drug Use

Transmission associated with intravenous drug use includes both use of intravenous drugs and sexual contact with male intravenous drug users (Chiasson et al., 1990). A recent study in New York City (Marmor et al., 1990) found that HIV seropositivity among female drug users was 37%, and a multiple logistic regression analysis indicated that a significant predictor of HIV infection among women included both a history of sexual contact with a male intravenous drug user and the recent past use of intravenous drugs. Among males and females enrolled in a methadone treatment program, the presence of positive HIV antibody status was associated with number of injections per month, percentage of injections with used needles, average number of injections with cocaine per month, and percentage of injections with needles that were shared (Schoenbaum et al., 1989). These findings are supported by studies conducted in the New York City area, in which frequency of drug injection was linked to seropositivity (Des Jarlais, Friedman, & Stoneburner, 1988).

Once HIV is prevalent among intravenous drug users, the risk for heterosexual transmission increases. Over 87% of heterosexual transmission cases in New York City have occurred from an intravenous drug user to a sexual partner who does not use intravenous drugs (Des Jarlais et al., 1987). Although it may seem unlikely that women who do not inject drugs themselves would have regular male sexual partners who do, Des Jarlais et al. (1988) reported that this is quite common; approximately 75% of the intravenous drug users in the United States are heterosexual males, and the majority of these men have their primary sexual relationships with females who do not inject drugs. Also, many male intravenous drug users may have multiple female sexual partners. Among one sample of such men, over 60% had had more than five female sexual partners during the previous 5 years, and 73% never used condoms—indicating potential for widespread secondary transmission of HIV (Lewis, Watters, & Case, 1990).

Transmission through Sexual Contact

The second most common transmission category for women with AIDS is heterosexual contact with an HIV-infected person; this form of transmission currently accounts for one-third of all female and adolescent cases in the United States (CDC, 1991).

A person's risk of acquiring HIV infection through sexual contact is influenced by the number of different partners, the likelihood of HIV infection in these partners, and the probability of virus transmission during sexual contact with the infected partner. Virus transmission itself may in turn be affected by a number of factors, including: (1) concurrent sexually transmitted disease infections in either partner; (2) behavioral factors (e.g., type of sex practice and use of condoms); and (3) level of infectivity in the sexual partner based on clinical stage of the disease. Currently, approximately 60% of worldwide HIV transmission is through heterosexual contact; by the turn of the century it is estimated that 75–80% of HIV cases will result from heterosexual intercourse (World Health Organization, 1991).

Factors Influencing Virus Transmission   Sexually transmitted diseases have been hypothesized to increase the probability of transmission of HIV by penetration of the virus through skin ulcerations or by increasing susceptibility of the immune system. Several studies have reported correlations between a history of sexually transmitted diseases and HIV infection (Chiasson et al., 1990; Quinn et al., 1990). Though some have argued that sexually transmitted diseases are only indicators of sexual promiscuity—and that is why they show a relation to HIV infection—others have noted that associations between sexually transmitted diseases and HIV infection have persisted after adjustment for number of sexual partners (European Study Group, 1989). Quinn et al. (1990) reported that of all potential risk factors for HIV infection in a population of male and female patients at inner-city sexually transmitted disease clinics in Baltimore the variable that was most consistently correlated with HIV infection was syphilis, and that this was independent of age, gender, number of sexual partners in the preceding month, intravenous drug use, or male homosexual activity.

Type of sexual practice influences virus transmission rates. Penile-vaginal contact is a well-documented risk, although it is a less efficient means of transmission than penile-anal intercourse (Padian, Wiley, & Winkelstein, 1987). Anal intercourse clearly has been found to increase the risk of male to female transmission (European Study Group, 1989), which is consistent with the fact that anal intercourse among homosexual men is a well-known transmission risk factor. In one study, women who reported having anal intercourse with an infected partner were 2.3 times more likely to be infected than women who reported only vaginal intercourse (Padian, Marquis et al., 1987). No other sexual practices have been associated with risk of transmission, but there has been little research to determine risks associated with oral-genital contact. Complicating the study of oral-genital sex risk are two factors: (1) oral sex is strongly associated with other sexual practices, and (2) usually only a very small number of couples report oral-genital practices; thus risk would have to be extremely high to detect differences through the power of statistical tests.

Level of infectivity in the sexual partner based on clinical stage of the disease may affect virus transmission (Centers for Disease Control [CDC], 1989). For example, the European Study Group (1989) found that men with full-blown AIDS seemed to be more infective than carriers without symptoms.

Risk Rates of Heterosexual Transmission   Though sexual transmission of HIV is not as efficient as the transmission of other sexually transmitted diseases (e.g., syphilis or gonorrhea), with repeated contact the risk of infection increases.

As is probably becoming apparent, the link between drug use and sexual contact as modes of transmission of HIV is strong. Females may trade sex for money to obtain drug or for drugs themselves (Sterk, 1988). They may not see themselves in a high-risk category if they are trading sex for non-IV drugs, and yet they are at risk due to the type of partner chosen (males involved in selling drugs) or the number of partners they may have to obtain sufficient money to maintain their drug habit. In a study of female prostitutes in Florida (Fischl, Dickinson, Flanagan, & Fletcher, 1987), factors associated with HIV antibody included greater number of clients per week, greater number of black clients, participation in vaginal intercourse, syphilis, and number of pregnancies. Negative association occurred with several factors, including fellatio.

There has been some question regarding the range of risk of heterosexual transmission, as well as whether risk is equal for male to female and female to male. The studies on range of risk for heterosexual transmission have varied. The range of risk for spouses of seropositive hemophiliacs and bisexual men has been estimated to be between 7 and 21% (Peterman & Curran, 1986). Rates of approximately 40% were found in one study of transmission of HIV from intravenous drug users with AIDS to their heterosexual partners (Fischl et al., 1987), and seropositivity rates of over 50% have been reported for female partners of intravenous drug users. There have been attempts to examine the relationship between HIV serostatus and the total number of exposures (Padian, Marquis et al., 1987). Ninety-seven females were studied for serostatus after partner infection. Vaginal, oral, and anal intercourse could not be assessed separately because only 3 subjects reported engaging only in vaginal intercourse, and none engaged in only oral or anal intercourse. Study findings indicated that seropositive women were 4.6 times more likely than seronegative women to have had more than 100 sexual exposures with the infected partner. Although there have been attempts to determine formulas that provide an exact probability value for transmission (e.g., transmission probability based on a single penile-vaginal contact), it must be fairly evident from this section that numerous factors other than number of sexual contacts can influence transmission, and that all of these appear to influence likelihood of transmission.

Male to female transmission is approximately twice as efficient as female to male transmission (European Study Group, 1992), as is the case with other sexually transmitted diseases such as gonorrhea. For example, Padian, Shiboski, & Jewell (1990) reported that among a sample of 219 white couples that female-to-male transmission was less efficient than male-to-female transmission; it appears that the odds ratio comparing male-to-female with female-to-male transmission, adjusted for number of contacts, was 12.31 to 1.0.

For women who have contracted the virus, through whatever mode of transmission, a long and possibly extremely stressful course of clinical disease progression may await. The next section discusses both the medical progression of HIV infection and the psychological issues involved in being diagnosed as HIV positive.

PROGRESSION OF HIV INFECTION IN WOMEN

Medical Progression of HIV Infection

Acquired immune deficiency syndrome (AIDS) is caused by a retrovirus that attacks and severely weakens part of the immune system. After some debate over a name for the virus, it was termed the human immunodeficiency virus (HIV). HIV infects and attacks certain types of white blood cells, principally CD4 + T-lymphocytes. The CD4 + T-lymphocyte coordinates a number of important immunologic functions (CDC, 1992), and a loss of these functions results in progressive impairment of the immune system. The CD4 + T-lymphocyte is the primary target for HIV infection, because there is an affinity of the virus for the CD4 surface marker. So, as HIV binds to the lymphocytes, it causes them to lose their normal ability to activate other immune system cells. Such binding can also cause the lymphocytes to die precipitately. The CD4 + T-cell count is used as an indicator of disease progression among physicians; however, these cell levels are subject to fairly wide variations within a single patient. For that reason, consistent trends in CD4 + T-cell counts over time are typically used.

HIV infection may be detected in three ways: (1) by culture of the virus; (2) by identification of viral proteins or genetic material; and (3) by measurement of antibodies produced to defend against the virus. HIV is most commonly tracked by the presence of serum antibodies. Individuals are said to be seropositive when HIV antibodies are detected in their blood serum.

Although HIV was found to be present in AIDS patients, it soon became evident in early research that milder conditions were appearing in the same populations that were at risk for AIDS. That is, an individual does not just suddenly develop a full-blown clinical case of AIDS. HIV, like other infectious diseases, causes a wide variety of clinical symptoms. The following discussion centers on clinical description of positive serostatus. Following these descriptions is a summary of the CDC's 1993 Revised Classification System.

Human Immunodeficiency Virus Infection: Asymptomatic Status   Infection with HIV may occur symptomatically or asymptomatically (Tindall et al., 1988). Initial acute infection with HIV is often characterized as a mononucleosis-like syndrome (Moss & Bacchetti, 1989); antibodies to HIV are observed, and occasionally hematologic abnormalities are present (CDC, 1987). Symptoms may appear 2–6 weeks after laboratory seroconversion, and include transient fever, headache, diarrhea, sore throat, and neurological manifestations. Persistent antibodies to HIV typically develop in approximately 3 months, although this period varies. These symptoms are often shortlived and, for a majority of people, are followed by an extended asymptomatic period of time (Glasner & Kaslow, 1990), in which for some people the only evidence of infection is a positive test result for antibodies to HIV. These people show no acute infection, are asymptomatic, and may remain clinically well for a long period of time.

Human Immunodeficiency Virus Infection: Symptomatic Status   At some point during HIV infection, an individual may begin to experience symptoms that to not meet criteria for a full-blown AIDS diagnosis. The conditions are attributed to HIV infection—they are indicative of a weakness in cell-mediated immunity or are considered by physicians to have a clinical progression complicated by HIV infection (CDC, 1992). These symptoms include a wide variety of conditions (e.g., fever or diarrhea lasting more than one month, pelvic inflammatory disease, peripheral neuropathy). Disease progression among HIV-infected individuals does not always follow a well-defined pattern. For these reasons, many investigators believe that there is no single, discrete disease stage corresponding to the label "AIDS related complex" (ARC), which was formerly diagnosed when an infected individual had one or more of a wide variety of symptoms and laboratory abnormalities, but did not have a specific infection, cancer, or symptom complex diagnostic of AIDS. However, the general label of ARC is rarely used in the research literature any more.

Acquired Immune Deficiency Syndrome   AIDS stands for acquired immune deficiency syndrome. AIDS is the end-stage outcome of HIV infection (Tindall et al., 1988). The CDC criteria for diagnosis of AIDS define a syndrome that is most likely to occur late in the progression of HIV infection. AIDS has been defined as a reliably diagnosed opportunistic disease or infection that is predictive of cellular immune deficiency, and that occurs in a person without preexisting illness that would produce immunosuppression (Haverkos & Drotman, 1984; Jaffe, Bregman, & Selik, 1985). Immunodeficiency illnesses can develop when the virus invades and destroys a sufficient number of CD4 + T-lymphocytesemthe cells that activate many immune responses (Groopman, 1985). AIDS onset is thought to occur when there has been a large reduction of CD4 + T-lymphocytes, which leaves an individual unable to resist diseases and opportunistic secondary infections. Because AIDS is a disease in which immunodeficiency is the central problem, symptoms vary across individuals, reflecting the different underlying opportunistic infections. Opportunistic infections may be viral, fungal, bacterial, or protozoan. Common infections include Candida infection of the mouth or gastrointestinal tract and *Pneumocystis carinii* pneumonia. In addition, persons with AIDS have an unusually high incidence of an uncommon cancer—Kaposi's sarcoma—and of some types of lymphomas. Other late symptoms of HIV include neurological manifestations, dermatological conditions, and constitutional symptoms such as "HIV wasting syndrome." Over 30% of people with AIDS eventually develop clinically significant dementia that affects cognition, behavior, and motor function; most AIDS dementia patients develop moderate to severe dementia approximately 3 months after symptoms first appear (McArthur, 1990).

In early studies, general estimates of mortality have been found to exceed 80% within 2 years from the time of diagnosis of AIDS (Curran, Morgan, Starcher, Hardy, & Jaffee, 1985). However, antiviral regimens initiated early in the disease course have extended this time in recent years, and progress in antiviral research is continuing at a rapid rate. Although advances are being made, the prognostic picture for women remains poorer than that for men. Ickovics and Rodin (1992) reviewed a number of mortality studies, and found that women have been found to die significantly sooner after an AIDS diagnosis than men. Brown and Rundell (1990) found that progression was three times as fast among a group of 20 employed, educated, seropositive women than in a comparable male sample. Similarly, Rothenberg et al. (1987) found that the probability of survival, especially during the first year of illness, was affected by gender, with women having poor early prognosis. Gender accounted for 8% of excess risk. As Ickovics and Rodin noted, these survival differences may be due to a number of factors: (1) diagnosis and treatment occurring later in the disease process; (2) lack of information about clinical course of HIV infection in women; or (3) inability to obtain treatment in a timely manner due to less health care access for females.

Early reports suggested that only a minority of infected individuals would progress to clinical AIDS. It now is becoming apparent that investigators underestimated the long average latency time from HIV infection to AIDS. The prognosis for progression to AIDS by individuals who are HIV positive has been studied, although no investigations have focused specifically on women (Peterman et al., 1988). It is currently believed that infected individuals will progress to AIDS within an average of 7 to 10 years from infection (Giesecke, Scalia-Tomba, Hakansson, Karlsson, & Lidman, 1990; Moss & Bacchetti, 1989). Predicted course for the majority of AIDS patients is development of severe complications followed by death. Autopsy series suggest that opportunistic infections are responsible for almost 90% of deaths (Niedt & Schinnella, 1985).

Although a number of laboratory markers for disease progression have been studied (Moss & Bacchetti, 1989; Peterman et al., 1988), no epidemiological evidence for any infectious disease cofactor has yet been demonstrated. Those factors hypothesized to influence acceleration of progression to AIDS that affect women include pregnancy, older age, and having other sexually transmitted diseases. Although it is not known whether pregnancy increases an HIV seropositive woman's risk for developing AIDS, it is hypothesized that pregnancy is associated with suppression of cell-mediated immunity and increased susceptibility to other viral diseases (Lifson, Rutherford, & Jaffe, 1988).

CDC 1993 Revised Classification System for HIV Infection. In December of 1992, the CDC published a revised classification system for HIV infection and expanded the surveillance case definition for AIDS among adolescents and adults. The revised CDC classification system for HIV infection categorizes persons on the basis of clinical conditions associated with HIV *and* on CD4+ T-lymphocyte counts. This represents a major change from the classification system published in 1986, which included only clinical disease criteria. That system was developed before the widespread use of CD4+ T-cell testing. The new classification system is based on three ranges of CD4+ T-lymphocyte counts (which are numbered 1, 2, and 3), and three clinical categories (which are noted by the letters A, B., and C); thus, there is a matrix of nine mutually exclusive categories. The three CD4+ T-lymphocyte categories are: (1) > 500 cells per microliter of blood; (2) 200-499 cells per microliter; and (3) < 200 cells per microliter. The clinical categories are: (A) Asymptomatic, acute (primary HIV or PGL (persistent generalized lymphadenopathy); (B) symptomatic, not (A) or (C) conditions; and (C) AIDS-indicator conditions. Thus, and individual in category B2 would be symptomatic, with 200-499 CD4+ T-cells per microliter of blood.

The expanded AIDS surveillance case definition the accompanied the revised classification system should have a significant impact on the number of reported cased, especially among women. For example, given that several recent studies have found an increased prevalence of cervical dysplasia—which is a precursor lesion for cervical cancer—among HIV-infected women, invasive cervical cancer has been added to the list of AIDS-indicator diseases.

Obviously, the progressive course of this disease is severe and would be dreaded by patients knowledgeable about probable future clinical course. Not only do HIV-infected patients have to contend with a widespread variety of serious physical symptoms, but they have unique psychological sequelae to their illness. As will be seen in the following section, HIV infection produces a series of interacting psychosocial stressors.

Psychological Complications of HIV Infection

Although there appears to be only one study conducted to investigate the emotional consequences that follow a diagnosis of HIV among women, there have been several studies among male patients. Anxiety has been found to be one of the most common reactions to HIV seropositivity (Coates, Morin, & McKusick, 1987). Over 50% of homosexual males studied experienced significant anxiety, insomnia, and memory problems following HIV diagnosis (Joseph et al., 1987). In addition, studies with homosexual men have found that they experience significantly higher levels of anger than men who are seronegative or unaware of HIV status (McCusker et al., 1988); they report higher levels of psychosomatic distress and more physical symptoms (Cochran, 1987); and they often deny their HIV seropositive status, which may preclude making behavioral changes to prevent transmission (Joseph et al., 1987). They also report significantly higher levels of depression (Coates et al., 1987). In one study of 13 AIDS patients seen by a psychiatric consultation service, 2 met DSM-III major depression criteria,

1 had dysthymic disorder, and 7 had adjustment disorder with depressed mood (Dilley, Ochitill, Perl, & Volberding, 1985).

It is typical for many patients to experience anxiety, depression, guilt, and fear; the common symptoms may include sleeplessness, fatigue, sadness, lethargy, loss of libido, difficulty with memory and concentration, hyperactivity, tremors, and rapid heart rate (Coates & Lo, 1990). More serious symptoms of generalized anxiety due to extreme stress may include nightmares, sleep disturbance, and intrusive thought, which may come about due to social isolation, guilt, or a sense of dread (Coates & Lo, 1990). Complicating these issues is the fact that HIV patients may be asymptomatic or have only mild symptoms, and may cope with years of uncertainty about when they will develop serious illness (Kelly & St. Lawrence, 1988). In fact, results of at least one study have indicated that psychosocial distress may be higher among asymptomatic HIV-infected patients and patients with some symptoms than among patients with full-blown AIDS (Chuang, Devins, Hunsley, & Gill, 1989).

Common psychological themes among male HIV-infected individuals include dealing with a life-threatening illness, uncertainty about the implications of an AIDS diagnosis, social isolation, and guilt over their life style (Dilley et al., 1985). Not only do HIV-seropositive individuals experience psychosocial distress, but as Kelly and his colleagues (e.g., Kelly, St. Lawrence, Hood, Smith, & Cook, 1988; Kelly, St. Lawrence, Smith, Hood, & Cook, 1987) have reported, social support systems appear to be less likely for persons with AIDS than for patients with other serious illnesses.

Although many HIV patients experience psychological distress, it is also clear from the figures given in the above studies that not all patients exhibit clinically significant levels of distress. In addition, these studies have been conducted among males and may not be applicable to females. In the one study to date that investigated psychiatric morbidity in 20 employed, educated, HIV-infected women (Brown & Rundell, 1990), 50% were found to have an Axis I diagnosis; none developed major depression or drug dependence; 5% abused alcohol; 15% exhibited mild cognitive decline; sexual functioning was disrupted in the majority of patients; and safe sex practices were adhered to in only 40% of the sample. Progression of HIV infection was found to be three times as fast as in a comparable male sample. To the surprise of the investigators, none of the women required psychiatric hospitalization, no suicide attempts or completions were made, and there were continued high levels of occupational functioning. However, these findings may be of limited value in terms of generalization to the majority of HIV seropositive women in the United States since the sample was a non-drug-using, employed, educated population who discovered their HIV status as part of the U.S. Air Force mandatory screening program. In addition, mean length of time for knowledge of serostatus was only 14.4 months.

In addition to the psychological consequences for individuals diagnosed as HIV positive, significant others such as parents, siblings, spouses, lovers, and children are affected by the diagnosis. The most frequent sources of stress among family members have been fears of contracting AIDS and a sense of helplessness and grieving (Frierson, Lippmann, & Johnson, 1987). Although fears of contracting AIDS can be somewhat alleviated by factual information, families often feel a loss of control, given the unpredictability in the relationship between exposure to the virus and the latency to development of the syndrome.

Although the issues that impact on men may facilitate the development of investigations of psychological distress for women, women may face very different issues when diagnosed with HIV. For example, currently most studies involving group support for HIV patients have drawn mainly upon homosexual male subjects; thus HIV-infected women may have difficulty finding support systems. Women, in addition to having to worry about contracting the virus that causes AIDS themselves, have the unique and added burden of the possibility of transmitting the virus to their children. The majority of pediatric AIDS cases are contracted from the mother; the ethnic distribution of pediatric AIDS cases reflects the proportions found for adult women. Given that this issue is unique to women—and that the consequences of HIV infection can cause tremendous guilt in and of themselves, but are exacerbated when a woman feels responsible not only for her own diagnosis but also for that of one or more of her children— issues of pediatric AIDS will be discussed briefly.

PEDIATRIC AIDS

Given the rapidly rising number of women who are seropositive, the estimated rates of pediatric cases have also increased. As of July, 1992, there were 3,898 cases of pediatric AIDS reported to the CDC (1992). Based on projected estimates of rates of reproductive females who will test HIV positive, it is predicted that the number of cases of pediatric AIDS in the United States will increase dramatically over the next several years. As we shall see in the following sections, this will have repercussions not only for health service care, but also for psychological and social services for both mothers and their children. How the virus is transmitted from mother to child will first be described. In addition, diagnosis of HIV in infants and the course of the disease in children will be discussed, keeping in mind the psychological consequences these issues may have for mothers.

Maternal Transmission

Research on maternal transmission of HIV indicates that it is possible for the virus to be transmitted vertically from mother to child, either in utero, intrapartum, or possibly postpartum as a result of breastfeeding. (HIV infection of a newborn may be termed congenital or perinatal, but since the timing and mechanism of transmittal are unknown, the more general term of vertical transmission may be more appropriate.) Although the general timing is unknown, intrauterine transmission may occur early in a pregnancy, as suggested by studies showing viral recovery from fetal products at abortion (Sprecher, Soumenkoff, Puissant, & Degueldre, 1986). The risk of transmission during the delivery process has not been established, although the use of cesarian section has been hypothesized to reduce the rate of transmission, given that HIV has been detected in vaginal secretions and cervical mucous (Lee, Tsai, & Wu, 1988). Finally, although HIV has been cultured from the cell-free fraction of breast milk from seropositive women (Thiry et al., 1985), mothers with HIV have breastfed their babies without infecting them (Halsey, cited in Nicholas, Sondheimer, Willoughby, Yaffe, & Katz, 1989). Obviously, further investigation is needed, although current recommendations are that seropositive women refrain from breastfeeding (Rodgers, 1988).

If a pregnant woman is HIV seropositive, does she always transmit the virus to her infant? Original studies estimated the rate of vertical transmission of infection from women with the disease or at risk for it to offspring to be as high as 65% (Minkoff, Nanda, Menez, & Fikrig, 1987). However, more recent studies in both Europe and the United States estimate the rate of vertical transmission to be 24–40% (Andiman et al., 1990; Blanche et al., 1989; Johnson et al., 1989). Factors hypothesized to influence in-utero transmission include preterm delivery, increased maternal age, immune and clinical status of the mother, level of HIV infection and the virulence of the infecting strain, infection with other viruses, complications of pregnancy, premature delivery, and fetal immune status (Andiman & Modlin, 1991; Lambert, 1990).

Diagnosis of Infants

Complicating the possibly bleak picture for infants born to seropositive or high-risk mothers is that in contrast to adults—in whom infection with HIV can be diagnosed simply by detection of antibodies or antigens specific for HIV—serological diagnosis in infants is more difficult due to the fact that maternal antibodies specific for HIV cross the placenta. The length of time maternal antibodies persist is not known, although it has been estimated that 15 months are required before demonstration of antibody against HIV indicates infant infection (CDC, 1987). Viral cultures, antigen determination, and the early identification of infant anti-HIV antibodies have not provided reliable diagnostic results. Currently, the status of an asymptomatic child born to a seropositive mother can only be confirmed following 15 to 18 months of evaluation, with the disappearance of maternal antibodies (Hankins, 1990; Nadal et al., 1989). Developing sensitive diagnostic tests that can identify HIV infection in early infancy is important in order that children be eligible for more and earlier treatment interventions.

Course of the Disease in Infants

Even more alarming than the new estimates on pediatric AIDS cases in the United States are the facts that (1) the incubation period for perinatally acquired illness is usually much shorter than in adults, and (2) postdiagnosis survival is also briefer than for adults, with approximately one-half of pediatric cases dying within 9 months of diagnosis (Cooper, Pelton, & LeMay, 1988). In addition, there is a wide spectrum of presentations of HIV-mediated disease in children (Nicholas et al., 1989; Shannon & Amman, 1985). Infants born to mothers with HIV are more often premature and have lower birth weights in comparison to infants of seronegative mothers; this is even more likely to occur in seropositive mothers with advanced HIV-related illness (Ryder et al., 1989).

Given the variety and severity of illness that a child with HIV may experience, the ability of mothers who are likely themselves to be seropositive to care for their children also becomes an issue. As Abrams and Nicholas (1990) have noted, pediatric HIV is basically a family disease. Approximately 81% of pediatric AIDS cases reported to the CDC identify perinatal exposure as the mode of transmission. In one of their studies, Abrams and Nicholas reported that of 200 children identified as having HIV and tracked since 1985 only 46% were able to remain with a natural parent. This was because many of the mothers were actively using drugs and were unable to provide for the complicated needs of an HIV-infected child.

Even if a mother is able to care for her HIV-infected child—since the incubation period for perinatally acquired illness is usually much shorter than in adults and the postdiagnosis survival is also briefer than for adults—this only means that a great many mothers will have to watch their children die, knowing that they passed the virus to the child. In addition, an HIV-infected mother caring for a child with AIDS can only help be reminded that she is also facing serious illness and death.

PREVENTION AND TREATMENT

The issues of prevention and treatment for HIV are multifaceted and complex. As can be seen from previous sections of this chapter, there are not only medical issues involved in prevention and treatment, but also serious psychological and social issues. In addition, the word "treatment" can be used to describe the course taken by medical or mental health personnel from the time a person comes in and asks for HIV testing through the entire course of post-test results, asymptomatic seropositive status, symptomatic seropositive status, and full-blown AIDS. This section will focus mainly on prevention of HIV infection and psychological treatment for women diagnosed with HIV; a thorough review of counseling issues for pre- and post-HIV testing and the ethical issues surrounding such testing is available (Mantell, Thomas, Rosenthal, Solomon, & Moss, 1988).

The emphasis throughout this section will be on psychosocial issues pertinent to prevention and treatment of HIV infection for women.

Prevention Strategies for Women at Risk for HIV Infection

Although there is no vaccine or prophylactic therapy for HIV, there have been some effective prevention modalities developed for certain populations. The major prevention intervention involves teaching people how to modify their behavior to reduce risk of infection; several surveys have reported decreased risk behavior among gay men in AIDS epicenters following intervention (e.g., Kelly, St. Lawrence, Hood, & Brasfield, 1989; McKusick, Coates, Wiley, Morin, & Stall, 1987). However, as Ickovics and Rodin (1992) have noted, the epidemiologic shifts and projections regarding HIV infection among women raises questions regarding the generalizability of prevention findings with other populations to women. Prevention interventions designed specifically for women are just beginning, and may offer unique challenges to investigators in the field.

Issues of Condom Use among Women   In a recent survey of 759 women attending contraceptive care clinics, 37% expressed uncertainty of their ability to initiate condom use, and 22% believed they would be "too embarrassed" to purchase condoms in a drug store (Valdiserri, Arena, Proctor, & Bonati, 1989). The majority of the women in this study were white (85 percent), and over half were between the ages of 19 and 25. Only 15% were married, and another 15% were living with a male partner. Although a majority of women endorsed condom use as an important means to reduce AIDS, only 14% reported using condoms in addition to another form of contraception to prevent sexually transmitted diseases. Women who did not use condoms felt that most men did not like them and that intercourse would not be enjoyable. These women also were less likely to report peer acceptance of condoms. Murphy et al. (1993) found in a sample of 188 inner-city women that only 14% of the sample reported using condoms for birth control; "no form of birth control" was chosen by 23% of the sample as the type of birth control most often used, and this outranked condom use. This lack of condom use despite knowledge of risk is especially true of young women (Cochran, Keidan, & Kalechstein, 1990).

Male cooperation is critical for maintained condom use, and therefore the empowerment of women by development of a prophylaxis that relies on the woman and is under her control is seen as a top priority by some investigators (Stein, 1990). Stein (1990) has argued that the most effective methods of pregnancy prevention have depended upon women, and that these findings should convince us that women-controlled barrier methods should be developed. Other studies confirm the need for development of barriers that are woman controlled. Of 112 women interviewed in Rwanda, 75% opted for a method that they could use themselves without obtaining male cooperation for AIDS risk reduction (e.g., a spermicidal cream); only 25% opted for condom use (Allen et al., 1988). However, the efficacy of spermicidal cream to prevent HIV infection is not known. Although the spermicide nonoxynol-9 at certain concentrations has been reported to inactivate the HIV virus in vitro (Hicks et al., 1985), more studies are needed in this area. There is a female condom under preliminary development (Leeper, 1990), and studies involving over 500 couples in close to 5,000 uses have been conducted. Exposure to semen was significantly less than for male condoms, and the female condom was reported to be well accepted by those concerned about AIDS.

Literature on sexual attitudes and responses in females may facilitate effective interventions. Kyes (1990) reported that viewing a film of an erotic demonstration of condom placement had a positive effect on attitudes toward condoms and an increased willingness in women to have their partners use them. This change in attitudes was found for women regardless of whether they were classified by a sexual opinion survey as erotophilic or erotophobic. M. Z. Solomon and DeJong (1989) have also reported that a soap opera style videotape that portrays using condoms as socially acceptable, normative behavior can improve attitudes regarding condom use, especially among subjects with less formal education and subjects who had never used condoms.

Cultural and Social Issues Related to Intervention   Interventions targeted at women need to be consistent with the cultural and social context in which these women live. For example, according to Cochran and Mays (1989), some ethnic women report experiencing verbal and physical abuse when they advocate condom usage; among some cultural groups this issue may be considered the male's province. In many Latin American communities, it is not considered appropriate for women to discuss sex (Worth & Rodriguez, 1987). Female attractiveness is equated with sexual inexperience; thus a woman prepared to use condoms may be perceived as unattractive and promiscuous. This becomes something of a double-bind, because if the man proposes measures for safer sex, the woman may perceive herself as a sexual conquest rather than a potential marriage partner.

One major issue among the growing HIV population of women is that of poverty. Many minority women have no or inadequate health insurance. Single women with children face the added issue that many services offered do not provide child care and thus may effectively be useless to these women. In addition, AIDS prevention may hardly be of concern to a woman who is struggling to maintain a minimal existence for herself and her children. Factors other than poverty and poor education may prevent women from seeking education or health care related to HIV, such as language barriers or a reluctance in some cultures to obtain information from outside the family or ethnic group. In addition, anecdotal report suggests that many of these women do not perceive themselves to be at risk; therefore, they may have stronger denial reactions when diagnosed.

When women contract HIV, they may be exposed to social ostracism and blamed for infecting children, or, if they are prostitutes, for infecting men. Such social ostracism will exacerbate the problems such women already face. Women may also find it more difficult to obtain psychological support services since many programs have targeted gay men almost exclusively thus far. As noted earlier, most HIV-infected women are poor, minority, and uneducated. However, women with HIV may be extremely diverse in cultural and ethnic background. Their diversity may increase their problems in finding social services, create further social isolation, and make it difficult for them to form a community as gay men have. Tunstall et al. (1990) found that among 63 high risk women, feelings of inertia, isolation, and stigmatization diminished their sense of self-efficacy and thus impeded risk reduction or development of social networks where education could be obtained. Similarly, Nyamathi (1991) found that among 327 women recruited from a drug program and homeless shelters, high risk behaviors were less frequent among women with high self-esteem.

A number of medical treatments now recommended for males and females (e.g., cholesterol-lowering drugs, antidepressants, AIDS interventions) have been studied practically exclusively in men. In a society in which many states do not provide any public funds for abortion, and little money is spent to research effective contraceptives with fewer side effects, low-income women in the United States do not even have control over their bodies. Added to this, their poverty prevents them from making up for these deficits: currently three out of five of the nation's 16 million "displaced homemakers" live at or below the poverty level; women still earn only $0.70 to a male's $1.00 in stereotypically female jobs (Ehrenreich, 1990). The findings in this section read like a horror story for women; the lack of empowerment and poverty among women in this country and other countries has always been a problem for appropriate health care, but has worsened now that AIDS is increasing among females. Providing AIDS prevention programs is only a modest part of what needs to be accomplished for such women, and no programs will have an impact in the AIDS crisis unless these cultural and socioeconomic factors are taken into account.

Findings from Other Behavioral Medicine Research Areas   Research findings from a variety of health and social topic areas may be relevant to the preparation of prevention interventions for women at risk for HIV infection. For example, gender differences in coping skills should influence development of prevention interventions for women. In a review of the stress, coping, and social support systems related to women (L. J. Solomon & Rothblum, 1986), it was noted that women use less active coping strategies than men do. Women have been found to use selective ignoring, which can exacerbate stress; women are also more likely to use avoidance as a strategy. These gender differences, with women using more passive coping styles that may be associated with more psychological distress, should be addressed when developing AIDS prevention treatment for women. In addition, women who alter their sexual behavior have been found to be more sexually experienced than those women who have not reduced risk; the best predictor is a history of being treated for a sexually transmitted disease (Cochran & Peplau, cited in Cochran & Mays, 1989). Thus women who are vulnerable from personal experience are more likely to alter behavior, whereas predictors of behavior change in men have been found to be related to cognitions (e.g., perceptions of being at risk). This finding receives some confirmation from a study conducted by Middlestadt and Fishbein (1990), in which intention to use a condom was assessed among 101 female university students. Intention was predominantly under normative (subjective norm) control among sexually experienced women; intention was primarily under attitudinal control (attitude toward the behavior) among sexually inexperienced women.

Research Findings on Prevention Intervention for Women   There appear to be few published studies of the efficacy of prevention interventions developed specifically for women. A brief description of an AIDS education program in county Woman, Infants, and Children (WIC) clinics has been published (McDonald, Kleppel, & Jenssen, 1990), but no evaluation of the program has been conducted. The intervention consisted of a brief 20-minute class in which a video that presented information on AIDS was shown, and the class ended with the distribution of safe-sex kits.

One prevention program focused on young adults of both sexes (Cochran et al., 1990), but it was conducted with a well-educated sample of college students, and 44% of the sexually experienced subjects reported during follow-up that they had not changed their behavior to reduce HIV infection. A program to change high-risk sexual behaviors of female sexual partners of intravenous drug users was somewhat successful (Trapido, Chitwood, McKay, & Vogel, 1990). Almost half of the subjects made positive changes in sexual behaviors; however, 10% of the women made changes that increased their risks for AIDS and the remainder made no changes at all. The most significant change was reduction of the number of sexual partners. Kelly et al. (1993) offered a behavior change intervention to inner-city women who were sexually active with multiple or high-risk partners. Women who received the HIV/AIDS intervention increased in risk knowledge, and accuracy of risk estimation at three-month follow-up, relative to women in the control group. More importantly, occurrences of unprotected sexual intercourse significantly declined and condom use increased from 20% to 60% of all intercourse occasions among intervention group participnats; women in the comparison group showed no change.

Among sex partners of intravenous drug users, 65% reported that family members were their closest friends, and 50% reported that their families and children were the most important things in their life (Pappas, Gaulard, Winterhalter, & Christen, 1990). Sabogal, Sabogal, and Gilad (1990) reported high levels of acceptance and comprehension of a program offered to 156 Hispanic women. The program involved using Hispanic models within a family context in their education program. Thus, for some populations, prevention efforts that emphasize family will be more effective than general prevention programs.

Proposed Prevention Intervention for Women   Given the information thus far, and the fact that we are not at a stage in which a totally effective woman-controlled barrier method is available, *what* prevention methods should be taught to women at risk for HIV infection and *how* should they be presented? AIDS education and prevention strategies that are appropriate for gay men are not always appropriate for heterosexual women. Women at risk for HIV infection could be recruited through clinics where they currently receive their primary health care and placed in group sessions focusing on AIDS education. The use of their primary clinic as the site of recruitment and counseling is thought to be essential since women will be familiar with the clinic and potentially less threatened if they are referred to a group by their own physician (e.g., when they come in for sexually transmitted disease testing). McDonald, Kleppel, and Jenssen (1990) reported that using the WIC clinic to reach possible high-risk women was effective. Kelly and St. Lawrence (1988) have already noted the importance of community educational programs using innovative outreach programs.

Components comprising an education/prevention/treatment intervention for women should include AIDS education, group social support, assertion training with behavioral rehearsal, and problem solving. One particularly strong component of any planned prevention package is that of assertiveness training: in group sessions women can practice bringing up topics that may be traditionally the male's province, such as safe sex practices and the use of condoms. Choi, Wermuth, and Sorensen (1990) found that recent discussion of condom use with a partner and partner's neutral or positive reaction was significantly associated with condom use among women who had intravenous drug users as sexual partners. These two foci—a group intervention format and emphasis on behavioral rehearsal—are consistent with previous studies with other at-risk populations.

Coates et al. (1988) outlined three important dimensions to peer support: general social support, peer expectations and support for behavior change, and the availability of support when needed. Lack of social support has been found to be related to high-risk sex. In addition, Coates et al. stated that having the social skills necessary to negotiate with partners is necessary to reduce high risk practices. This emphasis on skills training is also consistent with studies among gay men indicating that AIDS awareness *alone* may show little corresponding reduction in risk behavior—although there is some evidence that knowledge among intravenous drug users may be associated with lowered risk behaviors (Feldman & Biernacki, 1987; Valdiserri et al., 1989). Currently, the risk-reduction intervention for urban women at the Medical College of Wisconsin's Community Health Behavior Program cited above (Kelly et al., 1993) includes the components suggested in this section. Preliminary data indicates that socially disadvantaged women can be assisted in making changes to reduce risk for contracting HIV infection. The treatment protocol stems from a 1986 National Institute of Mental Health funded research project ("Behavioral Training to Reduce AIDS Risk Activities") called Project ARIES (Kelly et al., 1990), which was developed to study the efficacy of an intervention program to assist groups of gay or bisexual men in reducing behaviors that placed them at high risk for HIV infection.

Treatment for HIV-Seropositive Women

As the number of HIV-infected women grows, so will the need for treatment focused specifically for this population. The psychological issues facing women who are diagnosed with HIV have been described. In addition, literature on other serious illnesses and stressful life events indicate the need for social support among women diagnosed with HIV. It appears that seropositive males who are involved in socially supportive community organizations are better able to cope (Krieger, 1988; Mandel, Coates, Wiley, Bart, & Woods, 1987). Clinical interventions that have been found useful for other illnesses—such as relaxation training, self-guided imagery, thought stopping, positive self-talk, and goal setting—may be helpful. In an evaluation of stress management with a group of male HIV patients, Coates, Morin, & McKusick (1987) found that treatment reduced anxiety and depression and lowered rates of high-risk behavior.

One problem unique to women who are diagnosed with HIV is the issue of whether to continue a pregnancy or to begin one, if one was planned. Because women have constituted a small percentage of total HIV patients, few studies have examined women's attitudes regarding this issue. Johnstone et al. (1990) reported that knowledge during pregnancy that they had HIV antibodies and subsequent counseling did not alter women's original intentions regarding continuing or terminating their pregnancy. When a woman wanted the pregnancy, this took precedence over other considerations. The authors speculated that the women may have been influenced by their own lack of clinical illness and the possibility that their child would not be infected. In another study of 1,860 New York City women, among those with perceived risks for AIDS, 83% said they would terminate a pregnancy if they tested HIV positive (Balanon, Fordyce, & Stoneburner, 1990). Women with negative attitudes toward people with AIDS, unmarried women, and non-Hispanic women were more likely to say they would terminate pregnancy. However, only 35% of women actually at risk for AIDS expected to terminate such a pregnancy. The obstacles that women who are seropositive and pregnant may face are immense, and counseling that clearly delineates these obstacles is imperative so that women can make an informed decision as to whether to continue with their pregnancy.

Although stress management, social support, and counseling for depression and anxiety may be of primary importance for HIV-infected women who are asymptomatic, there may be further complications when patients become ill. Symptomatic patients become acutely aware of their physical symptoms. In addition, manifestations of the disease such as lesions, "wasting," and hair loss can take a tremendous toll on self-image (Beckett & Rutan, 1990), and these may be especially salient issues for women. Symptomatic patients may feel more and more out of control. Coates and Lo (1990) have suggested that a regimen of good health habits (e.g., smoking cessation, physical activity, decrease in alcohol and drug use) may give patients a sense of control and possibly improve quality of life. Kelly and St. Lawrence (1988) have also emphasized establishment of a sense of control and, in addition to suggestions made by Coates and Lo, recommended that patients follow through with therapy tasks, adopt healthful nutrition and rest patterns, and avoid sexual or drug use practices that could result in further re-exposure to help foster a sense of control. Even though this does not alter disease progression, these changes may lower susceptibility to certain opportunistic infections. Given that there have so far been few controlled studies of psychotherapy methods with seropositive women, an approach that encompasses all of the components reviewed here will probably be more effective than one that focuses exclusively on a single component.

FUTURE RESEARCH DIRECTIONS

As can be seen throughout this entire review of the psychological impact of AIDS on women's health, many important research questions have not yet been addressed. First, further research needs to be conducted on the transmission rates of HIV, as well as the factors that influence transmission probability. Second, although common psychological themes among HIV seropositive males have been investigated, much less research has focused on females with HIV. Gender differences in this area need to be explored so that appropriate psychotherapies can be developed. Third, development of a reliable, woman-controlled prophylaxis is an important issue. Fourth, developing reliable diagnostic tests that can identify HIV infection in early infancy is critical, in order to begin early treatment and establish eligibility for pediatric enrollment into clinical drug trials, which may be the only access route to free treatment for many children. Fifth—and possibly most important—prevention interventions specifically for women need to be developed and evaluated in methodologically sound, controlled studies. These interventions need to have a primary goal of sensitivity to the cultural and social context of the women they serve. Effective prevention efforts among gay men have appeared to help to slow down the spread of the virus. Therefore, finding efficacious prevention for women should perhaps be of top priority for researchers. Sixth, and finally, as increasing numbers of women are diagnosed with HIV, there will unfortunately be a female population available for whom to evaluate therapies aimed specifically at female patients who are asymptomatic and symptomatic. Progression of HIV infection in women needs to be tracked, and effective counseling for women to improve quality of life and to decrease psychosocial stress is urgently needed. As with prevention efforts, these approaches need to be sensitive to gender, cultural, and socioeconomic issues. Such psychological intervention will indeed be needed, to help the thousands of women that are estimated will be diagnosed in the United States in the 1990s.

REFERENCES

Abrams, E. J., & Nicholas, S. W. (1990). Pediatric HIV infection. *Pediatric Annals, 19*, 482–487.

Allen, S., Serufilira, A., Carael, M., Nsengumuremgi, F., Fortney, J., Black, D., & Hulley, S. (1988, June). *Acceptability of condoms and spermicides in population-based sample of urban Rwandan women.* Paper presented at the Fourth International Conference on AIDS, Stockholm.

Andiman, W. A., & Modlin, J. F. (1991). Vertical transmission. In P. A. Pizzo & C. M. Wilfert (Eds.), *Pediatric AIDS: The challenge of HIV infection in infants, children, and adolescents* (pp. 140–155). Baltimore: Williams & Wilkins.

Andiman, W. A., Simpson, J., Olson, B., Dember, L., Silva, T. J., & Miller, G. (1990). Rate of transmission of human immunodeficiency virus type 1 infection from mother to child and short-term outcome of neonatal infection. *American Journal of Diseases in Children, 144*, 758–766.

Balanon, A., Fordyce, E. J., & Stoneburner, R. (June, 1990). *AIDS concerns and women's reproductive intentions: HIV testing and pregnancy choices.* Paper presented at the Sixth International Conference on AIDS, San Francisco.

Beckett, A., & Rutan, J. S. (1990). Treating persons with ARC and AIDS in group psychotherapy. *International Journal of Group Psychotherapy, 40*, 19–29.

Blanche, S., Rouzioux, C., Guihard Moscata, M.L., Veber, F., Mayaux, M.J., Jacomet, C., Tricoire, J., Deville, A., Vial, M., Firtion, G., de Crepy, A., Douard, D., Robin, M., Courpotin, C., Ciraru-Vigneron, N., le Deist, F., Griscelli, C., & The HIV Infection in Newborns French Collaborative Study Group. (1989). A prospective study of infants born to women seropositive for human immunodeficiency virus type 1. *New England Journal of Medicine, 320*, 1643–1648.

Brown, G. R., & Rundell, J. R. (1990). Prospective study of psychiatric morbidity in HIV-seropositive women without AIDS. *General Hospital Psychiatry, 12*, 30–35.

Centers for Disease Control (1992). 1993 Revised classification system for HIV infection and expanded surveillance case definition for AIDS among adolescents and adults. *Morbidity and Mortality Weekly Report, 41*, RR-17.

Centers for Disease Control (1992, July). *HIV/AIDS surveillance report.* Atlanta: Author.

Centers for Disease Control (1991). *HIV/AIDS surveillance report: Year end edition.* Atlanta: Author.

Centers for Disease Control. (1989). Update: Heterosexual transmission of acquired immunodeficiency syndrome and human immunodeficiency virus infection—United States. *Morbidity and Mortality Weekly Report, 34,* 507–514.

Centers for Disease Control. (1987). Revised case definition for acquired immunodeficiency syndrome. *Morbidity and Mortality Weekly Report, 36,* 142–145.

Chiasson, M. A., Stoneburner, R. L., Lifson, A. R., Hildebrandt, D. S., Ewing, W. E., Schultz, S., & Jaffe, H. W. (1990). Risk factors for human immunodeficiency virus type 1 (HIV-1) infection in patients at a sexually transmitted disease clinic in New York City. *American Journal of Epidemiology, 131,* 208–220.

Chin, J. (1990). Current and future dimensions of the HIV/AIDS pandemic in women and children. *Lancet, 336,* 221–224.

Choi, K., Wermuth, L., & Sorensen, J. (1990, June). *Predictors of condom use among women sexual partners of intravenous drug users.* Paper presented at the Sixth International Conference on AIDS, San Francisco.

Chu, S. Y., Buehler, J. W., & Berkelman, R. L. (1990). Impact of the human immunodeficiency virus epidemic on mortality in women of reproductive age, United States. *Journal of the American Medical Association, 264,* 225–229.

Chuang, H. T., Devins, G. M., Hunsley, J., & Gill, M. J. (1989). Psychosocial distress and well-being among gay and bisexual men with human immunodeficiency virus infection. *American Journal of Psychiatry, 146,* 876–880.

Coates, T. J., & Lo, B. (1990). Counseling HIV seropositive patients: An approach for medical practice. *Western Journal of Medicine, 153,* 629–634.

Coates, T., J., Morin, S. F., & McKusick, L. (1987, June). *The efficacy of stress management in reducing high risk behavior and improving immune function in HIV antibody positive men.* Paper presented to the Third International Conference on AIDS, Washington, DC.

Cochran, S. D. (1987, June). *Psychosomatic distress and depressive symptoms among HTLV III/LAV seropositive, seronegative, and untreated homosexual men.* Paper presented at the Third International Conference on AIDS, Washington, DC.

Cochran, S. D., Keidan, J., & Kalechstein, A. (1990). Sexually transmitted diseases and acquired immunodeficiency syndrome: Changes in risk reduction behaviors among young adults. *Sexually Transmitted Diseases, 17,* 80–86.

Cochran, S. D., & Mays, V. M. (1989). Women and AIDS-related concerns: Roles for psychologists in helping the worried well. *American Psychologist, 44,* 529–535.

Cooper, E. R., Pelton, S. I., & LeMay, M. (1988). Acquired immunodeficiency syndrome: A new population of children at risk. *Pediatric Clinics of North America, 35,* 1365–1387.

Curran, J. W., Morgan, W. M., Starcher, E. T., Hardy, A. M., & Jaffee, H. W. (1985). Epidemiological trends of AIDS in the United States. *Cancer Research, 45,* 4602–4604.

Des Jarlais, D. C., Friedman, S. R., & Stoneburner, R. L. (1988). HIV infection and intravenous drug use: Critical issues in transmission dynamics, infection outcomes, and prevention. *Review of Infectious Diseases, 10,* 151–158.

Des Jarlais, D. C., Wish, E., Friedman, S. R., Stoneburner, R., Yancovitz, S. R., Midvan, D., El-Sadr, W., Brady, F., & Cuadrade, M. (1987). Intravenous drug use and heterosexual transmission of the human immunodeficiency virus: Current trends in New York City. *New York State Journal of Medicine, 87,* 283–286.

Dilley, J. W., Ochitill, H. N., Perl, M., & Volberding, P. A. (1985). Findings in psychiatric consultations with patients with acquired immune deficiency syndrome. *American Journal of Psychiatry, 142,* 82–85.

Ehrenreich, B. (1990, Fall). Sorry, sisters, this is not the revolution. *Time* (Special issue—Women: The road ahead), p. 15.

European Study Group. (1989). Risk factors for male to female transmission of HIV. *British Medical Journal, 298,* 411–415.

Feldman, H. W., & Biernacki, P. (1987, June). *AIDS community outreach for intravenous drug users].* Paper presented at the Third International Conference on AIDS, Washington, DC.

Fischl, M. A., Dickinson, G. M., Flanagan, S., & Fletcher, M. A. (1987, June). *Human immunodeficiency virus (HIV) among female prostitutes in south Florida.* Paper presented at the Third International Conference on AIDS, Washington, DC.

Fischl, M. A., Dickinson, G. M., Scott, G. B., Klimas, N., Fletcher, M. A., & Parks, W. (1987). Evaluation of heterosexual partners, children, and household contacts of adults with AIDS. *Journal of the American Medical Association, 257,* 640–644.

Frierson, R. L., Lippmann, S. B., & Johnson, J. (1987). AIDS: Psychological stresses on the family. *Psychosomatics, 28,* 65–68.

Giesecke, J., Scalia-Tomba, G., Hakansson, C., Karlsson, A., & Lidman, K. (1990). Incubation time of AIDS: Progression of disease in a cohort of HIV-infected homo- and bisexual men with known dates of infection. *Scandinavian Journal of Infectious Diseases, 22,* 407–411.

Glaser, J. B., Strange, T. J., & Rosati, D. (1989). Heterosexual human immunodeficiency virus transmission among the middle class. *Archives of Internal Medicine, 149,* 645–649.

Glasner, P. D., & Kaslow, R. A. (1990). The epidemiology of human immunodeficiency virus infection. *Journal of Consulting and Clinical Psychology, 58,* 13–21.

Groopman, J. E. (1985). Clinical spectrum of HTLV-III in humans. *Cancer Research, 45,* 4649–4651.

Guinan, M. E., & Hardy, A. (1987). Epidemiology of AIDS in women in the United States: 1981 through 1986. *Journal of the American Medical Association, 257,* 2039–2042.

Hankins, C. A. (1990). Issues involving women, children, and AIDS primarily in the developed world. *Journal of Acquired Immune Deficiency Syndromes, 3,* 443–448.

Haverkos, H. W., & Drotman, D. P. (1984). The epidemiology of the acquired immunodeficiency syndrome. *Diagnostic Immunology, 2,* 67–72.

Hicks, D. R., Martin, L. S., Getchell, J. P., Heath, J. L., Francis, D. P., McDougal, J. S., Curran, J. W., & Voeller, B. (1985). Inactivation of HTLV-III/LAV-infected cultures of normal human lymphocytes by nonoxynol-9 in vitro. [Letter to the editor]. *Lancet, 2,* 1422–1423.

Ickovics, J. R., & Rodin, J. (1992). Women and AIDS in the United States: Epidemiology, Natural History, and Mediating Mechanisms. *Health Psychology, 11,* 1–16.

Jaffe, H. W., Bregman, D. J., & Selik, R. M. (1985). Acquired immune deficiency syndrome in the United States: The first 1000 cases. *Journal of Infectious Diseases, 148,* 339–345.

Johnson, J. P., Nair, P., Hines, S. E., Seiden, S., Alger, L., Revie, D. R., O'Neil, K. M., & Hebel, R. (1989). Natural history and serologic diagnosis of infants born to human-immunodeficiency virus-infected women. *American Journal of Diseases in Children, 143,* 1147–1163.

Johnstone, F. D., Brettle, R. P., MacCallum, L. R., Mok, J., Peutherer, F., & Burns, S. (1990). Women's knowledge of their HIV antibody state: Its effect on their decision whether to continue the pregnancy. *British Medical Journal, 300,* 23–24.

Joseph, J. G., Montgomery, S., Kessler, R. C., Ostrow, D. G., Emmons, C. A., & Phair, J. P. (1987, June). *Two-year longitudinal study of behavioral risk reductions in a cohort of homosexual men.* Paper presented at the Third International Conference on AIDS, Washington, DC.

Kelley, P. W., Miller, R. N., Pomerantz, R., Wann, F., Brundage, J. F., & Burke, D. S. (1990). Human immunodeficiency virus seropositivity among members of the active duty U.S. Army 1985–89. *American Journal of Public Health, 80,* 405–410.

Kelly, J. A., Murphy, D. A., Washington, C. D., Wilson, T. S., Koob, J. J., Davis, D. R., Ledezma, G., & Davantes, B. (1993). HIV/AIDS prevention for women seen in urban primary health care clinics: Effects of intervention to change high-risk sexual behavior patterns. Manuscript submitted for publication.

Kelly, J. A., & St. Lawrence, J. S. (1988). AIDS prevention and treatment: Psychology's role in the health crisis. *Clinical Psychology Review, 8,* 255–284.

Kelly, J. A., St. Lawrence, J. S., Brasfield, T. L., Hood, H. V., Bahr, G. R., & Stevenson, L. Y. (1990). *Behavioral group intervention to teach AIDS risk reduction skills.* Jackson, MS: University of Mississippi Medical Center.

Kelly, J. A., St. Lawrence, J. S., Hood, H. V., & Brasfield, T. L. (1989). Behavioral intervention to reduce AIDS risk activities. *Journal of Consulting and Clinical Psychology, 57,* 60–67.

Kelly, J. A., St. Lawrence, J. S., Hood, H. V., Smith, S., Jr., & Cook, D. J. (1988). Nurses' attitudes towards AIDS and homosexual patients. *Journal of Continuing Education in Nursing, 19,* 78–83.

Kelly, J. A., St. Lawrence, J. S., Smith, S., Hood, H. V., & Cook, D. L. (1987). Stigmatization of AIDS patients by physicians. *American Journal of Public Health, 77,* 789–791.

Krieger, I. (1988). An approach to coping with anxiety about AIDS. *Social Work, 33,* 263–264.

Kyes, K. B. (1990). The effect of a "safer sex" film as mediated by erotophobia and gender on attitudes toward condoms. *Journal of Sex Research, 27,* 297–303.

Lambert, J. S. (1990). Maternal and perinatal issues regarding HIV infection. *Pediatric Annals, 19,* 468–472.

Lee, S. D., Tsai, Y. T., & Wu, T. C. (1988). Role of cesarian section in prevention of mother-infant transmission of hepatitis B virus. *Lancet, 2,* 833–834.

Leeper, M. A. (June, 1990). *Update on the WPC-333 female condom.* Paper presented at the Sixth International Conference on AIDS, San Francisco.

Lewis, D. K, Watters, J. K, & Case, P. (1990). The prevalence of high-risk sexual behavior in male intravenous drug users with steady female partners. *American Journal of Public Health, 80,* 465–466.

Lifson, A. R., Rutherford, G. W., & Jaffe, H. W. (1988). The natural history of human immunodeficiency virus infection. *Journal of Infectious Diseases, 158,* 1360–1367.

Mandel, J. S., Coates, T. J., Wiley, J., Bart, T., & Woods, W. J. (1987, June). *Disclosure of health concerns and homosexuality among 671 men at risk of AIDS.* Paper presented at the Third International Conference on AIDS, Washington, DC.

Mantell, J. E., Thomas, P. A., Rosenthal, S., Solomon, K., & Moss, D. (1988). *HIV counseling and antibody testing of women and their sexual partners in the United States.* Unpublished manuscript. Available from Inter-Agency AIDS Planning and Research, New York City Department of Health.

Marmor, M., Krasinski, K., Sanchez, M., Cohen, H., Dubin, N., Weiss, L., Manning, A., Bebenroth, D., Saphier, N., Harrison, C., & Ribble, D. J. (1990). Sex, drugs, and HIV infection in a New York City hospital outpatient population. *Journal of Acquired Immune Deficiency Syndromes, 3,* 307–318.

McArthur, J. (1990). AIDS dementia: Your assessment can make all the difference. *RN, 53,* 36–41.

McCusker, J., Stoddard, A. M., Mayer, K. H., Zapka, J., Morrison, C., & Saltzman, S. D. (1988). Effects of HIV antibody test knowledge on subsequent sexual behaviors in a cohort of homosexually active men. *American Journal of Public Health, 78,* 462–467.

McDonald, M., Kleppel, L., & Jenssen, D. (1990). Developing AIDS education for women in county WIC clinics. *American Journal of Public Health, 80,* 1391–1392.

McKusick, L., Coates, T. J., Wiley, J. A., Morin, S. F., & Stall, R. (1987, June). *Prevention of HIV infection among gay and bisexual men: Two longitudinal studies.* Paper presented to the Third International Conference on AIDS, Washington, DC.

Middlestadt, S. E., & Fishbein, M. (June, 1990). *Factors influencing experienced and inexperienced college women's intentions to tell their partners to use condoms.* Paper presented at the Sixth International Conference on AIDS, San Francisco.

Minkoff, H., Nanda, D., Menez, R., & Fikrig, S. (1987). Pregnancies resulting in infants with acquired immunodeficiency syndrome or AIDS-related complex: Follow-up of mothers, children, and subsequently born siblings. *Obstetrics & Gynecology, 69,* 288–291.

Moss, A. R., & Bacchetti, P. (1989). Editorial review: Natural history of HIV infection. *AIDS, 3,* 55–61.

Murphy, D. A., Kelly, J. A., Washington, C. D., Wilson, S. T., Koob, J. J., Ledzema, G., Davantes, B. R., & Davis, D. R. (1993). *Psychological, behavioral, and relationship characteristics of inner-city women at risk for HIV infection.* Manuscript submitted for publication.

Nadal, D., Hunziker, U. A., Shupbach, J., Wetzel, J. C., Tomasik, Z., Jendis, J. B., Fanconi, A., & Seger, R. A. (1989). Immunological evaluation in the early diagnosis of prenatal or perinatal HIV infection. *Archives of Disease in Childhood, 64,* 6632–6669.

New York City Department of Health. (1989, February). *Report of the expert panel on HIV seroprevalence estimates and AIDS case projection methodologies.*

Nicholas, S. W., Sondheimer, D. L., Willoughby, A. D., Yaffe, S. J., & Katz, S. L. (1989). Human immunodeficiency virus infection in childhood, adolescence, and pregnancy: A status report and national research agenda. *Pediatrics, 83*, 293–308.

Niedt, G. W., & Shinnella, R. A. (1985). Acquired immunodeficiency syndrome: Clinicopathologic study of 56 autopsies. *Archives of Pathological Laboratory Medicine, 109*, 727–734.

Nyamathi, A. (1991). The relationship of resources to emotional distress, somatic complaints, and high risk behaviors in drug recovery and homeless minority women. *Research in Nursing and Health*, 14, 269–277.

Obtoby, M. J. (1990). Perinatally acquired himan immunodeficiency virus infection. *Pediatric Infectious Disease Journal, 9*, 609–619.

Padian, N., Marquis, L., Francis, D. P., Anderson, R. E., Rutherford, G. W., O'Malley, P. M., & Winkelstein, W. (1987). Male-to-female transmission of human immunodeficiency virus. *Journal of the American Medical Association, 258*, 788–790.

Padian, N., Shiboski, S., & Jewell, N. (1990, June). *The relative efficacy of female-to-male HIV sexual transmission*. Paper presented at the Sixth International Conference on AIDS, San Francisco.

Padian, N., Wiley, J., & Winkelstein, W. (1987, June). *Male-to-female transmission of human immunodeficiency virus (HIV): Current results, infectivity rates, and San Francisco population seroprevalence estimates*. Paper presented at the Third International Conference on AIDS, Washington, DC.

Pappas, L., Gaulard, J., Winterhalter, S., & Christen, P. (1990, June). *Survey of female sexual partners of male IDU's in preparation for HIV prevention campaign*. Paper presented at the Sixth International Conference on AIDS, San Francisco.

Peterman, T. A., Cates, Jr., W., & Curran, J. W. (1988). The challenge of human immunodeficiency virus (HIV) and acquired immunodeficiency syndrome (AIDS) in women and children. *Fertility and Sterility, 49*, 571–581.

Peterman, T. A., & Curran, J. W. (1986). Sexual transmission of human immunodeficiency virus. *Journal of the American Medical Association, 256*, 2222–2226.

Quinn, T. C., Cannon, R. O., Glasser, D., Groseclose, S. L., Brathwaite, W. S., Fauci, A. S., & Hook, E. W. (1990). The association of syphilis with risk of human immunodeficiency virus infection in patients attending sexually transmitted disease clinics. *Archives of Internal Medicine, 150*, 129–-1302.

Quinn, T. C., Groseclose, S. L., Spence, M., Provost, V., & Hook III, E. W. (1992). Evolution of the human immunodeficiency virus epidemic among patients attending sexually transmitted disease clinics: A decade of experience. *Journal of Infectious Diseases, 165*, 541–544.

Rodgers, M. R. (1988). Pediatric HIV infection: Epidemiology, etiopathogenesis, and transmission. *Pediatric Annals, 17*, 324–331.

Rothenberg, R., Woelfel, M., Stoneburner, R., Milberg, J., Parker, R., & Truman, B. (1987). Survival with the acquired immunodeficiency syndrome: Experience with 5833 cases in New York City. *New England Journal of Medicine, 317*, 1297–1302.

Ryder, R. W., Wato, N., Hassig, S. E., Behets, F., Rayfield, M., Ekungola, B., et al. (1989). Perinatal transmission of the human immunodeficiency virus type 1 to infants of seropositive women in Zaire. *New England Journal of Medicine, 320*, 1637–1642.

Sabogal, F., Sabogal, R., & Gilad, R. B. (1990, September). *Development of a culturally appropriate AIDS prevention guide for the Hispanic family.* Paper presented at the Annual Meeting of the American Public Health Association, New York, NY.

Shannon, K. M., & Amman, P. J. (1985). Acquired immune deficiency syndrome in childhood. *Journal of Pediatrics, 106,* 332–342.

Shapiro, C. N., Schulz, S. L., Lee, N. C., & Dondero, T. J. (1989). Review of human immunodeficiency virus infection in women in the United States. *Obstetrics and Gynecology, 74,* 800–808.

Solomon, L. J., & Rothblum, E. D. (1986). Stress, coping, and social support in women. *Behavior Therapist, 9,* 199–204.

Solomon, M. Z., & DeJong, W. (1989). Preventing AIDS and other STDs through condom promotion: A patient education intervention. *American Journal of Public Health, 79,* 453–458.

Sprecher, S., Soumenkoff, G., Puissant, F., & Degueldre, M. (1986). Vertical transmission of HIV in 15 week fetus [Letter to the editor]. *Lancet, 2,* 288–289.

Sterk, C. (1988). Cocaine and HIV seropositivity. *Lancet, 1,* 1052–1053.

Stein, Z. A. (1990). HIV prevention: The need for methods women can use. *American Journal of Public Health, 80,* 460–462.

Sweeney, P. A., Onorato, I. M., Allen, D. M., Byers, R. H., and the Field Services Branch (1992). Sentinel surveillance of human immunodeficiency virus infection in women seeking reproductive health services in the United States, 1988–1989. *Obstetrics and Gynecology, 79,* 503–510.

Thiry, L., Sprecher-Goldberger, S., Jonckheer, T., Levy, J., Van de Perre, P., Henrivaux, P., Cogniaux-LeClerc, J., & Clumeck, N. (1985). Isolation of AIDS virus from cell-free breast milk of three healthy virus carriers. *Lancet, 2,* 891–892.

Tindall, B., Barker, S., Donovan, B., Barnes, T., Roberts, J., Kronenberg, C., Gold, J., Penny, R., Cooper, D., & the Sydney AIDS Study Group. (1988). Characterization of the acute clinical illness associated with human immunodeficiency virus infection. *Archives of Internal Medicine, 148,* 945–949.

Trapido, E., Chitwood, D., McKay, C., & Vogel, J. (June, 1990). *AIDS risk behavior change in female sexual partners of IVDUs.* Paper presented at the Sixth International Conference on AIDS, San Francisco.

Tunstall, C., Cooper, F., Oliva, G., Stein, E., Kegeles, S., & Darney, P. (1990, June). *Addressing psychological barriers to the prevention of HIV infection in high-risk women.* Paper presented at the Sixth International Conference on AIDS, San Francisco.

Valdiserri, R. O., Arena, V. C., Proctor, D., & Bonati, F. A. (1989). The relationship between women's attitudes about condoms and their use: Implications for condom promotion programs. *American Journal of Public Health, 79,* 499–501.

Weinberg, D. S., & Murray, H. W. (1987). Coping with AIDS—The special problems of New York City. *New England Journal of Medicine, 317,* 1469–1473.

World Health Organization predicts up to 30 million world AIDS cases by year 2000. (1991, January). *The Nation's Health,* American Public Health Association, pp. 1, 8.

Worth, D., & Rodriguez, R. (1987). Latina women and AIDS. *SIECUS Report,* January-February, 5–7.

Part Six

Directions for Research in Women's Health

We began this book with a discussion of the impact of the male standard on women's health. In the final chapter of this book, Sheryle Gallant, Helen Coons, and Patricia Morokoff add to our understanding of the notion of the male standard and review several research areas to illustrate the negative impact adherence to this standard has had on the understanding of women's health.

To accomplish this, Gallant, Coons, and Morokoff discuss in detail the failure to consider gender differences in psychosocial measures of coping and social support. They provide a number of cogent examples of how a male-oriented perspective on research in these areas has led to a neglect of dimensions relevant to understanding women's health. For example, measures of coping have tended to confound emotion-focused coping—which women are more likely to use to cope with stress than men but which has been associated with greater distress—with psychopathology. However, some recent work indicates that emotion-focused coping, when separated from psychopathology, is linked with improved coping for women but not for men.

Gallant et al.'s review of the social support literature provides other examples of the failure to use the female experience to inform the measurement of social support. One example from this review focuses on the question, "Is number of visits with family members a good measure of social support, or do researchers need to look at whether those visits are 'obligatory' or 'discretionary'?'' Recent research suggests that obligatory visits are associated with greater distress and not social support. Thus, Gallant, Coons, and Morokoff use the failure to assess the full range of women's experience and to incorporate the female perspective into health research to exemplify the role of the male standard in impeding a fuller understanding of women's health.

Gallant, Coons, and Morokoff carefully document the recent and current interest on a national, governmental level in redressing the gender bias in research and in increasing the number of women in scientific careers. They also review contemporary areas of specific progress and concern regarding women's health, particularly the areas of breast cancer and AIDS. Nevertheless, they make painfully clear that if the barriers to the success of women in scientific careers are not understood and removed, it is unlikely that sufficient numbers of women will be available to undertake the research necessary to understand more fully women's health from a woman's perspective. Finally, Gallant, Coons, and Morokoff point out that despite the current efforts to gain a better understanding of gender differences in health and health behaviors, researchers will need to adjust their methodologies to permit consideration of the multiple interacting factors influencing health and health behaviors.

Chapter 12

Psychology and Women's Health: Some Reflections and Future Directions

Sheryle J. Gallant
Helen L. Coons
Patricia J. Morokoff

INTRODUCTION

Women's health issues have been the subject of increasing attention during the last several years. This book attests to the growth of behavioral science research in this area. In the past 2 years, several leading psychological and medical journals have published special issues on women's health (e.g., *Health Psychology*, 1991, Vol. *10(2)*; *Journal of the American Medical Association*, 1992, Vol. *268[B]*), and new journals devoted to women's health have appeared (e.g., *Journal of Women's Health*, published by M. A. Liebert, and *Women's Health Issues*, published by the Jacobs Institute of Women's Health). In addition, groups of scholars and professionals have formed to advocate research and policy on

A similar analysis could be developed for behavioral measures. For example, much of the research suggesting the benefits of physical fitness in improving overall health and reducing the risk of cardiovascular disease and other diseases has investigated exercise in men, and the standard measures for assessing activity level and fitness were developed from that perspective. A. C. King (1991) has discussed the need to develop measures sensitive to women's physical activity patterns and experiences. For many women this involves unscheduled, home-based, intermittent short periods of exercise, and lighter, more diverse forms of daily activity (e.g., child care, household chores), rather than the programmed high intensity endurance exercise that has been the primary focus of intervention research.

women's health that reflect the importance of psychosocial and behavioral as well as biomedical factors (see, e.g., Society for the Advancement of Women's Health Research, 1991; Howes, 1992). Several major conferences on women's health have been held (e.g., the National Institutes of Health 1980–1991 series on women and health and the National Heart, Lung, and Blood Institute 1991 Conference on Women, Behavior, and Cardiovascular Disease), and the American Psychological Association Committee on Women is planning a National Conference on Psychology and Women's Health for 1994.

The demand for greater attention to women's health issues has come from several domains, including the lay public, the Women's Congressional Caucus, and investigators in the behavioral, social and biomedical sciences. This interest has spurred new initiatives in research and pressured major funding agencies into paying greater attention to diseases and conditions that affect women. Outcomes of this effort include the Office of Research on Women's Health (ORWH) that has been established within the National Institutes of Health (NIH), and the plans that are underway for a large clinical trial (the Women's Health Initiative) that will focus on three of the most important health problems of adult women: breast cancer, cardiovascular disease, and osteoporosis (Healy, 1991a; Kirschstein, 1991). In addition, there is a recognized need to increase the number of women researchers in health and to address barriers to advancement to high decision-making roles (Healy, 1992b). There is also interest in establishing a women's health specialty in medicine (Johnson, 1992). In a recent directive, the Senate Appropriations Labor Health and Human Services Subcommittee requested a study of medical school curricula to determine the extent of coverage of women's health issues and to formulate recommendations for a model curriculum that includes attention to behavioral factors (1992, pp. 142–143).

Given the surge of activity related to women's health issues, it is appropriate to take stock and reflect upon where we are headed. The goals of this chapter are: (1) to review important changes taking place relating to the creation of the Office of Research on Women's Health and the Women's Health Initiative; (2) to discuss methodological and research directions for studying psychosocial factors in women's health; (3) to highlight understudied populations of women at risk for physical and psychosocial problems; (4) to examine some important gender issues that must be addressed to promote the study of women's health; and (5) to examine factors affecting career success of women researchers.

RESEARCH ON WOMEN'S HEALTH:
PAST AND PRESENT

Broad-based interest and support for research on women's health is new. Researchers, including psychologists, working in this area can easily recall when the topic was considered non-mainstream and of relatively little importance, and when those doing the work were often viewed as having a political rather than a scientific agenda. Currently, research on women's health issues and gender differences in health has a higher priority and is more often seen as a legitimate focus of study. The change that is underway reflects greater awareness of the extent to which health problems specific to women have been overlooked (Cotton, 1990; Healy, 1991b). Professional and advocacy groups have lobbied Congress to mandate that NIH research priorities and funding practices insure that women's health concerns are addressed. There has also been a significant increase in media attention to the lack of funding for research in many areas of women's health, including breast and lung cancer and AIDS, where rates of disease are increasing. This attention has raised concern in the general public that important health problems of women are being ignored (e.g., Butler & Ohland, 1991; Neuman, 1992).

The exclusion of women from major health studies of conditions that affect both men and women has drawn sharp criticism from Congress and the scientific community (e.g., Society for the Advancement of Women's Health Research, 1992; Public Health Service Task Force, 1985). The failure to include women or sufficient numbers of women to assure that gender effects can be examined has resulted in confusion as to whether findings based on male samples can be generalized to women. Even many recent studies show this pattern (e.g., Cambien et al., 1992; Grobbee et al., 1990; Physician's Health Study Group, 1989; Jialal & Grundy, 1992). For example, a study of aspirin and cardiovascular disease involved 22,071 male physicians (Physician's Health Study Group, 1989). Results showed that those who took aspirin had a significantly lower incidence of heart attacks. However, since no women were included, it is unclear whether this preventive strategy would help, harm, or have no effect on women. Similarly, a recent Finnish study (Salonen et al., 1992) found a positive relationship between blood levels of iron and risk for heart attack in men. The implications of the findings for women are undetermined since no women were studied, but potentially important since women are often encouraged to consume iron supplements.

The Office of Research on Women's Health

Congressional pressure on NIH concerning the need for more attention to women's health issues and the problem of underrepresentation of women in major clinical trials led to the creation of the Office of Research on Women's Health (ORWH) within NIH. The ORWH was established in September 1990 in the office of the current director of NIH, Dr. Bernadine Healy. She is the first woman to head this institution and has publicly stated strong support for a women's health research agenda (e.g., Healy, 1991a, Healy, 1992a). The goal of the ORWH is to promote NIH efforts to address the health problems of women. The role of the office is to increase NIH supported research on women's health, to assure the participation of women in biomedical and biobehavioral research and clinical trials funded or conducted by NIH, and to develop opportunities and address issues related to the advancement of women in health science careers (Kirschstein, 1991; Pinn, 1992).

A focus on women's health issues within the NIH is of major importance. NIH is the principal federal agency supporting biomedical and behavioral research in the United States. Its budget in 1990 was over 7.5 billion. In 1985, a Public Health Service Task Force on Women's Health recommended that "biomedical and behavioral research should be expanded to insure emphasis on conditions and diseases unique to or more prevalent in women in all age groups" (Public Health Service Task Force, 1985). NIH policy urging that women be included in research has been "on the books" since 1986. However, a 1990 Government Accounting Office review found that NIH had made little progress in implementing the policy (Nadel, 1990). This led to a rewording of the requirement in stronger language and to a revision of NIH grant application forms to require information about the enrollment of women (National Institutes of Health [NIH] Guide to Grants and Contracts, 1990). These changes have increased the likelihood that future studies will have sufficient power in terms of the number of women participants to examine effects in women and to test for gender differences.

The Women's Health Initiative (WHI): Pluses and Minuses

The Women's Health Initiative (WHI), if implemented as planned, will be the largest study of its kind ever undertaken in the United States. It is of tremendous potential significance not only because of its size but because it specifically targets women's health problems. The WHI will focus on three leading causes of death and disability in women age 45 and older: cardiovascular disease (CVD), cancer (i.e., breast and colorectal), and osteoporosis. Specific attention will be given to including minority and underserved populations. The WHI is expected to take 10 to 14 years to complete and to cost about 600 million dollars. The study has three components: (1) a randomized clinical trial involving 60,000–70,000 women aged 50–79, that will test the efficacy of three preventive approaches (i.e., hormone replacement therapy (HRT), low-fat dietary pattern, and calcium/vitamin D supplementation); (2) a prospective epidemiological study of more than 100,000 women that will examine specific biomarkers for disease; and (3) a randomized community prevention study to assess the effects of a community-based intervention for risk factor modification and health promotion in adult women (Harlan & Kirschstein, 1991).

From a behavioral science prospective, there are several positive features of the WHI. One is the recruitment of adequate numbers of minority participants to allow comparison of results for these groups. Another is the focus on evaluating the efficacy of life style modifications (i.e., lower dietary fat and increased calcium) and the opportunity to assess the efficacy of these behavioral interventions compared to a pharmacological treatment (HRT). Each of the interventions may influence several outcomes. For example, HRT may affect occurrence of CVD and osteoporotic fractures; lower dietary fat may affect rates of CVD and breast and colorectal cancer; and calcium may impact both osteoporosis and colorectal cancer. Studying all three will give a more comprehensive picture of total benefits than would be gained if each were studied separately (Harlan & Kirschstein, 1991). In addition, because some women will receive all three interventions it will be possible to evaluate the combined benefit/risk ratio. Some positive effects may be additive (e.g., HRT and lower dietary fat effects on CVD, HRT and calcium effects on osteoporosis), or there may be risks that cancel out benefits, (e.g., HRT may decrease occurrence of CVD but increase rates of breast or endometrial cancer).

The role of psychosocial factors will be most broadly studied in the community trial, where there will be attempts to assess change in health cognitions, attitudes, and behaviors as a result of the intervention. The community trial will involve women of different age, ethnic, racial, and socioeconomic groups. Twenty matched pairs of communities with populations of 30,000 or more and with at least 30% minority or underserved will be randomly assigned to receive the intervention or serve as a comparison community. The intervention will involve educational, mass media, community organization, and environmental strategies directed toward improved physical activity levels, smoking cessation and the avoidance of passive smoke, healthy diet (lower fat and salt, increased fiber and calcium), and participation in recommended screenings (e.g., for breast and cervical cancer, blood pressure, and cholesterol). A stratified random sample of women will be surveyed before, halfway through, and at the end of the intervention to assess the degree of reduction in risk factors for CVD, cancer, and osteoporosis. One goal is to produce models of effective behavior change that encompass sociocultural factors and personal health behavior. Most studies of health promotion have involved samples of convenience drawn from clinics, hospitals, or other limited groups. This population-based study with its prospective design provides a unique opportunity to increase our understanding of important factors related to behavior change for women.

A public hearing on the WHI was held at NIH in the fall of 1991. Psychologists and other behavioral researchers raised concerns about the proposed design. One had to do with the design of the clinical trial. The dietary intervention has an exercise component, but because these are linked no information will be forthcoming concerning the potential beneficial effects of exercise or diet by itself. This is important given recent data suggesting no significant effects of a low-fat diet on risk for breast cancer (Willett et al., 1992). Further, research suggests that exercise may be an independent contributor to lower risk for CVD and other diseases (A. C. King, 1991), and exercise has been shown to increase maintenance of smoking cessation in women (Marcus et al., 1991). Since the population of women to be studied is one of the most sedentary and least often studied with regard to exercise, there is a strong rationale for evaluating the effects of exercise separately from those of diet.

Another concern was the lack of attention to important psychosocial variables that may contribute to the risk of cancer and heart disease, including stress, social support, and coping. These variables may be important mediators of the outcomes of the interventions. For example, high levels of stress might reduce the impact of HRT and diminish the effect of this intervention (American Psychological Association, 1991). Further, the role of social support in adherence is important. It has been shown to be a positive predictor of smoking abstinence, particularly for women (Gritz, 1991), and an important factor influencing adoption and maintenance of regular physical activity (A. C. King, 1991). Failure to measure these variables may make it difficult to evaluate or understand some findings from the interventions.

A third weakness of the proposed design from a psychological standpoint was that it did not provide for collecting data on depressive symptoms or other negative mood states. This is problematic for several reasons. There is evidence that depression is a risk factor for CVD morbidity and mortality in men, but it is unclear if a similar relationship exists for women (Carney, Freedland, Smith, Rich, & Jaffe, 1991). Further, it can be anticipated that HRT may increase depressive symptoms in some women and that increased physical activity may diminish negative psychological states. These would be important intermediate outcomes and ones that could affect rates of adherence. If not assessed, problems in the interpretation of study findings may result. In addition to depression, hostility has shown interesting but complex relationships to risk factors for CVD in women (e.g., Helmers, Krantz, Howell, Klein, & Baire, 1991; Siegman & Johnson, 1991). Suppressed anger has also been found to be a significant predictor of women's mortality, coronary heart disease(CHD), and cancer after adjusting for traditional risk factors (Harburg, Schonk, & DiFrancisco, 1991). The etiology of CVD, cancer, and osteoporosis is multifactorial, and traditional medical risk factors explain only a portion of the incidence. Considering the scope of the WHI, its projected costs, and the fact that this could be the only study of its kind for many years to come, it should provide an opportunity for examining the role of important psychosocial variables. Since at this time plans for the WHI are still being finalized, it is possible that some of the initial design will be remedied.

MULTIDIMENSIONAL MODELS AND METHODS IN RESEARCH ON WOMEN'S HEALTH

Much has been written about the need for biopsychosocial models of illness and disease. Such models would facilitate studying health problems in a contextual perspective that addresses the relationships between biomedical, psychological, and sociocultural factors (e.g., Engels, 1977; Lewontin, Rose, & Kamin, 1984). This is important for understanding disease processes and for developing prevention and treatment strategies that address differences as a function of gender, ethnicity, age, and socioeconomic factors. A contextual perspective is particularly appropriate in the area of women's health because it places relationships with others at the center rather than the periphery of factors that can affect health. However, actually doing this type of research poses a significant challenge for many health researchers who are unfamiliar with theories of women's development from a relational perspective or who are uncomfortable with the designs, methods, and procedures for data analysis that are required.

For many investigators the most familiar methodological designs are neat, simple experiments, and the most often used statistical procedures are those that look at part effects (i.e., varying one factor and keeping as many others as possible constant, varying X to see the impact on Y, Z, etc.). This approach has produced many important and useful findings. However, the integration of these findings is often difficult. In the area of women's health, one problem arising from this approach is the panoply of confusing and sometimes conflicting recommendations concerning certain health issues. For example, there is research that suggests that modest alcohol consumption may reduce the risk of heart disease. However, other data suggest that it may increase the risk of breast cancer. Similarly, there is research showing that lower fat in the diet may reduce the risk of CHD and breast cancer, but other data suggest no effect on breast cancer risk and suggest that people on a low-fat diet or cholesterol-lowering drugs may be more prone to violence and have a higher risk of suicide (e.g., Frick et al., 1987; Lipid Research Clinics Program, 1984). To address the relative risks and benefits, one must examine these findings in relationship to one another.

In his presidential address to the American Psychiatric Association, Lawrence Hartmann (1992) asserts that many of us are reductionists at heart and assume that an understanding of complex phenomena is most appropriately achieved by investigating component parts. Although most researchers would agree that nothing exists in isolation and that every organism is influenced by the context of which it is a part, accepting this complexity means abandoning a view of disease as involving simple cause and effect relationships, and embracing the notion of mutual bidirectional causality. This is the reality of our environment, but most of our models, including those most prominent in health research, are still solidly unidirectional, with greater emphasis placed on biological determinants than on psychosocial, relational, or cultural factors.

The importance of a contextual perspective for understanding aspects of women's health and well-being is suggested in research on the effects of circumstances and involvement with others. For example, Coyne and Smith (1991) found that the degree of distress wives experienced in relation to their husband's myocardial infarction (MI) was significantly influenced by the prior quality of their marital relationship and by the nature of their contact with medical personnel, as well as by the severity of the event and their coping responses. Similarly, work at the Karolinska Institute has demonstrated the value of a "holistic" approach that acknowledges on an operational level that individuals exist in a biological, sociocultural, and psychological context (Orth-Gomer, 1991). They have developed a multilevel model for investigating direct and indirect pathways in illness that includes sociocultural factors, psychosocial and behavioral variables, and physiological and somatic variables, with the endpoint being disease manifestation. Research on CVD has shown the utility of this approach for assessing multiple bidirectional effects and interactions. In one study of CVD mortality, low socioeconomic status effects were found to be mediated by lack of social support and social isolation. The effects of Type A behavior were not significant when looked at in isolation, but were strong predictors when entered into the model and were found to add to the effects of social isolation and to identify a group at extreme mortality risk. This study is important for demonstrating the utility of a multidimensional biopsychosocial approach. However, since only men were included, it is unclear what aspects of this model would be significant for women.

There are many examples where studying a problem from a contextual perspective may be crucial to achieving more positive health outcomes for women. However, one that appears particularly important at the present time is AIDS-risking behavior. Without explicit consideration of the context of sexual exploitation and violence that is the "home" environment of many women at high risk, programs cannot successfully address the barriers to change in substance abuse and other behaviors central to AIDS-risking behavior in these women (Morokoff, Grimley, Harlow, & Quina, 1992). Similarly, understanding the role of the interpersonal context in risky sexual behavior appears equally critical. For women whose economic or physical survival depends on their sexual availability to their partner or whose sense of emotional stability is strongly linked to having a relationship with a man, high-risk sexual behavior may seem a reasonable trade-off. Interventions that focus only on the importance of saying no to sex without condoms or insisting on the use of barrier contraceptives are not likely to be successful. Research is needed that addresses the full complexity of sexual relationships for women and that examines factors related to risky sexual behavior within this framework.

Future Research on Psychological Aspects of Women's Health

The following sections considers several issues in women's health that warrant additional research. The discussion is by no means comprehensive or exhaustive. Instead, topics were chosen to call attention to important measurement issues in research on women's health, and to complex and controversial issues in biomedical technology and treatments that affect women's health.

Gender Sensitive Measurement in Research on Women's Health   Psychologists interested in women's health issues have called attention to the importance of examining psychosocial and behavioral variables. However, to advance our knowledge of these factors in women's health requires addressing certain measurement issues. To a large extent, gender differences in health have been examined in relation to phenomena as they are defined in men, with little consideration of whether the measures adequately assess dimensions central to women's functioning and behavior. Simply standardizing or collecting normative data on measures for women as well as men is not sufficient to assure appropriate conceptualization from a gender perspective. Constructs need to be operationalized in ways that are sensitive to the full range of women's experience. There are many measures for which this argument is relevant, but we will focus on psychosocial measures of coping and social support because of their prominence and importance in health research.

Coping and Women's Health   It is well accepted that individuals facing a stressful event appraise the threat, assess their resources, engage in coping, and experience positive or negative outcomes (e.g., Coyne & Lazarus, 1980; Lazarus & Folkman, 1984). Coping has been related to health and well-being in many studies (e.g., Dunkel-Schetter, Feinstein, Taylor, & Falke, 1992; Folkman, Lazarus, Gruen, & DeLongis, 1986), and understanding how coping influences women's health is an important area of research. However, traditional models of coping and resultant measures were developed without specific consideration of the importance of women's roles, socialization, or status within society. Further, there has been little examination of whether measures of coping might be biased toward an overly narrow range of coping that does not encompass aspects of particular importance for women. A distinction is often made between problem-focused coping, involving behaviors directed at modifying the stressor, and emotion-focused coping, involving regulation of one's affective responses (e.g., Endler & Parker, 1990; Lazarus & Folkman, 1984). Several studies suggest that emotion-focused coping is associated with greater psychological distress (Carver, Scheier, & Weintraub, 1989; Endler & Parker, 1990). However, recent research on emotion-focused coping (Stanton & Danoff-Burg, 1992) underscores the limitations of current measures for assessing women's experience of coping through emotional expression.

In one study, Stanton and Danoff-Burg (1992) found that many items on current coping scales confound emotion-focused coping with emotional reactions and with symptoms of psychopathology. Items reflecting psychopathology assessed symptoms of psychological distress or contained self-deprecating, self-blaming content (e.g.,"focused on my general inadequacies," "blamed myself for being too emotional about the situation," Endler & Parker, 1990). The authors also found an absence of items assessing positive aspects of emotional coping such as attempts to identify or understand emotions, disclosure of emotions, or efforts at working through emotions. This omission is particularly important for women because processing of emotional reactions is often of central concern, and some research suggests that women are more likely than men to use emotion-focused strategies to cope with stress (e.g., Stone & Neale, 1984). In a subsequent study, Stanton and Danoff-Burg (1992) measured emotion-focused coping with items tapping the acknowledgment, expression, and understanding of feelings and examined the effects on physical and psychological well-being. Results indicated that when emotion-focused coping was unconfounded with psychopathology, it enhanced adjustment in the face of stress for women but not men. Women who used emotion-focused coping experienced significantly less depression and hostility and higher well-being, with results for physical symptoms in the same direction but not significant.

Another dimension of coping that is not well assessed by current measures but is important for understanding women's functioning and behavior can be described as relationship-focused coping. This involves engaging in behavior in a stressful situation that protects one's partner or significant others (e.g., children) from stress and is aimed at restoring, maintaining, or enhancing the stability of the couple or family. An example is provided in research by Smith and Coyne (1988) and Coyne and Smith (1991), who examined responses in married couples in which the husband had experienced a myocardial infarction (MI). Results indicated that the wife's use of relationship-focused coping (e.g., protecting husband from her fears about the MI or encouraging husband to initiate activities despite worries) contributed significantly to the husband's recovery but increased her own distress. This kind of "self-sacrificing" behavior may appear dysfunctional unless the relational context and the impact on the couple or family as a unit is appreciated.

These research findings suggest the need for further study of dimensions of coping that may be particularly important for women's health and the development of measures that are adequately sensitive to possible gender differences in coping processes. This is an undeveloped area in the coping literature and an important direction for future research.

Social Support as a Predictor of Women's Health   There is a large literature linking social support to physical and mental health (e.g., Cohen & Syme, 1985; Shumaker & Czajkowski, in press; Wallston, Alagna, DeVellis, & DeVellis, 1983). Lower support has been linked to higher morbidity and mortality (e.g., Berkman & Syme, 1979; Orth-Gomer & Johnson, 1987). However, these data are strongest for men. Weaker and more complex relationships between social support and physical health have been found for women (Shumaker & Hill, 1991). For example, men who are socially isolated are at increased risk of CHD mortality and other mortality independent of most major CVD risk factors. However, in studies of women, controlling for major risk factors significantly reduces the relationship between social isolation and negative health outcomes (Berkman & Vacarino, 1991). Further, in several studies, higher social support was associated with increased mortality among women in certain age groups (e.g., Berkman & Syme, 1979). In one study, the Tecumseh, Michigan Community Health Study (House, Robbins, & Metzner, 1982), the role of social support was examined in a sample of 1,322 men and 1,422 women. Social support was assessed by measuring several aspects of their social networks including marital status, visits with friends and relatives, and participation in formal organizational meetings. After controlling for baseline morbidity and health risk behavior, the relationship of social support to mortality was significant for men but not for women. Is social support less important for women's health? Perhaps, but there are indications that the weaker relationship for women may reflect inadequate conceptualization and measurement of social support in relation to gender issues.

Shumaker and Hill (1991) discuss possible differences in men's and women's support networks that are not adequately assessed by current measures. Women are more likely than men to be support providers as well as support recipients, and women are more likely than men to provide support that places emotional burdens and demands on them (e.g., caregiving). Women's networks tend to be larger than men's, providing more opportunity for support but increasing the potential demands on their resources that may negate potential benefits. Women are more likely than men to be "network tenders," i.e., to "nurture" the network that supports both men and women (Schumaker & Hill, 1991). Thus it appears that women are more often exposed to negative aspects of network involvement. The research by Coyne and Smith (1991) and Smith and Coyne (1988) described earlier found that wives may choose to engage in protective buffering, even at the cost of increasing their own distress. Unfortunately, few measures of social support assess dimensions of network strain as well as gain. Since current measures were largely developed on male populations, it is not surprising that they may fail to include features important for understanding social support effects in women. In addition to the need for measures of social support that tap both positive and negative aspects of social networks, Berkman and Vacarino (1991) suggest that women may experience their networks differently than men, so that frequency counts of visits to family members, relatives or friends are less relevant for them. A recent study by Bolger and Eckenrode (1991) found that social visits with friends and neighbors buffered against anxiety in the face of stress only if contacts were "discretionary" and not "obligatory." In fact, obligatory contacts with family members and relatives were associated with greater distress. To the extent that older women have more care obligations in their network and thus greater potential for obligatory contacts, this may be reflected in the weaker relationship of social support to physical health for women in certain age groups.

P. S. Derry (personal communication, 1992) has discussed the importance of the transactional character of women's support networks. She points out that the role of power in relationships has been ignored in the study of social support, and she relates this to the history of the concept (see also Derry & Baum, 1992). Researchers initially conceptualized social support as the opposite of "social stress" defined in terms of social disconnection and alienation, and thus left power relationships, discrimination, and inequity out of its formulation. P. S. Derry (personal communication, 1992) maintains that particularly for women it may be important to have social support measures that characterize the nature of transactions in one's social network. Definitions of social support often involve a priori assumptions about what makes relationships supportive but which may overlook essential aspects. For example, a recent study of stress in employed mothers (Reifman, Biernat, & Lang, 1991) measured social support with questions such as whether the husband helped with child care or encouraged the wife's career. Derry points out that asking whether a husband "helps" with child care implicitly assumes that this is not part of his normal role. However, the presence of child care as a normal part of the husband's role may be as or more important to the mother's health and well-being than the husband's willingness to help when asked. To be more appropriate, measures of social support need to encompass structural aspects of relationships that are truly beneficial to women.

Effects of Medical Advances on Women's Health   Advances in biomedical technology and treatments during the past several decades have had a significant impact on women's health. Synthetic hormones have increased women's control over reproductive decisions; hormone replacement therapy (HRT) has decreased symptoms associated with menopause and may reduce the risk of coronary heart disease as well as osteoporosis. In addition, screening mammography and Pap smears have resulted in increased detection of early stage breast and cervical cancer. Breast conservation followed by radiation therapy is now considered an effective treatment alternative to mastectomies for a portion of women with early-stage breast cancer. These biomedical advances have the potential to positively affect women's physical and emotional well-being. However, each has also been the source of significant controversy and as such represents a potential area of conflict and distress for women.

There is only limited knowledge about the ways confusing or controversial information concerning the benefits and long-term health risks of a given screening procedure, diagnostic test, or treatment option may affect women's health behavior. It seems likely, however, that some women may be reluctant to follow medical recommendations or may delay undergoing screening exams if recommendations are not clear. In addition, many women may not have access to adequate information about medical technologies and treatment pros and cons to facilitate decision making in the face of controversial and complex issues. Differential exposure to information is of particular concern for women in lower socioeconomic groups who often have limited access to medical care or receive inadequate care. The extent to which information about health benefits and risks of a given diagnostic test or treatment option is presented consistently to women in different racial/ethnic and socioeconomic groups and across medical settings and providers is largely unresearched. In addition, the degree to which women give consent to diagnostic tests or treatments based on accurate and detailed knowledge of the benefits and health risks is unclear (see Travis, 1988). There is also little empirical data on the psychosocial impact of decision making in the face of confusing information about screening and treatment options for women at risk for life-threatening conditions. There are many other areas of women's health in which clear recommendations are lacking. In the following section, we present several examples of the type of complex information that women must confront and some directions that research should take to help resolve this.

One area of confusion involves synthetic hormones, which are widely prescribed as an effective means of birth control, and to decrease distressing symptoms experienced during menopause. These interventions are controversial, however, because long-term use of these medications may be associated with increased risk of breast cancer in some women depending on their health history and behavior (Rodin & Ickovics, 1990; Travis, 1988). Oral contraceptive use among women who smoke may be associated with increased risk of coronary heart disease (Mattson & Herd, 1988; Rosenberg et al., 1980). Matthews, Bromberger, and Egeland (1990) found that use of HRT was associated with multiple correlates of health status, including social class, ethnicity, body weight, past contraceptive use, and blood pressure. Additional research is needed to examine the range of health behavior of women who elect long-term use of synthetic hormones in contrast to those who chose other means of birth control or symptom reduction during menopause (Matthews, 1989; Matthews, Bromberger, & Egeland, 1990). Research is also needed to determine whether women of diverse age, ethnicity, education and socioeconomic status are consistently provided detailed information about the benefits and risks of these medications.

The National Cancer Institute recently initiated the Breast Cancer Prevention Trial to evaluate the ability of tamoxifen (an antiestrogen and estrogen-agonist) to reduce the incidence of breast cancer in 16,000 women at risk because of their familial history of the disease. Tamoxifen has been found to reduce the rate of recurrence and mortality in the treatment of breast cancer (Early Breast Cancer Trialists' Collaborative Group, 1992). Women at high risk often feel vulnerable (Alagna, Morokoff, Bevett, & Reddy, 1987; Royak-Schaler & Benderly, 1992; Wellisch, Gritz, Schain, Wang, & Siau, 1991), and anxious (Kash, Holland, Halper, & Miller, 1992; Royak-Schaler, & Benderly, 1992) about the possibility of developing breast cancer in the future. As a result, many are interested in strategies or treatment options such as tamoxifen that may potentially reduce the chance of their developing cancer (Daly, Seay, Balshem, Lerman, & Engstrom, 1992). However, while tamoxifen's side effects have been evaluated in postmenopausal women with breast cancer (Davidson, 1992; Love 1991; Love et al., 1991; Love et al., 1992). Information about its long-term health risks for premenopausal women without cancer is at this point extremely limited. The clinical trial currently underway will include pre- and postmenopausal women ages 35–78 who will be randomized in a double-blind, placebo-controlled design (Davidson, 1992). Little is known about the types of women who will choose to participate in such a drug prevention trial in spite of the medication's potential negative effects. Research is needed that examines the characteristics of women who choose to participate as well as those of women who chose non-pharmacological risk-reducing strategies such as lowering their dietary fat intake instead of or in addition to the medication trial (Engstrom, 1991).

Another area of confusion for many women is that of guidelines associated with screening exams such as mammography. Although mammograms are recommended on an annual basis for women over 50, there is controversy surrounding the frequency with which asymptomatic, premenopausal women between 40 and 50 should be screened. Conflicting findings from studies on the effectiveness of mammography for detection of breast cancer in this age group as well as recent revisions in recommendations for screening by the American Cancer Society (1992) and the National Cancer Institute have added to the confusion about the necessary frequency of screening for women who are premenopausal. Research is needed that examines the extent to which changes in screening guidelines contribute to delay in obtaining mammograms. Confusing or controversial recommendations may be particularly distressing and disruptive of optimal screening behavior among women at high risk for breast cancer.

Controversy is also attached to breast conservation procedures as an alternative to mastectomy for early breast cancer. First, it is unclear how consistently women are offered the option of breast-conserving surgery and radiation as a surgical alternative to mastectomy even when tumor size, tumor location, and overall stage of the disease make this a feasible treatment option. Further, although women who undergo limited resection and radiation therapy may experience better body image, sexual functioning, and overall adjustment compared to women who have mastectomies, few studies have examined effects in diverse subgroups, and results across studies are inconsistent (Kiebert, de Haes, & van de Velde, 1991; Levy, Herberman, Lee, Lippman & d'Angelo, 1989; Morris & Ingham, 1988; Morris & Royle, 1988; Rowland & Holland, 1991). Finally, in the United States and Great Britain, some women are offered the choice of surgical procedures; others are presented with options by their physicians, who retain the main decision making power; some agree to participate in randomized trials; and some are entirely excluded from the decision-making process (Morris & Ingham, 1988; Morris & Royle, 1988). Research is needed to determine factors affecting women's decisions about surgery, and in what way physicians differ in how they present options or share decision-making power depending on their medical specialty or their beliefs about the importance of women's participation in treatment planning (Kiebert, de Haes, & van de Velde, 1991; Morris

& Ingham, 1988; Morris & Royle, 1988; Rowland & Holland, 1991). A recent area of significant controversy concerns the long- term health risks associated with silicone breast implants. These implants are used during reconstructive surgery following mastectomy or for cosmetic reasons (i.e., breast augmentation). Although some research suggests that many women are satisfied with the outcome of their reconstructive surgery for personal and practical reasons (Rowland & Holland, 1991), the risks associated with silicone implants remains unresolved, and there are heated opinions on both sides in the medical and scientific community. Recent hearings conducted by the Food and Drug Administration on the safety of implants and the subsequent attention to this issue by the media have resulted in an airing of contradictory views. This is likely to increase the conflict that women experience in deciding about breast implants and may impact the frequency with which women elect reconstructive surgery following mastectomy. Research is needed that carefully and thoroughly evaluates whether there are long-term physical health risks associated with silicone implants and that examines the psychological sequalae of these procedures.

Understudied Women at Risk

While correlates of health and illness of women in general have not been adequately researched, particular populations such as women of color have received almost no attention. The Public Health Service (1990) has identified three broad goals associated with "Healthy People 2000." These include (1) to increase the span of healthy life for Americans, (2) to reduce the health disparities among Americans, and (3) to achieve access to preventive service for all Americans. Consistent with these objectives, research is needed that rigorously addresses the biomedical, behavioral, sociocultural, environmental, economic, and medical care factors that affect the health status of women who are financially disadvantaged, and of women of color (N. B. Anderson, 1991). These are complex and interrelated issues that need to be examined with regard to the prevention, diagnosis, and treatment of acute, chronic, and life-threatening conditions. Poor women of color, for example, are less likely to have access to adequate health care. They consequently are less likely to undergo screening and diagnostic tests. In a retrospective analysis of a large sample of African-American and Hispanic women with breast cancer, Freeman and Wasfie (1989) found that over half the patients had symptoms for 3 months or longer prior to seeking care. In addition, half of the sample had advanced disease at the time of diagnosis. Not surprisingly, the long-term survival rate of these women is significantly shorter than the rate for Caucasian women. A similar analysis could be made for hypertension, which is more prevalent and associated with higher morbidity and mortality among poor African-American women than Caucasian women.

Women at Risk of HIV/AIDS   Women now account for approximately 12% of all cases of AIDS in the United States, and the HIV seroprevalence among females has been increasing at an alarming rate (Centers for Disease Control [CDC], 1992). Over seventy percent of women with AIDS are African-American or Hispanic (CDC, 1991), and AIDS is currently the leading cause of death of black women between the ages of 24–44 in New York City and New Jersey. In spite of these trends, relatively little empirical data is available regarding the natural course of HIV infection and AIDS in women (Hawkins & Hardley, 1992). Although women are at risk for the common physical complications observed in men, their symptom experience is not identical (Hankins & Handley, 1992; Ickovics & Rodin, 1992; Spence & Reboli, 1991). Gender-specific problems such as chronic fungal vaginitis (e.g., candidiasis), pelvic inflammatory disease, and cervical dysplasia may develop secondary to immunosuppression associated with HIV disease. There is little research on the psychological sequelae of these problems. In addition, despite the biomedical advances in the treatment of HIV infection and AIDS, women have only recently been included in clinical trials of antiviral agents (Campbell, 1990; Ickovics & Rodin, 1992). There is consequently little empirical data on how their disease course is altered by early intervention.

Although "women of color are disproportionately represented among those with HIV and AIDS, few studies have investigated behavioral and psychosocial issues related to prevention and treatment of HIV infection among ethnic groups. The minimal attention paid to research on women and HIV and AIDS has resulted in a serious and damaging vacuum of information regarding prevention and intervention strategies that are effective for women" (J. R. Anderson, Landry, & Kerby, 1991, p. 24). Women who are seropositive, for example, have rarely been included in studies of the psychosocial and neuropsychiatric sequelae of HIV infection or AIDS. Both of these areas have been the focus of multiple investigations whose samples have consisted primarily of men (e.g., Baer, 1989; Clifford, Jacoby, Miller, Seyfried, & Glickman, 1990; Hays, Turner & Coates, 1992; Hintz, Kuck, Peterkin, Volk, & Zisook, 1990; King, 1989; Perdices & Cooper, 1990; Rubinow et al., 1988). Furthermore, there has been far too little research on the practical, informational, and treatment needs of women with HIV/AIDS or on factors associated with noncompliance with treatment regimens for HIV/AIDS or poor attendance at clinic visits, and there has been very little research on the relationship between biological correlates of HIV/AIDS and psychosocial and neurocognitive functioning in women.

Eighty-five percent of women who are HIV positive are also in their reproductive years (i.e., 15–44 years of age) (Ellerbrock, Bush, Chamberland, & Oxtoby, 1991). Many of these women already have children, and others will give birth to infants who may become seropositive. Many of these children will need to be cared for by other family members, friends, and social service agencies. This issue underscores the need for research that examines the physical and emotional status of women who are caring for relatives of all ages who are ill with HIV/AIDS. Little is known, for example, about the health and well-being of women who must care for their grandchildren as a result of their daughters' life threatening illness. As a population this group is likely to be economically disadvantaged and underemployed and to have limited access to health care resources, all of which increase their risk for the development of physical and psychological difficulties.

Barriers to AIDS Prevention in Women   Because half of all women with AIDS become infected as a result of their IV drug use, the most important line of attack in preventing HIV infection is intervention directed at IV drug users. Data suggest that needle sharing is the most important transmission route for IV drug using women (rather than sexual transmission with an infected partner) (Morokoff, 1991). Needle exchange programs have been reported to work in European countries by lowering the rate of infection while not increasing the number of IV-drug-using citizens. Political considerations make it unlikely that such a policy will be adopted on a widespread basis in the United States. Nevertheless, this is an option that deserves careful study. If methodologically sound data can be collected that document the positive changes described, this may impact on American policy makers.

The best current option is improvement of chemical dependence treatment programs. However, significant barriers exist to women's treatment in such programs. The greatest barrier is the fact that alcohol and drug addiction has traditionally been considered a male problem. Many programs are thus designed for men and assume a male clientele. According to the U.S. House of Representatives Select Committee on Children, Youth, and Families, of California's 366 publicly funded drug treatment programs, only 67 (18%) treat women. In addition to the reduced availability of programs for women, programs that can accommodate children are especially rare. Of California's 67 programs that treat women, only 16 (4% of the total) can accommodate their children. Similarly, Ohio has 16 women's recovery programs, only 2 of which can accommodate children. Many women with children find the prospect of being separated or finding placements for children unacceptable or impossible. This effectively constitutes discrimination against women. Further, according to Chavkin (1990), National Institute on Drug Abuse (NIDA) sponsored surveys of drug treatment programs revealed that

> male program staff and participants were often hostile to women clients, employed a confrontational "therapeutic" style uncomfortable for women, and directed them into gender stereotyped tasks and training. . . . Moreover, they did not address the environment of sexual exploitation and violence in which female addicts often lived. (p. 485)

The pregnant substance abuser often faces the greatest difficulty in chemical dependence treatment. Of 78 drug treatment programs surveyed in New York City, 54 percent exclude all pregnant women, 67 percent will not accept pregnant women on Medicaid, and 87 percent will not accept pregnant crack-addicted women on Medicaid (Chavkin, 1989). Programs exclude pregnant women in part because of uncertainty over their optimal medical management and in part because of issues of criminal liability. As of 1990, according to American Civil Liberties Union data, over 30 women have been criminally charged for drug use during pregnancy for delivery of drugs to a minor. A Florida woman has been convicted of delivery of a controlled substance to a minor via the umbilical cord in the seconds after delivery before it was clamped. This was a felony drug charge with a possible 30-year sentence. Hundreds more pregnant substance abusers have been civilly charged for alleged child abuse. Four states (Florida, Illinois, Oklahoma, Rhode Island) have amended definitions of child abuse to include drug use during pregnancy, and three states (Indiana, Nevada, Utah) have included alcohol and drug use during pregnancy; one state (Minnesota) has amended its definition of criminal child neglect to include prenatal exposure to controlled substances, and three states (Minnesota, Oklahoma, Utah) now require doctors to report if either the mother or the child has a positive urine toxicology screen (Kennedy, 1990). This litigious approach to pregnant substance abusers in the face of the severe lack of appropriate chemical dependence treatment for these women amounts to cruel and unusual punishment. It is likely to deter such women from seeking treatment and to increase the risk of physical, mental, and emotional harm to their children.

Barriers to changes in sexual behaviors may be as detrimental to preventing HIV infection in women as barriers to changes in substance abuse behaviors. Substance-abusing and non-substance-abusing women need to be able to negotiate safer sex with partners. Recent research at the Women and AIDS Research Project at the University of Rhode Island indicates some of the reasons why sexual behavior change may be particularly difficult for women. A study of 430 undergraduate women was undertaken to determine predictors of AIDS-risking sexual behaviors. A multidimensional model was designed to predict HIV-related risky sex in women from a set of behavioral, interpersonal, and psychoattitudinal measures. Three sets of dependent measures were assessed: partner-related risk, unprotected vaginal sex, and anal sex. Structural modeling methods were used to relate predictors to dependent variables (Harlow, Grimley, Quina, & Morokoff, 1992). The finished model indicates that engaging in unprotected vaginal sex was predicted by low sexual assertiveness and high levels of sexual experience. In other words, both less assertive and more sexually experienced women were likely to engage in unprotected vaginal sex. Choice of a risky partner was predicted by low sexual assertiveness, substance use, history of victimization, sexual experience, psychosocial functioning, and psychosexual attitudes. Overall, results provided good support for the model, explaining 54 percent of variance with the three types of predictors. Behavioral and interpersonal factors accounted for 2–3 times the risk of the psychoattitudinal factors (including hopelessness, demoralization, stress, meaninglessness, and enjoyment of sexuality). The behavioral factors of sexuality experience and substance abuse were related to all three dependent variables, and interpersonal factors of sexual assertiveness and victimization were most associated with choice of a risky partner.

Results of this study indicate that it is *not* intrapsychic characteristics that most determine a woman's ability to protect herself sexually from either unwanted pregnancy or sexually transmitted diseases. Unfortunately, the focus of much research on predictors of contraceptive use has focused on just such intrapsychic variables (e.g., self-esteem). Rather it is sexual abuse and victimization history plus the relational context of the sexual activity that is most important in determining her behaviors. The traditional model assumes that satisfaction of internal drives motivates humans to sexual activity. It is time to add to this the realization that there is a relational context to sex that is especially important for women, whose survival often depends on the successful negotiation of a sexual relationship. If a woman, at least in part, engages in sex in order to attain relationship or survival goals, then insistence on sex in a way that is objectionable to a partner will be inconsistent with her goals. Thus failure to insist on condom or contraceptive use may not be irrational. A woman who is exchanging sex for drugs or rent money is not in a position to insist on condom use against the wishes of her partner. Neither is a woman who views the relationship with her man as the most important goal of her life. These data coincide with the theoretical view that enabling women to protect themselves against HIV and AIDS requires empowerment of women and significant societal changes in women's dependence on sexual relationships for emotional and economic survival.

Gender Issues in the Psychological Study of Women's Health

In this section we will discuss ways in which psychological research on women's health may be biased or flawed as a result of inadequate attention to gender issues.

Cultural Biases or Medical Realities?   A multitude of studies have examined effectiveness of interventions to improve women's health. Cultural concepts support the characterization of women as in need of improvement. The prototype for this belief is that women need to beautify themselves. A multibillion-dollar cosmetics industry is ample evidence of this norm. The argument has frequently been made that this cultural expectation derives from a patriarchal society in which women, as subordinates, must alter themselves to accommodate the desires of the dominants. Interestingly, there is an interface between the power dynamics of aesthetics and medicine. First, medicine may be the means by which beautification is achieved, as in plastic surgery. Second, a scientific or medical rationale may be provided to support the cultural expectation of a slim body. Thus cultural norms for thinness are supported by the medical opinion that excess fat is unhealthy. In addition, body fat is the focus of research on preventable causes of breast cancer, but environmental toxins have barely begun to be studied, despite provocative evidence of a relationship between exposure and increased risk. It is not our intent to evaluate the evidence for a link between body fat and morbidity or mortality, but simply to suggest that we should look with caution at medical hypotheses that provide support for gender-biased cultural norms. Furthermore, such issues should be considered when designing interventions to improve women's health.

Capability of Subordinates to Effect Change   Health promotion interventions for women include those designed to increase use of mammograms, change family foods to a low-fat, low-sodium diet, reduce weight, participate in exercise programs, insist on condom use, and obtain prenatal care. In designing and evaluating such interventions, it is necessary to take into account women's capacity to implement or follow the recommended program. Interventions across these diverse content areas may be difficult to put into practice due to women's lack of structural resources or lack of interpersonal power. For example, a low-income woman may have to choose between obtaining a mammogram and feeding children or grandchildren in her household. She may also not be able to leave her job in order to attend a daytime appointment. A woman's subordinate position in her family may not allow her to prepare low-fat foods for family meals, for example, if her husband demands certain meats or gravy and can back up his demands with the threat of force. Similarly, some women may not be able to insist on condom use in a relationship in which her partner objects to using a condom with risking physical abuse. For women in ongoing relationships, status in the relationship may determine ability to make a contraceptive demand, and for women in dating relationships, there may be the cost associated with condom preparedness of being perceived as sexually loose.

Devaluation of Women's Needs and Characteristics   Women's medical needs have traditionally been devalued. For example, the need to aggressively treat cardiac disease in women is only recently being acknowledged. Physicians are more likely to interpret possible cardiac symptoms in women as evidence of anxiety or emotional distress than as a cardiac problem (Czajkowski, 1992). Furthermore, research suggests that women receive less pain medication than men (Calderone, 1990). Only recently has research begun to examine behavioral interventions to improve labor and delivery outcomes and decrease pain during labor. Significant improvement on these variables was demonstrated by having doulas (women who provided continuous emotional support) present during labor and delivery (Kennell, Klaus, McGrath, Robertson, & Hinkley, 1991). The

Centers for Disease Control are only now revising AIDS criteria to include female manifestations of the disease.

In addition, in psychological research examining the relationship between personality characteristics/styles and health, characteristics associated with women may be devalued or pathologized. Numerous studies have demonstrated sex-role stereotyping of mental health standards (Aslin, 1977; Broverman, Broverman, Clarkson, Rosenkrantz, & Vogel, 1970; Maslin & Davis, 1975). Separation, differentiation, and autonomy are part of the male stereotype and have been accorded higher mental health status than characteristics of caring and attachment, interdependence, relationship, and attention to context, traditionally associated with women (McGoldrick, 1988). A good example of how such stereotypes may impact on research is measurement of emotion-focused coping already discussed. Emotional relatedness, emotionality, and dependency, characteristics usually associated with women, tend to be devalued in our society. Thus when researchers devise measures of emotion-focused coping, they may write items that tap a pathologized version of emotional focus, which may then turn out to be negatively associated with better health outcomes. As previously discussed, when emotion-focused coping was unconfounded with psychopathology, it was associated with enhanced adjustment in the face of stress for women.

Women as Emotional and Physical Caretakers   Women's traditional gender role demands that women provide emotional support and nurturance to family members as well as care of the sick. Women still have the primary responsibility for childrearing (McGoldrick, 1988). Jobs in our society have been structured based on the assumption that the (male) worker will be supported by the family. Although the majority of women now work outside the home so that men and women share the burden of providing financial support for the family, the burden of taking care of housework and family responsibilities is not typically shared. Averaging estimates from major studies conducted in the 1960s and 1970s, Hochschild (1989) discovered that women worked (adding together paid work, housework, and childcare) roughly 15 hours longer each week than men. This translates into an extra month of 24-hour days a year. Despite this burden, women still attempt to fulfill the gender expectation that they support and nurture their husbands. In addition to these tasks, women nurse and visit the sick and dying. These activities are conducted without the cultural expectation of emotional support or affirmation. As previously noted, the relationship between social support for women and health outcomes is a complicated one. Typically, the larger a woman's social network or network of extended family, the greater her caretaking burdens. It may well be that women receive so little emotional support and are the recipients of so little caretaking that the positive benefits of high levels of such support cannot be measured.

WOMEN RESEARCHERS IN WOMEN'S HEALTH

Attention has focused on the need to increase funding for research on women's health issues and to assure adequate representation of women in research studies. Attention has also focused on the need to increase the number of women scientists in women's health research and to reduce barriers to career advancement. Barriers include not only the potential inequalities that women scientists face moving up the career ladder, but the negative consequences, often including derailment of one's career, psychological distress, isolation, and financial hardship, that confront women seeking redress for discrimination. To address the peripheral status of women in science, we need to examine the psychosocial and behavioral as well as institutional aspects of this problem. This is important to the health of science, the science of health particularly women's health, and the mental, emotional, and physical health of women scientists.

It is widely recognized that recruitment of women scientists has increased. However, factors that can stall one's career (e.g., heavy teaching loads that leave little time for research; family and child care responsibilities) affect women disproportionately and result in their not advancing at rates comparable to men or to their increased numbers in the overall pool of entering scientists. In examining the problem of underfunding of research on women's health, the Congressional Caucus on Women's Issues noted the marked absence of women in high decision-making ranks. This concern was also raised by the Public Health Service Task Force on Women's Health in 1985, which recommended that the numbers of women in prominent positions in research and administration be increased. Advancement of women in science careers is one of three top priorities of the ORWH, which recently convened a Task Force to obtain information on factors that facilitate or impede advancement and to hold a workshop to address strategies and develop an agenda for action (National Institutes of Health, Office of Research on Women's Health, 1992).

It is anticipated that as women advance to leadership positions, they will foster the career development of other women and that increasing the number and status of women in health science research will increase the amount of research focusing on issues that affect women. Several strategies have been recommended, including reaching out to girls before and during adolescence to increase the extent to which research careers in health are viewed as open to them. More research is needed on how gender socialization puts girls and women at a disadvantage in pursuing careers in science, and on the various factors that result in a disproportionate number of women Ph.D. candidates dropping out before they finish. There is also a need for intervention to prepare women for the research battlefield with regard to promotion and tenure.

In the last decade there have been several studies of the careers of women and men scientists (Zuckerman, Cole, & Bruer, 1991). In a review of current research, Zuckerman (1991) found many similarities: intellectual capacity as measured by standardized tests and academic performance is equivalent for women and men doctorates entering science careers; women are as likely as men to be admitted to prestigious graduate programs in science, to get degrees from top-ranking research universities, and to be offered postdoctoral fellowships at good places; and women are as likely as men to succeed in funding of grant applications (although many fewer apply). Further, women become assistant professors at a rate equal to men, even at top universities, and there is salary parity at the beginning assistant professor level. However, review of these studies also showed that women publish significantly less than men, a difference that begins early and grows with professional age; that having had a prestigious fellowship is less predictive of getting a subsequent tenure-track position for women than men; and that at every level of productivity women are less likely to receive tenure and promotion (Zuckerman, 1991). Gender has been found to be significantly related to academic rank, even after controlling for number of publications and rates of citation (e.g., Bayer & Astin, 1975). Further, women who have made important contributions are less likely to be considered to have had a major influence than comparable men (Cole, 1979). Women are also less likely to be journal editors or associate editors, to be on grant review panels, or to be in other important power and policy-making positions. Finally, there is a substantial salary differential between women and men, and about 50% of this remains after controlling for years of professional experience, field, race, and sector of employment (National Science Foundation, 1986). These data indicate that women are getting in the door in larger numbers but not up the ladder in career advancement as they should. Attention has been focused on recruitment, but much less research has addressed factors related to retention and advancement. Entry gains can be attributed in large measure to the success of affirmative action, which has focused pressure on hiring but has been much less effective in facilitating equitable treatment beyond entry.

Feldt (1985), in a study of scientists at the University of Michigan, found that male assistant professors received higher levels of research support, more startup funds, and better space than women at the same level. This kind of initial difference contributes to a snowball effect for men (i.e., a pattern of escalating cumulative advantage), but a revolving door effect for women. Astin and Davis (1985) found that productive male researchers identified structural factors (access to graduate research assistants, equipment, space) as related to their productivity, whereas women researchers cited hard work and motivation. Cole and Singer (1991) assert that gender disparities emerge early and build, culminating in the lack of recognition in awards and tenured positions at the most prestigious institutions. A recent examination of the Distinguished Scientist Award given by the American Psychological Association revealed a total of 117 recipients in the history of the award, only 11 of whom were women; and of these 11, 3 shared the award with a man.

What is going wrong that women with dedication and strong commitment to a career in science and with credentials equivalent to their male peers are not making it to the top? Women are getting in the door in larger numbers. Why not up the ladder? Concerns have been raised about sexism, racism, discrimination, and the glass ceiling, but we need to know more about how these social forces retard success for women. Blatant exclusionary policies have diminished. In some ways they were easier to tackle because they could more readily be observed and documented. Today's constraints appear more subtle and difficult to articulate. We see the outcome, but the determinative processes are not clear. There is sexism, discrimination, and sexual harassment, but often differential treatment takes a more subtle form involving ignoring or minimizing women's accomplishments. Career success appears to be as much a social product as an intellectual product. The current system of communication and interaction gives women fewer opportunities than their male peers to participate in professional activities that increase visibility, such as invited presentations, peer review panels, journal associate editorships, collaborative writing projects, books with major players, and NIH funding. It is not any one of these, but each of these that matters. Only when we have a better understanding of the ways women can successfully work the system and programs in place to assist women in achieving equity in career status can we expect the numbers of women researchers in health to increase substantially.

CONCLUSIONS

The growing interest in women's health is a source of great excitement and hope. Women have carried the burden of the nurturance and support of men and children with little affirmation, emotional support, or societal interest in their health issues and the effects of these burdens on health and well-being. Increased funding for women's health problems by the National Institutes of Health such as the Women's Health Initiative signal an important change. The opening of the Office of Research on Women's Health provides further evidence that policy makers view women's health issues seriously. It is clear that a women's health agenda will be most vigorously advanced when women are in policy-making and research positions. However, women encounter substantial difficulties in their efforts to advance academic and scientific careers. It is our challenge to find ways to overcome such difficulties.

This chapter has highlighted several areas in which future research on psychological aspects of women's health is needed. We have also underscored some of the gender biases that make such research or implementation of research findings difficult. Although women's health problems such as AIDS, cardiovascular disease, and breast cancer present a grim reality to us, they also present an opportunity to take women's suffering seriously, to make significant improvements in gender inequities, and to enhance the ability of society to care for women.

REFERENCES

Alagna, S. W., Morokoff, P. J., Bevett, J. M., & Reddy, D. M. (1987). Performance of breast self-examination by women at risk for breast cancer. *Women and Health, 12,* 29–47.

American Cancer Society. (1992). *Guidelines on screening for breast cancer: An overview.* American Cancer Society Professional Education Publication. Silver Spring, MD.

American Psychological Association and the Federation of Behavioral, Psychological and Cognitive Sciences on the Women's Health Initiative. (1991). Testimony before the cochairs of the Scientific and Technical Committee on the Women's Health Initiative. Bethesda, MD: National Institutes of Health.

Anderson, J. R., Landry, C. P., & Kerby, J. L. (Eds.). (1991). *AIDS: Abstracts of the Psychological and Behavioral Literature, 1983–1991* (3rd ed.). Washington, D.C.: American Psychological Association.

Anderson, N. B. (1991, March). *Addressing ethnic minority health issues: Behavioral medicine at the forefront of research and practice.* Paper presented at the Annual Meeting of the Society of Behavioral Medicine, Washington, DC.

Aslin, A. L. (1977). Feminist and community mental health center psychotherapists' expectations of mental health for women. *Sex Roles, 3,* 537–544.

Astin, H. S., & Davis, D. (1985). Research productivity across the life and career cycles: Facilitators and barriers for women. In M. F. Fox (Ed.), *Scholarly writing and publishing issues, problems and solutions* (pp. 147–160). Boulder, CO: Westman Press.

Baer, J. (1989). Study of 60 patients with AIDS or AIDS-Related Complex requiring psychiatric hospitalization. *American Journal of Psychiatry, 10,* 1285–1288.

Bayer, A. E., & Astin, H. S. (1975). Sex differentials in the academic reward system. *Science, 188,* 796–802.

Berkman, L. F., & Syme, S. L. (1979). Social networks, host resistance, and mortality: A nine year follow-up study of Alameda County residents. *American Journal of Epidemiology, 109,* 186–204.

Berkman, L. F., & Vacarino, V. (1991). *Social support and CVD morbidity and mortality in women.* Paper presented at the National Heart, Lung, and Blood Institute sponsored conference, *Women, Behavior, and Cardiovascular Disease,* Bethesda, MD.

Bolger, N., & Eckenrode, J. (1991). Social relationships, personality, and anxiety during a major stressful event. *Journal of Personality and Social Psychology, 61,* 440–449.

Broverman, I. K., Broverman, D. M., Clarkson, F. E., Rosenkrantz, P., & Vogel, S. R. (1970). Sex-role stereotypes and clinical judgments of mental health. *Journal of Consulting Psychology, 34,* 1–7.

Butler, K., & Ohland, G. (1991). Agenda at risk: The state of women's health care in America. *LA Weekly,* January 18–24.

Calderone, K. (1990). The influence of gender on the frequency of pain and sedative medication administered to postoperative patients. *Sex Roles, 23,* 713–725.

Cambien, F., Poirer, O., Lecerf, L., Evans, A., Cambon, J. P., Luc, G., Bard, J. M., Bara, L., Richard, S., Tiret, L., Amouyel, P., Gelas, F.A.C., Soubrier, F. (1992).

Deletion polymorphism in the gene for angiotension converting enzyme is a potent risk factor for myocardial infarction. *Nature, 359,* 641–644.

Campbell, C. A. (1990). Women and AIDS. *Social Science and Medicine, 30,* 407–415.

Carney, R. M., Freedland, K. E., Smith, L. J., Rich, M. W., & Jaffe, A. S. (1991). *Depression, anxiety, and coronary heart disease in women.* Paper presented at the National Heart, Lung, and Blood Institute sponsored conference, *Women, Behavior, and Cardiovascular Disease,* Bethesda, MD.

Carver, L. S., Scheier, M. F., & Weintraub, J. K. (1989). Assessing coping strategies: A theoretically based approach. *Journal of Personality and Social Psychology, 56,* 267–283.

Centers for Disease Control. (October 1992). *HIV/AIDS surveillance.* Report 1-18. Atlanta: U.S. Department of Health and Human Services.

Chavkin, W. (1989, July 18). Help, don't jail addicted women. *New York Times,* p. A21.

Chavkin, W. (1990). Drug addiction and pregnancy: Policy crossroads. *American Journal of Public Health, 80,* 483–487.

Clifford, D. B., Jacoby, R. G., Miller, J. P., Seyfried, W. R., & Glicksman, M. (1990). Neuropsychometric performance of asymptomatic HIV-infected subjects. *AIDS, 4,* 767–774.

Cohen, S., & Syme, S. L. (Eds.) (1985). *Social support and health.* New York: Academic Press.

Cole, J. R. (1979). *Fair science: Women in the scientific community.* New York: Free Press.

Cole, J. R., & Singer, B. (1991). A theory of limited differences: Explaining the productivity puzzle in science. In H. Zuckerman, J. R. Cole, & J. T. Bruer (Eds). *The outer circle: Women in the scientific community* (pp. 277–310). New York: W. W. Norton.

Cotton, P. (1990). Is there still too much extrapolation from data on middle-aged white men? *Journal of the American Medical Association, 263,* 1049–1050.

Coyne, J. C., & Lazarus, R. S. (1980). Cognitive style, stress perception and coping. In I. L. Kutach & L. B. Schlesinger (Eds.), *Handbook on stress and anxiety* (pp. 144–158). San Francisco: Jossey-Bass.

Coyne, J. C., & Smith, D. A. F. (1991). Couples coping with a myocardial infarction: A contextual perspective on wives' distress. *Journal of Personality and Social Psychology, 61,* 404–412.

Czajkowski, S. M. (1992, August). Women, biobehavioral factors and cardiovascular disease: New paradigms for research. In S. M. Czajkowski (Chair), *Biobehavioral influences on women's health: Research and policy perspectives.* Symposium conducted at the meeting of the American Psychological Association, Washington, DC.

Daly, M., Seay, J., Balshem, A., Lerman, C., & Engstrom, P. (1992). Feasibility of a telephone survey to recruit health maintenance organization members into a tamoxifen chemoprevention trial. *Cancer Epidemiology, Biomarkers & Prevention, 1,* 413–416.

Davidson, N. (1992). Tamoxifen—panacea or Pandora's Box. *New England Journal of Medicine, 326,* 885–886.

Derry, P. S. (1992) The transactional character of women's support networks. Personal communication.

Derry, P. S., & Baum, A. (1992). Social support: A history of the concept. *Psychosomatic Medicine*, in review.

Dunkel-Schetter, C., Feinstein, L. G., Taylor, S. E., & Falke, R. L. (1992). Patterns of coping with cancer. *Health Psychology, 11*, 79–87.

Early Breast Cancer Trialists' Collaborative Group. (1992). Systemic treatment of early breast cancer by hormonal, cytotoxic, or immune therapy. *Lancet, 339*, 1–15, 71–85.

Ellerbrock, T. V., Bush, T. J., Chamberland, M. E., & Oxtoby, M. J. (1991). Epidemiology of women with AIDS in the United States, 1981 through 1990: A comparison with heterosexual men with AIDS. *Journal of the American Medical Association, 265*, 2971–2975.

Endler, N. S., & Parker, J. D. A. (1990). Multidimensional assessment of coping: A critical evaluation. *Journal of Personality and Social Psychology, 58*, 844–854.

Engels, G. L. (1977). The need for a new medical model: A challenge for biomedicine. *Science, 196*, 129–135.

Engstrom, P. (1991). Specific compliance issues in an antiestrogen trial of women at risk for breast cancer. *Preventive Medicine, 20*, 125–151.

Feldt, B. (1985). *An analysis of productivity of nontenured faculty women in the medical and related schools: Some preliminary findings.* Ann Arbor, Mich.: University of Michigan, Office of Affirmative Action.

Folkman, S., Lazarus, R. C., Gruen, R. J., & DeLongis, A. (1986). Appraisal, coping, health status, and psychological symptoms. *Journal of Personality and Social Psychology, 50*, 571–579.

Freeman, H. P., & Wasfie, T. J. (1989). Cancer of the breast in poor black women. *Cancer, 63*, 2562–2569.

Gritz, E. R. (1991). *Biobehavioral factors in smoking and smoking cessation in women.* Paper presented at the National Heart, Lung, and Blood Institute sponsored conference, *Women, Behavior, and Cardiovascular Disease*, Bethesda, MD.

Grobbee, D. E., Rimm, E. B., Giovannucci, E., Colditz, G., Stampfer, M., & Willett, W. (1990). Coffee, caffeine and cardiovascular disease in men. *New England Journal of Medicine, 323*, 1026–1032.

Hankins, C. A., & Handley, M. A. (1992). HIV disease and AIDS in women: Current knowledge and a research agenda. *Journal of Acquired Immune Deficiency Syndromes, 5*, 957–971.

Harburg, J. M., Schonk, M. A., & DiFrancisco, W. (1991). *Role of marital stress and suppressed anger for women and wives on health factors and mortality.* Paper presented at the National Heart, Lung, and Blood Institute sponsored conference, *Women, Behavior, and Cardiovascular Disease*, Bethesda, MD.

Harlan, W. R., & Kirschstein, R. L. (1991). *Women's Health Initiative* (prospectus). Department of Health and Human Services. Bethesda, MD: National Institutes of Health.

Harlow, L. L., Grimley, D., Quina, K., & Morokoff, P. (1992). *Behavioral, interpersonal, and psycho-situational predictors of HIV-risk in women.* Paper presented at the meeting of the Society of Behavioral Medicine, New York.

Hartmann, L. (1992). Presidential address: Reflections on humane values and biopsychosocial integration. *American Journal of Psychiatry, 149*, 1135–1141.

Healy, B. (1991a). Women's health, public welfare. *Journal of the American Medical Association, 266*, 566–568.

Healy, B. (1991b). The Yentl syndrome. *New England Journal of Medicine, 325*, 274–276.

Healy, B. (1992a). A celebration and new resolve. *Journal of Women's Health, 1*, xvii.

Healy, B. (1992b). Women in science: From panes to ceiling. *Science, 255*, 1333.

Helmers, K. F., Krantz, D. S., Howell, R. H., Klein, J., & Bairey, C. N. (1991). *Hostility and myocardial ischemia: Gender differences.* Paper presented at the National Heart, Lung, and Blood Institute sponsored conference, *Women, Behavior, and Cardiovascular Disease*, Bethesda, MD.

Hintz, S., Kuck, J., Peterkin, J. J., Volk, D. M., & Zisook, S. (1990). Depression in the context of HIV infection: Implication for treatment. *Journal of Clinical Psychiatry, 51*, 497–501.

Hochschild, A. (1989). *The second shift.* New York: Avon.

House, J. S., Robbins, C., & Mejzner, H. L. (1982). The association of social relationships with mortality: Prospective evidence from the Tecumseh Community Health Study. *American Journal of Epidemiology, 116*, 123–140.

Howes, J. M. (1992). The Society for the Advancement of Women's Health Research. *Journal of Women's Health, 1*, xxi.

Ickovics, J. R., & Rodin, J. (1992). Women and AIDS in the United States: Epidemiology, natural history and mediating mechanism. *Health Psychology, 11*, 1–16.

Jialal, I., & Grundy, S. M. (1992). Effect of dietary supplementation with alpha-tocopherol on the oxidative modification of low density lipoprotein. *Journal of Lipid Research, 33*, 889–906.

Johnson, K. (1992). Women's health: Developing a new interdisciplinary specialty. *Journal of Women's Health, 1*, 95–99.

Kash, K. M., Holland, J. C., Halper, M. S., & Miller, G. (1992). Psychological distress and surveillance behaviors of women with a family history of breast cancer. *Journal of the National Cancer Institute, 84*, 24–30.

Kennedy, M. (1990). *Women, addiction, and perinatal substance abuse: Fact sheet.* U.S. House of Representatives, Select Committee on Children, Youth, and Families.

Kennell, J., Klaus, M., McGrath, S., Robertson, S., & Hinkley, C. (1991). Continuous emotional support during labor in a U.S. hospital. *Journal of the American Medical Association, 265*, 2197–2201.

Kiebert, G. M., de Haes, J. C. J. M., & van de Velde, C. J. H. (1991). The impact of breast-conserving treatment and mastectomy on the quality of life of early-stage breast cancer patients: A review. *Journal of Clinical Oncology, 9*, 1059–1070.

King, A. C. (1991). *Biobehavioral variables, exercise and CVD in women.* Paper presented at the National Heart, Lung, and Blood Institute sponsored conference, *Women, Behavior, and Cardiovascular Disease*, Bethesda, MD.

King, M. B. (1989). Psychosocial status of 192 out-patients with HIV infection and AIDS. *British Journal of Psychiatry, 154*, 237–242.

Kirschstein, R. L. (1991). Research on women's health. *American Journal of Public Health, 81*, 291–293.

Lazarus, R. S., & Folkman, S. (1984). *Stress, appraisal, and coping.* New York: Springer.

Lewontin, R. C. Rose, S., & Kamin, L. J. (1984). *Not in our genes: Biology, ideology, and human nature.* New York: Parthenon.

Love, R. R. (1991). Antiestrogen chemoprevention of breast cancer: Critical issues and research. *Preventive Medicine, 20*, 64–78.

Love, R. R., et al. (1991). Effects of tamoxifen on cardiovascular risk factors in postmenopausal women. *Annals of Internal Medicine, 115*, 860–864.

Love, R. R., et al. (1992). Effects of tamoxifen on bone mineral density in postmenopausal women with breast cancer. *New England Journal of Medicine, 326*, 852–856.

Luborsky, L., McClelland, A., Childress, M., O'Brien, L., et al. (1983). *Guide to the Addictions Severity Index*. Treatment Research Monographs. Washington, DC: National Institute on Drug Abuse.

Marcus, B., Albrecht, A. E., Niaura, R. S., Thompson, P. D., & Abrams, D. B. (1991). *Physical exercise improves maintenance of smoking cessation in women*. Paper presented at the National Heart, Lung, and Blood Institute sponsored conference, *Women, Behavior, and Cardiovascular Disease*, Bethesda, MD.

Maslin, A., & Davis, J. L. (1975). Sex-role stereotyping as a factor in mental health standards among counselors-in-training. *Journal of Counseling Psychology, 22*, 87–91.

Matthews, K. A. (1989). Interactive effects of behavior and reproductive hormones on sex differences in risk for cardiovascular heart disease. *Health Psychology, 8*, 373–387.

Matthews, K. A., Bromberger, J., & Egeland, G. (1990). Behavioral antecedents and consequences of the menopause. In S. Korenman (Ed.), *Biological and clinical consequences of ovarian failure: Evaluation and management*. New York: Plenum Press.

Mattson, M. E., & Herd, J. A. (1988). Cardiovascular disease. In E. A. Blechman & K. D. Brownell, (Eds.), *Handbook of behavioral medicine for women* (pp. 160–177). New York: Pergamon Press.

McGoldrick, M. (1988). Women and the family life cycle. In B. Carter & M. McGoldrick (Eds.), *The changing family life cycle: A framework for family therapy*. New York: Gardner.

Morokoff, P. J. (1991). AIDS: Special issues in prevention for women. In S. J. Gallant (Chair), *Women's health issues and directions for the future*. Symposium presented at the Annual Meeting of the American Psychological Association, San Francisco.

Morokoff, P. J., Grimley, D., Harlow, L., & Quina, K. (1992). Aids prevention in women: Behavioral change efforts and public policy. In S. M. Czajkowski (Chair), *Biobehavioral influences on women's health: Research and policy perspectives*. Symposium presented at the Annual Meeting of the American Psychological Association, Washington, DC.

Morris, J., & Ingham, R. (1988). Choice of surgery for early breast cancer: Psychosocial considerations. *Social Science and Medicine, 27*, 1257–1262.

Morris, J., & Royle, G. T. (1988). Offering patients a choice of surgery for early breast cancer: A reduction in anxiety and depression in patients and their husbands. *Social Science and Medicine, 26*, 583–585.

Nadel, M. V. (1990). National Institutes of Health: Problems in implementing policy on women in study populations. GAO testimony before the Subcommittee on Health and the Environment, Committee on Energy and Commerce, House of Representatives.

National Institutes of Health. (1990, August). *NIH Guide to Grants and Contracts*, Vol. 19. Bethesda, MD.

National Institutes of Health. Office of Research on Women's Health. (1992). *Overview*. Bethesda, MD.

National Science Foundation. (1986). *Women and minorities in science and engineering*. Washington, DC: Author.

Neuman, E. (1992). Cancer: The issue feminists forget. The breast cancer battle. *Insight on the News*, February 24.

NIH Guide to Grants and Contracts (1990, August). Vol. 19. Orth-Gomer, K. (1991). *Linking psychosocial factors to CVD in women. A theoretical framework*. Paper presented at the National Heart, Lung, and Blood Institute sponsored conference, *Women, Behavior, and Cardiovascular Disease*, Bethesda, MD.

Orth-Gomer, K., & Johnson, J. V. (1987). Social network interaction and mortality: A six year follow-up study of a random sample of the Swedish population. *Journal of Chronic Disease, 40,* 949–957.

Perdices, M., & Cooper, D. A. (1990). Neurophysical investigation of patients with AIDS and ARC. *Journal of Acquired Immune Deficiency Syndromes, 3,* 555–564.

Physician's Health Study Group, Steering Committee. Final report on the aspirin component of the ongoing physician's health study. (1989). *New England Journal of Medicine, 321,* 129–135.

Pinn, V. (1992). Biobehavioral factors and women's health: A policy perspective. In S. M. Czajkowski, (Chair), *Biobehavioral influences on women's health: Research and policy perspectives*. Symposium presented at the Annual Meeting of the American Psychological Association, Washington, DC.

Public Health Service. (1990). *Healthy people 2000* (PHS Report). Washington, DC: U.S. Department of Health and Human Services.

Public Health Service. Task Force on Women's Health Issues. (1985). *Women's Health Report. Public Health Report, 1,* 74–106.

Reifman, A., Biernat, M., & Lang, E. (1991). Stress, social support and health in married women with small children. *Psychology of Women Quarterly, 15,* 431–445.

Rimm, E. B., Giovannicii, E. L., Willett, W. C., Colditz, G. A., Ascherio, A., Rosner, B., & Stompfer, M. J. (1991). Prospective sutdy of alcohol consumption and risk of coronary disease in men. *Lancet, 338,* 464–468.

Rodin, J., & Ickovics, J. R. (1990). Women's health: Review and research agenda as we approach the 21st century. *American Psychologist, 45,* 1018–1034.

Rose, D. P., & Connolly, J. M. (1990). Dietary prevention of breast cancer. *Medical Oncology Tumor Pharmacotherapy, 7,* 21–30.

Rosenberg, L., Hennekens, C. H., Rosner, B., Belanger, C., Rothman, C., & Speizer, F. E. (1980). Oral contraceptive use in relation to nonfatal myocardial infarction. *American Journal of Epidemiology, 111,* 59–66.

Rowland, J. H., & Holland, J. C. (1991). Patient rehabilitation and support. In J. R. Harris, S. Hellman, I. C. Henderson, & D. W. Kinne (Eds.), *Breast disease* (pp. 849–866). Philadelphia: J. B. Lippincott.

Royak-Schaler, R., & Benderly, B. L. (1992). *Challenging the breast cancer legacy: A program of emotional support and medical care for women at risk.* New York: Harper Collins.

Rubinow, D. R., Joffe, R. T., Brouwers, P., Squillace, K., Lane, H. C., & Mirsky, A. F. (1988). Neuropsychiatric impairment in patients with AIDS. In T.P. Bridges (Ed.), *Psychological, neuropsychiatric and substance abuse aspects of AIDS* (pp. 111–116). New York: Raven Press.

Salonen, J. T., Nyyssonen, K., Korpela, H., Tuomilehto, J., Seppanen, R., & Salonen, R. (1992). High stored iron levels are associated with excess risk of myocardial infarction in eastern Finnish men. *Circulation, 86,* 803–811.

Shumaker, S. A., & Czajkowski, S. M. (Eds.). (In press). *Social support and cardiovascular disease.* New York: Plenum Press.

Shumaker, S. A., & Hill, D. R. (1991). Gender differences in social support and physical health. *Health Psychology, 10,* 102–111.

Siegman, A. W., & Johnson, G. S. (1991). *Structured interview derived hostility scores and thallium stress test results in men and women.* Paper presented at the National Heart, Lung, and Blood Institute sponsored conference, *Women Behavior, and Cardiovascular Disease,* Bethesda, MD.

Smith, D. A. F., & Coyne, J. C. (1988). Coping with a myocardial infarction: Determinants of patient self-efficacy. Symposium presented at the 96th Annual Convention of the American Psychological Association, Atlanta, GA.

Society for the Advancement of Women's Health Research. (1991). *Towards a women's health research agenda: Findings of the scientific advisory meeting.* Washington, DC.

Speizer, F. E. (1980). Oral contraceptive use in relation to nonfatal myocardial infarction. *American Journal of Epidemiology, 111,* 59–66.

Spence, M. R., & Reboli, A. C. (1991). Human immunodeficiency virus infection in women. *Annals of Internal Medicine, 115,* 827–829.

Stanton, A. L., & Danoff-Burg, S. (1992). *(Mis)measurement of emotion-focused coping: Problems of conceptualization and confounding.* Paper presented at the Annual Meeting of the American Psychological Association, Washington, DC.

Stone, A. A., & Neale, J. M. (1984). New measures of daily coping: Development and preliminary results. *Journal of Personality and Social Psychology, 46,* 892–906.

Travis, C. B. (1988). *Women and health psychology: Biomedical issues*(pp. 203–228). Hillsdale, NJ: Lawrence Erlbaum Associates.

United States Public Health Service Task Force on Women's Health Issues (1985). Women's health: Report of the Public Health Service Task Force on Women's Health Issues. Public Health Reports, 100(1). Washington, D. C.: U. S. Department of Health and Human Services.

U.S. Senate Appropriations Labor, Health and Human Services Subcommittee. (1992). *Appropriations Bill HR 5677* (Report No. 102-397).

Wallston, B. S., Alagna, S. W., DeVellis, B. K., & DeVellis, R. F. (1983). Social support and physical health. *Health Psychology, 2,* 367–391.

Wellisch, D. K., Gritz, E. R., Schain, W., Wang, H. J., & Siau, J. (1991). Psychological functioning of daughters of breast cancer patients. Part 1: Daughters and comparison subjects. *Psychosomatics, 32,* 324–336.

Willett, W. C., Hunter, D. J., Stompfer, M. J., Colditz, G., Manson, J. E., Spiegelman, D., et al. (1992). Dietary fat and fiber in relation to breast cancer: An eight year follow-up. *Journal of the American Medical Association, 268,* 2037–2044.

Zuckerman, H. (1991). The careers of men and women scientists: A review of current research. In H. Zuckerman, J. R. Cole, & J. T. Bruer (Eds.), *The outer circle: Women in the scientific community* (pp. 27–56). New York: W. W. Norton.

Zuckerman, H., Cole, J. R., & Bruer, J. T. (Eds.). (1991). *The outer circle: Women in the scientific community.* New York: W. W. Norton.

Index